D0989538

THE GOSPEL ACCORDING TO JOHN

The Gospel According to John

VOLUME III
(Chapters 15-21)

by

Oliver B. Greene

The Gospel Hour, Inc., Oliver B. Greene, Director
Box 2024, Greenville, South Carolina 29602

Printed in the United States of America

First printing, April 1967—10,000 copies
Second printing, October 1968—15,000 copies
Third printing, July 1970—15,000 copies
Fourth printing, December 1971—15,000 copies
Fifth printing, June 1973—15,000 copies

$6.00

FOREWORD

The key verses to *The Gospel of John* are found in this third and last volume of studies in that Gospel:

"And many other signs truly did Jesus in the presence of His disciples, which are not written in this book: *but these are written, that ye might believe that Jesus is the Christ, the Son of God; and that believing ye might have life through His name*" (ch. 20, vv. 30,31).

This has been the aim of these studies. They are not intended to be examples of rhetorical accomplishment or literary genius. The ultimate purpose of these three volumes has been to present our Lord and Saviour Jesus Christ as the only begotten Son of God, the Living Word, that those who read these pages may believe on Him, and believing, "might have life through His name."

This entire series of studies is offered with a sincere prayer that through the divine truths of God's Word, sinners may be saved and Christians led into a closer walk with the Christ whom John so clearly presents.

The Author

FOREWORD

CONTENTS

THE GOSPEL ACCORDING TO JOHN

CHAPTER XV

1. I am the true vine, and my Father is the husbandman.

2. Every branch in me that beareth not fruit he taketh away: and every branch that beareth fruit, he purgeth it, that it may bring forth more fruit.

3. Now ye are clean through the word which I have spoken unto you.

4. Abide in me, and I in you. As the branch cannot bear fruit of itself, except it abide in the vine; no more can ye, except ye abide in me.

5. I am the vine, ye are the branches: He that abideth in me, and I in him, the same bringeth forth much fruit: for without me ye can do nothing.

6. If a man abide not in me, he is cast forth as a branch, and is withered; and men gather them, and cast them into the fire, and they are burned.

7. If ye abide in me, and my words abide in you, ye shall ask what ye will, and it shall be done unto you.

8. Herein is my Father glorified, that ye bear much fruit; so shall ye be my disciples.

9. As the Father hath loved me, so have I loved you: continue ye in my love.

10. If ye keep my commandments, ye shall abide in my love; even as I have kept my Father's commandments, and abide in his love.

11. These things have I spoken unto you, that my joy might remain in you, and that your joy might be full.

12. This is my commandment, That ye love one another, as I have loved you.

13. Greater love hath no man than this, that a man lay down his life for his friends.

14. Ye are my friends, if ye do whatsoever I command you.

15. Henceforth I call you not servants; for the servant knoweth not what his lord doeth: but I have called you friends; for all things that I have heard of my Father I have made known unto you.

16. Ye have not chosen me, but I have chosen you, and ordained you, that ye should go and bring forth fruit, and that your fruit should remain: that whatsoever ye shall ask of the Father in my name, he

may give it you.
17. These things I command you, that ye love one another.
18. If the world hate you, ye know that it hated me before it hated you.
19. If ye were of the world, the world would love his own: but because ye are not of the world, but I have chosen you out of the world, therefore the world hateth you.
20. Remember the word that I said unto you, The servant is not greater than his lord. If they have persecuted me, they will also persecute you; if they have kept my saying, they will keep your's also.
21. But all these things will they do unto you for my name's sake, because they know not him that sent me.
22. If I had not come and spoken unto them, they had not had sin: but now they have no cloke for their sin.
23. He that hateth me hateth my Father also.
24. If I had not done among them the works which none other man did, they had not had sin: but now have they both seen and hated both me and my Father.
25. But this cometh to pass, that the word might be fulfilled that is written in their law, They hated me without a cause.
26. But when the Comforter is come, whom I will send unto you from the Father, even the Spirit of truth, which proceedeth from the Father, he shall testify of me:
27. And ye also shall bear witness, because ye have been with me from the beginning.

This chapter of John's Gospel is familiar to believers; it is read often—but I wonder just how much of its teaching most of us really understand? For instance, why does the Lord Jesus Christ liken Himself to a *vine*? What is *the main thought* suggested by this parable? What does Jesus mean when He says, "Every branch in me that beareth not fruit He taketh away"? And what is the "*fruit*"? What is the meaning of His statement, "If a man abide not in me he is cast forth as a branch, and is withered; and men gather them, and cast them into the fire, and they are burned"?

As we study this chapter we must also keep in mind the following questions: *Who are the persons* Jesus had in mind as He gave this parable to the disciples? And *what is the central thought or topic* in the message given here?

It is not difficult to discover to whom Jesus was speaking. He was not addressing a mixed multitude here; he was not speaking to unbelievers. He was speaking to believers only—the message was given to the eleven apostles.

In the two chapters immediately preceding this one, Jesus taught His disciples what He would be doing for them—and for all believers—while He was away from them. He is seated in heaven at the right hand of the Father; He is interceding for us; He is our Mediator and our Intercessor, our great High Priest. And while He is there, He is preparing a place for us, and in the fulness of time He will return for us. Until that time, He will manifest Himself to us in the Person of the Holy Spirit who abides within us; and *through* the Holy Spirit He supplies our every need and we are complete in Him.

Now in our present chapter Jesus presents the other side of the truth concerning believers and Himself. In this chapter we learn what *we* are to *do* and what we are to *be* for Jesus while He is absent from us.

In chapters 13 and 14 Jesus assured His disciples that the grace of God is sufficient—not only to redeem us from the eternal penalty of sin, but also to provide every need from the moment we are born again until we are safe with Jesus in Paradise. But in our present chapter Jesus sets forth the responsibility of the individual believer—the responsibility to bear fruit, much fruit, *more* fruit, thereby glorifying God the Father.

The closing words of chapter 14 were "*Arise, let us go hence.*" Only a few minutes before, Jesus had said to His disciples, "Peace I leave with you, my peace I give unto you"—and only moments before He gave this tremendous promise supplied by divine grace, He had presented the emblems of His death—the unleavened bread and the fruit of the vine. There could BE no peace apart from His shed blood. We have peace with God through the finished work and the shed blood of His only begotten Son.

Immediately following His announcement that He would

give them peace, Jesus rose from the table and said, "Let us go hence"—and it was on the way to the Garden of Gethsemane that He gave the address we will study in this chapter. He opened the discourse by saying, "I am the true vine, and my Father is the Husbandman." You see, we cannot go forth to bear fruit until we know Jesus in the power of His resurrection. There can be no fruit-bearing until we have experienced the resurrection-life that connects us to the true Vine, the Lord Jesus Christ. Therefore *the central theme and paramount truth set forth here* is not salvation from sin; it is not how to be saved or how to keep from *losing* salvation. *The theme here is fruit-bearing* and the conditions under which the believer *bears* fruit.

The word "fruit" occurs no less than eight times in chapter 15, and *eight* is the *resurrection number.* Jesus rose on the first day of the week. The Jewish Sabbath is the seventh day, Sunday is the eighth day—and Jesus rose on Sunday. "Eight" in Scripture is associated with a new beginning, and of course the resurrection of Jesus was the beginning of the new day, the Day of Grace. If He had *not* risen we would have no salvation, because "if Christ be not risen, then is our preaching vain, and your faith is also vain" (I Cor. 15:14). Study the entire fifteenth chapter of I Corinthians.

Many times in the Old Testament Scriptures Israel had been likened unto a vine, and Jesus knew that His disciples would be familiar with His use of the vine as a figure here. The vine serves no other purpose than to bear fruit; it is worth very little for anything else. *Trees* produce building materials, but vines are practically worthless unless they produce fruit. Vineyards were a familiar sight in Palestine, and Jesus is here teaching the relationship between Himself and believers on earth. Vines grow out of the earth, and a *dead* vine certainly could not bear fruit. Jesus speaks here of a fruit-bearing vine, therefore a *living* vine—born again believers, those who are alive in Christ.

The word "abide" is found nine times in the first ten

verses of this chapter. Abiding has reference to fellowship, not redemption. Only born again people can have fellowship with the Father and with the Lord Jesus Christ.

The vine, and branches connected *to* the vine, express oneness, *unity.* Certainly believers are in Christ, and He is in us (Rom. 8:1; Col. 1:27). We are saved to bear fruit and we glorify God only when we DO bear fruit. It is true that fruit-bearing has nothing to do with redemption, but it has *everything* to do with reward at the end of this life. If we are faithful stewards, if we have been fruitful, we will receive a reward; and if we have been *unfaithful and careless* in our stewardship we will suffer loss.

In chapter 14 Jesus comforted His disciples by promising them another Comforter after He should return to the Father, and He assured them that at the appointed time He would Himself return to receive them, that where He is, there all believers would be, to spend eternity with Him.

In chapter 15 He assures them of their union with Himself, and shows them that their connection with Him and with each other would not be broken, dissolved, or weakened. True, the *outward* bond that had held them together for more than three years would be severed, the Shepherd would be smitten and the sheep scattered (Zech. 13:7); but there is a deeper bond, a more intimate connection. To illustrate this and make it plain to them, He compared Himself to the vine and His children to the branches. They knew and understood that the branch is connected to the vine, and the sap which is essential to life proceeds from the vine into the branches. In other words, because HE lives, WE live—and *without* Him we would have no life eternal.

In chapter 12, verse 24, He had taught them that "except a corn of wheat fall into the ground and die, it abideth alone: but if it die, *it bringeth forth MUCH fruit*"—and it is "much fruit" that glorifies the Father. Fruit was the end of the Father's commandment, and this was accomplished through the obedience of Jesus the Son (John 10:17,

18). God set forth Jesus to die on the cross, that He might bring many sons into glory. His spotless, sinless life could never have saved us; it was a divine imperative that He *die*. Christ died for our sins "according to the Scriptures" (I Cor. 15:1–4), and we are saved through His death.

Discourse on the Way to the Garden

Verse 1: *"I am the true vine, and my Father is the Husbandman."*

Here again is *"I AM."* Jehovah God is the great I AM, and Jesus was God in flesh, therefore He could truthfully say, *"I AM the true vine."*

We find the word "true" in several other passages and verses describing the Lord Jesus:

In chapter 1 verse 9, He is the *true LIGHT*.

In chapter 6 verse 32, He is the *true BREAD*.

In Hebrews 8:2 He is "a minister of the sanctuary, and of the *true TABERNACLE.*"

In our present verse, "true" is not used as in opposition to "false," but rather that Christ was the perfect, sinless, righteous, holy, essential and enduring reality of which all other vines are only types and shadows. The vine, being created and constituted as it is, is a fit and perfect representation of Christ, together with believers bringing forth fruit to the glory of God the Father. (For the use of the word "true" in a similar way, see John 6:32—"the true Bread.") We need not suppose that Jesus selected a vine as a figure from among a multitude of other things just because there was one *visible* at that moment. Is it not more likely that He had in view the places in the Old Testament where Israel is referred to as a vine—as in Isaiah chapter 5, verses 1, 2, and 7?

"Now will I sing to my well beloved a song of my beloved touching His vineyard. My well beloved hath a vineyard in a very fruitful hill: and He fenced it, and gathered out the stones thereof, and planted it with the choicest vine, and built a tower in the midst of it, and also made a winepress therein: and He looked that it should bring forth grapes, and it brought forth *wild* grapes. . . For the vineyard of the Lord of hosts is the house of Israel, and the men of Judah His pleasant plant: and He looked for judgment, but behold oppression; for righteousness, but behold a cry" (Isaiah 5:1,2,7).

Also in Psalm 80:8,9 we read, "Thou hast brought a *vine* out of Egypt: thou hast cast out the heathen, and planted it. Thou preparedst room before it, and didst cause it to take deep root, and it filled the land."

These passages show Israel as the vine, the type. Israel failed, but Jesus *the TRUE vine* did not fail. In Jeremiah 2:21 we read, "Yet I had planted thee a noble vine, wholly a right seed: how then art thou turned into the degenerate plant of a strange vine unto me?"

And in Hosea 10:1, "Israel is an empty vine, he bringeth forth fruit unto himself: according to the multitude of his fruit he hath increased the altars; according to the goodness of his land they have made goodly images."

Israel, the Old Testament vine, failed miserably; but Jesus the true vine satisfied every jot and tittle of the law (Matt. 5:17). And because He was TRUE He could not fail, He could not disappoint the heavenly Father.

I have already mentioned that we are studying a parable here. We know the Lord Jesus Christ was not a literal vine, we know believers are not literal "branches," and we know that Jehovah God the Eternal Spirit is not literally a husbandman; but Jesus used the vine, the branches, and the husbandman as an illustration, to reveal to our poor, weak minds and our limited capacities the truth He wanted us to know concerning the connection between Himself, and believers, and the heavenly Father.

Jesus used the vine to show His discouraged disciples that true believers are closely united to Jesus the Saviour and God the Father. Spiritual life—as well as fruitbearing—*depends* upon our union with the Lord Jesus Christ through the miracle of the new birth, the indwelling of the Holy Spirit.

Up to this time, *Israel* had been the vine, and all who worshipped God could worship only as they were grafted into the vine, the nation Israel. All others were strangers to the covenants, aliens to the commonwealth of Israel, and without hope; but *now* Jew and Gentile alike must be saved by grace, connected to the vine through the miracle of the new birth and the Holy Spirit. Now *Jesus* is the true vine, and all other vines are types and shadows.

In this illustration He was saying to His disciples, "As the *vine* is the true source of its branches, so am I the source of your spiritual life. You are entirely dependent upon me, and because I live, YOU live. As the branch depends upon the vine for food and sustenance, so do you depend upon me. It is only by, through, and in me that you have spiritual life; therefore our relationship is the same as that which exists between the vine and its branches."

In the same illustration, Jesus showed the disciples that God the Father takes the same tender interest and care about believers as the vineyard keeper, the husbandman, takes concerning the branches of the vines in his vineyard. The husbandman continually watches, prunes, fertilizes, and cares for the branches—and just so, the heavenly Father continually looks upon us and cares for us through our wonderful Lord and Saviour, supplying our spiritual life and our every need. And certainly, since God is doing all that for us, we should *bring forth fruit,* more fruit, and *much* fruit to glorify Him.

In the Old Testament, God the Father is seen as the proprietor—or the owner—of the vineyard, as shown in the passage just quoted from Isaiah 5; but in our present chapter He is referred to as the husbandman, the cultivator, the one who prunes and cares for the vineyard. Jesus would have us understand God's love—first for His only begotten Son, then for believers. Christ took upon Him the form of a servant, He took a body of humiliation, He took a place of dependency upon the Father, and God the Father watched over and protected the Son as He grew up before Him "as a tender plant, and as a root out of a dry ground" (Isa. 53:2).

For example, even before Jesus was born, when Joseph was about to put Mary away, God sent an angel and instructed Joseph concerning the Lord Jesus Christ, and made it plain to him that the conception of His Son was of the Holy Ghost in the womb of the virgin Mary (Matt. 1:18–20).

Then shortly after Jesus was born, when wicked King Herod would have destroyed Him, "the angel of the Lord appeareth to Joseph in a dream, saying, Arise, and take the young child and His mother, and flee into Egypt, and be thou there until I bring thee word: for Herod will seek the young child to destroy Him" (Matt. 2:13).

If God the Father so loved the TRUE vine, then we have divine assurance that He also loves the branches. This is proved in the fact that He prunes and cares for the branches that they might be fruitful. I am so thankful that God did not commit to men—to ministers, priests, popes, or bishops—the task of pruning, correcting, and instructing. I am glad it is God the heavenly Father who cares for the vine and its branches, for His care is tender and faithful.

Verse 2: *"Every branch in me that beareth not fruit He taketh away: and every branch that beareth fruit, He purgeth it, that it may bring forth more fruit."*

This Scripture is often misinterpreted and abused. Comparing spiritual things with spiritual, we learn that *"taketh away"* here has nothing to do with eternal destruction and damnation. If the meaning here were that a blood-washed, born again, saved-by-grace believer should be plucked away from the vine simply because that believer was not bearing fruit, it would be in direct contradiction to scores of other plain, understandable statements recorded—not only in the Gospel of John, but in the Epistles as well. For example:

In *John 4:14* we read, *"Whosoever drinketh of the water*

that I shall give him SHALL NEVER THIRST; but the water that I shall give him shall be in him a well of water springing up into *EVERLASTING LIFE.*"

John 10:28: "And I give unto them ETERNAL LIFE; AND THEY SHALL NEVER PERISH, NEITHER SHALL ANY MAN PLUCK THEM OUT OF MY HAND."

John 18:9: "That the saying might be fulfilled, which He spake, *Of them which thou gavest me HAVE I LOST NONE.*"

Romans 5:9,10: "Much more then, *being now justified by His blood, WE SHALL BE SAVED FROM WRATH THROUGH HIM.* For if, when we were enemies, we were reconciled to God by the death of His Son, *MUCH MORE, BEING RECONCILED, WE SHALL BE SAVED BY HIS LIFE.*"

Romans 8:31—39: "What shall we then say to these things? If God be for us, who can be against us? He that spared not His own Son, but delivered Him up for us all, how shall He not with Him also freely give us all things? Who shall lay anything to the charge of God's elect? It is God that justifieth. Who is he that condemneth? It is Christ that died, yea rather, that is risen again, who is even at the right hand of God, who also maketh intercession for us.

"WHO SHALL SEPARATE US FROM THE LOVE OF CHRIST? Shall tribulation, or distress, or persecution, or famine, or nakedness, or peril, or sword? As it is written, For thy sake we are killed all the day long; we are accounted as sheep for the slaughter.

"Nay, in all these things we are more than conquerors through Him that loved us. *For I am persuaded, that neither death, nor life, nor angels, nor principalities, nor powers, nor things present, nor things to come, nor height, nor depth, NOR ANY OTHER CREATURE, shall be able to separate us from the love of God, which is in Christ Jesus our Lord!*"

Ephesians 4:30: "Grieve not the holy Spirit of God,

whereby ye are SEALED UNTO THE DAY OF REDEMPTION."

When we come to difficult passages in the Word of God, the best commentary on that passage IS the Word of God. Paul wrote to the believers in Corinth, "What man knoweth the things of a man, save the spirit of man which is in him? Even so the things of God knoweth no man, but the Spirit of God.

"Now we have received, not the spirit of the world, but the spirit which is of God; that we might know the things that are freely given to us of God. Which things also we speak, not in the words which man's wisdom teacheth, but which the Holy Ghost teacheth; comparing spiritual things with spiritual. But the natural man receiveth not the things of the Spirit of God: for they are foolishness unto him: neither can he know them, because they are spiritually discerned" (I Cor. 2:11–14).

The only possible way to understand and correctly interpret the Bible is to compare Scripture with Scripture. Many times a passage that seems vague, or that is hard to understand, can be better understood if we consider the persons to whom the words were addressed. I know that all Scripture is given by inspiration and is profitable to us (II Tim. 3:16); but we must rightly divide the Word. For instance, God commanded Noah to build an ark, and if Noah had not *obeyed* God he would not have saved his house and become "heir of the righteousness which is by faith" (Heb. 11:7). But God has not commanded ME to build an ark—and if I *built* an ark I would be the laughing stock of my community.

Likewise, when Jesus gave the threefold parable in Luke 15, He was speaking to His enemies (Luke 15:2). He was not speaking to His disciples, giving them a lesson on backsliding. No, in the threefold parable from the fifteenth chapter of Luke, He was teaching concerning the sinner and how the sinner is saved. The shepherd went after the lost sheep, the woman searched for the lost coin, the father of the prodigal son kept looking for the son's homecoming. Many ministers teach that in this passage the sheep and the coin are *lost,* and then they say the son was a *backslider*—but not so. The father, in welcoming his son, said, *"This my son was DEAD"*—and a true Bible backslider is not dead; he has done what Peter did, denied the Lord and followed Christ afar off. The prodigal son was not a backslider, he was LOST; but in our present Scripture we must keep in mind that those to whom the Lord was speaking were *saved* people, His own disciples, and He was not speaking to them of salvation, but of stewardship and fruit-bearing.

"Every branch in me that beareth not fruit He taketh away." There is no point in suggesting that this refers to people who were in the visible church but not in the *true* Church, because Jesus said, *"every branch IN ME."* The branch referred to here is definitely IN the vine, and Jesus is the true vine. Most believers are so accustomed to concentrating on their own salvation and so *little* accustomed to dwelling upon the glory of God and His glory in US, that there is a sad tendency to apply many of these Scriptures to the unsaved, instead of rightly dividing the Word and letting them point to true believers in warning, rebuke, reproof and correction, as well as for instruction in righteousness.

According to Hebrews 12:6,8 Jesus chastens every believer: "For whom the Lord loveth He chasteneth, and scourgeth *every son* whom He receiveth. . . . But if ye be *without* chastisement, whereof all are partakers, then are ye bastards, and not sons." Therefore, if we be without chastisement we are not born again at all. Many believers fail to recognize the fact that we are saved not just to miss hell, *but to glorify God.*

In verse 5 of this chapter Jesus said to His disciples, *"YE are the branches,"* and in our present verse He made it clear to whom He was referring when He said, "Every branch IN ME that beareth not fruit He taketh away."

There is no way to misunderstand this. When the Bible says, "in ME . . . in HIM . . . in CHRIST," it is speaking only to born again, blood-washed children of God. And since this phrase points to the believer, and since it does not mean that the believer will be taken away to perish in the lake of fire, then what DID Jesus mean here?

The Greek reads, "Every branch in me *not bearing fruit.*" Jesus was speaking of a branch that had once been fruitful but *ceased to bear fruit.* If we look at the literal vine of the earth we know there are several things—such as disease, insects, drought—that will cause a branch not to bear fruit. By comparison, there are several things that will cause a believer (a branch in the *spiritual* sense) not to bear fruit. Peter tells us that we are "partakers of the divine nature, having escaped the corruption that is in the world through lust. And beside this, giving all diligence, add to your faith virtue; and to virtue knowledge; and to knowledge temperance; and to temperance patience; and to patience godliness; and to godliness brotherly kindness; and to brotherly kindness charity. *For if these things be in you, and abound, THEY MAKE YOU THAT YE SHALL NEITHER BE BARREN NOR UNFRUITFUL in the knowledge of our Lord Jesus Christ*" (II Pet. 1:4–8).

In Titus 3:14 Paul said, "Let our's also learn to maintain good works for necessary uses, *that they be not unfruitful.*"

A natural vine that produces only leaves may be beautiful, but it is extremely unprofitable to its owner. Even if the leaves were harvested they would be of no value. In the spiritual sense, it is a sad thing indeed when a believer speaks great swelling words and gives great testimony, but offers no fruit—only leaves. Such a person is not a soul-winner and will not glorify God because he bears no fruit.

We have even further proof that the sinner is not referred to in this verse, because we are plainly told that it is the "husbandman" (the heavenly Father) who takes away the unfruitful branch—and Jesus said, "*The FATHER judgeth NO man, but hath committed ALL judgment unto the*

SON" (John 5:22). It is *Jesus the Son,* not Jehovah God, who will say to the condemned, "Depart from me, ye cursed, into everlasting fire, prepared for the devil and his angels" (Matt. 25:41).

"Who is he that condemneth? It is Christ that died, yea rather, that is risen again, who is even at the right hand of God, who also maketh intercession for us" (Rom. 8:34). According to this Scripture, it is Jesus who condemns if there is to BE any condemnation; and it is the Lord Jesus Christ who will sit upon the Great White Throne in that final judgment day, to judge the wicked (Rev. 20:11–15)—but no born again believer will appear there. Believers will be judged and rewarded *for their stewardship* at an earlier time.

In I Corinthians 9:19–27 Paul gives instructions concerning the method and the reward of true spiritual stewardship or ministry:

"For though I be free from all men, yet have I made myself servant unto all, that I might gain the more. And unto the Jews I became as a Jew, that I might gain the Jews; to them that are under the law, as under the law, that I might gain them that are under the law; to them that are without law, as without law, (being not without law to God, but under the law to Christ,) that I might gain them that are without law. To the weak became I as weak, that I might gain the weak: I am made all things to all men, that I might by all means save some. And this I do for the Gospel's sake, that I might be partaker thereof with you. Know ye not that they which run in a race run all, but one receiveth the prize? So run, that ye may obtain. And every man that striveth for the mastery is temperate in all things. Now they do it to obtain a corruptible crown; but we an incorruptible. I therefore so run, not as uncertainly; so fight I, not as one that beateth the air: But I keep under my body, and bring it into subjection: *lest that by any means, when I have preached to others, I myself should be a CASTAWAY.*"

The Greek word here translated *"castaway"* should be rendered *disapproved,* and to be disapproved of God does not mean that the *soul* is lost. Paul was writing of *service,* not salvation. He was speaking of *reward,* not of redemption. He makes this plain in I Corinthians 3:11–15:

"For other foundation can no man lay than that is laid, which is Jesus Christ. Now if any man build upon this foundation gold, silver, precious stones, wood, hay, stubble; every man's work shall be made manifest: for the day shall declare it, because it shall be revealed by fire; and the fire shall try every man's work of what sort it is. If any man's work abide which he hath built thereupon, he shall receive a reward. *If any man's work shall be burned, he shall suffer loss: BUT HE HIMSELF SHALL BE SAVED; YET SO AS BY FIRE!"*

According to this passage from God's Word, there will be believers who will be saved but all of their works will be consumed and they will lose their reward.

I believe the Bible teaches that a truly born again child of God *WILL bear fruit*—perhaps not a hundredfold, but sixty or even thirty; and *if* a believer allows the cares of the world, the deceitfulness of riches, or the lust for other things to crowd out fruitbearing in his life, God will definitely place that believer on the shelf, disapprove him as a good steward, and render him inactive. Then unless that believer repents, he may commit the sin unto death and God will be forced to cut him off; but it will be the *body* that is destroyed, not the soul.

We are clearly instructed that there IS a sin unto death, and that there is no use to pray for one who has *committed* that sin:

"If any man see his brother sin a sin which is not unto death, he shall ask, and He shall give him life for them that sin not unto death. There is a sin unto death: I DO NOT SAY THAT HE SHALL PRAY FOR IT" (I John 5:16).

"And every branch that beareth fruit, He purgeth it, that it may bring forth more fruit." This does not mean that

the branch is pruned or caused to suffer through chastisement, although God *does* chasten wayward believers who depart from the straight and narrow way of dedicated living. *"Purging"* does not necessarily mean suffering. The same Greek word can be translated "cleanseth," and we know that the Word is the living water (Eph. 5:26). The very next verse in our present text declares, *"Now ye are clear through the WORD* which I have spoken unto you."

In the natural vineyard the husbandman cleanses the branches by spraying them with water and some form of cleanser to wash away and destroy the insects, blight, and mildew. For the *spiritual* branch, the Word of God carries the message of the cleansing blood of Jesus Christ which not only cleanses (redeems) us when we believe, but *continually* cleanses us day by day. The ministry of the blood is not finished when we are saved; it continues in our daily lives:

"This then is the message which we have heard of Him, and declare unto you, that God is light, and in Him is no darkness at all. If we say that we have fellowship with Him and walk in darkness, we lie, and do not the truth: but if we walk in the light, as HE is in the light, we have fellowship one with another, *and the blood of Jesus Christ His Son cleanseth us from all sin"* (I John 1:5–7).

Since believers are purged (cleansed) through the Word, we are to hear the Word, receive the Word, and live by the Word, that it might wash away or cleanse us from anything that would hinder the flow of the love of God and the Spirit of God in us and through us as the branches that bear fruit. We are commanded to study the Word, desire the sincere milk of the Word, feed upon the bread of the Word, quench our thirst through the water of the Word, and *walk in the light of the Word.* By so doing, we will be purged and cleansed, that we may be fruitbearing branches.

Bear in mind that "purging" here has nothing to do with making the believer fit for heaven. Rather, it fits him for fruitbearing and effective stewardship whereby he will glorify God. In I Corinthians 10:31 we are commanded, *"Whether therefore ye eat, or drink, or whatsoever ye do, do all to the glory of God."*

There is absolutely no way to estimate the importance of the Word of God.

We are *saved* by grace through faith, and faith comes by hearing the *Word* (Eph. 2:8; Rom. 10:17).

We are *born again* through the Word (I Pet. 1:23).

We are *begotten* through the Word (James 1:18).

The Word is *the power of God unto salvation* (Rom. 1:16).

We are *cleansed* by the Word (John 15:3).

We are *sanctified* by the Word (Eph. 5:26).

We grow in grace by *feeding* upon the Word (I Pet. 2:2).

No wonder the devil hates the Word of God and is doing everything in his diabolical power to discredit the Word through liberals, modernists, new translations and revisions, adding to and taking from the Word!

Many pages could be written concerning the purging of believers by the Husbandman, but we do not have time or space here for a full discussion of the subject. The following references must suffice:

I Peter 1:7: "That the trial of your faith, being much more precious than of gold that perisheth, though it be tried with *fire,* might be found unto praise and honour and glory at the appearing of Jesus Christ."

James 1:2—4: "My brethren, count it all joy when ye fall into divers temptations; knowing this, that the trying of your faith worketh patience. But let patience have her perfect work, *that ye may be perfect and entire, wanting nothing.*"

Romans 5:3—5: "...we glory in tribulations also: knowing that tribulation worketh patience; and patience, experience; and experience hope: and hope maketh not ashamed; because the love of God is shed abroad in our hearts by the Holy Ghost which is given unto us."

Verse 3: *"Now ye are clean through the Word which I have spoken unto you."*

The Greek here reads, "Now ALREADY ye are clean . . . ." The purging (or daily cleansing) of a believer has to do with *our state of being,* but "now *already* ye are clean" has to do with our standing before God. The *state* of the believer is progressive, but *the standing is absolute and final;* it will not be altered—and here is Scripture to prove that statement:

"Seeing ye have purified your souls in obeying the truth through the Spirit unto unfeigned love of the brethren, see that ye love one another with a pure heart fervently: Being born again, not of corruptible seed, but of incorruptible, by the Word of God, which liveth and abideth for ever" (I Pet. 1:22,23).

Those of us who have obeyed the Word of God and are born of God through the incorruptible seed, have purified our souls—that is, our souls are pure because we have obeyed the Word through the Spirit, but we need to continually purify ourselves: "Every man that hath this hope in him purifieth himself, even as He is pure" (I John 3:3). This purifying comes through daily reading and absorbing the living water of the Word. All believers are washed (I Cor. 6:11); but Jesus clearly taught that pilgrims need their feet bathed daily. Some days—depending on the journey—the feet need bathing more than once. It is not the entire body that needs to be cleansed, but the feet—*the daily walk.*

All Scripture is God-breathed; and in His sovereignty and omniscience God knew there would be false teachers who would wrongly divide the Word; so the Holy Ghost inserted this tremendous verse to bring unshakable assurance to born again believers. Jesus had just told His disciples, "The branch that beareth not fruit, He taketh away"—and then He assured them, *"YE are clean!"* The disciples to whom He was speaking were redeemed, they were true believers; but Jesus was teaching them that they would need purging (cleansing) in their daily walk, that they might bear fruit, *more* fruit—yea, even *MUCH fruit.*

Verse 4: *"Abide in me, and I in you. As the branch cannot bear fruit of itself, except it abide in the vine; no more can YE, except ye abide in me."*

The words "abide" or "remain" are found ten times in the first eleven verses of this chapter. *"Abide"* implies constant remaining, continuing in one identical place without moving. A truly born again believer is IN CHRIST (Rom. 8:1; Col. 1:27). The believer is in Christ in the same way a person dwells (or abides) inside the walls of a fortified city—closed in, kept, and protected.

Jesus instructed His disciples, *"Abide in ME."* That is, "Cling to me, cast your whole weight upon me; let ME bear your burdens and carry your load. Be rooted and grounded in me, just as the branch is connected to the vine." Jesus will never leave us nor forsake us, He will go with us all the way, and He will supply our every need, regardless of what that need might be.

We cannot fully appreciate the truth set forth in *this* verse unless we fully understand the previous verse. Jesus declared to the disciples, "Ye are clean—you have been washed, cleansed, you are clean *already.*" Thus the One who knows all things, the One who testifies what He has seen, declares that believers are every whit clean, *every spot removed:*

"Come now, and let us reason together, saith the Lord: though your sins be as scarlet, they shall be as white as snow; though they be red like crimson, they shall be as wool" (Isa. 1:18). Yes, we are made as white as snow when we are cleansed by the blood of Jesus; and even though as a branch we contact impurities that can hinder fruitbearing, this has nothing to do with our being "every whit clean" IN CHRIST.

God cannot bless us as He *wants* to bless us until we fully realize our oneness with the Lord Jesus Christ and our cleanness in Him by and through His precious Word. Jesus did not wash Peter's feet until Peter first recognized the fact that he was *already cleansed* and that only his *feet* needed washing (see John 13:2–12). We who are branches connected to the vine through the miracle of the new birth cannot learn and understand what is needful as having to do with fruitbearing unless we first fully understand and accept the statement Jesus made to His disciples: *"Ye are already clean through the Word I have spoken unto you."* When we realize this, we are ready for further instruction in fruitbearing.

There is no such thing as *"abiding"* in Christ until we are IN Christ, and we are "in Christ" *through the miracle of the new birth.* We are born of God, saved by grace—"not of works, lest any man should boast. For we are His workmanship, created in Christ Jesus unto good works, which God hath before ordained that we should walk in them" (Eph. 2:8–10).

Also, "If any man be in Christ, he is a new creature: old things are passed away; behold, all things are become new" (II Cor. 5:17).

There is no place in the New Testament where believers are admonished, "BE in Christ," because all believers ARE in Him; but we find several verses which admonish us to *abide* in Him—as in I John 2:28: "And now, little children, abide in Him; that, when He shall appear, we may have confidence, and not be ashamed before Him at His coming."

What does it mean to abide in Christ? It means that the believer has surrendered to Him *fully*—soul, spirit, and body. It means that whatever we do or say is to His honor and glory. Very few believers enjoy their spiritual birthright of "abundant life" as set forth in John 10:10, which comes only through abiding in Christ. The branch must abide in the vine if it is to live and bear fruit, and the same is true of believers: we must constantly abide in Christ if we hope to bear fruit.

Jesus said, "He that eateth my flesh, and drinketh my blood, dwelleth in me, and I in him" (John 6:56). We become Christians by believing on the Lord Jesus Christ, and the initial act of believing is described as coming TO Him:

"*Come unto me,* all ye that labour and are heavy laden, and I will give you rest" (Matt. 11:28).

". . . him that *cometh to me* I will in no wise cast out" (John 6:37).

"Jesus said unto them, I am the bread of life: he that *cometh to me* shall never hunger; and he that believeth on me shall never thirst" (John 6:35).

"Abiding in Him" means continual feeding upon His Word, continual appropriation and assimilation of the Word, taking it into the inner man. Thus will we walk in the light, thus will we walk in the Spirit; and whatever we do or say will be done and said to the glory of God.

"Abide in me, and I IN YOU." Our abiding in Jesus and His abiding in us are closely connected yet distinctly *different.* In other words, there is definitely a difference between being redeemed and being a good steward (abiding). *Christ IN us is perpetual:* when the Lord Jesus comes in, He comes to stay; He does not move in and out—but *His abiding FULNESS* may be interrupted by careless living on the part of the believer. Christ is in us because of grace, but it is our responsibility to keep the vessel clean. We are the tabernacle in which the Holy Spirit abides, but in order for Him to fill our lives we must be clean—sanctified, soul, spirit, and body (I Thess. 5:23). Jesus is IN every believer, but not every believer enjoys the fulness of His presence. Jesus came that we might have life, and every believer HAS life—howbeit some Christians remain *babes* in Christ, enjoying only God's second or third best instead of enjoying the abundant life that is their birthright.

Ephesians 5:18 commands us to be "FILLED with the Spirit"—but before we can be filled with the Spirit we must first be emptied of all else. No vessel can be *completely filled* with one thing until it is completely emptied of another—i. e., a five-hundred-gallon tank cannot be completely filled with water if there is one grain of sand in it; it will contain water *plus sand.* The same is true in the life of the Christian: in order for us to enjoy the abiding, filling presence of Jesus we must be emptied of self and of all things that would *crowd out* His fulness. The sanctified believer knows the happy, conscious recognition of the presence of Jesus at all times; and such a believer also knows the assurance of Christ's sufficient grace, His goodness, and His keeping power.

"As the branch cannot bear fruit of itself, except it abide in the vine; no more can ye except ye abide in me." A branch apart from the vine bears no fruit—and so it is with the Christian. The only way to be truly happy in Jesus is to be *fully surrendered* to Him, abiding, emptied of all things and filled with His Spirit, His love, and His divine presence. Thousands of believers complain that they do not have the joy other Christians have—but they fail to place the lack of joy at the right source. Such believers are not filled with "joy unspeakable and full of glory" because their communion with Christ is so meagre. They seek fruit-bearing and joy in church activities, or in doing something for the community and for their fellowman; but the abundance of God's grace and the fulness of joy come only when whatsoever we do, be it little or great, is done solely to the glory of God.

The Psalmist has truly said, "Those that be planted in the house of the Lord shall flourish in the courts of our God. They shall still bring forth fruit in old age; they shall be fat and flourishing" (Psalm 92:13,14). The believer cannot bear fruit by trying to work up stewardship in his own way, doing for clubs, community affairs, civic organizations—nor even for the church. The only fruit that brings glory to God comes from a heart wholly surrendered to Jesus, doing all things through Him and to glorify His precious name. Abiding in Jesus (and Jesus abiding in the believer) produces fruit. Walking in fellowship with Jesus is a divine imperative if we would bring forth fruit, because *HE is the source* of all fruitbearing.

Verse 5: *"I am the vine, ye are the branches: He that abideth in me, and I in him, the same bringeth forth much fruit: for without me ye can do nothing."*

Here our Lord repeats the predominant thought set forth in the first verse of this chapter, and by His repetition we recognize the extreme importance of His teaching here—that is, the relationship between Christ and the Christian must be the same as the relationship between a vine and its branches. The divine secret of bearing "much fruit" (and being what the Lord would have us to be) is abiding in Jesus, experiencing close communion with Him every moment of every day, seeking only His will, doing only those things that will bring glory and honor to His precious name rather than bringing glory and honor to self or to one's fellowman.

"I am the vine, ye are the branches." In other words, it is not *our* ability or *our* sufficiency that produces a fruit-bearing believer. We need to admit that we are unworthy and insufficient. What Jesus is saying here is that *within ourselves* we are no better than a branch severed from the vine. Such a branch is dry, dead, and certainly fruitless; but the branch connected to the vine is alive, bringing forth fruit.

"Without me ye can do nothing." Here we see that we are totally dependent upon Christ, and our fruitbearing is through His power, His ability, His sufficiency. A branch has no resources from which to bring forth fruit except it be connected to the vine. The *vine* provides life, power, ability to produce fruit. The born again believer is connected to the true vine, the Lord Jesus Christ—and it is through Him, by His power, that we are enabled to produce fruit.

The Apostle Paul said, "I am crucified with Christ: nevertheless I live; *yet not I, but Christ liveth in me:* and the life which I now live in the flesh *I live by the faith of the Son of God,* who loved me, and gave Himself for me" (Gal. 2:20).

In a vineyard, the branch bears clusters of grapes, but the branch does not *produce* the grapes, and *were it not for the vine* there would be no clusters. The same is true in the life of the believer. We need to recognize our own weakness, our own insufficiency, our own inability to serve God within ourselves. We need to recognize the full truth of Philippians 4:13 and say with Paul, "I can do all things *through Christ* which strengtheneth me."

"Without me ye can do nothing" in the Greek reads, "Separate from me, or *severed* from me, ye can do nothing" —but this statement has nothing to do with the divine union existing between the Lord Jesus Christ and the born again believer, a union that can never be broken (Rom. 8:38,39). Jesus was speaking here of the *interruption of fellowship* and of our entire dependency upon Him. The Christian cannot do anything spiritually good, he cannot speak right, think right, or live as he ought to live unless he is an *abiding* Christian. Severed from fellowship with Jesus, the believer cannot hope to glorify Him by producing fruit.

In Ephesians 5:22–32 Jesus and the Church are compared to husband and wife. According to the Word of God, husband and wife are no longer twain, but ONE flesh. Yet it is altogether possible (and not uncommon) that a married couple who love each other dearly may suffer broken fellowship, lacking communication when in each other's company; but *they are still married,* and when fellowship is restored they do not go to the minister to be married all over again! Fellowship is restored because they ARE married and they love each other.

The same is true with a born again believer. We love Jesus, and He loves US a million times more than we could ever love Him! He longs for fellowship with us far more than we could ever know, and when fellowship is *broken* between Jesus and the Christian, the Holy Spirit convicts the Christian and woos him back. For instance, *Peter* was not cast out from the Lord insofar as his discipleship was concerned; but when he *denied* Jesus, his fellowship with his Lord was severed. Then when Jesus looked at Peter with such tenderness as to cause him to go out and weep in bitter repentance, that fellowship was restored—and the Word of God makes it plain that Peter became a mighty spiritual giant before the end of his ministry. He was a child of God *before* He denied the Lord, and he did not cease to be a child of God even when fellowship was broken. He was not cut off from his established relationship with Jesus; *fellowship* between them was severed.

Beloved, we need to be ever alert lest the devil cause us to center our minds on something aside from Jesus, thus causing us to break fellowship with Him; and if the master deceiver can cause us to become occupied with ourselves, self-willed and self-centered, our fruitbearing will be drastically crippled! The most pathetic and painfully deluded person on earth is a Christian who, in witnessing for Christ, feeds upon his own fruit and glories in his own attainments and victories. The more fully we are dedicated to Christ, the more fully He controls us—soul, spirit, and body—the less respect we will have for ourselves and the more honor and glory we will bestow upon His precious name.

Verse 6: *"If a man abide not in me, he is cast forth as a branch, and is withered; and men gather them, and cast them into the fire, and they are burned."*

This is another verse that has been widely misunderstood and misinterpreted; but I repeat, if we study and rightly divide the Word we will have no problem seeing just what the Lord Jesus taught here.

"If a man abide not in me . . . ." Some commentators and teachers point out the word *"man"* in this phrase, but Greek scholars tell us that "man" is not found in the orig-

inal at all. In the Greek the phrase reads, "Unless *anyone* abide in me, he is cast out as a branch."

What Jesus meant by these words is simply that if a believer continues out of fellowship with Him, that believer is "cast forth." Now certainly these words could not be spoken of an *unbeliever,* nor of one who only *professed* to be saved. Jesus was speaking here of the branches connected to the vine, and any branch (any believer) who does not bear fruit and who continues out of fellowship with Him is *cast forth*—but that does not mean that the believer is lost, cut off and doomed to spend eternity in the lake of fire. It means that such a believer has reached the point of uselessness insofar as stewardship and fruitbearing are concerned.

Let us look more carefully into the truth our Lord taught here: We must bear in mind that He was speaking of the Christian and of the Christian's pilgrimage through this world, and the main object of the believer on earth is to bring forth fruit—"more fruit, yea, MUCH fruit," thereby bringing glory and honor to God the Father.

We must also keep in mind the fact that when Jesus spoke of the fruitless believer being "cast forth," the casting forth is to be done by the "husbandman," God the Father, and therefore refers to the taking away of gifts which were given to the believer but which he failed to develop or use to God's glory. It refers to opportunities which were offered but which the Christian failed to use. In Luke 8:18 Jesus said, "Take heed therefore how ye hear: for whosoever hath, to him shall be given; and whosoever hath not, *from him shall be taken even that which he seemeth to have.*"

In Matthew 5:13 Jesus said to His disciples, "Ye are the salt of the earth: but if the salt have lost his savour, wherewith shall it be salted? It is thenceforth good for nothing, but to be cast out, and to be trodden under foot of men." When salt loses its purifying quality it is useless, and so it is with the Christian who has lost his power to win souls, bear fruit, and glorify God in daily living.

In II John, verse 8, we are admonished, "Look to yourselves, that we lose not *those things which we have WROUGHT,* but that we receive a full reward." This admonition could have nothing to do with redemption, because certainly we did not "wrought" our redemption. Jesus *purchased* redemption through His shed blood, and when we receive His finished work and trust in His shed blood, we are redeemed and cleansed. But John was speaking of rewards and stewardship when he said, "lest we lose those things which we have wrought." Therefore to be "cast forth" means that the believer is laid aside, put on the shelf, so to speak—unfruitful and unprofitable to God.

"Men gather them, and cast them into the fire, and they are burned." Notice here the change from singular to plural—*"men... them... they."* Jesus did not say, "A *man* (singular) gathers *him* (singular), and casts *him* into the fire." He said, "*Men* (plural) gather *them* (plural), and cast *them* into the fire." Reading this verse from the Greek we find, "Unless anyone abide in me, he is cast forth as a branch, and men gather *them* and cast *them* into the fire *and they are burned."* It is easy to see that "them" and "they" issue from the one who is "cast forth."

We find more light on this in I Corinthians 3:11–15: "Other foundation can no man lay than that is laid, which is Jesus Christ. Now if any man build upon this foundation gold, silver, precious stones, wood, hay, stubble; every man's work shall be made manifest: for the day shall declare it, because it shall be revealed by fire; *and the fire shall try every man's work of what sort it is.* If any man's work abide which he hath built thereupon, he shall receive a reward. *IF ANY MAN'S WORK SHALL BE BURNED, HE SHALL SUFFER LOSS: BUT HE HIMSELF SHALL BE SAVED; YET SO AS BY FIRE."* A born again believer who is not an *abiding* believer produces dead works, and it is to dead works that "them" and "they" refer—works that are classed as "wood, hay, and stubble."

Jesus is the foundation, but men build ON that foundation. Some build gold, silver, precious stones—and the more these are burned, the brighter they shine! They will not be consumed. But men also build wood, hay, and stubble, and certainly these will burn freely. It is true that born again, blood-washed believers sometimes build works (stewardship) that are no good, and those works will be burned. That man will therefore "suffer loss"—not the loss of his soul—(*he himself shall be saved, yet so as by fire*)—but loss of reward. He will have no crowns or trophies to lay at the feet of Jesus in that great crowning day! *Lot,* nephew of Abraham, is a good example of the truth set forth here. According to the New Testament, Lot was a righteous man (II Pet. 2:7,8); but he chose the cities of the plains, he chose the world, moved into Sodom—and backslid. It cost him everything he had. His works were burned, but Lot himself was saved. You will find the record in Genesis 19.

In Matthew 13:41,42 we read, "The Son of man shall send forth His angels, and they shall gather out of His kingdom all things that offend, and them which do iniquity; and shall cast them into a furnace of fire: there shall be wailing and gnashing of teeth." Yes, the angels will gather *"all things that offend,"* and then they will gather *"them which do iniquity."* The things that offend will be gathered and burned at the judgment seat for believers, as described in II Corinthians 5:10: "For we must all appear before the judgment seat of Christ; that every one may receive the things done in his body, according to that he hath done, whether it be good or bad." "Them which do iniquity" will be gathered and cast into the lake of fire at the Great White Throne judgment of Revelation 20:11–15: "And I saw a great white throne, and Him that sat on it, from whose face the earth and the heaven fled away; and there was found no place for them. And I saw the dead, small and great, stand before God; and the books were opened: and another book was opened, which is the book of life: and the dead were judged out of those things which were written in the books, according to their works. And the sea gave up the dead which were in it; and death and hell delivered up the dead which were in them: and they were judged every man according to their works. And death and hell were cast into the lake of fire. This is the second death. And whosoever was not found written in the book of life was cast into the lake of fire."

There is a solemn warning here for all Christians: There is no such thing as "the middle of the road" where God is concerned. We are either bringing forth fruit to His glory, or we are producing wood, hay, and stubble that will be consumed. The things we do, the places we go, the company we keep, the way we spend our time and our money—in other words, *our daily living*—will determine whether we are bringing forth fruit to His glory, or producing stewardship that will be burned.

Beloved, *salvation* is the miracle of God's grace; Christ IS our salvation. But *fruit-bearing* is an altogether different subject. In John 3:16 we read, "For God (who is the husbandman in our present passage) so loved the world, that He gave His only begotten Son (who is the true vine in our present passage), that whosoever believeth in Him should not perish, but have *EVERLASTING life.*" In John 5:24 we read, "He that heareth my Word, and believeth on Him that sent me, *hath EVERLASTING life,* and shall NOT come into condemnation; but is passed from death unto life."

Yes, God gives the believer *eternal, EVERLASTING life,* imperishable life, and this divine fact is settled in the Word of God. Jesus said, "My sheep hear my voice, and I know them, and they follow me: *and I give unto them ETERNAL LIFE; and they shall NEVER perish, neither shall any man pluck them out of my hand. My Father, which gave them me, is greater than all; and no man is able to pluck them out of my Father's hand*" (John 10: 27–29).

The everlasting, imperishable life possessed by the believer is also declared through the inspired pen of Paul:

"Who shall separate us from the love of Christ? Shall tribulation, or distress, or persecution, or famine, or nakedness, or peril, or sword? . . . Nay, in all these things we are more than conquerors through Him that loved us. *For I am persuaded, that neither death, nor life, nor angels, nor principalities, nor powers, nor things present, nor things to come, nor height, nor depth, NOR ANY OTHER CREATURE, shall be able to separate us from the love of God, which is in Christ Jesus our Lord*" (Rom. 8:35–39).

Who could ask for a clearer, more definite and understandable statement? God knew in the beginning that man would need a Saviour; He knew man could not save himself, nor could man keep himself saved after God saved him. Therefore, God made provision for redemption, and for *victory* after redemption.

The power of the new birth is given by Almighty God: "As many as received Him, to them gave He power to become the sons of God, even to them that believe on His name: Which were born, not of blood, nor of the will of the flesh, nor of the will of man, but of God" (John 1:12, 13). According to Romans 1:16, this power comes *through the Word:* "For I am not ashamed of the Gospel of Christ: for *it is the power of God unto salvation to every one that believeth;* to the Jew first, and also to the Greek."

The power of God that "borns" us also *keeps* us *after* we are born from above:

"Blessed be the God and Father of our Lord Jesus Christ, which according to His abundant mercy hath begotten us again unto a lively hope by the resurrection of Jesus Christ from the dead, to an inheritance incorruptible, and undefiled, and that fadeth not away, reserved in heaven for you, *WHO ARE KEPT BY THE POWER OF GOD through faith unto salvation ready to be revealed in the last time*" (I Pet. 1:3–5).

According to I John 5:4,5, "Whatsoever (whosoever) is

born of God *overcometh the world*: and this is the victory that overcometh the world, even our faith. Who is he that overcometh the world, but he that believeth that Jesus is the Son of God?"

The Scripture makes it plain that we are saved *by grace through faith,* we are *kept* by grace through faith, and we *overcome* by faith. This much is true of all believers, but not all believers will have a reward from the standpoint of stewardship. As Christians we overcome the devil that would damn us, but many times self-will, selfishness, the cares of this world, the deceitfulness of riches and other things crowd out fruit-bearing. Fruit cannot be produced through human effort or power. Paul declared, "I am crucified with Christ: nevertheless I live; *YET NOT I, but Christ liveth in me:* and the life which I now live in the flesh I live by the faith of the Son of God, who loved me, and gave Himself for me" (Gal. 2:20).

Paul also said, "By the grace of God I am what I am: and His grace which was bestowed upon me was not in vain: but I laboured more abundantly than they all: YET NOT I, BUT THE GRACE OF GOD WHICH WAS WITH ME" (I Cor. 15:10).

Jesus used the vine as an illustration for His disciples because they were familiar with the grape vineyards in Palestine and they clearly understood what it meant for a branch to wither and become fruitless. A branch which does not consistently and continually feed upon the life-giving substance of the vine will soon wither and become unfruitful. In the same way, in a *spiritual* sense, if we as believers do not continually draw upon the life-giving bread and meat of the Word we will wither and become spiritually anemic and fruitless. To continue thus means that God must remove such a believer from active service, and then if that Christian does not repent, God will call him home! He will not allow one of His born again children to remain upon this earth and live a fruitless life. Just as it is the purpose of a natural branch to bear fruit, so

Christians are saved to serve, saved to win others—and if we do not produce fruit the Lord God prunes, purges, and does all in His power to cause us to *become* productive. If we still do not bear fruit, He will then call us home. This is the sin unto death, and believers are the only persons who can commit such sin.

Notice that John says, *"If any man see his BROTHER sin a sin which is not unto death,* he shall ask, and He shall give him life for them that sin not unto death. There is a sin unto death: I do not say that he shall pray for it" (I John 5:16). This Scripture definitely refers to *brothers in Christ,* the "little children," the born ones. The "sin unto death" is committed by Christians, believers who continually walk out of fellowship with the Lord, refusing to repent of known sin.

Verse 7: *"If ye abide in me, and my words abide in you, ye shall ask what ye will, and it shall be done unto you."*

The new birth which makes us one with Christ is a miracle of God's grace, and the purging of the branch is also a miracle of God's grace *through the WORD;* but "abiding" is definitely the believer's responsibility. Throughout the New Testament we are admonished to be alert and watchful ("sober, vigilant"), as in I Peter 5:8. We are urged to present our bodies, living sacrifices (Rom. 12:1); we are invited to yield our members as instruments of righteousness (Rom. 6:13). We are told to abstain from all appearance of evil (I Thess. 5:22), to have no fellowship with the unfruitful works of darkness (Eph. 5:11); and finally, Paul declares, "*Whatsoever* ye do in word or deed, do all in the name of the Lord Jesus, giving thanks to God and the Father by Him" (Col. 3:17). In I Corinthians 10:31 we are told, "Whether therefore ye eat, or drink, or whatsoever ye do, *do ALL to the glory of God.*"

After God works the miracle of the new birth, after we are purged through the power of the Word, it is our own responsibility to abide daily, moment by moment, "that, when He shall appear, we may have confidence, and not be ashamed before Him at His coming" (I John 2:28).

The invitation of Jesus to the sinner is, "Come unto me . . ." (Matt. 11:28). His command to the believer is, *"ABIDE in me."* I would emphasize again that *abiding* has nothing to do with redemption, the salvation of the soul. It has to do with *rewards.* I confess that I cannot comprehend what it will be like to be in heaven with no reward, but according to God's Word there *will* be souls there without any reward at all. They will be saved "as by fire," they will be snatched as brands from the burning (Zech. 3:2), and the Scripture declares that they will suffer loss. I do not know what it will mean to suffer loss throughout eternity because of works burned, but I do know it is a very serious thing for a believer to fail to abide and bring forth fruit to God's glory.

There are many people—yes, *truly born again Christians*—who live in uncertainty and doubt. They do not enjoy their spiritual birthright because they have broken fellowship with the Lord Jesus Christ. If they would only turn their eyes from themselves to the blood of Jesus, they would forget their doubts and become happy Christians, possessing "the peace of God, which passeth all understanding" (Phil. 4:7). The only way to have assurance and victory over the torturing uncertainty of spiritual things is to forget self and look only to the Lord Jesus Christ, believing wholeheartedly in His saving blood, trusting in His precious Word. The believer who abides faithfully in Jesus, feeding upon the Word, assimilating it through study, humbly submitting to the Spirit as the *truth* of the Word is revealed, will find peace, satisfaction, happiness, and victory. Isaiah 26:3 promises, "Thou wilt keep him *in perfect peace,* whose mind is stayed on thee: because he trusteth in thee."

By contrast, the believer who does *not* have assurance and satisfaction of heart has only himself to blame, because God has set the table before us and has invited—yea, *com-*

manded—that we feed. Therefore if we refuse to eat and be satisfied we have no one but ourselves to blame, and we will suffer loss when God rewards His children for their stewardship.

In verses 4 and 5, Jesus exhorted the disciples to abide in Him, and in verse 6 He warned them of the consequences of *failing* to abide. Now in verse 7 He returns to the blessings that will be theirs if they obey His admonition:

"Ye shall ask what ye will, and it shall be done unto you." The abiding believer has a divine guarantee that God will answer his prayers. This does not mean that he can ask God for a new automobile, a new home, or a fat bank account and expect God to readily grant such requests. The abiding believer will not pray foolish prayers; he will pray *according to the will of God.* I John 5:14 promises, "This is the confidence that we have in Him, that, if we ask any thing *according to His will, HE HEARETH US!"*

There are two conditions in verse 7 which must be met if we expect God to keep His promise:

(1) *"If ye abide in ME,* and (2) *my words abide in YOU."* Abiding in Christ means full surrender of heart, spirit, and body. Such a believer maintains heart-communion with the Lord Jesus Christ at all times. Then, the abiding believer must continually feed upon the Scriptures and be occupied with a deep desire to know more of God's Word. The Christian who is fully surrendered to Jesus and who constantly maintains heart-communion with God can claim the promise of this verse, for the Christian who meets the two conditions set forth here will pray in the Spirit and according to the will of God. Therefore he can ask what he will, and it shall be done unto him.

The believer who lives in constant fellowship with Christ will heed the words of Paul in II Corinthians 10:5, "casting down imaginations, and every high thing that exalteth itself against the knowledge of God, *and bringing into captivity every thought to the obedience of Christ."*

The believer who expects God to answer prayer will also

keep in mind instructions concerning prayer, as found in God's Word:

James said, ". . . ye have not, because ye ask not. Ye ask, and receive not, because ye ask amiss, that ye may consume it upon your lusts" (James 4:2b,3).

Also in James 5:16 we read, "Confess your faults one to another, and pray one for another, that ye may be healed. The effectual fervent prayer of a righteous man availeth much."

Instructing His disciples regarding prayer, Jesus said, "When thou prayest, thou shalt not be as the hypocrites are: for they love to pray standing in the synagogues and in the corners of the streets, that they may be seen of men. Verily, I say unto you, They have their reward. But thou, when thou prayest, enter into thy closet, and when thou hast shut thy door, pray to thy Father which is in secret; and thy Father which seeth in secret shall reward thee openly. But when ye pray, use not vain repetitions, as the heathen do: for they think that they shall be heard for their much speaking. Be not ye therefore like unto them: for your Father knoweth what things ye have need of, before ye ask Him" (Matt. 6:5–8).

Verse 8: *"Herein is my Father glorified, that ye bear much fruit; so shall ye be my disciples."*

As Jesus tabernacled among men, the glory of the heavenly Father was uppermost in His mind at all times. He came into the world to do the Father's will and to complete the work the Father gave Him to do; and when He returned to the Father He left instructions with His disciples, instructions which have been passed on to us. It is His desire that we, the children of God, glorify, honor, and magnify God in all that we do. An unfruitful believer is a dishonor to the heavenly Father, and it should be the heart's desire of each and every Christian to abide in Christ. The Psalmist expressed it in these words:

"Blessed is the man that walketh not in the counsel of

the ungodly, nor standeth in the way of sinners, nor sitteth in the seat of the scornful. But his delight is in the law of the Lord; and in His law doth he meditate day and night. And he shall be like a tree planted by the rivers of water, that bringeth forth his fruit in his season; his leaf also shall not wither; and whatsoever he doeth shall prosper.

"The ungodly are not so: but are like the chaff which the wind driveth away. Therefore the ungodly shall not stand in the judgment, nor sinners in the congregation of the righteous. For the Lord knoweth the way of the righteous: but the way of the ungodly shall perish" (Psalm 1).

The Father is glorified when we bear *"much fruit."* What IS the fruit of which Jesus spoke here? Suppose we return to the vine:

Jesus said, "I am the true vine, ye are the branches." The specific purpose of the branch is to bear fruit, but the fruit does not originate *outside* the branch; it is the product of the life-giving quality which proceeds from the vine *through* the branch. Fruit on a branch testifies that the branch is connected to the living vine which feeds the branch and produces fruit from within. Some Christians make a big outward show—but the inner life is lean and fruitless. They do what they do to bring glory and honor to *themselves* and for the praise of man, rather than serving to please God and bring honor to *Him.*

True, a fruit-bearing Christian will certainly *manifest* fruit—for Jesus said, "Let your light so shine before men, *that they may see your good works, and glorify your Father which is in heaven*" (Matt. 5:16); but when we are motivated solely by the desire to bring glory to God, those around us will take notice that we have been with Jesus, as was the case in Acts 4:13: "Now when they saw the boldness of Peter and John, and perceived that they were unlearned and ignorant men, they marvelled; *and they took knowledge of them, that they had been with Jesus.*"

Paul gives us a picture of God's fruitbasket in Galatians

5:22–26: "The fruit of the Spirit is love, joy, peace, longsuffering, gentleness, goodness, faith, meekness, temperance: against such there is no law. And they that are Christ's have crucified the flesh with the affections and lusts. If we live in the Spirit, let us also walk in the Spirit. Let us not be desirous of vain glory, provoking one another, envying one another."

It is extremely important that we recognize the divine truth that *fruit* in the life of a Christian is the outflow of the union we possess in Christ. When we are born of His Spirit, indwelt by the Spirit, led by the Spirit, and filled with the Spirit, we will bear the *fruit* of the Spirit.

In Philippians 1:11 Paul speaks of *"being filled with the fruits of righteousness, which are by Jesus Christ, unto the glory and praise of God."*

In II Corinthians 5:14,15 Paul said, "The love of Christ constraineth us; because we thus judge, that if One died for all, then were all dead: and that He died for all, *that they which live should not henceforth live unto themselves, but unto Him which died for them, and rose again."*

Believers who are filled with the fruit of righteousness are filled by Jesus Christ to the praise and glory of God. Believers who possess true love possess it because the love of Christ is in them. Believers who demonstrate joy unspeakable and full of glory do so because Christ's joy is in them. Believers who possess peace that goes beyond all earthly understanding have this peace because of Jesus; and believers who are meek, humble, gentle, and kind are so because of Jesus.

To the Apostle Paul, Christ was all in all. He testified, *"I will not dare to speak of any of those things which Christ hath NOT wrought by me,* to make the Gentiles obedient, by word and deed" (Rom. 15:18). In II Corinthians 13:3,4 he said, "Since ye seek a proof of Christ speaking IN me, which to you-ward is not weak, but is mighty in you. For though He was crucified through weakness, yet He liveth by the power of God. For we also are weak in Him, but we shall live with Him by the power of God toward you."

In Galatians 2:8 Paul testified, "He that wrought effectually in Peter to the apostleship of the circumcision, the same was mighty in me toward the Gentiles." In Philippians 4:13 he said, *"I can do all things through Christ which strengtheneth me."* And when he came to the end of this life's journey he said, "I am now ready to be offered, and the time of my departure is at hand. I have fought a good fight, I have finished my course, I have kept the faith: Henceforth there is laid up for me a crown of righteousness, which the Lord, the righteous Judge, shall give me at that day: and not to me only, but unto all them also that love His appearing" (II Tim. 4:6–8).

Before we can bear the fruit that will glorify God, we must, like Paul, recognize our total dependence upon Him. We must recognize the fact that we cannot depend upon our own strength and wisdom, we must exclude all selfishness and self-glory from our stewardship. Only then will the Lord Jesus Christ become all in all to us, only then will our fruit-bearing be to the praise and honor of God.

"So shall ye be my disciples." Abiding in Jesus and continuing in the Word is not a *condition* of discipleship, but is rather the *evidence* of it. Faith without works is dead, and a person is in error who testifies that he has exercised faith unto salvation and yet *bears no fruit.* ALL born again believers bear fruit—not all a hundredfold, not all sixty, but where there is spiritual life there is *some evidence* of that life in fruit-bearing.

Jesus warned His disciples, "Beware of false prophets, which come to you in sheep's clothing, but inwardly they are ravening wolves. Ye shall know them by their fruits. Do men gather grapes of thorns, or figs of thistles? Even so every good tree bringeth forth good fruit; but a corrupt tree bringeth forth evil fruit. A good tree cannot bring forth evil fruit, neither can a corrupt tree bring forth good fruit. Every tree that bringeth not forth good fruit is hewn down, and cast into the fire. *Wherefore by their fruits ye shall know them"* (Matt. 7:15–20).

Good fruit on a tree does not *make* the tree good, but rather, good fruit is testimony that the tree IS good. Likewise, fruit-bearing in the life of a believer does not *redeem* that believer, but the fruit of the Spirit is testimony that such a person is *born* of the Spirit, *indwelt* by the Spirit, and *led* by the Spirit.

Verse 9: *"As the Father hath loved me, so have I loved you: continue ye in my love."*

"As the Father hath loved me . . . ." How did the Father love Jesus? He loved Him from the beginning, for Jesus was in the beginning *with* the Father. God loved Him with a special, unchanging, everlasting love: and in this same manner Jesus loves every born again believer. In Jeremiah 31:3 we read, "The Lord hath appeared of old unto me, saying, Yes, I have loved thee with an everlasting love: therefore with lovingkindness have I drawn thee."

"Continue ye in my love." I am so glad Jesus' love for us is not affected by our changeableness. The Giver of every good and perfect gift is unchanging (James 1:17). However, if we hope to enjoy our spiritual birthright of abundant life and joy unspeakable, we must *continue* in His love. This has nothing to do with redemption; it has to do with abiding moment by moment in His love—and to *abide* in the love of God is to be *occupied* with the love of God, depending upon and resting in His love, *never doubting.*

God's love for us is not measured by our love for Him—if it were, we would be most pitiable. Writing to the believers at Ephesus Paul said, "Wherefore I desire that ye faint not at my tribulations for you, which is your glory. For this cause I bow my knees unto the Father of our Lord Jesus Christ, of whom the whole family in heaven and earth is named, that He would grant you, according to the riches of His glory, to be strengthened with might by His Spirit in the inner man; that Christ may dwell in your hearts by faith; *that ye, being rooted and grounded in love, may be able to comprehend with all saints WHAT IS THE BREADTH, AND LENGTH, AND DEPTH, AND HEIGHT; AND TO KNOW THE LOVE OF CHRIST, WHICH PASSETH KNOWLEDGE, that ye might be filled with all the fulness of God"* (Eph. 3:13–19).

Verse 10: *"If ye keep my commandments, ye shall abide in my love; even as I have kept my Father's commandments, and abide in His love."*

"If ye keep MY commandments . . . ." Jesus is speaking here of the commandments in the New Testament, His own commandments—not the Law of Moses, for "by the deeds of the law there shall no flesh be justified in His sight" (Rom. 3:20). The law was not given to save us; "the law was our schoolmaster to bring us unto Christ, that we might be justified by faith" (Gal. 3:24). Jesus is the only person who ever kept the law perfectly; therefore "Christ is *the end of the law* for righteousness to every one that believeth" (Rom. 10:4). Our Lord was speaking here of His own commandments, and the New Testament has scores of verses which pertain to those commandments. Note what Paul says in writing to the believers in Corinth:

"For though I be free from all men, yet have I made myself servant unto all, that I might gain the more. And unto the Jews I became as a Jew, that I might gain the Jews; to them that are under the law, as under the law, that I might gain them that are under the law: to them that are without law, as without law, (being not without law to God, but under the law to Christ,) that I might gain them that are without law. To the weak became I as weak, that I might gain the weak: I am made all things to all men, that I might by all means save some" (I Cor. 9:19–22).

Several times in his letter to the Christians in Rome, Paul deals with this subject. In Romans 13:10 we read, "Love worketh no ill to his neighbour: therefore love is the fulfilling of the law." In Romans 7:22 and 25 he said, "I delight in the law of God after the inward man. . . I thank God through Jesus Christ our Lord. So then with the mind I myself serve the law of God; but with the flesh the law of sin."

Then in Romans 8:1–4 he said, "There is therefore now no condemnation to them which are in Christ Jesus, who walk not after the flesh, but after the Spirit. For the law of the Spirit of life in Christ Jesus hath made me free from the law of sin and death. For what the law could not do, in that it was weak through the flesh, God sending His own Son in the likeness of sinful flesh, and for sin, condemned sin in the flesh: *That the righteousness of the law might be fulfilled in us, who walk not after the flesh, but after the Spirit.*"

"If ye keep my commandments, ye shall abide in my love." The fact that Jesus said this to His disciples does not put us in bondage under the Law of Moses—although God has not destroyed the law. We are law-keepers IN CHRIST, but *only* in Christ. There is a vast difference, however, between the commandments God gave to Moses and the commandments spoken by Jesus to His disciples and to believers in this present day.

For example, in John 13:34 He said, "A new commandment I give unto you, That ye love one another; as I have loved you, that ye also love one another." In John 14:15 He said, "If ye love me, *keep* my commandments." And in Matthew 28:19,20 He said, "Go ye therefore, and teach all nations, baptizing them in the name of the Father, and of the Son, and of the Holy Ghost: *Teaching them to observe all things whatsoever I have commanded you*: and, lo, I am with you alway, even unto the end of the world."

"Even as I have kept my Father's commandments, and abide in His love." Jesus, very God in flesh, walked according to the Father's commandments. He did not speak or act independently of the heavenly Father, but as the Father directed. "For even Christ pleased not Himself; but,

as it is written, The reproaches of them that reproached thee fell on me" (Rom. 15:3).

Jesus came into the world to declare God to man, and His need was to do the *will* of God. When He came to the end of His earthly ministry He said to His Father in heaven, "I have glorified thee on the earth: *I have finished the work which thou gavest me to do.* And now, O Father, glorify thou me with thine own self with the glory which I had with thee before the world was" (John 17:4,5).

Obedience on the part of the believer assures fellowship with Jesus. The Christian who disregards the commandments of Jesus is not walking in the will of God nor abiding in the love of Jesus. The true believer does not despise or ignore the Law of Moses, but rather realizes and acknowledges that IN CHRIST we fulfill every jot and tittle of the law, and *without HIM we can do nothing!*

The commandments of Jesus include the entire inspired Word of God, with the exception of the rituals and political statutes under the old economy. These had to do with another dispensation, and the old passed away when the new came into power. Jesus fulfilled the law—including political statutes and religious rituals and offerings. He offered *one sacrifice*—once, for all, forever—the sacrifice that satisfied God completely as having to do with all of the ceremonial laws and statutes under the old covenant.

However, we must keep in mind that we are to study and rightly divide the Word of Truth—for instance, God gave Noah specific commandment to build an ark, and He commanded Abraham to go up on the mountain and offer Isaac as a sacrifice; but He has not commanded US to build an ark or to offer our sons in like manner as Abraham offered Isaac—nor will He do so. These commandments have been fulfilled; they have nothing to do with grace and our salvation insofar as we are individually concerned—but apart from such commandments, statutes and rituals, we are subject to all of the Word of God. "All Scripture is given by inspiration of God, and is profitable for doctrine, for reproof, for correction, for instruction in righteousness: that the man of God may be perfect, throughly furnished unto all good works" (II Tim. 3:16,17).

Christ's obedience to the *Father's* commandments was an obedience of love, and *our* obedience to Jesus must be the same. We love Him because He first loved us—and it is not difficult to obey one whom we love. *External* obedience is not a demonstration of love at all. If we do what we do because of what people may think about us, or because of what the Church may say about us; if we are seeking praise and respect from our fellowman, then we are not serving to the glory of God. Some people refrain from certain habits, or stay away from certain places, because they fear what others will say about them. Such abstinence is no good; it is vain and empty. We need to do—or *abstain* from doing—*because we love Jesus.*

The dedicated believer does not keep the commandments of Jesus because he MUST keep them, but because, *loving Him,* it is a joy to do those things which please Him. Jesus was faithful to the heavenly Father from the beginning to the end of His earthly life; He obeyed every word and fulfilled every desire of the great heart of God. He was faithful unto death, even the death of the cross—and we will be likeminded if we love Him as we should. Jesus said, "No man, having put his hand to the plough, and looking back, is fit for the kingdom of God" (Luke 9:62). And we have His promise, "To him that overcometh will I grant to sit with me in my throne, even as I also overcame, and am set down with my Father in His throne" (Rev. 3:21).

No matter how dedicated we may be, we need to get on our knees and pray for God to empty us of all selfishness, self-will, and all things that hinder the Spirit from having right-of-way in our lives.

Verse 11: *"These things have I spoken unto you, that my joy might remain in you, and that your joy might be full."*

In chapter 14, verse 27 of this study, Jesus promised

double peace—"Peace I leave with you, MY peace I give unto you . . . ." Now in our present verse we find *double JOY*—the joy of Christ Himself, and the joy we have IN HIM. ("And now come I to thee; and these things I speak in the world, that they might have my joy fulfilled in themselves"—John 17:13.)

Since Jesus was abiding in His Father's love, He had a joy the world knew nothing of. True, He was the "Man of sorrows" (Isa. 53:3), but He possessed a unique and singular joy as He tabernacled among men. HIS joy was to do the Father's will, to glorify the name of the Father and finish the work the Father had sent Him to do.

"Wherefore seeing we also are compassed about with so great a cloud of witnesses, let us lay aside every weight, and the sin which doth so easily beset us, and let us run with patience the race that is set before us, looking unto Jesus the author and finisher of our faith; *who for the joy that was set before Him endured the cross, despising the shame, and is set down at the right hand of the throne of God*" (Heb. 12:1,2).

This twofold joy of Jesus is mentioned in Psalm 16:8,9: "I have set the Lord always before me: because He is at my right hand, I shall not be moved. Therefore my heart is glad, and my glory rejoiceth: my flesh also shall rest in hope." Jesus knew and possessed the joy of perfect communion and perfect obedience to God the Father who sent Him into the world: "Thou wilt shew me the path of life: in thy presence is fulness of joy; at thy right hand there are pleasures for evermore" (Psalm 16:11).

Sin in the life of a believer breaks fellowship with the Father and destroys the joy which is our spiritual birthright. *David* sinned, thereby breaking fellowship between himself and his God. Joy departed from him and he prayed, "Restore unto me the joy of thy salvation; and uphold me with thy free Spirit" (Psalm 51:12).

Notice that David did not pray, "Lord, *save* me," or "Lord, restore my *salvation.*" He had not lost his salvation; he had lost his *joy* in the Lord. Therefore he prayed, "*Restore unto me the JOY of thy salvation!*" Sin destroys the joy believers should possess when they abide in the Lord and walk in the paths of righteousness for His name's sake.

Peter is another example of a Christian who sinned and lost the joy of salvation. He declared that he would go into Jerusalem and *die* with his Lord. He boldly declared, "Lord, I am ready to go with thee, both into prison, and to death!" (Luke 22:33). Jesus warned Peter that before the cock crew he would deny Him three times—and he did. He lost the joy of fellowshipping with his Lord, and in Luke 22:61,62 when Jesus turned and looked at Peter, "Peter went out, *and wept bitterly!*"

No person can be happy and rejoice in sin if he has been truly born of the Spirit, washed in the blood, and saved by God's grace. A believer out of fellowship with God is of all people most miserable.

"These things write we unto you, *that your joy may be full*" (I John 1:4). *Full joy* is the spiritual birthright of every believer, and the entire First Epistle of John was written that we might *enjoy* that birthright. Remember, beloved, *the first desire of the devil is to damn us;* but when we are born again he knows he cannot accomplish our damnation, so he sets about to rob us of our power, our usefulness to God, our joy, and our eternal reward. But there is victory! We can be more than conquerors *through Jesus Christ our Lord* if we will only trust and obey, abide in Him and allow Him to lead us moment by moment.

The only *real* joy is in Jesus. "Rejoice in the Lord alway: and again I say, Rejoice" (Phil. 4:4). The *world* can rejoice when all is well, but the Christian rejoices regardless of circumstances. Paul and Silas rejoiced and sang praises to God when they were arrested, beaten, and thrown into a dungeon, their feet made fast in the stocks in the inner prison; and their rejoicing brought a response from

God that led to the salvation of the Philippian jailer and his entire household! No matter what the circumstance, Christians can rejoice because Christ abides in our hearts and we abide in HIM. We are seated with Him in heavenly places (Eph. 2:6), and we "rejoice with joy unspeakable and full of glory" (I Pet. 1:8).

Verse 12: *"This is my commandment, That ye love one another, as I have loved you."*

This is a commandment, not a suggestion. We are to love our fellow believers as God has loved US. If we do this, if we love our fellow Christians as Jesus loved us, what will be our actions *toward* other Christians? The answer is found in Paul's letter to the believers at Rome:

"Love worketh no ill to his neighbour: therefore love is the fulfilling of the law" (Rom. 13:10).

In God's loveletter to His "little children" we find the kind of love that we should show toward our fellow believers:

"For this is the message that ye heard from the beginning, that we should love one another. Not as Cain, who was of that wicked one, and slew his brother. And wherefore slew he him? Because his own works were evil, and his brother's righteous. Marvel not, my brethren, if the world hate you. We know that we have passed from death unto life, because we love the brethren. He that loveth not his brother abideth in death. Whosoever hateth his brother is a murderer: and ye know that no murderer hath eternal life abiding in him. Hereby perceive we the love of God, because He laid down His life for us: and we ought to lay down our lives for the brethren.

"But whoso hath this world's good, and seeth his brother have need, and shutteth up his bowels of compassion from him, how dwelleth the love of God in him? My little children, let us not love in word, neither in tongue: but in deed and in truth.

"And hereby we know that we are of the truth, and shall

assure our hearts before Him. For if our heart condemn us, God is greater than our heart, and knoweth all things. Beloved, if our heart condemn us not, then have we confidence toward God. And whatsoever we ask, we receive of Him, because we keep His commandments, and do those things that are pleasing in His sight. And this is His commandment, That we should believe on the name of His Son Jesus Christ, and love one another, as He gave us commandment.

"And he that keepeth His commandments dwelleth in Him, and He in him. And hereby we know that He abideth in us, by the Spirit which He hath given us" (I John 3: 11–24).

What is the message? That we should love one another, and we know we are believers *because* we love one another. If we have this world's goods and our fellow believer is in need, and we refuse to help him, how dare we say the love of God dwells in us? We are to love *unbelievers*—that is, we are to love them in Christ, witness to them, and do all in our power to win them to Jesus; but we are to love our fellow believers with a *special* love, *as God has loved US.* And we should prove this love before the world in our attitude toward other Christians.

Jesus supported this command by His own example. We are to love as HE loved. The frequent repetition of the command to love one another proves the importance of Christian love—and there is entirely too little of it today! Great religious leaders, esteemed in the eyes and hearts of tens of thousands of church people, preach great sermons and teach great lessons; but all too often in private life they do not demonstrate the love of God.

Verse 13: *"Greater love hath no man than this, that a man lay down his life for his friends."*

In this verse Jesus teaches the *measure* of love believers should have for each other. As born again children of God, our love should be self-sacrificing—yes, even to death if need be. Christ died for US because He loved us. He proved His love by His death on the cross—but remember, HE died not only for His friends, but for His enemies as well!

"For when we were yet without strength, in due time Christ died for the ungodly. . . God commendeth His love toward us, in that, while we were yet sinners, Christ died for us" (Rom. 5:6,8). Love can go no further. Dying for one whom we love is the greatest possible demonstration of love.

In I John 4:7—21 we read, "Beloved, let us love one another: for love is of God; and every one that loveth is born of God, and knoweth God. He that loveth not knoweth not God; for God is love. In this was manifested the love of God toward us, because that God sent His only begotten Son into the world, that we might live through Him.

"Herein is love, not that we loved God, but that He loved us, and sent His Son to be the propitiation for our sins.

"Beloved, if God so loved us, we ought also to love one another. No man hath seen God at any time. If we love one another, God dwelleth in us, and His love is perfected in us.

"Hereby know we that we dwell in Him, and He in us, because He hath given us of His Spirit. And we have seen and do testify that the Father sent the Son to be the Saviour of the world. Whosoever shall confess that Jesus is the Son of God, God dwelleth in him, and he in God. And we have known and believed the love that God hath to us. God is love; and he that dwelleth in love dwelleth in God, and God in him.

"Herein is our love made perfect, that we may have boldness in the day of judgment: because as He is, so are we in this world. There is no fear in love; but perfect love casteth out fear: because fear hath torment. He that feareth is not made perfect in love.

"We love Him, because He first loved us. If a man

say, I love God, and hateth his brother, he is a liar: for he that loveth not his brother whom he hath seen, how can he love God whom he hath NOT seen? And this commandment have we from Him, That he who loveth God love his brother also."

Verse 14: *"Ye are my friends, if ye do whatsoever I command you."*

In the deeper intimacy which Jesus established between Himself and believers in the discourse recorded here, He unfolds more fully what was involved in the disciples' being called His "friends." He had already made it clear that it meant doing His will, doing those things that pleased Him; but they were to do more than this. Later, in some of the epistles, the disciples referred to themselves as "servants" (bondslaves) (see II Peter 1:1, Jude 1, and Romans 1:1). For true believers, the capacity of being a servant goes further than serving in the position of a bondslave; it carries with it the intimacy and communion of true friendship.

Verse 15: *"Henceforth I call you not servants; for the servant knoweth not what his lord doeth: but I have called you friends; for all things that I have heard of my Father I have made known unto you."*

"The servant knoweth not what his lord doeth." The servant (as such) does not have full knowledge of what his master is doing; his knowledge is limited to his *duties*. But when the master takes the servant into his confidence, the situation is changed and the servant then occupies the position of communion and friendship. That is what Jesus is saying here: *"I have called you FRIENDS."*

"For all things that I have heard of my Father I have made known unto you." All things that were needful to the welfare and spiritual good of the disciples, all things they were able to receive and understand at that moment, Jesus made known to them. In chapter 16, verses 12 and

13, Jesus said to these men, "I have yet many things to say unto you, *but ye cannot bear them now.* Howbeit when He, the Spirit of truth, is come, HE will guide you into ALL truth: for He shall not speak of Himself; but whatsoever He shall hear, that shall He speak: *and He will shew you things to come.*" But what Jesus meant in our present verse was that He had made known to them all things they were capable of understanding up to that time.

The grand, glorious, and high privilege of being a believer is set forth here by the Lord Jesus Christ. The Christian is a friend of Christ as well as a child of God. There are times when most of us feel that we do not have a friend—but we do! We have a Friend in heaven, a Friend who never changes, a Friend who "sticketh closer than a brother."

It is noteworthy that in all of the Old Testament Scriptures, only one man is named whom God called "friend." We read in Isaiah 41:8, "But thou, Israel, art my servant, Jacob whom I have chosen, the seed of *Abraham my friend.*"

James, writing for New Testament believers, referred to this remarkable friendship when he said, "Abraham believed God, and it was imputed unto him for righteousness: *and he was called the Friend of God*" (James 2:23).

We are saved by grace—just as saved as we will ever be; but the spiritual life is progressive, and we are commanded to grow in grace and increase in faith. We see this progressive intimacy between Jesus and His disciples as we study John's Gospel: In chapter 13, verse 13, Jesus said, "Ye call me Master and Lord: and ye say well; FOR SO I AM." In chapter 15, our present verse, He calls the disciples "friends," and in chapter 20, verse 17, He calls them "brethren."

Verse 16: *"Ye have not chosen me, but I have chosen you, and ordained you, that ye should go and bring forth fruit, and that your fruit should remain: that whatsoever ye shall ask of the Father in my name, He may give it you."*

Bible scholars do not fully agree on the full meaning of this verse. Some believe that "I have chosen" speaks of election unto salvation and therefore speaks to all who are saved by grace. Others believe that it speaks only of election insofar as the service (choosing of an office) of the *apostles* is concerned. Personally, I am inclined to agree with the latter. I believe Jesus was speaking specifically to the eleven concerning their stewardship. They were already believers, He had called and ordained them apostles. His instructions to *"go and bring forth fruit"* seem to apply in a very special and peculiar way to them, as did the commission given in Matthew 28:19,20.

"That your fruit should remain" applies to a lasting and abiding work done by these men when they were sent forth throughout the known world, preaching the Gospel of the grace of God; but I believe there is also a lesson here for Christians today. In Hebrews 2:3,4 Paul asked the heart-searching question, *"How shall we escape, if we neglect so great salvation;* which at the first began to be spoken by the Lord, and was confirmed unto us by them that heard Him; God also bearing them witness, both with signs and wonders, and with divers miracles, and gifts of the Holy Ghost, according to His own will?"

Yes, God wrought special miracles by the hands of the apostles, and since Paul's day some of these miracles have never been repeated. No preacher since Paul has raised the dead—but *we* do not need signs and wonders today because we have the perfect law of liberty, the complete Scriptures, and "when that which is perfect is come, then that which is in part shall be done away" (I Cor. 13:10). The day of miracles is not over, to be sure. The greatest miracle on earth—even greater than raising the dead—is the conversion of a sinner. But since we have "Thus saith the Lord" we do not need to see signs and wonders. When we hear His Word and believe on Jesus, we have everlasting life. As we study and appropriate His Word, our faith is strengthened and increased. The apostles were ordained to a special and peculiar ministry during the transition from law to grace.

Jesus definitely chose the apostles, He called each of them individually; they did not choose HIM. He ordained the apostles (Luke 6:13), and since the calling and ordination of the Apostle Paul there has not *been* an apostle. *Sons of God?* Yes. *Ministers of the Gospel?* Indeed so. *Missionaries?* Certainly. *Apostles?* NO. They were special ministers ordained of God at a special time for a special ministry.

"Chosen" here speaks of choosing one for an office. It is the same truth set forth in John 6:70 when Jesus said to the disciples, "Have not I *chosen you twelve,* and one of you is a devil?" Jesus chose these men and set them apart for the specific purpose of preaching the Gospel of the grace of God. And since they did not have the New Testament as we have it, they had no written Scripture other than that of the Old Testament, He encouraged them by promising, *"Whatsoever ye shall ask of the Father in my name, He may give it you."* Jesus chose and ordained them, He was sending them forth to bear fruit, and whatever they needed to effectively fulfill their ministry, they would find supplied by the heavenly Father if they asked in the name of His dear Son.

"That your fruit should remain" is comforting to me. While I believe this was given specifically to the apostles, we do have the assurance in Revelation 14:13, *"Blessed are the dead which die in the Lord from henceforth: Yea, saith the Spirit, that they may rest from their labours; AND THEIR WORKS DO FOLLOW THEM."*

I believe this verse of Scripture declares that *if we who are in Christ* die before the Rapture, we will go to be with Jesus—blessed and happy in Paradise. The body will return to dust, and the spirit will go back to God who gave it. Then the work that we have accomplished here in faith, in the Spirit and to the glory of God, will remain and continue to bring forth fruit *until the last soul is saved and the Church is raptured!* For example, when in the Gospel Hour ministry I lead someone to Jesus, it is not I alone, but all who have had a part in my ministry, all who have helped to make it possible for me to be on the radio or in revivals, or to send out our literature. Each person who has a part in the Gospel Hour ministry has a part in the salvation of souls won *through* this ministry.

The souls we lead to Jesus will lead others to Him, and we will have a part in the reward for every soul won by those *we* win for Christ. That is why not one believer in the New Testament Church can be rewarded for individual stewardship until *all* believers are gathered at the marriage supper of the Lamb. All believers who have died during the Dispensation of Grace are resting in Paradise, waiting until that glorious day when the Church will be complete and caught up to meet Jesus in the clouds in the air, where we will be rewarded, every one, for our stewardship.

"He that reapeth receiveth wages, and gathereth fruit unto life eternal: that both he that soweth and he that reapeth may rejoice together" (John 4:36).

It is true that we are chosen of the Lord unto salvation (Rom. 5:8)—but not in the sense that some are chosen to be saved while others are chosen to be damned. II Peter 3:9 plainly tells us that God is "not willing that any should perish, but that all should come to repentance," and the invitation in Matthew 11:28 is "Come unto me, ALL ye that labour and are heavy laden . . . ." No one believes in the sovereignty of God more than I do. I believe in Bible election and Bible predestination—I believe the Church *as a body* was elected before the foundation of the world; but the Church is made up of individuals who believe on the Lord Jesus Christ AFTER hearing His Word. God did not choose some to be saved and others to be damned. *"God so loved THE WORLD"*—and that takes in everyone, it excludes no one.

I believe God chooses, calls, and ordains men today—pastors, teachers, evangelists, missionaries, deacons. Not all are called to be full time Christian workers. God saves all who will come to Him by the Lord Jesus Christ, and then out of the millions of born again ones He calls and ordains individuals to minister. Such is His program in this Day of Grace. ALL believers are stewards, and all believers *should be* soul winners, witnessing and sowing the seed of the Gospel; but not all believers are called to be pastors, teachers, evangelists, or missionaries.

We might note here that Jesus never called a disciple to serve Him *part* of his life, nor did He give His disciples the privilege of making the ministry a sideline while they participated in other things. "The gifts and calling of God are without repentance" (Rom. 11:29). When God calls a man into *full time service,* He calls him *fully.* The call to pastor a church, the call to be an evangelist or missionary, is not a "part time" calling, nor is it for so long as a person feels he is suited for it. God calls and ordains a man for as long as that man lives, and there is no such thing as retiring from a God-ordained ministry. Sometimes health or the passing of years prevents one from continuing to be as active as in the early days of a ministry, but God's calling is a lifetime calling.

Verse 17: *"These things I command you, that ye love one another."*

Personally, I believe *"these things"* points to the things Jesus is about to say, though some may interpret it to refer back to what has just *been* said. "I press on you these repeated charges to love one another, because the world will hate you." He did not say, "I *suggest* that you love one another if you find it profitable or convenient." He said, *"I COMMAND you,* that ye love one another." Again and again He has repeated the command that the disciples love one another. He warned them that they would be hated and despised by the world, for since the world hated HIM it would hate them too; and the more the world hated them, the more they should love one another, and *through* their love for each other they would prove to the world that they were disciples of Jesus and therefore were not OF the world.

The fact that the world will hate believers is mentioned seven times in the verses that follow. Jesus had just assured the disciples that they were His friends, and now He begins to describe their enemies and the *deadliness* of those enemies. He had set before the apostles the divine truth of His unchanging love for them; now He warns them of the certain hatred of the world for them.

He has given various reasons and motives for the disciples' loving one another, the main reason being the example He had set before them—His own love for them. Now He sets forth a new and different reason: Christians need to love one another, live in harmony, unity, and brotherly love, *because our enemy the world is definitely united in its hatred of true Christians!* You may rest assured that the closer you live to God and the more dedicated you are, the more you will be hated by the world. We hear much today about ministers being "good mixers," but the ministers of Jesus Christ are *good "separators."* We are to have no fellowship with the unfruitful works of darkness; we are to love not the world, neither the things that are IN the world. The world hated Jesus, and if we walk in His footsteps we will be hated too. The Holy Spirit warns, through the inspired pen of John the Beloved, "Marvel not, my brethren, if the world hate you" (I John 3:13).

Tenderly, graciously, and compassionately Jesus is here fortifying His disciples against the storms of persecution which He knew would strike soon after He left them. He had chosen them, ordained them, given them a mission and a ministry; and He knew the fulfillment of that ministry would bring persecution, not praise; crosses, not crowns. Insofar as the record shows, there was no severe persecution directed toward the disciples until after the crucifixion, resurrection, and ascension of our Lord. When He sent the seventy out to preach the Gospel, they evidently encountered no persecution, because Luke 10:17 tells us that "the seventy returned again with joy, saying, Lord, even the devils are subject unto us through thy name!"

The religious leaders of that day were offended when the apostles transgressed the tradition of the elders and the fathers, but instead of attacking them directly the religious leaders complained to Jesus, holding Him responsible for the actions of those who walked with Him: "Then came to Jesus scribes and Pharisees, which were of Jerusalem, saying, Why do thy disciples transgress the tradition of the elders? for they wash not their hands when they eat bread" (Matt. 15:1,2).

Even after the arrest and crucifixion of Jesus, the disciples were allowed to return to their nets and take up again their ordinary life in the community, unmolested. But Jesus knew that after His resurrection and ascension they would be severely persecuted. In John 16:33 He said to them, "These things I have spoken unto you, that in me ye might have peace. *In the world ye shall have tribulation: but be of good cheer; I have overcome the world.*" The Apostle Paul plainly told young Timothy, "Yea, and all that will live godly in Christ Jesus shall suffer persecution" (II Tim. 3:12).

Such words, penned down by holy men under inspiration of the Holy Spirit, certainly rebuke the popularity of many professing Christians today—even ministers, evangelists, and leaders in the church councils and organizations. Today religious leaders mix, mingle, and fellowship with men who openly deny the virgin birth of our Lord, the blood atonement, and the second coming. One outstanding religious leader of our day recently made the statement that it is not necessary to believe in the verbal inspiration of the Scriptures in order to be saved! If we do not believe in the verbal inspiration of the Scriptures, if we do not believe the Bible to be the Word of God, then who can tell us what part of it IS the Word of God and what part is NOT? We are living in an age when there are many false teachers, false apostles, and we need to try the spirits to see if they be of God: "Beloved, believe not every spirit, but try the spirits whether they are of God: because many false prophets are gone out into the world" (I John 4:1). If we who are truly born again befriend the enemies of Jesus, we will lose our reward. James said, "Ye adulterers and adulteresses, know ye not that the friendship of the world is enmity with God? Whosoever therefore will be a friend of the world is the enemy of God" (James 4:4).

How much plainer can it be made in the Word of God that those who claim to be followers of the Lord Jesus Christ and yet seek illicit love from liberals, modernists, and haters of God, stand before Him as spiritual adulterers and adulteresses? The same is true of church membership: If a born again Christian is a member of a church where the Gospel is not preached in all of its purity and power, even though the minister in that church may be popular, and social prestige may be there, the born again Christian is seeking and enjoying illicit love, spiritually speaking, if he supports such a church and such a pastor. Yet I know that some believers who will read these lines are members of churches that are pastored by liberals and modernists, and they will *remain* in those churches, even though the minister denies the virgin birth, the blood atonement, and other fundamentals of the faith. Such a believer will lose his reward!

Children of God and the World

Verse 18: *"If the world hate you, ye know that it hated me before it hated you."*

The subject of the world's hatred for believers is clearly introduced here. The world hates that which is not like itself. To be loved by the world one must act, think, and *be* like the world. Even though the persecution of the world is painful to bear, it is nevertheless evidence of a true stand for God. The disciples would suffer at the hands of the world simply because *Jesus* suffered before them; the world would hate *them* because it hated *Him*. They need not be perplexed or astonished when they realized that the masses would not treat them kindly. Yet—they must not retaliate, they must not fight back. God's Word commands us to live peaceably with all men insofar as is possible without compromising. Christians are not to return evil for evil. Let us turn again to the words penned down by the Apostle Paul:

"Let love be without dissimulation. Abhor that which is evil; cleave to that which is good. Be kindly affectioned one to another with brotherly love; in honour preferring one another; not slothful in business; fervent in spirit; serving the Lord; rejoicing in hope; patient in tribulation; continuing instant in prayer; distributing to the necessity of saints; given to hospitality.

"Bless them which persecute you: bless, and curse not. Rejoice with them that do rejoice, and weep with them that weep. Be of the same mind one toward another. Mind not high things, but condescend to men of low estate. Be not wise in your own conceits.

"Recompense to no man evil for evil. Provide things honest in the sight of all men. If it be possible, as much as lieth in you, live peaceably with all men.

"Dearly beloved, avenge not yourselves, but rather give place unto wrath: for it is written, Vengeance is mine; I will repay, saith the Lord. Therefore if thine enemy hunger, feed him; if he thirst, give him drink: for in so doing thou shalt heap coals of fire on his head. Be not overcome of evil, but overcome evil with good" (Rom. 12:9—21).

It should be of comforting assurance to the Christian to know that Jesus walked this path before He called upon us to walk it; and if we are hated, despised, and persecuted we know that He endured the same before us. John 10:4 tells us, "When He putteth forth His own sheep, He goeth before them, and the sheep follow Him: for they know His voice." We have the assurance today that the Holy Spirit not only goes *before* us, but also *abides with us* to lead us and guide us in the paths of righteousness for Jesus' sake.

No, we should not be sorrowful if we are hated and persecuted by the world. On the contrary, we should be concerned if we *escape* persecution, because if we stand up for Jesus we are sure to meet with condemnation from the world! The Psalmist said, "I had rather be a doorkeeper in the house of my God, than to dwell in the tents of wickedness" (Psalm 84:10); and in Psalm 37:16 we read, "A little that a righteous man hath is better than the riches of many wicked." If we compromise with the enemies of Jesus we will lose our reward and be partakers of their evil deeds (II John 7–11). May God help us when the world hates us and persecutes us, to rejoice and be glad, knowing that the world treated our blessed Saviour the same way before us!

"It is enough for the disciple that he be as his Master, and the servant as his Lord. If they have called the Master of the house Beelzebub, how much more shall they call them of His household? . . . Think not that I am come to send peace on earth: I came not to send peace, but a sword. For I am come to set a man at variance against his father, and the daughter against her mother, and the daughter in law against her mother in law. And a man's foes shall be they of his own household. . . And he that taketh not his cross, and followeth after me, is not worthy of me" (Matt. 10:25–38).

Verse 19: *"If ye were of the world, the world would love his own: but because ye are not of the world, but I have chosen you out of the world, therefore the world hateth you."*

It is most interesting to note that Jesus mentions "the world" five times in this verse.

"If ye were of the world, the world would love his own." God pity the Christian who desires the praise of the world! We are IN the world, but we are not OF the world because

Jesus has chosen us *out* of the world. We walk on earth, but our citizenship is in heaven; we are strangers and pilgrims on earth, seeking a city whose Builder and Maker is God. We no longer share the love of the world, we do not love what the world loves. We are not governed by the principles of the world, therefore the world hates us. We will be appreciated only by the spiritually minded; we will receive frowns, not smiles, from unbelievers.

Jesus said to His enemies, "Ye are from beneath; I am from above: ye are of this world; I am not of this world" (John 8:23). Now He points out to the disciples that they, too, are citizens of another world, with a home and an inheritance in heaven, and the world will treat them exactly like it treated HIM.

The world will not hate one who is *conformed to the world*, but believers are commanded, "Be *not* conformed to this world: but be ye *transformed* by the renewing of your mind, that ye may prove what is that good, and acceptable, and perfect, will of God" (Rom. 12:2).

The church member who takes part in all social and political events, indulges in pleasures of the world, belongs to all the civic organizations, and attends more parties than prayermeetings will not be persecuted; but the born again Christian who believes in a dedicated, Spirit-filled walk with Jesus, abstaining from the appearance of evil and having no fellowship with the unfruitful works of darkness, will be ostracized and persecuted! It is natural for the world to hate a consecrated believer—just as natural as it is for the sun to rise in the east or for water to run downhill. II Peter 1:4 tells us that believers possess divine nature, and certainly divine nature and the world cannot fellowship together. We are dead to the world, and the world is dead to us.

Paul cried out, "God forbid that I should glory, save in the cross of our Lord Jesus Christ, by whom the world is crucified unto me, and I unto the world" (Gal. 6:14). In other words, the fellowship existing between a consecrated

Christian and the world is the same fellowship that exists between two corpses in a morgue! If we should walk into a room where only two dead men lie, we would find unbroken silence—no activity, no fellowship, because both men are dead; they are dead *to each other.* The same is true in the Christian life: If we are what we should be for Jesus, we are dead to the world, and the world is dead to US. Therefore there is *no fellowship* between a Spirit-filled believer and the world.

Christians who walk in the footsteps of the rejected, crucified Christ will learn something of what it means to enter into "the fellowship of His sufferings" (Phil. 3:10). In the Sermon on the Mount Jesus said, "Blessed are they which are persecuted for righteousness' sake: for their's is the kingdom of heaven. Blessed are ye, when men shall revile you, and persecute you, and shall say all manner of evil against you falsely, for my sake. Rejoice, and be exceeding glad: for great is your reward in heaven: for so persecuted they the prophets which were before you" (Matt. 5:10–12).

Verse 20: *"Remember the word that I said unto you, The servant is not greater than his lord. If they have persecuted me, they will also persecute you; if they have kept my saying, they will keep your's also."*

"Remember the Word." Over and over again Jesus repeated these meaningful truths to His disciples—but since all Scripture is inspired and is profitable to us, we must consider that He was speaking also to you and to me. We are so prone to forget! We need to remember every word He said. The Psalmist declared, "Thy Word have I *hid in mine heart,* that I might not sin against thee" (Psalm 119:11).

"The servant is not greater than his lord." From the very outset of His ministry Jesus taught the disciples that they should not expect to be received more readily nor treated more kindly than He. They knew how the world had treated Him, and they should expect the same. WE need to remember this, also. Jesus was hated by the world

nineteen hundred years ago, and He is hated no less today. Therefore, if we live wholeheartedly for Him, we will be hated and persecuted by the same world that rejected the Saviour.

"If they have persecuted me, they will also persecute you." Believers should know what to expect from the world. If we are servants and followers of Jesus, then we must fellowship in His sufferings. Thank God for our present position in Christ! We are seated in heavenly places in Him, we are hid with Christ in God, there is no condemnation to us because we are in Christ Jesus, and Christ in us is the hope of glory. No wonder the world hates true believers! Many born again Christians suffer trouble and perplexity of spirit because they have wrong expectations concerning the world and a believer's relationship *with* the world. Jesus offers clear, down-to-earth, understandable words here, and as we walk with Him through this wilderness of sin we should *remember* His teaching. Did the world receive Jesus? Then the world will not receive US. Did they persecute Jesus? Then they will persecute us if we live for Him. Did the world hate Jesus? Then the world will hate US—and the closer we live to Him, the greater that hatred will be.

"If they have kept my saying, they will keep your's also." The Word of God is quick and powerful and sharper than any two-edged sword—it cuts going and coming, and the world hates Jesus because His Word condemns them. The Word of God is like the sun—the same sun that melts the ice also bakes the clay that makes bricks. Just so, the Word of God, if received, melts the hard heart; but if rejected, that same Word will make a heart as hard as stone.

"And this is the condemnation, that light is come into the world, and men loved darkness rather than light, because their deeds were evil. For every one that doeth evil hateth the light, neither cometh to the light, lest his deeds should be reproved. But he that doeth truth cometh to the light, that his deeds may be made manifest, that they are wrought in God" (John 3:19–21).

In I John 4:5,6 we read, "They are of the world: therefore speak they of the world, and the world heareth them. We are of God: *he that knoweth God heareth us; he that is NOT of God heareth not us.* Hereby know we the spirit of truth, and the spirit of error."

The Word of God is *light* to those who receive it, but it becomes *darkness* to those who reject it.

Verse 21: *"But all these things will they do unto you for my name's sake, because they know not Him that sent me."*

Here the Lord tells His disciples the primary reason the world would hate them: "*. . . for my name's sake.*" Jesus was soon to return to the Father, and the disciples would be His representatives on earth. They would preach salvation in His name (because "there is none other name under heaven given among men, whereby we must be saved"—Acts 4:12); and *because* the disciples would speak in His name, the world would hate them. It would not be their *persons* the world would hate, but the Person whom they would lift up and preach—the Lord Jesus Christ.

It is a grand and glorious thing to be a child of God; it is glorious to know the joy of salvation, to know that IN HIM we are complete and *through* Him our every need will be supplied; but it is *just* as glorious and wonderful to know that Christ allows us to share in His sufferings: "If ye be reproached for the name of Christ, happy are ye; for the spirit of glory and of God resteth upon you: on their part He is evil spoken of, but on your part He is glorified" (I Pet. 4:14).

From the Holy Scriptures we know that the apostles were arrested, threatened, commanded not to speak in the name of Jesus—but they preached His name daily, in prison or out. These first evangelists were like Moses, who esteemed "the reproach of Christ greater riches than the treasures in Egypt: for he had respect unto the recompence of the reward" (Heb. 11:26).

If we are what we should be spiritually, we too will esteem the reproach of Jesus far greater riches than anything the world has to offer. The church member, Sunday school teacher, deacon, steward, elder, minister, evangelist, or missionary who courts the praise of men rather than the smile of God is not *right* with God. In most instances, religious leaders who court the praises of the world are not saved men; they have simply taken up the ministry as a vocation instead of being called and ordained of God.

"Because they know not Him that sent me." The unbelieving Jews did not know God the Father—at least they did not know Him in the right way. They did not know that Christ was God in flesh—their Messiah, the Promised One, "that Prophet" whom God would send. In this state of blindness and ignorance, they persecuted Jesus and His followers. The hardness of heart and the judicial blindness of Israel as a nation are clearly set forth in Acts 3:17; 13:27; 28:25—27; I Corinthians 2:8; and II Corinthians 3:14.

Verse 22: *"If I had not come and spoken unto them, they had not had sin: but now they have no cloke for their sin."*

In this verse—and the three following verses—is seen the deep and peculiar guilt and terrible wickedness of the Jews in not believing Jesus to be their Messiah.

If He had not tabernacled among them, the Word in flesh, speaking and teaching as no man had ever spoken or taught; if He had not worked such miracles as had never been wrought before; if His identity had not been revealed in all that He did or said, they might have had some reason for rejecting Him. If He had been just an ordinary man—*but He was not;* there was nothing ordinary about Him. Everything He did and said was *extraordinary.* The Jews saw Him, they heard Him, He had tabernacled among them during the three and one-half years of His earthly ministry. Yet they rejected Him—*without excuse!*

Deuteronomy 18:18,19 records the words of Moses, written centuries before Jesus came: "I will raise them up a Prophet from among their brethren, like unto thee, and will put my words in His mouth; and He shall speak unto them all that I shall command Him. And it shall come to pass, that whosoever will not hearken unto my words which He shall speak in my name, I will require it of him."

"Now they have no cloke for their sin." The word here translated "cloke" would be better rendered "excuse." Having spoken as He did in their presence, having wrought the miracles He wrought before them, they had no excuse for their sin of rejecting Him.

When Jesus said "they had not sin" He was speaking of the degree of their guilt; He did not mean that they were not *sinners.* He meant that they would not have been guilty of the terrible sin of rejecting Him. But they had heard His words, they had witnessed His miracles, and therefore their guilt was far greater. In John 9:41 Jesus said to them, "If ye were blind, ye should have no sin: but now ye say, We see; therefore your sin remaineth." These people were proud, haughty, rebellious—and spiritually blind. They claimed to know Moses, they claimed to be children of Abraham; but Jesus clearly declared that had they known Moses or had they been children of Abraham, they would have recognized and accepted Him as their Messiah. In John 8:44 He told them in plain words, "Ye are of your father *the devil,* and the lusts of your father ye will do."

Beloved, I would lay upon your heart the awful truth that we as Christians will be held accountable for the opportunities we failed to buy up; we will be held responsible for the light we rejected and in which we refused to walk. To whom much is given, of him shall much be required. We can rest assured that when we stand before the judgment seat of Christ to receive our rewards for stewardship, we will be judged in righteousness and we will receive what is right!

The same is true concerning sinners. The degree of punishment in hell for the lost will be determined—not only by their refusal to receive Jesus, but according to the opportunities they had to be saved, opportunities they refused. Oh, yes—the Scriptures plainly teach that there will be degrees of punishment in hell. Jesus said, in Luke 12:47,48, "That servant, which knew his Lord's will, and prepared not himself, neither did according to His will, shall be beaten with many stripes. But he that knew not, and did commit things worthy of stripes, shall be beaten with few stripes. For unto whomsoever much is given, of him shall be much required: and to whom men have committed much, of him they will ask the more."

Verse 23: *"He that hateth me hateth my Father also."*

In this statement Jesus declared the unparalleled greatness of the sin of the Jews in rejecting Him as their Messiah. He was the Word Incarnate, God in flesh (John 1:1, 14; II Cor. 5:19), and the words He had spoken were not His words only, but the Father's words. The Jews professed to love God, but they hated Christ; and in rejecting Him they rejected God the Father also. They were the enemies of Christ, therefore they were the enemies of God, the God of their fathers whom they professed to know and serve.

John the Baptist declared, "No man hath seen God at any time; *the only begotten Son,* which is in the bosom of the Father, He hath declared Him" (John 1:18). Christ did reveal the Father. He was "the brightness of His glory, and the express image of His Person" (Heb. 1:3). To Philip Jesus said, "He that hath seen me hath seen the *Father*" (John 14:9).

The words of Jesus were the words of God, His doctrine was the doctrine of God, and in His life He put on display the *perfections* of God. No man could accuse Him of sin, and to hate Him was to hate God.

Verse 24: *"If I had not done among them the works*

which none other man did, they had not had sin: but now have they both seen and hated both me and my Father."

Only the virgin-born Son of God could make such a declaration! He was here declaring that the works He did placed Him far above any messenger, prophet, priest, or whomsoever might have preceded or followed Him.

The Jews enjoyed privileges and opportunities such as no other nation on earth enjoyed. Not only were they God's chosen people, but they had heard the words of Jesus, they had witnessed His mighty miracles—no doubt many of them were present when He fed the multitude with the loaves and fishes. Had they not been so privileged, their guilt in rejecting Him would have been much less.

"Now have they both seen and hated both me and my Father." The presence of Jesus, the only begotten Son of God, here on this earth in a body, presented the greatest opportunity man has ever had, the greatest privilege man has ever known—and when He was rejected, that rejection brought upon men the gravest result imaginable!

"God, who at sundry times and in divers manners spake in time past unto the fathers by the prophets, hath in these last days spoken unto us *by His Son, whom He hath appointed heir of all things, by whom also He made the worlds"* (Heb. 1:1,2). Therefore those who walked in His presence, listened to His words, and witnessed His miracles—yet rejected Him as Messiah—brought upon themselves the gravest and most severe condemnation possible. Truly, "Never *man* spake like *this Man"* (John 7:46), but we can also say that in Jesus, GOD spoke as He had never spoken before; and the greater guilt rested upon those who heard Him and yet refused to believe and receive Him as Messiah.

Verse 25: *"But this cometh to pass, that the Word might be fulfilled that is written in their law, They hated me without a cause."*

Why DID the Jews hate Jesus—*and why do men hate*

Him today? At His trial, Pilate declared, "I find no fault in Him at all." His character was faultless, the doctrines He taught were the doctrines of God and true to the Old Testament Scriptures. His commandments were holy, just, and good. He harmed no one—on the contrary He healed the sick, opened the eyes of the blind, straightened withered limbs, fed the hungry, clothed the destitute, restored the dead to life. All that He did was in the interest of others. He had no place on earth to call home, He even borrowed a boat for a pulpit from which to preach. Yet He was hated, persecuted, falsely accused of every foul thing reprobate minds could conceive. Why was He hated and rejected? Jesus Himself answers: *"They hated me WITHOUT A CAUSE!"* Thus He traced the enmity of the world back to its true source. There was no reason for the world to hate Him; such hatred proceeded from wicked, unregenerate hearts. *"The heart is deceitful above all things, and desperately wicked: who can know it?"* (Jer. 17:9). Jesus said, "Out of the heart proceed evil thoughts, murders, adulteries, fornications, thefts, false witness, blasphemies" (Matt. 15:19).

He knew that the disciples were wondering why a holy God would allow His Son to be persecuted and hated as they had known Jesus to be, and He wanted them to understand that the treatment the world was giving Him was in fulfillment of the Word of God—*"that the Word might be fulfilled that is written in their law."* This does not mean that the things mentioned happened *in order that the Word might BE fulfilled,* but by their happening, *the Word WAS fulfilled.*

The Holy Spirit and the Believer

Verse 26: *"But when the Comforter is come, whom I will send unto you from the Father, even the Spirit of truth, which proceeded from the Father, He shall testify of me."*

In the preceding verses Jesus had clearly told the disciples that the world hated Him, and that the same world would hate all believers. The apostles did not have the written Word as we have it in the New Testament today, and it was only natural for them to wonder how they could overcome such difficulty as would confront them after Jesus departed. They wondered how they could overcome their enemies. Jesus knew their thoughts and their perplexities, and He assured them that He did not expect them to overcome the world and carry out their ministry by their own power or by human efforts. On the contrary, He would send another Comforter who would guide them into all truth.

Notice that Jesus spoke of the Comforter as *"the Spirit of truth, which proceedeth from the Father."* Notice also that the Holy Spirit was not to testify of Himself; but Jesus said, *"He shall testify of ME."* All true ministers speak in the Spirit and testify of Jesus—not of themselves. All true ministers direct all worship, honor, glory, and praise to Jesus. They magnify *His* name—not themselves, their talents and their abilities. The Apostle Paul said, *"We preach not ourselves, but CHRIST JESUS THE LORD..."* (II Cor. 4:5). I believe in a special anointing of the Spirit, I believe in the filling of the Spirit for specific ministries; but I do not believe in the modern program of those who claim to possess that special anointing and yet talk so little of Jesus and so much of their own achievements and works! The more fully we are controlled by the Holy Spirit the more we will praise Jesus and glorify His name, and the less we will talk about ourselves, our talents, our knowledge, and our achievements.

In John 14:26 Jesus said that the Comforter was to be sent by the Father in the name of the Lord Jesus Christ. In our present verse, the Comforter proceeds from God the Father, and when we place these two statements side by side we see *the unity of the Godhead.* In the statement in our present verse the Comforter is sent BY the ascended Christ, sent FROM God the Father; and since the Holy

Spirit was sent by Christ after He ascended to the heavenly Father, the Spirit witnesses and testifies of *the heavenly glory* of the ascended Christ.

The Spirit of truth is the only One who *could* witness truthfully of Christ as He is seated at the right hand of the Majesty above, for only the Holy Spirit *knows* the glory, splendor, and magnificence of the position the Lord Jesus Christ occupies—glorified now with all the glory He had with the Father before the world was (John 17:5).

Verse 27: *"And ye also shall bear witness, because ye have been with me from the beginning."*

"Ye also shall bear witness." The Holy Spirit would not be manifested in a body of flesh as Jesus was, but would bear witness *in and through the disciples* whom the Lord had chosen and ordained to bring forth fruit. The Spirit would testify of that which He had seen in Jesus *from the beginning,* that which the disciples had already heard, for Jesus had spoken in their presence. The Holy Spirit would not deliver a *new* message, because the Gospel was in the beginning—the *Word* was in the beginning, and Jesus was the Word Incarnate. The Spirit would bring to their memory all things Jesus had said to them.

The hatred of the world and the hostilities of Christ's enemies could not dampen or quench His compassion toward a lost world; and in this closing verse of this chapter He continued to encourage His disciples, telling them that in spite of the hardness of the Jews with their unbelief and hatred toward Him, He would enable them to deliver the message of the Gospel and bear testimony to His divine mission on earth. Their testimony would be such as their enemies would be forced to recognize—not as idle words of ignorant men, but as *divine,* inspired of God. This was fulfilled in a very remarkable way in the first years of Christianity. If you will study the first seven chapters of The Acts of the Apostles you will see the power of the Gospel of the marvelous grace of God. For example:

On the Day of Pentecost, Peter preached a sermon which can be read in five minutes; but when he finished preaching, declaring that Jesus was the Christ, the Son of the living God, we read that "they that gladly received his word were baptized: *and the same day there were added unto them ABOUT THREE THOUSAND SOULS*" (Acts 2:41).

In the third chapter of Acts, Peter and John healed a man who had been lame from his mother's womb, and as the people gathered around them in wonder and amazement, Peter preached his *second* sermon, declaring that the name of Jesus, "through faith in His name hath made this man strong, whom ye see and know: yea, the faith which is by Him hath given him this perfect soundness in the presence of you all" (Acts 3:16).

Acts 4:13 tells us that when the people "saw the boldness of Peter and John, and perceived that they were unlearned and ignorant men, they marvelled; and they took knowledge of them, that they had been with Jesus."

In Acts 4:31 we read, "And when they had prayed, the place was shaken where they were assembled together; *and they were all filled with the Holy Ghost, and they spake the Word of God with boldness.*"

Acts 6:7 declares, "And the Word of God increased; and the number of the disciples multiplied in Jerusalem greatly; and a great company of the priests were obedient to the faith!" The *reason* thousands and tens of thousands were saved was because "with great power gave the apostles witness of the resurrection of the Lord Jesus: and great grace was upon them all" (Acts 4:33).

In this tremendous fifteenth chapter of John three things stand out:

First, Jesus taught the disciples concerning their relationship to Himself—they were related to HIM in the same way as branches are related to the vine, and they were to abide in close fellowship with Him in the same way branches abide in the life-giving vine.

Then He taught them concerning their relationship to

each other as children of God. They were to love one another with the same deep, sincere, self-sacrificing love with which *He* had loved *them*—and in so doing they would prove to a gainsaying world that they were His disciples.

In the third place He taught them concerning their relationship to *the present world.* They need not expect the world to receive them because the world had not received HIM. They could expect the world to reject, hate, and despise them. They need not be surprised when the world refused to hear their message, because the world had refused to hear HIS message. "He was in the world, and the world was made by Him, and the world knew Him not. He came unto His own, and His own received Him not" (John 1:10,11).

The disciples need not hope to win Israel, because HE, their Messiah, had been rejected by them, and the majority of them would turn down the message of the *disciples.* However, He assured them that they *would give out the message,* they would bear fruit, and they would glorify God in their ministries.

As this chapter closes, think on these things:

"As the Father hath loved me, *so have I loved you:* continue ye in my love" (v. 9). Who on earth can fathom or measure the unknowable love of God? And yet Jesus assured us that *as God the Father loved HIM,* just so much HE loves US.

"Then said Jesus to them again, Peace be unto you: as my Father hath sent me, *even so send I you"* (ch. 20, v. 21). When the Father sent Jesus into the world, it meant the humility of Bethlehem—a babe in a manger. It meant trial on the Mount of Temptation when He met the devil in person. It meant agony in the Garden of Gethsemane when He met all the forces of hell led by Satan himself. It meant suffering on Golgotha, the shame and disgrace of the cross. But the victory of resurrection was assured, and He endured the shame of the cross for the joy that was set before Him—the glory where He sits today at the Father's right hand (Heb. 1:3).

"As He is, so are we in this world" (I John 4:17). Because of the love of God and the shed blood of Jesus, we are one with Christ. Therefore we are identified with Him in the acceptance of His worth and the completeness of His atonement.

"As Moses lifted up the serpent in the wilderness, even so must the Son of man be lifted up: that whosoever believeth in Him should not perish, but have eternal life" (John 3:14,15). This was the divine necessity if we were to be one with Christ, if we would have a right to eternal life. The *necessity* for His death is summarized in "MUST." The *nature* of His death is suggested in "LIFTED UP." The serpent lifted up by Moses in the wilderness was *like unto* the serpents which bit the Israelites and caused them to die. In like manner, Jesus was made *in the likeness* of sinful man; He was made to be sin for us, that we in Him might be made the righteousness of God!

I do not understand it, beloved, but I accept and believe it because God said it:

"For He hath made Him to be sin for us, who knew no sin (*Jesus* knew no sin); that we might be made the righteousness of God in Him" (II Cor. 5:21). As I read those words, I feel that I should remove the shoes from my feet because truly, *I stand on holy ground!*

Fellow Christian, we need to realize that all we are, *God made us IN JESUS;* and since Jesus loves us with the same unknowable love with which God loved HIM, the least we can do is present our bodies, living sacrifices, and our members as instruments of righteousness, vessels to be filled and used to glorify God the Father who loves us and Jesus the Son who died for us!

CHAPTER XVI

1. These things have I spoken unto you, that ye should not be offended.

2. They shall put you out of the synagogues: yea, the time cometh, that whosoever killeth you will think that he doeth God service.

3. And these things will they do unto you, because they have not known the Father, nor me.

4. But these things have I told you, that when the time shall come, ye may remember that I told you of them. And these things I said not unto you at the beginning, because I was with you.

5. But now I go my way to him that sent me; and none of you asketh me, Whither goest thou?

6. But because I have said these things unto you, sorrow hath filled your heart.

7. Nevertheless I tell you the truth; It is expedient for you that I go away: for if I go not away, the Comforter will not come unto you; but if I depart, I will send him unto you.

8. And when he is come, he will reprove the world of sin, and of righteousness, and of judgment:

9. Of sin, because they believe not on me;

10. Of righteousness, because I go to my Father, and ye see me no more;

11. Of judgment, because the prince of this world is judged.

12. I have yet many things to say unto you, but ye cannot bear them now.

13. Howbeit when he, the Spirit of truth, is come, he will guide you into all truth: for he shall not speak of himself; but whatsoever he shall hear, that shall he speak: and he will shew you things to come.

14. He shall glorify me: for he shall receive of mine, and shall shew it unto you.

15. All things that the Father hath are mine: therefore said I, that he shall take of mine, and shall shew it unto you.

16. A little while, and ye shall not see me: and again, a little while, and ye shall see me, because I go to the Father.

17. Then said some of his disciples among themselves, What is this that he saith unto us, A little while, and ye shall not see me: and

again, a little while, and ye shall see me: and, Because I go to the Father?

18. They said therefore, What is this that he saith, A little while? we cannot tell what he saith.

19. Now Jesus knew that they were desirous to ask him, and said unto them, Do ye enquire among yourselves of that I said, A little while, and ye shall not see me: and again, a little while, and ye shall see me?

20. Verily, verily, I say unto you, That ye shall weep and lament, but the world shall rejoice: and ye shall be sorrowful, but your sorrow shall be turned into joy.

21. A woman when she is in travail hath sorrow, because her hour is come: but as soon as she is delivered of the child, she remembereth no more the anguish, for joy that a man is born into the world.

22. And ye now therefore have sorrow: but I will see you again, and your heart shall rejoice, and your joy no man taketh from you.

23. And in that day ye shall ask me nothing. Verily, verily, I say unto you, Whatsoever ye shall ask the Father in my name, he will give it you.

24. Hitherto have ye asked nothing in my name: ask, and ye shall receive, that your joy may be full.

25. These things have I spoken unto you in proverbs: but the time cometh, when I shall no more speak unto you in proverbs, but I shall shew you plainly of the Father.

26. At that day ye shall ask in my name: and I say not unto you, that I will pray the Father for you:

27. For the Father himself loveth you, because ye have loved me, and have believed that I came out from God.

28. I came forth from the Father, and am come into the world: again, I leave the world, and go to the Father.

29. His disciples said unto him, Lo, now speakest thou plainly, and speakest no proverb.

30. Now are we sure that thou knowest all things, and needest not that any man should ask thee: by this we believe that thou camest forth from God.

31. Jesus answered them, Do ye now believe?

32. Behold, the hour cometh, yea, is now come, that ye shall be scattered, every man to his own, and shall leave me alone: and yet I am not alone, because the Father is with me.

33. These things I have spoken unto you, that in me ye might have peace. In the world ye shall have tribulation: but be of good cheer; I have overcome the world.

Chapter 16 is a direct continuation of chapter 15; there

is no break or pause in the events recorded in these chapters.

In the first seven verses of this chapter Jesus made three statements which deserve special attention:

1. He delivered a remarkable prophecy concerning things to come, warning His disciples that they would be persecuted even unto death. He told them that they would be put out of the synagogue and that their persecutors, in killing them, would think they were doing God a special service.
2. He explained to His disciples *why* He warned them concerning the things that were soon to come upon them: He did not want them to be offended when they were persecuted, and by such warning He prepared them for the road of severe persecution they would be traveling.
3. He explained to them why it was divinely expedient for them that He leave them and return to the heavenly Father, for if He did not depart, the Comforter would not come.

Jesus made it clear to His disciples that He had told them "these things" in order to prepare them for the treatment they would receive at the hands of the unbelieving and hostile Jews, lest they become even more discouraged and despondent in the next few weeks and months, and stumble in their Christian walk. If the words seemed strange to them at that time, they would come to fully understand their Lord's prophecy as it was fulfilled in their daily lives.

The Disciples Warned of Persecution

Verse 1: *"These things have I spoken unto you, that ye should not be offended."*

"These things" present a twofold message: (1) A *warning* of persecution that was to come, and (2) *the promise of the Spirit* that would come after Jesus returned to the Father. The disciples' foreknowledge of the persecution and hatred of their enemies would eliminate the element of surprise

and prevent their becoming more despondent and discouraged when they actually encountered such persecution; and at the same time, the promise of the Holy Spirit would encourage them and give them strength to *face* whatever trials and hardships lay ahead.

"That ye should not be offended" acquainted the disciples with our Lord's *reasons* for announcing that persecution was sure to come. He did not want them to be *"offended"* (the Greek suggests "scandalized").

To be forewarned is to be *forearmed* if we listen to the voice of the Spirit and follow His leading. In Matthew 26:31 Jesus told His disciples, "All ye shall be offended because of me this night: for it is written, I will smite the Shepherd, and the sheep of the flock shall be scattered abroad." Jesus knew exactly what would come upon the disciples, and telling them in advance would strengthen their faith as well as giving them courage to face persecution.

How tenderly He loved them! He was concerned about every detail of their life in this unfriendly world. Verily, "having loved His own . . . *He loved* them unto the end" (John 13:1b)—and He is just as gracious to those who follow Him today.

We might ask, "*Why* did Jesus forewarn His disciples when in His omniscience He knew they *would be* offended? Why did He tell Peter, "Watch ye and pray, *lest ye enter into temptation*" (Mark 14:38) when He already knew that Peter would deny Him three times before the cock crew? And why did He command US to go into all the world and preach the Gospel to every creature when He Himself said, "many are called, but few are chosen" (Matt. 22:14)? *He did it to point out and enforce individual responsibility.* We are individuals created in the image of God, and each of us must give an account to God of himself: "For it is written, As I live, saith the Lord, *every knee* shall bow to me, and *every tongue* shall confess to God. So then *every one of us* shall give account of himself to God" (Rom. 14:11,12).

Paul said to young Timothy, *"Yea, and all that will live*

godly in Christ Jesus shall suffer persecution" (II Tim. 3:12). Many young Christians today have not been instructed properly, they have not been sufficiently forewarned—and not being fully established in the faith they have allowed persecution to cause them to stumble. Since Jesus *knew* this would be true, He took special care to instruct His disciples concerning the cross they must bear and the persecution they were sure to meet. He did not conceal the difficulties that would face Christians on the journey to heaven.

Verse 2: *"They shall put you out of the synagogues: yea, the time cometh, that whosoever killeth you will think that he doeth God service."*

"They shall put you out of the synagogues." Persecution does not always come through the underworld or the rulers of spiritual wickedness. It also comes from the religious world—and of course for the apostles, persecution was perpetrated primarily by the Jews. They *professed* to be the people of God; but *they hated Jesus,* and during the first days of Christianity they severely persecuted those who followed Him.

The same is true today. Some of the most cruel persecution encountered by true believers comes from "professing" (not "possessing") Christians. These persecutors are "church members," but they are not part of the one true Church; they are of the world, and they persecute those who are true to the fundamentals of the faith. When the daily walk of a believer condemns the daily walk of a professing Christian who is a church member but not a member of the body of Christ, then that church member persecutes the true believer, declaring him to be "fanatical," or saying that he has gone "overboard in religion."

To be put out of the synagogue in the days of the disciples meant much more than being excluded from admission to the temple, the place of worship. It meant that the person who was put out of the synagogue was cut off from all the privileges of Israel and from all association with family and friends. It meant complete severance of all former ties and made one an outcast shunned by those *in* the synagogue and disowned by one's own family. Such condemnation was almost more than a person could bear.

Today, people are sometimes excommunicated from certain churches, and because of liberalism and modernism many dear saints of God have been forced to leave a church they helped to build and where they have spent most of their lives. But excommunication today means no such persecution and ostracism as it did in the days of the disciples, for sometimes when Christians were put out of the synagogue they were shortly put to death. There was a group in those days called Zealots, and in their fanaticism and extreme desperation they thirsted after the blood of true believers. We find an example of this in the persecution of Paul after his conversion:

"And when it was day, certain of the Jews banded together, and bound themselves under a curse, saying that they would neither eat nor drink till they had killed Paul. And they were more than forty which had made this conspiracy" (Acts 23:12,13).

Nor were such cruel men necessarily of the lower class. Before His conversion Paul (then Saul of Tarsus), one of the best educated men of his day, was also one of the most zealous persecutors of the Church. In II Corinthians 11:22 he made it very clear that he was an Israelite, of the seed of Abraham. In Philippians 3:5,6 he said of himself, "Circumcised the eighth day, of the stock of Israel, of the tribe of Benjamin, an Hebrew of the Hebrews; as touching the law, a Pharisee; concerning zeal, persecuting the Church; touching the righteousness which is in the law, blameless."

Yet this unusual man, later to become a spiritual giant, is said to have breathed out "threatenings and slaughter against the disciples of the Lord," and at the time of his conversion he was on his way to Damascus to arrest Christians there, whether they be men or women, "that he might bring them bound unto Jerusalem" (Acts 9:1,2). According to Paul's own testimony before King Agrippa, he said, "I verily thought with myself, that I ought to do many things contrary to the name of Jesus of Nazareth. Which thing I also did in Jerusalem: and many of the saints did I shut up in prison, having received authority from the chief priests; and when they were put to death, I gave my voice against them. And I punished them oft in every synagogue, and compelled them to blaspheme; and being exceedingly mad against them, I persecuted them even unto strange cities!" (Acts 26:9–11).

It may be that before the Rapture of the Church the people of God will again encounter such persecution, more severe than we have known in the past centuries. In Matthew 24:3 the disciples asked Jesus, "What shall be the sign of thy coming, and of the end of the world?" He replied, "Take heed that no man deceive you. For many shall come in my name, saying, I am Christ; and shall deceive many. And ye shall hear of wars and rumours of wars: see that ye be not troubled: for all these things must come to pass, but the end is not yet. For nation shall rise against nation, and kingdom against kingdom: and there shall be famines, and pestilences, and earthquakes, in divers places. ALL THESE ARE THE BEGINNING OF SORROWS" (Matt. 24:4–8).

I believe we are NOW living in the time Jesus mentioned here as "the beginning of sorrows," but I do not know just how far into that time the Church will go before Christ comes for His own and catches the saints away.

The history of the blood bath Christians have suffered in the past manifests to us the awful depravity of the human heart and shows us just how cruel the heart of unregenerate man can be. In every age, pure godliness has met with hatred and hostility from demented and Satan-energized men. Godly, holy men have suffered since the day of Abel (I John 3:12). Solomon wrote, "An unjust man is an abomination to the just: AND HE THAT IS UPRIGHT IN THE

WAY IS ABOMINATION TO THE WICKED" (Prov. 29:27).

In Amos 5:10 we read, "They hate him that rebuketh in the gate, *and they abhor him that speaketh uprightly*!"

People of God have always suffered persecution, and this will be true until the Rapture of the Church when Christians will be taken out of the world. The more fully dedicated one is to Christ, the more the world will hate that person and the more he will suffer for Christ's sake; but this suffering is only for a season, for in the by-and-by we will enter that celestial city to be eternally with our Lord who suffered so much for us.

Verse 3: *"And these things will they do unto you, because they have not known the Father, nor me."*

Here Jesus traces the world's ill-will and hatréd to its true source. The world hates spiritually-minded believers simply because the world does not know God the Father nor Jesus the Son. In chapter 8 verses 32–44 of our present study we learned that the Jews claimed to be children of Abraham—but *they did not know the GOD of Abraham* except as a historical God. They did not know Him as God and Saviour, therefore when Jesus came they rejected Him. Spiritual ignorance is the source of persecution toward spiritually-minded believers. If the Jews had know *God the FATHER* they would have known and acknowledged Jesus the Son, the "Sent One." They would have received Him and would have worshipped Him, instead of demanding His death. Certainly if they had received Jesus they would have received His *disciples;* but since they *rejected* Jesus, they rejected all who worshipped and followed Him.

"This then is the message which we have heard of Him, and declare unto you, that God is light, and in Him is no darkness at all. If we say that we have fellowship with Him, and walk in darkness, we lie, and do not the truth" (I John 1:5,6).

Verse 4: *"But these things have I told you, that when the time shall come, ye may remember that I told you of them. And these things I said not unto you at the beginning, because I was with you."*

In verse 1 of the chapter Jesus gave His disciples His first reason for warning them of sure and certain persecution. He did it so they would not be offended when His prophecy came true. Now He gives them another reason: He made these things known to them that their faith might be strengthened and increased when persecution came. They would then remember that before He left them and returned to the Father He had prophesied exactly what happened. When they were put out of they synagogue, when they and their fellow Christians were persecuted, they would remember that these things were prophesied by Jesus while He was yet with them, and their faith would be increased.

Fulfillment of these prophecies would encourage the disciples to depend upon *every promise* He had made, and would deepen their assurance that Jesus was truly God, equal *with* God in every respect. When they saw the *evil* things He prophesied come to pass literally, they would know for sure that the *good* things He had promised would also come to pass. Thus His prophetic words were destined to strengthen them in their minds and increase their faith in Him.

"These things I said not unto you at the beginning, because I was with you." Here Jesus explains why He waited until this point in His earthly ministry to give them this warning rather than giving it at the very outset of His ministry when He first called them to follow Him. At that time, the full revelation of what was to occur would have been too much for them to bear; they could not have accepted it. Such overwhelming knowledge could have caused them to stumble and perhaps turn aside from their calling. God never allows anything to come upon us that we are not able to bear (I Cor. 10:13). He prepares us for persecution, disappointments, and heartaches that are sure to come. If we walk as the Spirit leads there is always strength to overcome.

Jesus knew the human frailties of His disciples, and therefore He revealed these things to them little by little as they were able to bear them. He gradually unfolded to them the program of the cross; He told them about their duties to Him as His disciples—and warned them that when they *performed* those duties strong persecution would confront them.

We read in I Peter 2:1,2 that God's Word is milk for the *babes* in Christ, but He also has *meat* for men who are strong (Heb. 5:13,14). When we are babes in Christ, the Holy Spirit feeds us with the "sincere milk of the Word"; and as we grow in grace and in our Christian experience He gives us *meat.* Just so, in the beginning of the Lord's ministry on earth He was *with* His disciples and there was no need for Him to make known to them the things that would confront them after He was gone, and He knew that after He returned to the Father they would be much stronger and more fitted to receive the prophecy He gave them.

Verse 5: *"But now I go my way to Him that sent me; and none of you asketh me, Whither goest thou?"*

"But now I go my way to Him that sent me." Jesus probably paused a moment here, then looked at His disciples and asked, *"And none of you asketh me, Whither goest thou?"*

In chapter 13 verse 36 Peter asked Jesus, "Lord, whither goest thou?"—but at that point in the Lord's ministry Peter probably thought Jesus was preparing to take an *earthly* journey. Then in chapter 14 verse 5 *Thomas* asked Him, "Lord, we know not whither thou goest; *and how can we know the way?"* In the words of Thomas we see indication of an objection—that is, "We do not know where you are going, so *how CAN we know the way?"* But in our present verse, Jesus wanted His disciples to lend a sympathetic and affectionate response to what He had just been saying to them. They were so overwhelmed and occupied with their present grief over the announcement that Jesus was going away, they could not even think of the blessing of the coming of the Comforter.

Actually, if they had faced the facts, they would have been happy; for even though they were about to lose Jesus insofar as His visible Person was concerned, their loss was definitely His gain and token of His victory because He was going back to the glory from whence He came. He was soon to take His seat at the right hand of the Majesty on high, and if the disciples had loved their Lord as they should have, this would have brought them great joy. When we love someone wholeheartedly it makes us happy when that person is blessed.

The words of Jesus here, though gentle and tender as always, were definitely a rebuke to the disciples concerning their selfishness. They were self-occupied, thinking only of themselves. If we would truly be Christ's disciples we must *forget self.* We must think first of Jesus, and then of others. *Self comes LAST.*

Verse 6: *"But because I have said these things unto you, sorrow hath filled your heart."*

It is human to magnify afflictions, and even the most spiritual of God's people are guilty of this human frailty. If we would only count our many blessings, "name them one by one," we would indeed be surprised at what the Lord has done for us. The disciples had many blessings to count, but they could not count them because they were so heavy with mourning, engulfed in a dark cloud of grief and despondency.

But their dark cloud had a silver lining, and they did not continue in their mournful mood indefinitely. A different spirit was theirs after they learned of the Lord's resurrection, and in Luke 24:50–53 we read, ". . . He led them out as far as to Bethany, and He lifted up His hands, and blessed them. And it came to pass, while He blessed them, He was parted from them, and carried up into heaven. *And they worshipped Him, and returned to Jerusalem WITH*

GREAT JOY: AND WERE CONTINUALLY IN THE TEMPLE, PRAISING AND BLESSING GOD!"

The disciples enjoyed forty days of unbroken fellowship with Jesus after He rose again, and that fellowship strengthened their faith and removed their doubts and fears.

Verse 7: *"Nevertheless I tell you the truth; It is expedient for you that I go away: for if I go not away, the Comforter will not come unto you; but if I depart, I will send Him unto you."*

"Nevertheless" bears out the thought that Jesus knew the grief and anxiety of His disciples as they thought of His returning to the Father and leaving them alone in a hostile, unfriendly world. But in spite of their sorrow He firmly assured them that His going was divinely needful for them.

". . . I tell you the truth." He could tell them nothing *less* than truth because He IS truth and it is impossible for God to lie (Heb. 6:18; Tit. 1:2).

"It is expedient for you that I go away." In other words, "My going is for your profit and to your advantage. You will gain by my departure."

Jesus knew what the disciples were thinking and what they were feeling. He knew they were reasoning that if He remained with them, the prophecies He had just made would not befall them. So He assured them that His departure was best and needful for them.

I do not doubt that the disciples wondered (though they did not express it audibly) what Jesus really meant when He said His going away would be their gain. Where was He *going?* Ultimately and finally He was going to the Father, but first He must go to the cross; He MUST be lifted up (John 3:14; 12:32). Thus we see a twofold meaning here: First, Jesus must go to Calvary; but it was not possible that death should hold Him. He would rise again and would return to the Father to take His seat at the right hand of the Majesty.

It was expedient for us that Jesus go to Calvary and die on the cross that we might have life and have it abundantly. This was foreordained before the foundation of the world (I Pet. 1:18–20). He was therefore actually telling His disciples, "Unless I leave you, unless I die on the cross and then return to my Father, *nothing else will be accomplished.*" The disciples would have continued as they were, the Jews would have continued under the Mosaic economy, and the whole world would have gone on in blindness under the sentence of sin and death! If Jesus had not gone to the cross, the prophecies of the Old Testament would have crumbled and the foundation of the Church would never have been laid. The death of Jesus was a divine imperative in order to provide the Stone upon which the Church is built. He died that through His death many sons might be born into God's family (Rom. 8:29; Heb. 2:10). I do believe that the primary meaning of the statement in this verse is that Jesus would return to the Father and the Holy Spirit would come on the Day of Pentecost as promised; *but He must go by way of the cross.*

Then, there are other ways in which it was expedient for the disciples that Jesus should return to His heavenly Father. The Scripture speaks of a *glorified* Christ, and if He were to be glorified, then He must return to the Father and to the glory that was His in the beginning. If He had remained on earth He would have been localized, because as long as He remained in His body of humiliation His presence was confined to one locality; but now, *by the Spirit,* He is omnipresent, He is *everywhere.* Where two or three are gathered together in His name, He is there (Matt. 18:20).

For example, two or three may be gathered together in America, and in England two or three are gathered together at the same time, the same being true in Hong Kong and Brazil—and in a hundred other places around the world. Jesus is in the midst of *each gathering,* but as long as He remained on earth in a body of flesh He was localized. You will recall that when Lazarus was sick and Mary and Martha sent for Jesus, He did not come to Bethany until four days after Lazarus died; but today when we pray for the sick, regardless of where they may be, Jesus is there with each and every one. He is there to listen, to hear the prayers offered by faithful believers on behalf of sick friends and loved ones. In His body of flesh He was limited to a locality, but now He is omnipresent.

The book of Acts testifies to the fact that after the departure of Jesus and the coming of the Holy Spirit, the disciples were new men. They did far more for Him after He left them than while He was with them in His body of humiliation. Yes, it was expedient for them, it was for their good and His glory, that He depart.

The Work of the Holy Spirit in Relation to the World

Verses 8–11: *"And when He is come, He will reprove the world of sin, and of righteousness, and of judgment: Of sin, because they believe not on me; of righteousness, because I go to my Father, and ye see me no more; of judgment, because the prince of this world is judged."*

In verses 8 through 15 we see two contrasting operations of the Holy Spirit: (1) as having to do with the world, and (2) as having to do with the disciples of our Lord.

"When He (the Holy Spirit) *is come, He will reprove the world."* The Holy Spirit will bring home to the individual the evils and gross errors of the natural man apart from the new birth.

"He will reprove the world of *sin... righteousness... judgment."* The three subjects pointed out here have to do with the *conscience* of the individual, the state and attitude of unregenerate man in regard to God and God's claims upon man whom He created in His own image. These three subjects—sin, righteousness, and judgment—are distinct factors in the age-long, continued warfare between God and man, a controversy that has not changed since sin entered the Garden of Eden; but *since Jesus came,* the righteousness of God was manifested in flesh because in Christ dwelt all the fulness of the Godhead bodily (Col. 2:9,10). Therefore, in Christ dwelt the *righteousness* of God, the *holiness* of God, the *purity* of God.

Conviction, then, in respect to *sin,* goes to the very *root of ALL sin*—the sin of *UNBELIEF.* Essentially, all sin is and always *has* been unbelief. Adam did not believe God, *Cain* did not believe God, *Lot* did not believe God, and we could go on down a long line of names from the Scriptures, names of people who did not believe God. Men are damned eternally in the lake of fire because of unbelief.

"He that believeth on Him is not condemned: *but he that BELIEVETH NOT is condemned already,* because he hath not believed in the name of the only begotten Son of God" (John 3:18).

Conviction in respect to *"righteousness"*: The Holy Ghost shall convince the world of the righteousness of Christ and of the fact that there IS no righteousness except IN Christ Jesus. "As it is written, There is none righteous, no, not one: There is none that understandeth, there is none that seeketh after God. They are all gone out of the way, they are together become unprofitable; there is none that doeth good, no, not one" (Rom. 3:10—12). All have sinned (Rom. 3:23). "All we like sheep have gone astray" (Isaiah 53:6). But *in the Lord Jesus Christ* righteousness was brought down and displayed to men in a body like unto man's body, sin apart. *IN CHRIST,* righteousness has been realized in man for the first time since the creation of Adam, for Jesus *fulfilled* every jot and tittle of the law, and just before He went to Calvary He said to the heavenly Father, "I have finished the work which thou gavest me to do" (John 17:4).

Therefore, righteousness in man is *IN the Man Christ Jesus;* and yet He was rejected by the masses to whom He presented Himself. He was hated and ridiculed by His own people, the Jews, and the world refused to recognize His righteousness. Those in whose presence He performed such miracles as no man had ever wrought, accused Him of being demon-possessed and said that He performed His miracles by the power of Beelzebub, prince of demons. They called Him a blasphemer, an illegitimate, they numbered Him "with the transgressors." But He whom they rejected was God's Christ, the only begotten of the Father, full of grace and truth.

True faith produces righteousness because true faith brings Christ into the heart, and Christ "is made unto us wisdom, and righteousness, and sanctification, and redemption" (I Cor. 1:30). When one exercises faith in the finished work of the Lord Jesus Christ—faith in His death, burial, resurrection, and ascension "according to the Scriptures"—righteousness is instantaneously imputed to the believer. Christ *is* our righteousness, and a life of practical righteousness is a witness to the world of what true Christianity is. Since Christianity is righteous living, when one believes with the heart unto righteousness, that individual, indwelt by the Holy Spirit, lives a life of practical righteousness. Thus the Holy Spirit convicts the world of its *unrighteousness.* That is why worldlings in the church—church members who have never been born again—are always hostile toward Spirit-filled, Spirit-led believers who fully consecrate themselves to the Lord and refuse to practice the habits of the world. Thus, in righteousness imputed to us when we believe, the Lord associates the life of a true believer with His presence *with* the Father.

Believers are associated with Christ, who is now seated at the right hand of the Majesty. Paul declared, "God, who is rich in mercy, for His great love wherewith He loved us, even when we were dead in sins, hath quickened us together with Christ, (by grace ye are saved;) and hath raised us up together, and made us sit together in heavenly places in Christ Jesus: That in the ages to come He might shew the exceeding riches of His grace in His kindness toward us through Christ Jesus" (Eph. 2:4—7).

Also, in Colossians 3:1–4 we read, "If ye then be risen with Christ, seek those things which are above, where Christ sitteth on the right hand of God. Set your affection on things above, not on things on the earth. FOR YE ARE DEAD, AND YOUR LIFE IS HID WITH CHRIST IN GOD. When Christ, who is our life, shall appear, then shall ye also appear with Him in glory."

According to God's Word, true believers NOW sit together in heavenly places in Christ Jesus, we are hid with Christ in God, and therefore every born again Christian is a testimony against this unbelieving world. When we are fully surrendered to Christ, when we "walk in newness of life," the world is convicted that it is still walking in the old path, serving the "old man," and living in unrighteousness.

The Holy Spirit is also to convict the world *"of judgment."* This is man's day, the time when man walks by the light of his own councils. "The natural man receiveth not the things of the Spirit of God: for they are foolishness unto him: neither can he know them, because they are spiritually discerned" (I Cor. 2:14). The natural man is wise in his own heart; but in respect to the things of God, he is *foolish.* He thinks he knows best and he is determined to map out his own way—as set forth in Proverbs 16:25: *"There is a way that seemeth right unto a man, but the end thereof are the ways of death!"*

Apart from God, man cannot choose the right way. His estimate is marred and out of perspective because sin has alienated him from God. *ALL men are born in sin and shapen in iniquity;* or, as John the Beloved summed it up in I John 5:19, "The whole world lieth in wickedness" (or "in the lap of the wicked one"). Yet the world does not know or recognize this fact.

In Ephesians 2:2 Paul refers to the devil as "the prince of the power of the air," and in II Corinthians 4:4 he speaks of him as "the god of this world"; but he is a defeated "prince" because he met his doom at Calvary. Oh, yes—he is still operating, but he is a defeated foe. Jesus came into the world to lay His life down to take away sin—please notice, S-I-N, *singular* (John 1:29), the sin of unbelief. He willingly went to Calvary and won the victory. "And having spoiled principalities and powers, He made a shew of them openly, triumphing over them in it" (Col. 2:15). Since Calvary, Satan has been a defeated "prince"—and he knows it. That is why he works with such untiring fervor and unbelievable cunning in this Day of Grace. Revelation 20:3 refers to him as the deceiver of the nations, but he was judged and defeated by Jesus at Calvary, and therefore believers, too, are *overcomers in Christ* (Rom. 8:37).

The world is to be convicted by the Holy Spirit in respect of judgment—convicted of the falseness of its *own* judgment, and of the *righteous* judgment of God. Not only does the Holy Spirit convict the *individual sinner* of sin unto salvation, but His very presence here convinces the *world* of sin. The presence of the Holy Spirit in the world *today* condemns the world. He is not *known* to the world, and the world cannot receive Him; but He is in the world today to take the place of our absent Lord (in relation to believers). Jesus abides in the heart of every born again believer in the Person of the Holy Spirit, and "if any man have not the Spirit of Christ, he is none of His" (Rom. 8:9). Therefore every truly born again believer is a witness against the world. The life of a righteous man convicts the world of guilt, sin, and unrighteousness.

The Greek word translated *"Comforter"* is *paracletos*—the same word rendered "Advocate" in I John 2:1. According to Webster's dictionary, an "advocate" is a counsellor, one who pleads another's cause, as a *lawyer* does. An advocate therefore produces a conviction by producing *concrete proof* of a crime, proof that cannot be denied; and such proof must be presented before a court. Thus we see that an advocate reproves objectively, not *sub*jectively. That is the truth set forth in our present passage: the very *presence* of the third Person of the Trinity on earth *objectively* reproves the world of sin, rebukes the world of unrighteousness, and convicts the world of iniquity. His very presence is *divine proof positive* that Jesus Christ was everything He claimed to be!

It is not necessary that a person hear the Gospel before he realizes that he is a sinner. The *heathen* knows that he does not live right; that is the reason he worships trees, monkeys, the moon, the sun. He has his heathen gods, and *he worships because he fears the enemy.* Never having heard the Gospel, he does not know the truth concerning Jesus and salvation; but he knows he is not living right and he offers sacrifices—sometimes *human* sacrifices—hoping thereby to appease the anger of his gods. I repeat—it is not necessary for one to hear the Gospel in order to know that he is not *living* right; *but for one to be BORN AGAIN it IS necessary that he hear the Word of God* (Rom. 10:17; Eph. 2:8,9; John 5:24; I Pet. 1:23). It is a divine impossibility for one to be born again apart from hearing the Gospel, but it is not impossible for people to know they are sinners and that they are not living righteously, even though they may never have heard the Word of God. The very presence of the Holy Spirit in the world convicts the world of its wrong living and wrong doing!

Also in our present passage we find clearly stated the *consequences* of the presence of the Holy Spirit in the world. In John 9:39 Jesus said, "For *judgment* I am come into this world, that they which see not might see; and that they which see might be made blind." But in John 3:17 we read, "For God *sent not His Son into the world to condemn the world;* but that the world through Him might be saved." Now these two passages seem to be in flat contradiction to each other, but not so! John 3:17 makes known *the mission* on which God sent Jesus into the world, and John 9:39 names one of the *consequences* which resulted from His coming into the world. The very presence of Jesus on earth judged everything and all things that were contrary to God and His holiness, because Jesus was God in flesh.

In the same manner, the presence of the Holy Spirit in this Dispensation of Grace judges the world and reproves the world of sin. In the bosom of all men there is a yearning to please a Supreme Being, someone higher than themselves, because they fear a judgment. History has discovered that the American Indians buried bows, arrows, and hunting equipment in the graves with their dead warriors, believing that those who departed this life were going to another land where they would continue their hunting. Superstition? Yes. But superstition and practice born of man's inherent belief in a Supreme Being and in judgment.

The Holy Spirit is here in the world—not to *improve* the world, not to bring in Utopia, not to erase poverty, disease, greed, and fear—but to *reprove* the world. He is here to furnish divine proof that the world is guilty of the blood of Jesus the Righteous One; and in so doing He vindicates the Lamb of God, the only begotten Son of God whom the world rejected and nailed to a cross.

The world has not changed. The world does not love Jesus any more today than it did twenty centuries ago. If Jesus were to return to this earth today, if He lived, taught, and preached as He did two thousand years ago, the world would hate Him just as vehemently, reject Him just as definitely, and nail Him to another cross! The world is still in ignorance as gross as when unbelievers demanded the crucifixion of the Lamb of God, "which none of the princes of this world knew: for had they known it, they would not have crucified the Lord of glory" (I Cor. 2:8). Yes, the whole world stands guilty before God—guilty because it refused to believe on Jesus.

The Work of the Holy Spirit in Relation to Believers; New Truth to be Revealed by the Spirit

Verse 12: *"I have yet many things to say unto you, but ye cannot bear them now."*

There is a divine economy in the process of God's revelation of truth to believers. Jesus had *"many things"* yet to say to His disciples, things the Holy Spirit would make known to them when the proper time came. Had Jesus *revealed* these things to them while He was with them, they could not have understood, they would not have known what He was talking about. But when the Holy Spirit came, HE would bring these unspoken truths to the minds of holy men, appointed and anointed of God to receive them.

Verse 13: *"Howbeit when He, the Spirit of truth, is come, He will guide you into all truth: for He shall not speak of Himself; but whatsoever He shall hear, that shall He speak: and He will shew you things to come."*

The Greek word here rendered *"He"* is an emphatic word—*ekinos*—and it speaks of a PERSON, not an influence. The Holy Spirit IS a Person, the third Person of the Holy Trinity. He is *"the Spirit of truth"*—His very *nature* is truth, and that is the divine guarantee of the character of the truth *taught* by the Holy Spirit.

Jesus told His disciples, *"When He* (the Holy Spirit) *is come, He will guide you into all truth."* The Holy Spirit would give them divine facts and the *meaning* of those facts—and He would do it by a divinely arranged process. Notice that the Holy Spirit was to guide them into *"ALL truth."* The disciples were *given* "all truth," and since God gave The Revelation to John the Beloved on the Isle of Patmos, no other divine revelations have been given to men to be penned down as doctrine dictated by the Holy Ghost from God. Jesus assured His disciples that *in their lifetime,* the Spirit of Truth would make known to them ALL divine truth. Nothing would remain to be added by the Church. Man has no right to add any doctrine or dogma to the doctrine of the New Testament Church, nor to make any addition to or subtraction from the Word of God. The truth the Holy Spirit would make known to the disciples would be sufficient unto all generations:

"Beloved, when I gave all diligence to write unto you of the common salvation, it was needful for me to write unto you, and exhort you *that ye should earnestly contend for the faith which was once delivered unto the saints.* For there are certain men crept in unawares, who were before of old ordained to this condemnation, ungodly men, turning the grace of our God into lasciviousness, and denying the only Lord God, and our Lord Jesus Christ" (Jude 3,4).

"He shall not speak of Himself; but whatsoever He shall hear, that shall He speak." Again and again Jesus taught the disciples that the words He spoke were words He heard from the Father. (See John 8:38 and 15:15.) The same is true of the Holy Spirit. He makes known the truth as given to Him by Jehovah God. The Holy Spirit is not *another* God, nor is He one to *originate* truth. But as the third Person of the Trinity He would make known the truth of God.

"He will shew you things to come." The Holy Spirit would make known to the disciples all things relative to the Church Age—and even the ages *beyond* the Church Age—ALL truth, excepting none. Our Bible is the Word of God, and it is all there IS of the Word of God. "That which is perfect" has come, and therefore we have the *perfect* Word of God, the "perfect law of liberty," and nothing can be added to perfection! All we need to know about man, sin, salvation; all we need to know about God, God's Son, and the Holy Spirit; all we need to know about things that are to come, we can find in the sixty-six books of our Bible.

Verse 14: *"He shall glorify me: for He shall receive of mine, and shall shew it unto you."*

The Holy Spirit was not to speak of Himself, but to bear witness of Jesus. His mission was to glorify God's Son, not Himself.

"He shall receive of mine, and shall shew it unto you." I can see no meaning in the word *"mine"* except the truth

concerning Christ. The Holy Spirit shall take this truth and reveal it to disciples of Jesus. The New Testament is proof of the fulfillment of these words. Then by means of both the Old Testament and the New, the Spirit of Truth is even this very day fulfilling these words to believers, and this will continue until the Rapture. There remain yet glorious and wonderful things in the ages to come, things so glorious it is impossible for the finite mind to comprehend them: "As it is written, Eye hath not seen, nor ear heard, neither have entered into the heart of man, the things which God hath prepared for them that love Him! But God hath revealed them unto us by His Spirit: for the Spirit searcheth all things, yea, the deep things of God" (I Cor. 2:9,10).

Verse 15: *"All things that the Father hath are mine: therefore said I, that He shall take of mine, and shall shew it unto you."*

Here again is pointed out the perfect unity between Father, Son, and Holy Spirit, as well as the unknowable vastness of the storehouse of divine provisions and the divine possessions from which revelations are made known by the Spirit of Truth in this Day of Grace.

The only possible way to understand the Scriptures is to be taught by the Holy Spirit. The Word of God is not learned in Bible schools under the teaching of earthly educators, although we should thank God for great men to whom He has revealed many deep and tremendous truths found in the Scriptures. But these great men of God know such truths and are able to teach others only because the Holy Spirit has revealed them as they have dedicated themselves to the study of God's Word!

"All things that the Father hath are mine." I am convinced that this statement is given here by inspiration, to prevent anyone's supposing that there can be any division or separation between the things of Christ and the things of God the Father. In His prayer of intercession Jesus said

to the Father, "All mine are thine, and thine are mine..." (John 17:10). He wanted us to know that when the Spirit reveals the things of Christ, He is at the same time revealing the things of God the Father. It is impossible for the Spirit to show the things of Jesus without showing the things of the Father because God the Father and God the Son are ONE. The Holy Spirit proceeds from the Father as well as from the Son, and there is perfect union between the three of them.

Jesus Speaks of His Death, His Resurrection, His Second Coming

Verse 16: *"A little while, and ye shall not see me: and again, a little while, and ye shall see me, because I go to the Father."*

In the verses we have just studied, Christ touched upon deep and mighty truths—lofty things; but in this verse He condescends to the necessary level to meet the specific needs of the apostles at that moment. They were rapidly approaching days of such trials, tribulations, disappointment and confusion as they had never known. After His ascension they would remember His words here, *"A little while, and ye shall not see me,"* and when they realized that this was literally fulfilled they would also remember His second "little while"—His promise that they *would* see Him again. Thus His words would comfort their hearts just as believers today are comforted through the message of the Blessed Hope in I Thessalonians 4:13—18:

"I would not have you to be ignorant, brethren, concerning them which are asleep, that ye sorrow not, even as others which have no hope. For if we believe that Jesus died and rose again, even so them also which sleep in Jesus will God bring with Him. For this we say unto you by the Word of the Lord, that we which are alive and remain unto the coming of the Lord shall not prevent them which are asleep. For the Lord Himself shall descend from heaven with a shout, with the voice of the archangel, and with the trump of God: and the dead in Christ shall rise first: Then we which are alive and remain shall be caught up together with them in the clouds, to meet the Lord in the air: and so shall we ever be with the Lord. *Wherefore comfort one another with these words.*"

"*A little while . . . .*" It is true that in a few hours our Lord was arrested in Gethsemane, taken from the presence of His disciples, and they would not see Him again until after His resurrection. Thus they would lose bodily sight of Him for a little while. I do not doubt that their *faith* was also eclipsed at this point, as shown by the testimony of the two disciples on the road to Emmaus: They said, "But *we trusted that it had been He* which should have redeemed Israel" (Luke 24:21).

Mark 16:9–14 enlightens us further concerning the eclipse of their faith: "Now when Jesus was risen early the first day of the week, He appeared first to Mary Magdalene, out of whom He had cast seven devils. And she went and told them that had been with Him, as they mourned and wept. *And they, when they had heard that He was alive, and had been seen of her, BELIEVED NOT.*

"After that He appeared in another form unto two of them, as they walked, and went into the country. And they went and told it unto the residue: NEITHER BELIEVED THEY THEM. Afterward (Jesus) appeared unto the eleven as they sat at meat, *and upbraided them with their unbelief and hardness of heart, because they BELIEVED NOT them which had seen Him after He was risen!*"

He was absent from them "for a little while," but after three days and nights He rose again exactly as He told them He would. He appeared to them for another season of forty days, and then "while they looked stedfastly toward heaven as He went up, behold, two men stood by them in white apparel; which also said, Ye men of Galilee, why stand ye gazing up into heaven? *This same Jesus, which is taken up from you into heaven, shall so come in like manner as ye have seen Him go into heaven"* (Acts 1:10,11).

While the above is true, I do not believe this is the deeper meaning of our Lord's words here in the sixteenth verse. If this interpretation is His only meaning it fails to explain the words "I go to my Father."

In light of the previous verses (where Jesus was encouraging His disciples against His departure and His promise to send them the Comforter) I believe He was saying, "In a little while I shall ascend up to heaven to my Father and in a little while you shall see me again at my second advent." It is my belief that throughout the entire passage the Lord is speaking not only to the eleven, but to the whole Church, until His coming again.

"I go to my Father." Here Jesus tells His disciples *where* He is going and why they will not see Him again for "a little while." He was returning to the Father in a very special character to perform a very special ministry. He was to return to the Father as the One who had finished the work the Father sent Him to do and who gloriously accomplished every minute detail of that which He had come to accomplish (John 19:30); and *because* of what He had accomplished, He was entitled to a rich reward, the highest reward of all—the highest seat in heaven at the right hand of God!

Can you realize, beloved, that this rich reward bestowed upon Jesus is shared by all born again believers? Since we sit together with Him in heavenly places, since we are hid with Him in God and since Christ is in us and we are in Him, we share this glorious reward!

Jesus guaranteed that the Holy Spirit would come: "Therefore being by the right hand of God exalted, and having received of the Father the promise of the Holy Ghost, He hath shed forth this, which ye now see and hear" (Acts 2:33); and Hebrews 2:9 testifies that all believers see Jesus with the eye of the inner man. But He did not return to the Father to remain there eternally. He will come again and receive us unto Himself, that where He is, we may be also (John 14:3).

Verse 17: *"Then said some of His disciples among themselves, What is this that He saith unto us, A little while, and ye shall not see me: and again, a little while, and ye shall see me: and, Because I go to the Father?"*

How little the disciples understood the meaning of the words Jesus had just spoken to them! His words sounded strange to them, and they began to discuss what seemed to them a paradox—i. e., if they should *not* see Him, and then see Him *again*, were His words not in flat contradiction to each other? The fact that He said "I go to my Father" was confusing to them, too, for they were convinced that Messiah would come and would remain upon the earth: "The people answered Him, We have heard out of the law that Christ abideth for ever: and how sayest thou, The Son of man must be lifted up? Who IS this Son of man?" (John 12:34).

They had not yet grasped the full truth although it had been set forth by our Lord many times as He taught them, and the Old Testament Scriptures plainly prophesied His suffering before His glory (read Isaiah 53 and Psalm 22). If the disciples had comprehended the teaching of the Old Testament prophecies concerning the suffering Saviour they would not have been so bewildered and perplexed.

Verse 18: *"They said therefore, What is this that He saith, A little while? We cannot tell what He saith."*

It is plain that the disciples wanted to ask Jesus what He meant, yet they refrained from asking. We can profit from their example here, because Jesus *wants* us to ask. The Scripture tells us that we *have* not because we ASK not (James 4:2)—and many times we *understand not* because we do not pray and seek God's will and His wisdom.

The Word of God is like no other book. Other writings can be mastered by study and research, but the Bible is not mastered in that way. It speaks in language that can be understood only as the Holy Spirit enlightens and directs us in our study. We should pray with the Psalmist, "Open thou mine eyes, that I may behold wondrous things out of thy law. I am a stranger in the earth: hide not thy commandments from me" (Psalm 119:18,19). *Job* prayed, "That which I see not teach thou me" (Job 34:32).

God will grant us any and all things we desire to make us better ministers, better soul-winners, more effective Christians. Anything we will ask in faith, believing—but many of us, like the disciples, *wish* for knowledge without *asking* for it.

Verse 19: *"Now Jesus knew that they were desirous to ask Him, and said unto them, Do ye enquire among yourselves of that I said, A little while, and ye shall not see me: and again, a little while, and ye shall see me?"*

Again we see Christ's omniscience, His perfect knowledge of the hearts and thoughts of all men. He knew His disciples *"were desirous to ask Him"* a question, and He knew exactly what it was they wanted to ask; but He did not reply directly to their unspoken question.

What perplexed them just now was His promised return—"a little while, and ye shall not see me . . . a little while, and ye shall see me." We may conjecture that they had accepted the fact that they were about to lose Him, they believed He was speaking of His death, telling them of the time when He must be offered; but if this be true, then what did He mean by promising that in a little while they would see Him again?

It should be observed that our Lord gives no reply to the disciples' question. Questions about times and dates are rarely answered in the Word of God. We are not to set dates, we are not to appoint time. "In the *fulness* of time" God always operates, and performs that which was foreordained before the foundation of the world. Read Galatians 4:4,5 and I Peter 1:18–23.

Jesus did not specifically answer the question His disciples would have liked to ask, but He did emphasize *"a little while."* Shortly after His return to the Father, which would be only a "little while," He would return to receive them unto Himself in the Father's house.

The Lord Jesus knows what every believer needs even before we can ask: "And it shall come to pass, that before they call, I will answer; and while they are yet speaking, I will hear" (Isa. 65:24). The same promise is to every born again, blood-washed believer!

It is very impressive that in these last verses the mention of "a little while" appears seven times. Even though as man counts time it has been almost two thousand years since Jesus ascended back to the Father, it has been only "a little while" by God's timeclock, and surely this little while is about over. We can expect His return at any moment, for there is absolutely *nothing* recorded in Scriptures that must occur before the Rapture of the Church. Christ's coming for believers is imminent; it *could* be this very day!

Verse 20: *"Verily, verily, I say unto you, That ye shall weep and lament, but the world shall rejoice: and ye shall be sorrowful, but your sorrow shall be turned into joy."*

There is a message here for the apostles in the day in which they lived, but I think the whole verse is meant to be a general description of the state of things between the first and second coming of Christ. The message is to all believers up to this hour and through the duration of this Day of Grace.

"Ye shall weep and lament." When Mary Magdalene came to the apostles to tell them that Jesus had risen, she found them mourning and weeping: "And she went and told them that had been with Him, *as they mourned and wept"* (Mark 16:10). When the Lord Jesus joined the two disciples on the road to Emmaus after His resurrection, He asked them, "What manner of communications are these that ye have one to another, as ye walk, *and are sad?"* (Luke 24:17).

But although the disciples would be sad and discouraged because of their Lord's crucifixion, their mourning would be shortly "turned into joy" at His resurrection. The meaning of the verse must not be limited to this short period, however. We must keep in mind that the weeping will be when *"I go to my Father,"* and *besides* this, during the three days the body of Jesus remained in the tomb.

It is not quite clear that the *enemies* of Jesus were *rejoicing* these three days if we judge by their anxiety over His prophesied resurrection. I believe "Ye shall weep and lament" applies to believers between the first and second coming of Christ—throughout the Church Age. During His absence all believers will have many reasons to mourn, like a bride separated from her husband. Meanwhile the wicked will rejoice; they will neither want nor expect the Lord's return. They will eat, drink, and be merry, taking no thought for the eternity that lies ahead. But one day Jesus *will* come again, and the joy of the wicked will be turned into sorrow while the sorrow of the godly will be turned into joy.

Fellow Christian, we must accept the fact that *sorrow* is connected with this earthly pilgrimage, even for dedicated believers. We are *identified* with the Man of Sorrows, the Man who was "acquainted with grief." Jesus said, "He that loveth father or mother more than me is not worthy of me: and he that loveth son or daughter more than me is not worthy of me. And he that taketh not his cross, and followeth after me, is not worthy of me" (Matt. 10:37,38).

This life is a time of sorrow; the joy is on the other side. It is true that we rejoice "with joy unspeakable and full of glory" (I Pet. 1:8), and born again believers are the only people who can smile through tears and rejoice with a broken heart; but this IS an age of sorrow and groaning. Paul said, "We know that the whole creation groaneth and travaileth in pain together until now. And not only they, but ourselves also, which have the firstfruits of the Spirit, even we ourselves groan within ourselves, waiting for the adoption, to wit, the redemption of our body" (Rom. 8:22,23).

"Your sorrow shall be turned into joy." The women who came to the empty tomb on the resurrection morning, finding the Saviour risen, "departed quickly from the sepulchre with fear AND GREAT JOY; and did run to bring His disciples word" (Matt. 28:8).

John 20:20 tells us that when Jesus "shewed unto (the disciples) His hands and His side, *Then were the disciples glad,* when they saw the Lord!" But *"your sorrow shall be turned into joy"* will find its completion in the people of God when Jesus comes to receive believers unto Himself in the Rapture. Yes, "weeping may endure for a night," but that night is far spent, and surely "joy cometh in the morning!" (Psalm 30:5).

Paul wrote these encouraging words to the believers in the Corinthian church: *"For our light affliction, which is but for a moment, worketh for us a far more exceeding and eternal weight of glory;* while we look not at the things which are seen, but at the things which are not seen: for the things which are seen are temporal; *but the things which are not seen are eternal"* (II Cor. 4:17,18).

Luke 6:24,25 paints a woeful picture for those who have refused to receive the Gospel and believe on the Lord Jesus Christ:

"Woe unto you that are rich! for ye have received your consolation. Woe unto you that are full! for ye shall hunger. Woe unto you that laugh now! for ye shall mourn and weep!"

If we take up the cross and follow Jesus faithfully, if we suffer for the cause of Christ, then we can say with Paul, "For I reckon that the sufferings of this present time are not worthy to be compared with the glory which shall be revealed in us" (Rom. 8:18).

We who serve Him faithfully will one day hear Him say, "Well done, good and faithful servant; thou hast been faithful over a few things, I will make thee ruler over many things: *enter thou into the joy of thy Lord"* (Matt. 25:23).

Verse 21: *"A woman when she is in travail hath sorrow, because her hour is come: but as soon as she is delivered of the child, she remembereth no more the anguish, for joy that a man is born into the world."*

This is an illustration of the state of the Church between the first and second coming of Christ. In other words, for the entire duration of this Dispensation of Grace, there will be a time of pain and anxiety, a time when believers will desire deliverance from trials, tribulations, and persecution sure to come upon all who live godly in Christ Jesus.

The Greek word translated *"sorrow"* literally means "the pains of a travailing woman." Groaning and travailing is the normal state of affairs for the Christian while our Saviour is absent from us. Only His return can bring peace on earth and good will toward men. When Jesus comes again, the knowledge of the Lord will cover the earth as the waters now cover the sea. The devil will be chained in the pit (Rev. 20:1–3). Then and only then will we have peace and security without trials and tribulations.

In Matthew 24:3 the disciples asked Jesus, "When shall these things be? and what shall be the sign of thy coming, and of the end of the world?" He answered, "Take heed that no man deceive you. For many shall come in my name, saying, I am Christ; and shall deceive many. And ye shall hear of wars and rumours of wars: see that ye be not troubled: for *all these things* must come to pass, but the end is not yet. For nation shall rise against nation, and kingdom against kingdom: and there shall be famines, and pestilences, and earthquakes, in divers places. *All these are the beginning of sorrows*" (Matt. 24:4–8).

I believe the Church will be raptured before the Tribulation period begins, and according to Scripture the Antichrist will not be revealed until after the Church is taken out of the world; but the Church today is certainly *living* in the period described by Jesus in the passage just quoted from Matthew. Just how much *longer* these days will last before the Rapture, we do not know; but we do know that the blessed hope of the Church is the glorious appearing of the great God and our Saviour, Jesus Christ.

Jesus is teaching here that the period of time between His first coming and His second coming (the Dispensation of Grace) will be a period of anxiety, sorrow, and pain—a period like unto the state of a woman about to be delivered in childbirth; but this period will come to an end when Jesus appears a second time to receive the Church unto Himself—and when that glorious day comes, when we see Jesus, the pain and sorrow will be turned into such great joy that all of the tribulations will be forgotten (II Cor. 4:17,18).

As soon as the woman is delivered of her child, she remembers no more the anguish of her delivery, because of her joy that a man-child is born into the world. This corresponds to the tremendous truth it declares. It portrays our sufferings and declares the surety and necessity for them. It points out their severity, but at the same time it assures us that the suffering such as this is for but a brief period, only a little while; and then it will be turned into joy. The anguish, suffering, and indescribable pain of a woman giving birth to a child are compensated when the child is born, and she knows boundless joy because of the fruit of her anguish—a child born into the world.

The believer must know fellowship with the sufferings of Jesus before he shares His glory: ". . . if so be that we suffer with Him, that we may be also glorified together" (Rom. 8:17b).

Notice that Jesus said, *"Because her HOUR is come."* He used the same figure of speech over and over again in connection with His own "hour," the hour of travail when He would lay down His life that we might be born into the family of God through His suffering, death, burial, and resurrection.

Verse 22: *"And ye now therefore have sorrow: but I will see you again, and your heart shall rejoice, and your joy no man taketh from you."*

The first part of this verse is but a summary of all our Lord had said, beginning with verse 15 up to this present teaching. He was, of course, speaking directly to the disciples, but His teaching also applies to all believers from His first coming until the Rapture of the Church.

"Your joy no man taketh from you." I cannot see how this could mean the short period of forty days after the resurrection, and certainly it could not refer to the times of trouble, tribulation, persecution, and death through which the Church passed in its infancy. We know from Scripture and from history that the early Church passed through sorrow, and that their joy was often broken as countless saints of God sealed their testimony with their blood. Read the seventh chapter of Acts (the stoning of Stephen). Acts 12:2 tells us that Herod "killed James the brother of John with the sword." The statement here therefore must refer to the second coming of Christ, the *only* time when universal, unbroken and unending joy will come to believers. It is "the great God and our Saviour Jesus Christ" who will *give* us this joy that no man can take away. He will wipe away all tears and there will *be* no more crying, nor sickness, nor pain and sorrow, and there will be no more *death!*

Verse 23: *"And in that day ye shall ask me nothing. Verily, verily, I say unto you, Whatsoever ye shall ask the Father in my name, He will give it you."*

"In that day" points to the day when Jesus will come the second time. *"Ye shall ask me nothing"* means, "Ye shall ask me no questions"—that is, they would not want to ask questions or make inquiries such as the ones they wanted to ask in verse 19, because that will be the glorious day when Jesus will appear bodily. He will be seen by all believers; we will be with Him in the clouds in the air, and we will sit at the marriage supper in the sky—the Bride of Christ with the Bridegroom.

When Jesus comes to receive His Church we will not *need* to ask questions because we will understand fully the meaning of the many things which perplex us now. Paul sums it up in I Corinthians 13:10: "When that which is perfect is come, then that which is in part shall be done away."

The promise in the latter part of our present verse is preceded by a "double verily," stressing the importance and the surety of the promise: *"Whatsoever ye shall ask the Father in my name, He will give it you!"* Here the Lord renews and emphasizes His former promise to the disciples concerning prayer, and this applies to all believers even in this present day. Whatsoever we ask in prayer in the name of Jesus, God will give it to us—but certainly this does not mean that believers will pray foolishly. When we pray in the Spirit, we can expect an answer. God may not answer in the way we expect, He may not answer in the way we think He *should* answer; but He will answer any and all of our prayers that are for our good and His glory.

I would emphasize that *"whatsoever"* is limited to whatsoever things are to the glory of God and the good of the believer—not foolish things such as one might ask for in the flesh, but the things we ask for as we are led by the Spirit in prayer. Jesus promised, "If ye abide in me, and my words abide in you, ye shall ask what ye will, and it shall be done unto you" (John 15:7).

The Greek word translated *"ask"* in the latter part of our present verse is entirely different from that used in the first part of the verse. *Here, it refers to "seeking or petitioning in prayer"*; but in the first part of the verse it speaks of *asking questions.*

Verse 24: *"Hitherto have ye asked nothing in my name: ask, and ye shall receive, that your joy may be full."*

"Hitherto have ye asked nothing." These words of Jesus mean that up to that present time the disciples had not prayed for anything through the name and mediation of Christ. They had followed Him as Teacher, they looked to Him as their Master, they loved Him; and with all the faith

they possessed at that time they believed He was the Messiah. But as yet they had not realized that He was the one Mediator between God and man.

Jesus was not reproving the disciples for failure to pray; they had not *needed* to pray, because He was present with them bodily. He was simply announcing one of the consequences of the great change that was about to take place. It was expedient that He return to the Father, and after His return they were to pray in His name and God would hear and answer their prayers.

"Ask, and ye shall receive, that your joy may be full." It is impossible for words to express the great privilege of prayer. Prayer is the key that unlocks heaven's storehouse. We are invited, "Ask, and it shall be given you; seek, and ye shall find; knock, and it shall be opened unto you" (Matt. 7:7).

The disciples were to pray—not only for deliverance from their despondency and perplexity, but *"that your joy may be full."* The Greek word translated *"full"* literally means "filled up," or "to fill or fulfill." The statement here clearly teaches that joy and happiness in the life of a believer are experienced in degrees—some have a greater degree of joy than others do. It is also possible for a believer to enjoy a higher degree of joy and happiness at times than at other times.

To the believers at Thessalonica Paul wrote, "Rejoice evermore! Pray without ceasing" (I Thess. 5:16,17). When a believer ceases to pray, that believer also ceases to rejoice. We *must* pray without ceasing if we hope to rejoice evermore. Paul said, "Be careful for nothing; but in every thing by prayer and supplication with thanksgiving let your requests be made known unto God. And the peace of God, which passeth all understanding, shall keep your hearts and minds through Christ Jesus" (Phil. 4:6,7).

The joy of a Christian depends to a great degree on earnest prayer—but to "pray without ceasing" does not mean that we are to go about all day praying aloud, nor that we should spend the entire day on our knees. It means that we should be in an *attitude* of prayer, a spirit of prayer, meditating, thinking prayerfully in the heart.

Verse 25: *"These things have I spoken unto you in proverbs: but the time cometh, when I shall no more speak unto you in proverbs, but I shall shew you plainly of the Father."*

Here Jesus revealed that there was to be *a change in the nature* of the revealing of truth. *"Proverbs"* means different modes of figurative speech, and He would no longer speak to them in figurative language. He would speak plainly of His Father. Speaking *"plainly"* means freedom of speech. The time for fulness of utterance, fulness of understanding, had come.

"The time cometh" refers to the time after His ascension to the Father when He would send the Holy Spirit to teach them of all things and bring to their remembrance all things He had said to them. Jesus began to show them of the Father even before Pentecost, before the Holy Spirit came, and it is most interesting to note that *there are no parables in the epistles.* It is the business of the Holy Spirit to take of the things of Christ and tell them out, making them known to us that they may actually become part of us.

On the very day Jesus rose from the grave He *Himself* taught the two disciples on the road to Emmaus. Luke 24:27 tells us that "beginning at Moses and all the prophets, He expounded unto them in all the Scriptures the things *concerning Himself.*" In Luke 24:45 *He* opened their understanding, "that they might understand the Scriptures." It was *He* who revealed to Mary Magdalene that His Father was also the Father of the disciples, His brethren (John 20:17). But the complete and final fulfillment of the promise made by Jesus came at Pentecost when the Holy Spirit was given—He who guides believers into *"all truth."* (Please read John 16:13—15; I Corinthians 2:9,10; I John 2:20,27).

There is no excuse for spiritual ignorance today. We will

never understand ALL of the Word of God, but every born again believer has the Teacher of the Scriptures in his heart (Rom. 8:9,14,16; Eph. 4:30). The Scriptures came by holy men as they were moved by the Holy Ghost and penned down the words God gave them as the Holy Ghost spoke. Therefore, since the Holy Spirit *gave* the Word of God, certainly He is able to teach us from its storehouse of spiritual truths. If we are willing to study to show ourselves approved unto God, if we are willing to be led by the Spirit, then certainly we can understand the things God would *have* us understand.

There are three interesting comparisons on prayer in our recent study:

In John 14:13,14, prayer is the proof of Christ's almighty influence with God the Eternal Father: "Whatsoever ye shall ask in my name, that will I do, that the Father may be glorified in the Son. If ye shall ask any thing in my name, I will do it."

In John 15:7, prayer is the proof of the disciples' living fellowship with the Lord Jesus Christ: "If ye abide in me, and my words abide in you, ye shall ask what ye will, and it shall be done unto you."

In our present chapter, verses 23–26, prayer is the proof of the believer's spiritual maturity, proof of his access in confidence as a child to the Father: "And in that day ye shall ask me nothing. Verily, verily, I say unto you, Whatsoever ye shall ask the Father in my name, He will give it you. Hitherto have ye asked nothing in my name: ask, and ye shall receive, that your joy may be full. These things have I spoken unto you in proverbs: but the time cometh, when I shall no more speak unto you in proverbs, but I shall shew you plainly of the Father. At that day ye shall ask in my name: and I say not unto you, that I will pray the Father for you."

Verse 26: *"At that day ye shall ask in my name: and I say not unto you, that I will pray the Father for you."*

"At that day . . . ." After the Lord's resurrection, when

the disciples fully understood the nature of His mission and His ministry on earth, they would pray to the heavenly Father in His name, though up until that time they had *not* prayed in His name because He was with them bodily.

"And I say not unto you that I will pray the Father for you." The meaning here is that it was not necessary for Jesus to say that He would pray to the heavenly Father to hear and answer the prayers of the disciples. Not only does He mediate between God and man, but the Father hears our prayers willingly (and in the next verse we find the *reason* He hears and answers prayers of His children). The promise is extended *to ALL believers,* even to you and me.

Hear the words of Jesus as He prays for His disciples and for all believers throughout the Church Age:

"I pray for them: I pray not for the world, but for them which thou hast given me; for they are thine. . . I pray not that thou shouldest take them out of the world, but that thou shouldest keep them from the evil. . . *Neither pray I for these alone, BUT FOR THEM ALSO WHICH SHALL BELIEVE ON ME THROUGH THEIR WORD"* (John 17:9,15,20).

Verse 27: *"For the Father Himself loveth you, because ye have loved me, and have believed that I came out from God."*

This verse is a continuation of the preceding verse. Here we see how mercifully the Lord acknowledges the grace of His weak, sad, discouraged disciples. In spite of their weakness He recognized grace in their hearts. The Jews as a nation rejected Jesus, but the eleven loved Him and believed in Him as their Messiah, the Promised One. How thankful we should be that the Lord Jesus does not forget to honor *true grace!* Regardless of our weaknesses and infirmities, when we believe in all sincerity, God does not overlook true faith in the hearts of any of His children.

So Jesus said to the eleven, "You need not doubt that

God our Father will do for you all that you ask in my name, believing. My heavenly Father loves you because you have loved me, because you have believed in me and in my divine mission on earth."

This is indeed a deep verse. It contains much more than is seen at first glance. The truth here points *back* to the Incarnation and points *forward* to the resurrection of Jesus and His ascension. Here are vital facts for faith to lay hold of and cling to without wavering.

First of all, if we would believe "the faith once delivered unto the saints" we must believe that Christ came from God the Father. Not only was He officially *sent forth* by God, He came also of His own free will and *willingly* laid His life down. He was not forced or driven to be a propitiation for our sins; He willingly came into the world, knowing *why* He was coming (John 10:17,18).

In the second place, we must believe that Jesus came into the world *for the primary purpose of saving sinners.* He came—not to be ministered unto, but to minister, and to give His life a ransom for many. He came to seek and to save that which was lost. He came to lay His life down that we might have life.

In the third place, if we would believe and receive the faith once delivered unto the saints, we must believe that Jesus was crucified, buried, that He rose again, and that He returned to the Father "according to the Scriptures" (I Cor. 15:1–4).

Verse 28: *"I came forth from the Father, and am come into the world: again, I leave the world, and go to the Father."*

Here with solemn yet simple emphasis, Jesus declared His divine origin and destiny. He came *into* the world as no one else ever came into the world, and He *left* the world as no other ever left it. He came into the world of His own will, and He *departed* of His own will. In this simple statement is summed up the eternal generation—the

Incarnation, the death, the resurrection, and the ascension of the Lord Jesus Christ, Son of God, yea, God in flesh.

Four facts are stated in our present verse:

1. *Jesus came from the Father.*
2. *He came into the world.*
3. *He was about to depart out of the world.*
4. *He would return unto the Father.*

These four facts summarize the history of God's Christ, our Saviour, the Lord Jesus. The first fact takes us to *the past eternity* of Christ. Greek scholars tell us there is a significant change in the preposition. In verse 27 Jesus said, "Ye have believed that I came forth from (the Greek preposition is *para,* meaning *from with*) the Father." Jesus came *from* the Father, yet He was *with* the Father. The deeper truth declares more than a recognition of the faith of the disciples. The Greek preposition *ek* indicates oneness of essence—oneness of the Father and the Son from all eternity. There are those who deny the pre-eternal Sonship of the Lord Jesus Christ and thus fail to see the oneness between God the Father and God the Son. Jesus did not become the Son at His birth—He was God's Son *in the beginning* before the Incarnation. When He was born of the virgin Mary He simply took a body like unto our bodies that He might die, and in dying pay the sin-debt.

"Who is he that condemneth? It is Christ that died, yea rather, that is risen again, who is even at the right hand of God, who also maketh intercession for us" (Rom. 8:34).

"Wherefore in all things it behoved Him to be made like unto His brethren, that He might be a merciful and faithful high priest in things pertaining to God, to make reconciliation for the sins of the people" (Heb. 2:17).

The second fact in our verse covers the virgin birth, the Incarnation, the death, burial, and resurrection of our Lord and Saviour Jesus Christ.

The third fact declares His departure from the earth, and the fourth fact declares His return to the heavenly Father, standing in the same relation to God as in the eternal past.

The fact that Jesus came out from the Father is inseparable from the fact that He *returned* to the Father. His Sonship—the fact that He came out from the Father—does not suggest that the Father ceased to be with Him. In John 10:30 He declared, "I and my Father are one," and in 8:29 He declared, "The Father hath not left me alone!"

Verse 29: *"His disciples said unto Him, Lo, now speakest thou plainly, and speakest no proverb."*

The confession made by the apostles here looks back to what Jesus had just said in verses 27 and 28. Although they did not fully understand all of His meaning, what they *did* understand encouraged them, refreshed them, and gave them new hope and assurance.

Verse 30: *"Now are we sure that thou knowest all things, and needest not that any man should ask thee: by this we believe that thou camest forth from God."*

The disciples here recognized Christ's omniscience. They realized that He had perceived the thoughts of their hearts. They did not fully understand what He had said, however, nor what He meant by returning to God the Father. *"Father"* suggests relationship between father and children, and the disciples at that point did not understand what relationship existed between themselves and Jehovah God. For that matter, they did not fully understand the relationship between *Jesus* and God the Father, although they recognized Jehovah God as the one *true* God, the one divine Being who is over all, Creator and sustainer of all things.

"We believe that thou camest forth from God." The confession the disciples made here goes no further than a confession that He was Messiah. For example, in John 3:2 *Nicodemus* called Jesus "Rabbi," and declared, "We know that thou art a teacher come from God." *The woman of Samaria* at Jacob's well realized that Jesus was more than man. She said, "Come, see a Man, which told me all

things that ever I did: Is not this the Christ?" (John 4:29). When Jesus fed the five thousand with five barley loaves and two little fishes, those who witnessed the miracle said, "This is of a truth that Prophet that should come into the world" (John 6:14).

Israel was looking for their Messiah, for the King of kings—but they had no conception of the drastic changes that would occur, changes that would be different from what they had thought and expected concerning the kingdom that was to be set up when Messiah came. The disciples had no idea how things on earth would be when Jesus returned to the heavenly Father and the Holy Spirit came to dwell on earth, and even up to the very last they hoped that Jesus would set up the kingdom and deliver Israel from the Romans. Yet in all of their confusion and lack of understanding, they readily confessed that He had come forth from God.

Verse 31: *"Jesus answered them, Do ye now believe?"*

By asking this question Jesus challenged their faith. It is true that in a real sense they did believe Him to be the promised Messiah, and they believed He came out from God; but under the severe testing that lay ahead, their faith would be shaken to its very foundations. Their faith was genuine, but not nearly as strong as they supposed it to be.

Notice how Jesus asked the question: *"Do ye NOW believe?"* In other words, "Ye believe while I am with you, but what will you do when I am arrested, condemned, and nailed to a cross? What will you do when I am pronounced dead and my body is laid in the tomb?"

Actually, He was warning them against self-confidence, a warning which even the most spiritual believer needs. We do not realize the extreme weakness of our own hearts. You will notice that Jesus never flattered His disciples. The true secret of spiritual strength and stability is not self-confidence, but self-distrust and deep humility. When we realize just how weak we really are, it is then that we are strong in the faith. In II Corinthians 12:10 the Apostle Paul declared, "I take pleasure in infirmities, in reproaches, in necessities, in persecutions, in distresses for Christ's sake: *for when I am weak, then am I strong!"*

Verse 32: *"Behold, the hour cometh, yea, is now come, that ye shall be scattered, every man to his own, and shall leave me alone: and yet I am not alone, because the Father is with me."*

"Behold!" Jesus used this to arrest the attention of the disciples. *"Ye shall be scattered."* Yes, the time had come when the Shepherd must be smitten and the sheep would be scattered, ". . . *every man to his own."* That is, every man would search for his own shelter, his own hiding place.

There *was* no hiding place for Jesus. If His mission on earth was to be fulfilled, if lost sinners were to be delivered from the wages of sin and death, He must face the trial, the scourging, the crown of thorns, the cross. He would be left alone by His disciples, yet He spoke words of comfort to them, even in this hour:

"I am NOT alone, because the Father is with me." Someone may ask, "Does not the prayer of Jesus on the cross contradict His statement here? When Jesus cried out, 'My God, my God, why hast thou forsaken me?' did not God actually *leave* Him?" Yes, God did forsake Him *as the Son of man.* Jesus was man just as we are man (Rom. 8:3; Heb. 2:9,17). He was man in all things as we are except for man's original sin. However, Jesus was *very God* as truly as He was man (John 1:1,18; 10:30; II Cor. 5:19). As man on the cross paying the sin-debt, He was forsaken by God. God cannot look on sin, and Jesus bore our sins in His own body and nailed them to the cross (I Pet. 2:24). Yes, God literally turned His head and Jesus died alone—but *as God's Eternal Son,* co-equal with the Father from the beginning, in the bosom of the Father (John 1:18), Christ was *not* forsaken by the Father. That eternal unity has never been broken—nor will it ever be.

These deep spiritual truths cannot be explained in the language of mortal man, but this makes it all the more wonderful. This testifies to the greatness of God. In Christ dwelt all the fulness of the Godhead bodily (Col. 2:9,10). *As GOD in flesh* Jesus was never forsaken by the Father; but as the Son of man in His humiliation, He was forsaken by God and man (Phil. 2:5–8).

Verse 33: *"These things I have spoken unto you, that in me ye might have peace. In the world ye shall have tribulation: but be of good cheer; I have overcome the world."*

There are trials, temptations, troubles IN the world, as well as FROM the world. *"In the world"* is the place of testing. As long as Christians live on this earth they will suffer from the weaknesses and frailties of humanity. But just as surely as *"in the world"* we shall have tribulation and heartache, just that surely *"IN CHRIST"* we have peace beyond all understanding. In Christ there is no condemnation. In Christ we have life eternal. In Christ we have assurance and hope, and in Him we will enter the Pearly White City. The world cannot rob us of our peace, nor can the prince of this world destroy it. But we must remember that the believer lives by faith, and peace comes *only* through the Lord Jesus Christ. "Therefore being justified by faith, we have peace with God through our Lord Jesus Christ" (Rom. 5:1).

"These things I have spoken unto you, that in me ye might have peace." Having made clear and final reference to the awful hour that was just ahead of Him, Jesus brought His message here to a close with words of encouragement, words that would assure the disciples of victory. The peace He spoke of here can be enjoyed only by communion with Him as we live in faith and walk by faith—and there is no doubt in my mind that when Jesus was arrested and His enemies led Him away to be crucified, the disciples learned that peace was in Him alone!

"In the world ye shall have tribulation"—but thank God for the rest of that verse: *"BE OF GOOD CHEER; I have overcome the world!"* Jesus left the Father's bosom, came into this world born of a woman, took a body like unto our body, was made in all things like unto His brethren (sin apart); and in that body He conquered the world, the flesh, the devil, death, hell, and the grave. No wonder John the Beloved wrote, "Greater is He that is in you, than he that is in the world!" (I John 4:4).

The devil is powerful, but our Christ is *ALL powerful.* He met Satan and conquered him (Matt. 4:1–11). Since this is true, then we have the assurance that we are more than conquerors through Him. We are IN the world, but we are not OF the world. We are in the world, but we do not walk according TO the world—nor do we walk alone. It is true that we will be tried, we will suffer persecution, we will undergo tribulation, but we can say with Paul, *"I am persuaded, that neither death, nor life, nor angels, nor principalities, nor powers, nor things present, nor things to come, nor height, nor depth, nor any other creature, shall be able to separate us from the love of God, which is in Christ Jesus our Lord"* (Rom. 8:38,39).

I thank God that we are not called upon to take one step that Jesus did not take before us. The world today is essentially the same as that into which He came, and Jesus Christ is the same today as He was then (Heb. 13:8). Therefore He is saying to us, as He said to His disciples, "Be of good cheer! I have overcome the world!" I John 5:4 tells us that "whatsoever is born of God overcometh the world: and this is the victory that overcometh the world, EVEN OUR FAITH."

And finally, in Revelation 3:21, we have the glorious promise: "To him that overcometh will I grant to sit with me in my throne, even as I also overcame, and am set down with my Father in His throne!"

In this last verse of chapter 16 the Lord Jesus sums up the reasons for speaking the things contained in this entire discourse: All things that He had spoken were for this one great end—that believers might have inward peace through faith in Jesus and through close communion with Him. *"He IS our peace"* (Eph. 2:14).

CHAPTER XVII

1. These words spake Jesus, and lifted up his eyes to heaven, and said, Father, the hour is come; glorify thy Son, that thy Son also may glorify thee:

2. As thou hast given him power over all flesh, that he should give eternal life to as many as thou hast given him.

3. And this is life eternal, that they might know thee the only true God, and Jesus Christ, whom thou hast sent.

4. I have glorified thee on the earth: I have finished the work which thou gavest me to do.

5. And now, O Father, glorify thou me with thine own self with the glory which I had with thee before the world was.

6. I have manifested thy name unto the men which thou gavest me out of the world: thine they were, and thou gavest them me; and they have kept thy word.

7. Now they have known that all things whatsoever thou hast given me are of thee.

8. For I have given unto them the words which thou gavest me; and they have received them, and have known surely that I came out from thee, and they have believed that thou didst send me.

9. I pray for them: I pray not for the world, but for them which thou hast given me; for they are thine.

10. And all mine are thine, and thine are mine; and I am glorified in them.

11. And now I am no more in the world, but these are in the world, and I come to thee. Holy Father, keep through thine own name those whom thou hast given me, that they may be one, as we are.

12. While I was with them in the world, I kept them in thy name: those that thou gavest me I have kept, and none of them is lost, but the son of perdition; that the scripture might be fulfilled.

13. And now come I to thee; and these things I speak in the world, that they might have my joy fulfilled in themselves.

14. I have given them thy word; and the world hath hated them, because they are not of the world, even as I am not of the world.

15. I pray not that thou shouldest take them out of the world, but that thou shouldest keep them from the evil.

16. They are not of the world, even as I am not of the world.
17. Sanctify them through thy truth: thy word is truth.
18. As thou hast sent me into the world, even so have I also sent them into the world.
19. And for their sakes I sanctify myself, that they also might be sanctified through the truth.
20. Neither pray I for these alone, but for them also which shall believe on me through their word;
21. That they all may be one; as thou, Father, art in me, and I in thee, that they also may be one in us: that the world may believe that thou hast sent me.
22. And the glory which thou gavest me I have given them; that they may be one, even as we are one:
23. I in them, and thou in me, that they may be made perfect in one; and that the world may know that thou hast sent me, and hast loved them, as thou hast loved me.
24. Father, I will that they also, whom thou hast given me, be with me where I am; that they may behold my glory, which thou hast given me: for thou lovedst me before the foundation of the world.
25. O righteous Father, the world hath not known thee: but I have known thee, and these have known that thou hast sent me.
26. And I have declared unto them thy name, and will declare it: that the love wherewith thou hast loved me may be in them, and I in them.

This is the most remarkable chapter in all the sixty-six books of the Bible; it stands alone. It records the prayer Christ prayed after His sermon to His disciples just after the institution of the Lord's Supper. It is a specimen of His intercession on behalf of His disciples and of all born again believers throughout the Church Age.

This chapter embraces the longest recorded prayer of our Lord while He was on earth. No doubt He prayed other prayers as lengthy as this, for we know He spent much time in prayer and in communion with His heavenly Father; but God did not see fit to give these other prayers to us as the Holy Ghost spoke to holy men. We have many of the sermons of Jesus, many of His parables; but only this one lengthy prayer.

As we study this passage, we immediately recognize the fact that Jesus not only "*spake* as never man spake," He also *prayed* as no man has *ever* prayed, or ever could pray. This was His prayer just before Judas betrayed Him with a kiss, just before His own disciples forsook Him and fled, just before He walked the last mile to Golgotha to be nailed to a cross and bring His earthly ministry to a climax.

We are not told where Jesus was when He prayed this prayer. Some suggest that He was still in the upper room, but this is not according to reason, because in the last verse of chapter 14 He said to His disciples, "Arise, *let us go hence.*" Then between the arising and "going hence" and our present chapter, He gave His disciples the dissertation on the vine and the branches, as set forth in chapter 15, and the discussion on the coming of the Holy Spirit and persecutions of the Christians as given in chapter 16. It would seem, then, that the prayer recorded in this chapter was prayed somewhere outside the walls of Jerusalem—probably just before He crossed the brook Cedron (John 18:1).

This intercessory prayer of Jesus leads us into the holiest of all. This is one of the portions of God's Word which makes me feel that I should remove the shoes from my feet because I stand on holy ground, like Moses before the burning bush (Ex. 3:5). We should bow our heads and humble our hearts in adoration and worship as we read the holy words recorded here—words that fell from the holy lips of Jesus. We can feel the pulsations of love that flowed from His great *heart* of love as He prayed to His heavenly Father in the words recorded here.

We might note here His threefold references to the Father in this prayer:

In verse 1 He called God *"Father."*

In verse 11 He addressed God as *"Holy Father."*

In verse 25 He called God *"Righteous Father."*

From the first verse through the last verse of this holy prayer, we see the oneness which exists between God the Father and God the Son, and consequently we see the holy oneness *believers* have with both the Father and the Son through the grace brought down to man and the redemption Jesus purchased through His shed blood.

The Intercessory Prayer

Verse 1: *"These words spake Jesus, and lifted up His eyes to heaven, and said, Father, the hour is come; glorify thy Son, that thy Son also may glorify thee."*

"These words spake Jesus." This points back to the opening statement in verse 33 of the previous chapter and refers to the entire message Jesus had delivered to His disciples in the three preceding chapters. Then having completed His message to the disciples He lifted His eyes and His heart to God, to talk to His heavenly Father.

I believe Jesus gave us an example here: He had been preaching to His disciples, giving them words of warning, words of comfort, and wonderful words of promise; and when He finished speaking to them, He lifted His eyes to the heavenly Father to pray. After we have delivered the Word of God to our listeners, we should pray that the Holy Spirit will take the Word and bear it home to the hearts of those to whom we have spoken. We need to pray that the Holy Spirit will use our words to convict, convince, and draw sinners to Christ and to comfort and encourage the hearts of believers.

Jesus *"lifted up His eyes to heaven."* It stands to reason that while He was speaking to His disciples His eyes were fixed upon them; and then as He addressed His heavenly Father He lifted His eyes toward heaven, *looking UP,* not at the persons or things around Him. His eyes and heart were fixed on God the heavenly Father. I believe there are times when we should *close* our eyes when we pray—when we are praying in the assembly or when things around us might claim our attention; but at other times it is perfectly scriptural to pray with our eyes open. The individual should be led in his own heart concerning his manner and method of prayer.

When we lift our eyes to heaven it suggests that we are thinking of things above rather than of things on earth. David said, "Unto thee, O Lord, do I lift up my soul" (Psalm 25:1).

In Psalm 121:1,2 we read, *"I will lift up mine eyes* unto the hills, from whence cometh my help. My help cometh from the Lord, which made heaven and earth." And in Psalm 123:1 we read, *"Unto thee lift I up mine eyes,* O thou that dwellest in the heavens."

It is interesting as well as significant that Jesus here addressed the Eternal God as "Father." He did this, first of all, because it was God who gave Him His human nature: "Wherefore when He cometh into the world, He saith, Sacrifice and offering thou wouldest not, *but a body hast thou prepared me"* (Heb. 10:5). The angel of the Lord said to Mary, "The Holy Ghost shall come upon thee, and the power of the Highest shall overshadow thee: therefore also that holy thing which shall be born of thee shall be called the Son of God" (Luke 1:35).

In the second place, Jesus addressed God as "Father" because God stands as Father in relationship to our Lord and Saviour Jesus Christ, the divine head and representative of the family of God here on earth, that family being made up of all redeemed ones. Jesus is "the firstborn among many brethren" (Rom. 8:29; Heb. 1:5,6).

In the third place, Jesus addressed God as "Father" because of their relationship to each other in the beginning. Jesus was with the Father, He was God's Christ, in the beginning; He became man's Jesus when He was born of the virgin. The opening of this prayer points out specifically and clearly that Jesus is the Son of God in a definite and peculiar sense, such as no other one has ever been the son of God. He was the *ONLY begotten* Son.

When Jesus said "Father" those who *heard* Him immediately realized that to speak to one as Father denoted relationship. Jesus was speaking as the Son to the Father, and as the Son of God He had a right to be heard, accepted, and believed by His followers. The fact that He addressed God as "Father" in His prayer was as though He were saying to Jehovah, the Eternal God, "Father, I was with you in unity, in essence, in perfection, in holiness, and in righteousness from the unbegun eternity. When the beginning began, I was with you; and because of your will and your power, I was clothed with human nature and came to earth to *declare* God to man. It is as the Son of the Eternal Father that I approach the throne of grace on behalf of these my disciples, and in behalf of all who *will* believe on me as the Son of the Eternal Father."

Addressing Jehovah God as "Father" indicated to the disciples that love existed between Jesus and God, and suggested the *trust* a son has in his father. This shows us that we need to trust in the wisdom, power, and faithfulness of God, knowing that He will hear our prayers because He IS our Father.

"The hour is come." This is the seventh and final time Jesus refers to this *"hour"*—the greatest of all the hours He spent on earth. This was the hour when the Lord Jesus Christ would terminate the work the Father had sent Him into the world to do, the hour when He would terminate His life by death on the cross. It was the hour when He was made sin for us, "that we might be made the righteousness of God in Him" (II Cor. 5:21). This was the hour when He would cry out, "It is finished!" Every jot and tittle of the law—prophecies, types, symbols set forth throughout the Old Testament—would be fulfilled. This was the hour foretold in Genesis 3:15 when the serpent would bruise His heel and He would bruise the serpent's head.

"Glorify thy Son." From the moment Jesus entered His public ministry until He said "It is finished" His one desire was to glorify God the Father and finish the work the Father had given Him to do. Here, He prayed that the heavenly Father would support Him on Calvary during the hours of horrible suffering, and afterward deliver Him from the

grave and give Him His rightful seat at the right hand of the Majesty on high. He was praying for glorification in victory through suffering, death, and the grave, thus bringing to completion the work He came to do here on earth, work that would glorify God and completely satisfy His justice, holiness, righteousness, mercy, and faithfulness.

Jesus was facing the darkest hour of His earthly ministry, yet on the very brink of that dark hour He looked beyond the sufferings to the glory that would be His on the other side of Calvary. He did not seek the glory of men, nor did He seek to be glorified BY men. He prayed to be glorified by the Father—and that should be *our* desire also. We should not seek the praise or glory of men. Whatever we do should be done to the honor and glory of God, and He in turn will glorify us. Jesus said, "No man can come to me, except the Father which hath sent me draw him: and I will raise him up at the last day" (John 6:44).

Verse 2: *"As thou hast given Him power over all flesh, that He should give eternal life to as many as thou hast given Him."*

Greek scholars tell us that "the language used in the original here is extremely peculiar. The Greek contains a nominative absolute, and it is next to impossible to literally translate this into English. The *nearest* exact translation would be, 'that with regard to all that body (the Church), or thing (the Church) which thou hast given Him, He should give eternal life to them.'" There is a definite distinction between the body *as a whole* and the *individual members* who make up the body as a whole. The body *in its entirety* was given to Christ by the Eternal Father before the world was; but the individuals who make up the body are called by the preaching of the Gospel throughout this Day of Grace. They are called separately, *one by one,* and God gives them eternal life when they hear and receive the Gospel.

God calls through the preaching of the Word, and no

man can come to Jesus except he be called:

"For whosoever shall call upon the name of the Lord shall be saved. How then shall they call on Him in whom they have not believed? and how shall they believe in Him of whom they have not heard? and how shall they hear without a preacher? and how shall they preach, except they be sent? As it is written, How beautiful are the feet of them that preach the Gospel of peace, and bring glad tidings of good things" (Rom. 10:13–15).

To be saved, one must *hear* the Gospel, *believe* the Gospel, and *receive* the Gospel by faith. *Grace saves us,* but grace becomes ours by faith, and faith to appropriate grace comes by hearing the Word of God (Rom. 10:17; John 5:24; I Pet. 1:23). The true Church is the body of Christ. We become members of that body through the new birth, born of the Spirit, united to the body by and through the Holy Spirit:

"Verily, verily, I say unto thee, Except a man be born of water and of the Spirit, he cannot enter into the kingdom of God" (John 3:5).

"For as the body is one, and hath many members, and all the members of that one body, being many, are one body: so also is Christ. For by one Spirit are we all baptized into one body, whether we be Jews or Gentiles, whether we be bond or free; and have been all made to drink into one Spirit" (I Cor. 12:12,13).

"Thou hast given Him power over all flesh" does not mean that the Son is inferior to the Father. The meaning is that in the eternal councils between Father, Son, and Holy Ghost, it was arranged that Jesus would carry out the work of redemption and, *through His finished work,* redeem all that the Father had given to Him to make up the body of the New Testament Church. Jesus was the "Lamb without blemish and without spot: who verily was foreordained before the foundation of the world" (I Pet. 1:19,20). Christ was never inferior to the Father. He was in the beginning *with* the Father, and as the Father had life in Himself, so

the Son had life in Himself. Then two thousand years ago, God's Christ became the Son of man, God Incarnate. He took a body like unto our body, sin apart, and in that body He did what the law had never done, what the law never *could* have done:

"There is therefore now no condemnation to them which are in Christ Jesus, who walk not after the flesh, but after the Spirit. For the law of the Spirit of life in Christ Jesus hath made me free from the law of sin and death. For what the law could not do, in that it was weak through the flesh, God sending His own Son in the likeness of sinful flesh, and for sin, condemned sin in the flesh: that the righteousness of the law might be fulfilled in us, who walk not after the flesh, but after the Spirit" (Rom. 8:1–4).

"All flesh" means all mankind. Not all will be saved, but Christ has *power* over all flesh. I believe the meaning here is the same as in John 3:16,17: "For God so loved the world, that He gave His only begotten Son, that *whosoever* believeth in Him should not perish, but have everlasting life. For God sent not His Son into the world to condemn the world; but that the world *through Him might be saved."* The whole world *could* be saved, but the world will not be saved because the world will not receive the Gospel. But *all who hear and believe* will become members of the body of the New Testament Church.

"That He should give eternal life to as many as thou hast given Him." Does this mean that some are elected to be saved while others are elected to be damned? Indeed it does not! This emphasizes that in the eternal councils of the Trinity, Father, Son, and Holy Spirit agreed on the plan for salvation—they agreed on the New Testament Church; and the Church *as a body* was elected, predestined, given to the Son; and all hell cannot stop the completion of the Church—spoken of in Acts 20:28 as "the Church of God . . . purchased with His own blood."

Since God is sovereign, omniscient, omnipotent, and omnipresent, He knows who will be saved, He knows *when* they will be saved, and all about it; but that does not change the free will of man. Jesus does give eternal life to all those who are given to Him; but that does not mean that some are predestined to be saved while others are predestined to be lost. Redemption is for "*whosoever will!*"

Verse 3: "*And this is life eternal, that they might know thee the only true God, and Jesus Christ, whom thou hast sent.*"

True believers are justified *now*, we are sanctified *now*, we have eternal life *now*, and the divine secret of the fact that we will be glorified *hereafter* consists in having a right knowledge, a *saving* knowledge, of the one true God, He who is from everlasting to everlasting; and in having knowledge of Jesus Christ whom God sent to save sinners through His finished work and His shed blood. To know God and Christ aright is to possess eternal life, and there is no such thing as eternal life *apart* from both the Father AND the Son: "Whosoever transgresseth, and abideth not in the doctrine of Christ, hath not GOD. He that abideth in the doctrine of Christ, he hath both the Father AND the Son" (II John 9).

This is not speaking of head-belief or head-knowledge. James 2:19 declares, "the *devils also believe,* and tremble." The knowledge referred to here is that which dwells in the *heart:*

"If thou shalt confess with thy mouth the Lord Jesus, and shalt believe *in thine heart* that God hath raised Him from the dead, thou shalt be saved. *For with the HEART man believeth unto righteousness;* and with the mouth confession is made unto salvation" (Rom. 10:9,10).

Proverbs 4:23 warns, "Keep thy heart with all diligence; *for out of it are the issues of life!*"

Since it is with the heart that man believes unto righteousness, and since it is from the heart that the issues of life proceed, to know Jesus in the heart will definitely influence the life. Jesus in the heart produces a NEW life, because in Christ we are new creations: "Therefore if any man be in Christ, he is a new creature: old things are passed away; behold, all things are become new" (II Cor. 5:17).

A true believer knows the Lord through heart-belief: "Whom having not seen, ye love; in whom, though now ye see Him not, *yet believing,* ye rejoice with joy unspeakable and full of glory" (I Pet. 1:8).

The twofold foundation of Christianity is to know God, the Eternal Father, Jehovah—to know His holiness, His purity, His hatred of sin; and to know God's Christ, God's only begotten Son—to know His redemption, His mediatorial office, His grace, and His love for sinners: "For when we were yet without strength, in due time Christ died for the ungodly. . . God commendeth His love toward us, in that, while we were yet sinners, Christ died for us" (Rom. 5:6,8).

The *right knowledge of God* is the root of all true salvation, and Proverbs 1:7 tells us that *"the fear of the Lord* is the *beginning* of knowledge." There is no true repentance without fear of God. In Genesis 1:3 we learn that *light* was the beginning of creation, and in the spiritual sense light is the beginning of salvation: "For God, who commanded the light to shine out of darkness, hath shined in our hearts, to give the light of the knowledge of the glory of God in the face of Jesus Christ" (II Cor. 4:6).

Believers need to be "renewed in knowledge after the image of Him that created him" (Col. 3:10). We should "be ready always to give an answer to every man that asketh . . . a reason of the hope that is in (us) with meekness and fear" (I Pet. 3:15). Paul said, "I know WHOM I have believed, and am persuaded that He is able to keep that which I have committed unto Him against that day" (II Tim. 1:12).

Do I know God aright? Do I know Christ aright? I need to ask myself these questions and allow the Holy Spirit to search my heart and give me the right answer. You, dear reader, need to ask yourself the same questions. To know God *apart from Christ* is to know Him as a consuming fire (Heb. 12:29). To know *Christ without God* would be of no value at all, even if such knowledge were possible; because it was Jehovah God who so loved the world that He set forth His Son to be a propitiation for sin:

"But now the righteousness of God without the law is manifested, being witnessed by the law and the prophets; even the righteousness of God which is by faith of Jesus Christ unto all and upon all them that believe: for there is no difference: For all have sinned, and come short of the glory of God; being justified freely by His grace through the redemption that is in Christ Jesus: *whom God hath set forth to be a propitiation* through faith in His blood, to declare His righteousness for the remission of sins that are past, through the forbearance of God" (Rom. 3:21–25).

It is essential that we see a holy, sin-hating God who set forth His only begotten Son, a loving, merciful, sin-atoning Saviour. We must see God the Father AND God the Son if we are born again, because according to II John 9, if we deny the Father we do not know the Son, and if we deny the Son we certainly do not know the Father. Life eternal is to know God and God's Christ. To know God without Christ, or to know Christ without God, is not to know *either* in salvation. God the Father so loved us that He sent Jesus the Son, and Jesus the Son so loved us that He died on the cross that redemption might be made possible for all who will believe. The only possible way to approach God is in Christ. The only possible way to be *accepted* by God is in Christ. In John 14:6 Jesus declared, "I am the Way, the Truth, and the Life: *no man cometh unto the Father, but BY ME!*"

Why did Jesus say, *"Thee, the only true God"*? Was He suggesting that *He* was *not* true God, that only the Father was true God? Not at all! By pointing out "the only true God" He excluded idols and false gods, and set forth the order and economy of God's great salvation. I John

5:21 warns, "Little children, keep yourselves from idols." John was here excluding idols and false gods from the lives of the Gentiles. In I Thessalonians 1:9 Paul said, "They themselves shew of us what manner of entering in we had unto you, *and how ye turned to God from idols to serve the living and true God.*"

The statement in our present verse makes definite declaration that Jehovah is the only true God, and since God the Father, God the Son, and God the Holy Spirit are one in essence, the second and third Persons of the Trinity are "true God" just as surely as Jehovah is true God. In John 10:30 Jesus emphatically declared, *"I and my Father are one."* And in verses 37 and 38 of that same chapter He said, "If I do not the works of my Father, believe me not. But if I do, though ye believe not me, believe the works: that ye may know, and believe, that *the Father is in me, and I in Him.*"

In I John 5:20 we read, "We know that the Son of God is come, and hath given us an understanding, that we may know Him that is true, and we are in Him that is true, even in His Son Jesus Christ. *This is the TRUE GOD,* and eternal life." However, this statement does not exclude God the Father any more than our present verse excludes God the Son. We must compare Scripture with Scripture if we hope to understand the Word of God (I Cor. 2:12–14).

In the economy of salvation, the Scriptures represent God the Eternal Father as One who has resided from all eternity: *"In the beginning, GOD . . ."* (Gen. 1:1). *Jesus the Son* fills the office of Mediator and Intercessor. It was in this capacity that He said, "My Father is greater than I" (John 14:28). In the same manner, during this Dispensation of Grace, the Holy Ghost is the servant of the Godhead. (Study Luke 14:17–23 and compare John 16:13.)

In the last phrase of our present verse we read, ". . . *and Jesus Christ, whom thou hast sent.*" "SENT" is very important here; it points to the deity of Christ (John 16:30) and also to His Incarnation (Gal. 4:4). It also points to

His office as Mediator and Redeemer (Heb. 3:1).

Verse 4: *"I have glorified thee on the earth: I have finished the work which thou gavest me to do."*

"I have glorified thee." In John 8:29 Jesus said, "He that sent me is with me: the Father hath not left me alone; *for I do always those things that please Him."* He glorified God in every detail of His life—in His words, in His miracles, in *all* things whatsoever He did while He was here on earth. He kept the law perfectly, fulfilling every jot and tittle. Satan could find no blemish in Him. He declared truth in opposition to the heresy and false teachings of the Jews. He completed and fully accomplished the work God gave Him to do.

"On the earth" would undoubtedly mean the entire time Jesus spent on earth, from the day He was born until He returned to the Father.

"I have finished the work which thou gavest me to do." This speaks of the work of redemption. Jesus came into the world on a singular mission: *to lay His life down*—which commandment He received from the heavenly Father (John 10:18). He began His public ministry with His eye singled on Calvary, and now that His mission was so nearly completed and He was so very near the cross, He prayed as though He had *already* been crucified and raised. He knew that He would die; He knew He would *conquer* death, hell, and the grave; He knew He would ascend to the glorious seat at the right hand of God. In His omniscience, Christ said here that He *had finished* that which He came to accomplish; and since He came to accomplish *redemption,* He most surely knew that He *would* accomplish that which He came to do; all hell could not stop Him. Centuries before the crucifixion of Jesus, the Psalmist—under inspiration—wrote concerning the nails in His hands:

"For dogs have compassed me: the assembly of the wicked have inclosed me: *they pierced my hands and my feet"* (Psalm 22:16).

In the councils of the everlasting Trinity, Jesus the Son was the Person whom God the Father commissioned to pay the sin-debt and purchase redemption for all who will come to God through the shed blood and finished work of Jesus. And when the Son entered this world, He said, "Lo, I come (in the volume of the Book it is written of me,) to do thy will, O God" (Heb. 10:7).

When Joseph and Mary found Him talking with doctors of the law in the temple at the age of twelve, Mary said to Him, "Son, why hast thou thus dealt with us? Behold, thy father and I have sought thee sorrowing." Jesus replied, "How is it that ye sought me? *Wist ye not that I must be about my Father's business?*" (Luke 2:48,49). Later, after entering His public ministry, He declared, "My meat is to do the will of Him that sent me, and to finish His work" (John 4:34). And now, just before He walked the last mile to Calvary, He cried out in victory, "I have finished the work which thou gavest me to do!"

He had kept the law perfectly—tempted in all points as we are, yet without sin, He had overcome sin and temptation and had brought in "everlasting righteousness" (Dan. 9:24). He had "put away sin by the sacrifice of Himself" (Heb. 9:26), and had restored that which He "took not away" (Psalm 69:4). He had truly glorified the Father here on earth, and therefore *He was in a position to be glorified:*

"Therefore will I divide Him a portion with the great, and He shall divide the spoil with the strong; because He hath poured out His soul unto death: and He was numbered with the transgressors; and He bare the sin of many, and made intercession for the transgressors" (Isaiah 53:12).

Verse 5: *"And now, O Father, glorify thou me with thine own self with the glory which I had with thee before the world was."*

The meaning here is simply, "Father, my earthly ministry is coming to a close, my work on earth is done, and now I am asking you to restore to me the glory I had with you before the world was. Restore unto me that place in the undivided Trinity, the co-equal position with you on the throne. The period of my humiliation is coming to a close. I have been obedient—and *will be* obedient even unto the death of the cross. Now let me share once more the glory that I had with you before the world began."

In Hebrews 12:2 we are told that Jesus is "the author and finisher of our faith; who for the joy that was set before Him endured the cross, despising the shame, and is set down at the right hand of the throne of God." And in Hebrews 1:1–3 we read, "God, who at sundry times and in divers manners spake in time past unto the fathers by the prophets, hath in these last days spoken unto us by His Son, whom He hath appointed heir of all things, by whom also He made the world; *who being the brightness of His glory, and the express image of His person, and upholding all things by the word of His power, when He had by Himself purged our sins, SAT DOWN ON THE RIGHT HAND OF THE MAJESTY ON HIGH.*"

The pre-existence of Christ is clearly taught here, but it is also clearly taught that Father and Son are two distinct Persons, Persons with equal glory. These are divine and eternal truths. When Jesus said, *"Glorify thou me"* He was speaking as Mediator, as the Man Christ Jesus (I Tim. 2:5). As *Jesus* He had been humiliated, and now as *Jesus Christ* He was praying to be glorified. There is a Man in heaven now—a Man with a body of flesh and bones, glorified indeed! and that Man, the Man Christ Jesus, now sits on the throne at the right hand of God. In connection with this, please study Luke 24, the entire chapter.

In Acts 2:32–36 we read from Peter's sermon on the Day of Pentecost, "This Jesus hath God raised up, whereof we all are witnesses. Therefore being by the right hand of God exalted, and having received of the Father the promise of the Holy Ghost, He hath shed forth this, which ye now see and hear. For David is not ascended into the heavens: but he saith himself, The Lord said unto my Lord, Sit thou on my right hand, until I make thy foes thy footstool. Therefore let all the house of Israel know assuredly, that *God hath made that same Jesus, whom ye have crucified, both Lord and Christ!*"

To the Philippians Paul wrote, "Let this mind be in you, which was also in Christ Jesus: Who, being in the form of God, thought it not robbery to be equal with God: but made Himself of no reputation, and took upon Him the form of a servant, and was made in the likeness of men: and being found in fashion as a man, He humbled Himself, and became obedient unto death, even the death of the cross. *Wherefore God also hath highly exalted Him, and given Him a name which is above every name: that at the name of Jesus every knee should bow, of things in heaven, and things in earth, and things under the earth; and that every tongue should confess that Jesus Christ is Lord, to the glory of God the Father*" (Phil. 2:5–11).

There are three things I would especially like us to notice in our present verse:

First, *the bestowment of honors* merited by (and consequent upon) Christ's finished and perfected work: *"Glorify thou me."* Through His finished work and because He did always those things that pleased God, Jesus *merited* glory—and He is the only One of whom that can be said.

In the second place, Jesus said, *"with thine own self"*—not *"BY thyself"* but *"WITH thyself,"* expressing presence with the Eternal God and everlasting Father. He was not asking just to be glorified *BY God,* but to be glorified *WITH God.*

In the third place, He prayed, *"with the glory which I had with thee before the world was"*—not the glory He had before He came to the world as Saviour, the Sent One, but the glory He had with the Father *before the world was made!* Such glory is the glory of essential, unoriginated Deity, the glory of a Being uncreated, *a Personal Being,* not an ideal existence. Jesus was here praying for restored glory which He HAD, not glory He *received.* He was praying for the restoration of the glory He had with the Father in the beginning before creation began.

Verse 6: *"I have manifested thy name unto the men which thou gavest me out of the world: thine they were, and thou gavest them me; and they have kept thy Word."*

In this and the following verses we will notice the persons for whom the Lord Jesus Christ intercedes. We will notice the characters in which He *presents* them in prayer, and the petitions He offers on their behalf. It is wonderful indeed to know that our Lord and Saviour comes to God His heavenly Father as Intercessor-Mediator, presenting His own along with Himself in prayer. This fact reminds us of the prophecy in Isaiah 8:18:

"Behold, I and the children whom the Lord hath given me are for signs and for wonders in Israel from the Lord of hosts, which dwelleth in Mount Zion."

In our present verse we have the fulfillment of what was foreshadowed by God's appointed and anointed high priest in Israel during the Mosaic economy: "And Aaron shall bear the names of the children of Israel in the breastplate of judgment upon his heart, when he goeth in unto the holy place, for a memorial before the Lord continually" (Ex. 28:29).

Christ is OUR great High Priest, He is our Intercessor, our Mediator; and it is AS our High Priest that He enters into the Father's presence in prayer, bearing our names on His heart. The glorification of the Lord Jesus Christ (which was consequent upon His finished work) makes this possible. He earned the position He now holds at the Father's right hand in glory.

In verses 6 through 8 of this chapter Jesus prayed a prayer of *presentation*, and in verses 10 through 12 He offered a prayer of *supplication*. In the opening statement of this verse the Lord was praying for His believing people: directly for His disciples—but indirectly *He was praying for ALL of His believing people throughout this Dispensation of Grace.*

It is interesting that Jesus did not begin His prayer for the disciples by asking God to bless and enrich them, although He *described* those for whom He was about to pray. He calls them *"the men which thou gavest me . . . thine they were . . . thou gavest them me . . . they have kept thy Word."* He speaks here of those who heard and believed the Word and were therefore children of God, having been *born* of the Word (the only possible way *to be born again*—I Pet. 1:23).

"I have manifested thy name unto the men which thou gavest me out of the world." This testified to the divine fact that Jesus had revealed God to man, had manifested God's character and put God's love, holiness, and perfection on display. "No man hath seen God at any time: the only begotten Son which is in the bosom of the Father, He hath declared Him" (John 1:18). Jesus came to declare God, to make God known to men, and He did just that. The Lord Jesus Christ—Son of God and God the Son—was the only person competent TO manifest God to men. Only *Christ* could say, "He that hath seen me hath seen the Father" (John 14:9).

"Thine they were." This does not mean that these were men whom God had elected to be saved while others were elected to be damned. ALL creatures are God's by creation; the devil certainly created nothing—but creation is not in view here. Jesus was speaking of born again believers, the peculiar people who are saved by God's grace through the miracle of the new birth, the miracle wrought by the Holy Spirit when one believes in the finished work and the shed blood of Jesus.

In Ephesians 1:4–6 we read: "According as He hath chosen us in Him before the foundation of the world, that we should be holy and without blame before Him in love: having predestinated us unto the adoption of children by Jesus Christ to Himself, according to the good pleasure of His will, to the praise of the glory of His grace, wherein He hath made us accepted in the Beloved." But this does not mean that some are elected to be saved while others are elected to be damned!

I have pointed out numerous times in these studies that the Church as a body was elected, chosen in Christ, before the foundation of the world. Because God is sovereign He knew in the beginning who would be saved and who would *not* be saved; but God's sovereignty and foreknowledge of all things in no way alters man's responsibility. Jesus said, "Go ye into all the world, and preach the Gospel to every creature" (Mark 16:15). I ask you, Would God send a disciple to preach the Gospel of grace to a person who is already elected to be damned? Definitely not! Jesus said, "Give not that which is holy unto the dogs, neither cast ye your pearls before swine, lest they trample them under their feet, and turn again and rend you" (Matt. 7:6). If God commissioned men to preach to those who were already elected to be damned then He would be commissioning men to give that which is holy unto dogs and to cast pearls before swine! But He did not do that. He commissioned the disciples to preach the Gospel to ALL people because it is not His will that *any* perish. I repeat—the Church as a body was elected and foreordained before God created the world; but that body is made up of individuals who believe on the Lord Jesus Christ *after hearing the Gospel of God's marvelous grace!*

"Thou gavest them me." In other words, why does God save us? When we call on God, when we ask Him to have mercy on us and forgive our sins, why does He hear and answer our prayer? The answer is found in Ephesians 4:32:

"Be ye kind one to another, tenderhearted, forgiving one another, *even as God FOR CHRIST'S SAKE hath forgiven you!*"

Also, in Ephesians 2:1–7 we read, "And you hath He quickened, who were dead in trespasses and sins: wherein in time past ye walked according to the course of this world, according to the prince of the power of the air, the spirit that now worketh in the children of disobedience: Among whom also we all had our conversation in times past in the lusts of our flesh, fulfilling the desires of the flesh and of the mind; and were by nature the children of wrath, even as others.

"*BUT GOD* (God the Eternal Father, not Jesus the virgin-born Son) *who is rich in mercy, for His* (God's) *great love wherewith He loved us, even when we were dead in sins, hath quickened us together with Christ, (by grace ye are saved;) and hath raised us up together, and made us sit together in heavenly places in Christ Jesus: THAT IN THE AGES TO COME HE* (GOD) *MIGHT SHEW THE EXCEEDING RICHES OF HIS GRACE IN HIS* (GOD'S) *KINDNESS TOWARD US THROUGH CHRIST JESUS.*"

"*And they have kept thy Word.*" In John 5:24 Jesus said, "Verily, verily, I say unto you, He that heareth *my word,* and believeth on Him that sent me, hath everlasting life, and shall not come into condemnation; but is passed from death unto life."

When most of His followers turned back and walked with Him no more, Jesus turned to the twelve and asked, "Will ye also go away?" Peter answered, "Lord, to whom shall we go? *Thou hast the WORDS of eternal life*" (John 6: 67,68).

We are discussing deep things, words that we must read with peculiar reverence and godly fear. These are words that the Son of God addressed to the Eternal Father, Jehovah God, words that have to do with born again believers. This passage contains divine doctrine and eternal truth that only the Godhead can handle with certainty, positiveness, and full understanding. We will never fully comprehend the depth of what we are now studying, but it gives us joy and indescribable comfort to know that the Man Christ Jesus, now seated at the right hand of God the Father, cares for His born again children whom the Father has given Him.

Verse 7: "*Now they have known that all things whatsoever thou hast given me are of thee.*"

Wonderful words these, especially when we consider of whom they were spoken—the eleven disciples, primarily. Their faith was weak, their knowledge limited, their spiritual lives shallow. How easily they fainted in their hearts and were afraid! Very shortly after Jesus spoke these words of commendation, they all forsook Him and fled (Matt. 26:56; Mark 14:50).

It should be most encouraging to us that the glorious requests Jesus made for the disciples (and for all believers) were made on the grounds of their having received *the Word.* They had received the testimony of Jesus concerning God the Eternal Father, they had believed in His love—and that is God's invitation to all men today. *Believe on the Lord Jesus Christ,* believe God's love, believe God's Word. As many as receive Jesus (and the only possible way to receive Him is on the terms of the Word) to them God gives power to become *sons born of God* (John 1:12,13).

To know Jesus is to know the Father, to know the Father is to know Jesus. It is not how many talents we possess, it is not the size of the ministry we have or the services we render in the name of Jesus, but *to know and love God* and to know and love *Jesus*—this is what distinguishes saints from sinners, believers from unbelievers, sons of God from sons of Satan.

Verse 8: *"For I have given unto them the words which thou gavest me; and they have received them, and have known surely that I came out from thee, and they have believed that thou didst send me."*

"For" at the beginning of this verse connects it with the "all things" in the previous verse. *"I have given unto them the words which thou gavest me."* The disciples had received Jesus as the Messiah while the world declared Him an impostor. The little company who walked with Him had learned through His wonderful words that He had come from God, and that the words He spoke were the words God had given Him.

"They have received them . . . they have believed that thou didst send me." The WORD was the one thing that *convinced* the disciples that God the Eternal Father sent Jesus into the world. Now we see why the Holy Spirit inspired Paul to pen down Romans 10:17: "So then faith cometh by hearing, and hearing by the Word of God!" Saving faith comes by hearing the Word of God. We *must* hear the Word before we can believe on Jesus unto salvation. Then after we are saved, our faith is strengthened, our Christian experience is deepened, our spiritual capacity is increased and enlarged as we *continue* to study the Word of God.

True spiritual knowledge and spiritual discernment are the fruit of hearing and receiving the Word of God—in fact, the importance of God's Word will never be known this side of heaven. No wonder Satan has done everything in His diabolical power to discredit and destroy the Word! How assuring it is to know *"For ever, O Lord, thy Word is settled in heaven"* (Psalm 119:89).

In this verse Jesus tells what He had taught His disciples: He had done exactly what was settled in the eternal councils of the Trinity concerning salvation of sinners. He had given His disciples the words, the truths, and the doctrines that God the Father had given Him to give to men. The words He spoke and the works He performed were the Father's words and the Father's works.

I think it would be well worth time and space in this study to look at some verses that have to do with the peculiar use of words to denote the doctrines and the truth taught by Jesus:

John 3:34: "For He whom God hath sent *speaketh the words of God: for God giveth not the Spirit by measure unto Him."*

John 6:68: "Then Simon Peter answered Him, Lord, to whom shall we go? *Thou hast the words of eternal life."*

John 12:48: "He that rejecteth me, and receiveth not my words, hath one that judgeth him: *the word that I have spoken, the same shall judge him in the last day."*

John 14:10: "Believest thou not that I am in the Father, and the Father in me? The words that I speak unto you I speak not of myself: but the Father that dwelleth in me, He doeth the works."

Only the words given to us as God gave them to Jesus are words that bring eternal life. The disciples had willingly *received* the words of truth Jesus gave them from God; they knew and freely acknowledged that He was the Messiah, and that He came from God. This little company of men believed these divine truths at the moment the vast majority of men refused to acknowledge that Jesus had come from God or that He was Messiah. I am so thankful that God does not despise or discredit weak faith. He honors faith and sincerity of faith, regardless of how weak it may be.

The disciples' faith was weak; but they *had* faith—and beloved, the important thing is not so much that we have *great* faith, but that we *have* faith in God. The disciples knew little of the sacrificial death Jesus was to die. They had expected Messiah who would deliver Israel from the Romans and set up a glorious kingdom; and when Jesus declared that He would die, they did not fully understand; they could not reconcile this with their expectations. But they knew He was the Redeemer and Saviour, they knew He came from God, they knew He spoke the words God gave Him to speak, they knew the miracles He worked were the miracles of God, and in spite of the weakness of their faith Jesus commended them.

He had previously rebuked the disciples for their weak faith, He had rebuked them for so poorly accepting His wonderful words of life, He had rebuked them *sharply* for their unbelief and for other faults. Yet in His prayer here, as He represented them to the heavenly Father in intercession, He did not *mention* their weakness, their blundering, or their faults. He simply announced to the heavenly Father, "They were thine, thou gavest them me, I gave them the Word, they *received* the Word, and they know of a truth that I am the Messiah—Saviour, Redeemer. They are assured that you sent me into the world."

Verse 9: *"I pray for them: I pray not for the world, but for them which thou hast given me; for they are thine."*

This verse begins the *intercessory* part of His prayer, and in the following verses Jesus named the things He asked for His disciples. He prayed that they might be—first, *kept*; second, *sanctified*; third, *united*; and fourth, *that they might be with Him in glory.*

We are reading here a recorded account of what Jesus, as our great High Priest and Intercessor, does for believers. I believe His intercession here on behalf of His disciples accurately gives Christ's mind toward all born again believers now as He sits at the right hand of God. It records His desires for us, His interests in us, and exhibits accurately the graces He would have us possess. All born again believers should seek the four things pointed out here, and as we *seek*, we know for sure that we have a Mediator, Intercessor, and great High Priest in heaven who will see to it that we do not pray in vain!

"I pray for them: I pray not for the world." Christ never makes intercession for sinners in the special way that He intercedes for His believing people. We stand and continue in grace because there is One in heaven who is interceding on our behalf.

Jesus loves all mankind. He died for the sin of the world, *He died for ALL;* and through His shed blood He provided *redemption sufficient for all.* All are invited to receive grace without money and without price. Grace is offered to all *unconditionally.* If I did not believe what I have just said, if I did not believe that "whosoever will" can be saved and that Jesus died for every sinner who has ever been born or ever will be born, I would never again enter the pulpit to preach the Gospel! But I also firmly believe that Jesus does a *special work* for believers. He is our

Mediator, our High Priest in heaven making intercession for us in a special way that He does not do for unbelievers.

Before you call me a false prophet, weigh these words and let the Spirit testify whether they be truth or falsehood: Jesus came into the world, and in order that He might die He took a body like unto our body except that He was sinless. The wages of sin is death, and it was a divine imperative that one pay the debt if any were to go free. Jesus was the only one who *could* pay the debt, so God's Son became the Son of man—yet He was God in flesh; and in a tabernacle of flesh He paid sin's debt, laid His life down for sinners. Through His death, burial, and resurrection, as prophesied from Genesis through Malachi, He fulfilled the work He came to do, and when He died, the Man Christ Jesus finished His work concerning the redemption of sinners. NOW (according to Ephesians 4:32) God saves sinners for Jesus' sake. The unbeliever hears the Gospel, he believes that Christ died for our sins according to the Scriptures, and that He rose again the third day according to the Scriptures. Believing the Gospel, the sinner is saved—by God's grace, through faith in the shed blood and the finished work of Jesus. Faith comes by hearing, and hearing by the Word. Jesus made known the Word, He WAS the Word, and when He died for the sin of the world He said, "It is finished!" He rose from the grave, and now the Man Christ Jesus, glorified in His resurrection body, sits at the right hand of God, our High Priest to make intercession for us. He clearly stated, "I pray for *them,* for my children, those whom you have given me. *I pray NOT for the world.*" He *died on the cross* to make salvation possible for sinners; He *lives* to make intercession for saints.

Man not only needs a Redeemer, he needs a *Saviour.* Hear the words of Paul:

"For when we were yet without strength, in due time Christ died for the ungodly. . . God commendeth His love toward us, in that, while we were yet sinners, Christ died for us. *Much more then,* being now justified by His blood, *we shall be saved from wrath through Him.* For if, when we were enemies, we were reconciled to God by the *death* of His Son, *MUCH MORE, being reconciled, WE SHALL BE SAVED BY HIS LIFE.* And not only so, but we also joy in God through our Lord Jesus Christ, by whom we have now received the atonement" (Rom. 5:6–11).

Notice please: *"We SHALL BE saved."* That is, because Jesus lives, WE live. Therefore, what Jesus is saying in our present verse is, "I pray for my disciples, my own people, that they may be kept, that they may be sanctified, that they may be united as we are united, and that they may be *glorified.* I pray this prayer for *my children, not for the world."* On the one hand we must not forget that Jesus as Mediator does a special work only for His believing people; we must not forget, on the other hand, that Jesus loves all and provided salvation for all.

Jesus prayed, "Father, forgive them; for they know not what they do" (Luke 23:34). But we must remember that this prayer was offered while He was on earth in the capacity of Saviour. The intercessory prayer which we are now studying was prayed as though He had already been crucified, buried, and was risen again. He prayed this prayer with the assurance that His death, burial, and resurrection was a certainty.

"The world" may be considered from two distinct aspects: John the Baptist said, "Behold the Lamb of God, which taketh away the sin of the world" (John 1:29), and Jesus Himself said, "God sent not His Son into the world to condemn the world; but that the world through Him might be saved" (John 3:17). Looking at the world (mankind) from this standpoint, certainly Jesus loved the whole world; He came to save "whosoever will," and while He was here on earth in the capacity of Jesus, Saviour, He prayed for the very men who nailed Him to the cross. But we must also see the world from another viewpoint:

The world, as such, is ruled predominantly by ungodly principles. When we view the world from this aspect and in this sense, we see clearly the meaning of John 14:17, where we read of "the Spirit of truth; whom the world cannot receive, because it seeth Him not, neither knoweth Him." To pray for the world when we view it in this aspect would be as vain as to pray for the *prince* of this world. When we draw a definite distinction between the *intercession* of the Man Christ Jesus, the one Mediator now seated at the right hand of God, and *the special work* He does for His own and the general and whole mediatorial work He does on behalf of mankind, we will find no conflict.

"I pray . . . for them which thou hast given me; for they are thine." Here is repeated the description of the eleven which Jesus had given previously. His disciples were those whom the Father had given Him—to redeem, to sanctify, to justify, teach, lead, and save. They were the Father's sheep; the Father entrusted them to the care of the Good Shepherd, and they thus became the Shepherd's *responsibility.* So Jesus was saying here, "I pray especially for my own, the sheep of my pasture. I am duty bound to pray for them, and to ask for them everything they need. I am the Good Shepherd, and a good shepherd takes care of his sheep, even unto dying for them if need be. Those which thou hast given me are my peculiar possession—but they are also my peculiar responsibility."

Verse 10: *"And all mine are thine, and thine are mine; and I am glorified in them."*

This statement seems to be parenthetical. Certainly it sets forth the divine truth concerning the perfect, unbroken unity between God the Father and Jesus the Son. Greek scholars tell us that the literal rendering here would be "things," *not persons.* Thus Jesus was saying to the heavenly Father, "All things are thy things, and all things are my things. These are not mine more than they are thine; neither are they thine more than they are mine." Throughout His ministry on earth Jesus continually declared the divine doctrine of perfect unity between the Persons of the Godhead, and at the same time kept a remarkable distinction between those Persons.

"I am glorified in them." I believe Jesus was speaking here primarily of the eleven. The Jews and the masses of those who heard Him hated and rejected Him; but this little company believed in Him, walked with Him, and obeyed Him. They honored Him, and thereby brought glory to Him. He therefore prayed a special prayer of intercession for them. Later in His prayer He specifically pointed out that He prayed not only for these, but for them also which would believe on Him later through the Word—and that portion of His prayer reaches even to you and me.

Verse 11: *"And now I am no more in the world, but these are in the world, and I come to thee. Holy Father, keep through thine own name those whom thou hast given me, that they may be one, as we are."*

What touching words we have here as Jesus committed His little company of believers into the heavenly Father's keeping! They would soon be deprived of His personal presence, they would soon encounter the persecution of which He had so recently told them. Up to this time He had been their Guardian, their all-sufficient, ever-present Friend. He had borne their infirmities, strengthened them when they were weak, protected them from harm, from danger, and from the evil one. Now the time of His departure was very near; the hour had arrived when He would be crucified, buried, raised, and in a few days would return to the Father to occupy the seat at His right hand. For this reason He committed His disciples to the Father's care.

"Holy Father, keep through thine own name those whom thou hast given me." This is the only place in the Gospels where Jesus addressed God as "Holy Father." *Holy* as used here points to and describes God's character. The root meaning of the word in the Greek is *"separation,"* and therefore signifies that God is completely removed from evil.

But this is only *negative.* We must consider that God is not only removed from evil, but He is elevated *high above* all evil, sin, and impurity. God cannot be tempted with evil because He is absolute holiness, essentially pure in Himself. God has always *been* pure, He has always been holy—and the fact that He IS holy shows that He is lifted high above all finite creatures:

"Who shall not fear thee, O Lord, and glorify thy name? *For thou only art HOLY:* for all nations shall come and worship before thee; for thy judgments are made manifest" (Rev. 15:4). *Absolute holiness* is the essence of our God.

In Scripture, the titles used in addressing God or speaking of Him *correspond to the request made of God.* For example, in Romans 15:5 Paul prayed for the Christians at Rome, "Now *the God of patience and consolation* grant you to be like-minded one toward another according to Christ Jesus." He prayed for the Thessalonians, "Now *the Lord of peace* Himself give you *peace* always by all means. The Lord be with you all" (II Thess. 3:16).

In our present verse, Jesus was praying that God would keep His disciples *holy,* and He therefore addressed Him as *"Holy Father"*—and since Jesus was asking for the deliverance, preservation, unification, and sanctification of His followers, He requested the Father to do for them that which was in strict accord with the character and nature of God. It is our Lord's desire that all believers hate sin and *keep on hating sin* with a *deeper* hatred as we live for Him day by day and grow in His grace: *"Ye that love the Lord, HATE EVIL:* He preserveth the souls of His saints; He delivereth them out of the hand of the wicked" (Psalm 97:10).

"Keep . . . those whom thou hast given me." It is noteworthy that seven times in this chapter Jesus spoke of believers as *those whom the Father had given Him.* He used this reference in verse 2, twice in verse 6, and in verses 9, 11, 12, and 24. His prayer for God to keep His "little born ones" shows the high value He places on believers and the

deep interest He has in each and every one of us. Here in verse 11 He is especially praying for the disciples. He was deeply concerned about and in sympathy with this little band who had followed Him while the multitudes had rejected Him and turned from Him.

Believers are God's love-gift to Jesus. In John 3:16 we learn how much God loved US, and in John 3:35 we behold His love to *His only begotten Son*—His Christ, our Saviour Jesus. God so loved *the world* that He gave His only begotten Son to *die* for the world. He so loves His only begotten Son that He has given Him the Church to be His bride. In that glorious day of the Rapture and the first resurrection, the Church will be given to Jesus, "a glorious Church, not having spot, or wrinkle, or any such thing . . . holy and without blemish" (Eph. 5:27).

Jesus prayed for the preservation of His disciples because He knew that He was leaving them in a hostile world. He knew they would be sorely tempted, tested, persecuted, hated; He knew that with the exception of John the Beloved they would each and every one seal their testimony with their life's blood—and even *John* was exiled to Patmos "for the Word of God, and for the testimony of Jesus Christ" (Rev. 1:9). Therefore Jesus asked His Father to keep the disciples from evil, to keep them from being overcome by Satan, to keep them from being crushed and destroyed by persecution—in other words, He prayed that they would be delivered *from every device of the devil.*

"That they may be one as we are." Oneness here speaks of divine power in operation in the hearts and lives of believers. All born again believers are partakers of divine nature: "Whereby are given unto us exceeding great and precious promises: that by these ye might be partakers of the divine nature, having escaped the corruption that is in the world through lust" (II Pet. 1:4).

In Acts 4:32 we read, "And the multitude of them that believed *were of one heart and of one soul:* neither said any of them that ought of the things which he possessed was his own; but they had all things common." The members of the early Church were of "one heart and of one soul." The same is true of born again believers today. We are one in Christ, we believe God's Word, we believe in the verbal inspiration and *final authority* of the Word, we believe in the Holy Trinity—Father, Son, and Holy Spirit. We believe in the finished work of Jesus as sufficient for salvation, we believe we are saved *BY GOD'S GRACE plus nothing.* All truly born again believers are ONE in that we are "looking for that blessed hope, and the glorious appearing of the great God and our Saviour Jesus Christ" (Tit. 2:13).

All born again believers are one in that we have all been baptized into the body of Christ by the Holy Spirit: "For as the body is one, and hath many members, and all the members of that one body, being many, are one body: so also is Christ. For by one Spirit are we all baptized into one body, whether we be Jews or Gentiles, whether we be bond or free; and have been all made to drink into one Spirit. *For the body is not one member, but many*" (I Cor. 12:12–14).

Verse 12: *"While I was with them in the world, I kept them in thy name: those that thou gavest me I have kept, and none of them is lost, but the son of perdition; that the Scripture might be fulfilled."*

"I kept them in thy name" is the same as in the preceding verse, which is rendered, *"through thine own name,"* meaning *preservation through the power and attributes of God the Father.* Under such keeping, no one could destroy them.

"Those that thou gavest me I have KEPT, and none of them is lost." The Greek word here translated "kept" is not the same as the word rendered "kept" in the first part of the verse. In the first part of the verse *kept* means *"preserved,"* while here it means "I have *guarded* them from harm and danger as a shepherd guards his sheep or as a

soldier guards a treasure."

Jesus had so carefully guarded His disciples that *not one of them* had perished, not one of them had been lost—*"but the son of perdition, that the Scripture might be fulfilled."* The "son of perdition" refers to Judas Iscariot. Then the question arises, "Was Judas a true believer? Was he one of those given to Jesus by the heavenly Father? *Was* Judas ever truly born again? Was he once *in* grace, and did he *fall from* grace?"

Those who believe that Judas was a true believer (and that he fell from grace) use this Scripture to teach that a person can be truly born again—washed in the blood, *saved by grace*—and then *fall* from grace, lose salvation, and spend eternity in hell. But if we *rightly divide* the Word, can this verse of Scripture really be used to prove the doctrine of falling from grace? Let us look more closely at the words of Jesus here:

The conjunction *"but"* in this verse is *adversitive* (opposite), not *exceptive.* The meaning is *not* "none of those given to me is lost, EXCEPT the son of perdition." I believe the literal meaning here is "Father, all that thou gavest me I have kept; *not one* of them is lost. *BUT* (however) *among the company there is one who IS lost*—Judas, the son of perdition."

Earlier in our study (chapter 6, verse 70) Jesus said to His disciples, "Have I not chosen you twelve, *and one of you is a devil?"* (In the original Greek, there is no "a" in this verse. Therefore what Jesus actually said was, "Have I not chosen you twelve, *and one of you is DEVIL?"*) Verse 71 then makes it clear that He was speaking of Judas Iscariot, "for he it was that should betray Him, being one of the twelve."

Satan is exactly the opposite of God, and the Antichrist will be exactly the opposite of Christ. In view of this fact, I ask you: Since the Holy Ghost overshadowed Mary and God's only begotten Son was thus born, is it impossible that the devil could have overshadowed a woman, and

Judas, *conceived of Satan,* could have been born in like manner?

Judas was a singular, exceptional case. I believe the Scriptures teach that he will one day minister again upon this earth—in the person of the Antichrist. Jesus never called any *man* "the son of perdition." He referred to wicked men as the *children of Satan, sinners,* or as *the ungodly*; but here He definitely pointed to Judas as *"the son of perdition."*

The question may then arise, "Why did Jesus choose Judas as one of the twelve?" The only answer I can give—and I give it with a humble spirit and a sincere heart—is Deuteronomy 29:29: "THE SECRET THINGS BELONG UNTO THE LORD OUR GOD . . . ."

". . . that the Scripture might be fulfilled" does not mean that Judas was lost in order to fulfill the Word of God. The meaning is that the Scripture *was fulfilled* by the loss of Judas. Please study Psalm 109, and note especially verse 8, which we quote here: "Let his days be few; and let another take his office."

Judas Iscariot was not saved; he never believed with the heart, he never accepted Jesus as the Son of God, very God in flesh. He was never given to Jesus by the Father. Judas Iscariot was a graceless man.

Some may ask, "Then why does the Scripture say that Judas *fell*?" The Scriptures *do* tell us that Judas fell—but he fell from an *office, NOT FROM GOD'S GRACE.* In Acts 1:15—26 we read where the apostles prayed concerning the choice of a man to replace Judas among the remaining eleven; and in verses 24 and 25 we read, "Thou, Lord, which knowest the hearts of all men, shew whether of these two thou hast chosen, *that he may take part of this ministry and apostleship, FROM WHICH JUDAS BY TRANSGRESSION FELL, that he might go to his own place."*

Judas fell from the ministry, from apostleship; *he did not fall from grace!* An apostle is a learner, one who follows another. Judas *followed* Jesus, he walked among the other apostles, but *he was never saved.*

Notice the last phrase in Acts 1:25: "*. . . that he might go to his own place.*" Certainly the *body* of Judas was buried in the potter's field; it was his *spirit* that went to "*his own place.*" Whether this refers to hell in general or to a special compartment in the underworld, I do not know; but I do know that such a statement is made of no other person in all the Word of God from Genesis through Revelation! When the *righteous* die, their spirits go to Paradise. The *wicked* die—and open their eyes in hell. The Bible does not say that Judas died *and went to hell.* It says he fell from the ministry and apostleship "that he might go to his OWN PLACE."

I am firmly convinced that the spirit of Judas Iscariot will dwell in the body of Antichrist, the man of sin—yes, *the devil in flesh*—and that he will carry out the ministry of Antichrist.

Paul wrote to the Thessalonian Christians of "*that man of sin, THE SON OF PERDITION,*" who would be revealed after the Rapture of the Church. He did not say simply "a man of sin," but "*THAT* (specific) *man of sin,* the son of perdition"—and Jesus plainly told us that "the son of perdition" was Judas Iscariot, who went "*to his own place.*" I believe—and teach without apology—that the spirit of Judas Iscariot will be embodied in the Antichrist—the devil incarnate. (Please study the entire passage of II Thessalonians 2:1–12, and Acts 1:15–20 in connection with this.)

I trust that you will not miss the high honor Jesus always put on the Old Testament Scriptures. Even as He prayed to the heavenly Father, He reverently referred to the written Word. He often quoted from Psalms, as did the writers of the New Testament. We cannot begin to realize the importance of the Word of God. The *devil* knows its importance, and that is why he does everything in his power to discredit and destroy "thus saith the Lord"!

Verse 13: "*And now come I to thee; and these things I*

speak in the world, that they might have my joy fulfilled in themselves."

Jesus prayed this prayer audibly in the presence of His disciples, that they might be instructed and comforted. He was soon to return to His own place at the right hand of the Majesty, and in departing from the world He was giving the disciples their place—the place He had occupied on earth: *they were to continue His work.* In chapter 14, verse 12, Jesus said to the disciples, *"He that believeth on me, the works that I do shall he do also; and greater works than these shall he do; because I go unto my Father."* This same truth is set forth throughout our present chapter.

Jesus had finished His work on earth, He had glorified God, and now He was ready to be accepted in glory to take His place at God's right hand. Since believers are united with Christ (Eph. 2:6; Col. 3:3), we must display the same character HE displayed on earth. We will never live the sinless, holy life Jesus lived, but we *can* be *blameless* (I Thess. 5:23). We can occupy the place He *left* for us to occupy as sons of God. We can make God known, we can sow the seed, give out the good news of salvation, and reap a harvest to the glory of God. We not only build on the foundation Jesus laid for us to build on, we not only occupy His place here below since He returned to the Father, but we also join Him in the same heavenly blessedness. Notice the statements He made in this chapter to give us this assurance:

"I have given unto them the words which thou gavest me" (v. 8).

"That they might have my joy fulfilled in themselves" (v. 13).

"They are not of the world, even as I am not of the world" (v. 16).

"As thou hast sent me into the world, even so have I also sent them into the world" (v. 18).

"I sanctify myself, that they also might be sanctified" (v. 19).

"The glory which thou gavest me I have given them" (v. 22).

"That the love wherewith thou hast loved me may be in them" (v. 26).

I cannot but exclaim, Hallelujah! What a Saviour! What position, privilege, honor, responsibility, and assurance believers have! No wonder we sing, "Amazing grace! How sweet the sound that saved a wretch like me." God's grace IS amazing.

Believers are not only blessed *through* Christ (His death, burial, and resurrection); we are also blessed *with* Christ. We are citizens of heaven, therefore strangers and pilgrims on earth. Notice in this chapter of John's Gospel how the Lord Jesus has identified believers with Himself:

"That they may be one, as we are one" (vv. 11,22).

"They are not of the world, even as I am not of the world" (v. 14).

"As thou hast sent me into the world, even so have I also sent them into the world" (v. 18).

"As thou, Father, art in me, and I in thee, that they also may be one in us" (v. 21).

"The glory which thou gavest me I have given them" (v. 22).

"That the world may know that thou hast sent me, and hast loved them, as thou hast loved me" (v. 23).

In the last part of our present verse Jesus prayed, *"that they might have my joy fulfilled in themselves."* In chapter 15 verse 11 He said, "These things have I spoken unto you, that *my joy* might remain in you, and that *your joy* might be full." This is a singular and peculiar joy, an inward comfort which Christ gives to believers. Peter refers to it as "joy unspeakable and full of glory" (I Pet. 1:8). Jesus imparts joy no earthly language can express; and since He was at this time on the verge of leaving His disciples in the world, He wanted them to know this singular, peculiar joy.

In this intercessory prayer, Christ makes known the position believers hold before God the Father. As the result of His finished work, His conquering the world, the flesh, the devil, death, hell, and the grave, every barrier has been removed, the veil has been rent from top to bottom, and a new and living way has been opened to all. We have access into the holy of holies, and we are invited to draw near "with a true heart in full assurance of faith." This is expressed in Hebrews 10:19–22:

"Having therefore, brethren, boldness to enter into the holiest by the blood of Jesus, by a new and living way, which He hath consecrated for us, through the veil, that is to say, His flesh; and having an high priest over the house of God; let us draw near with a true heart in full assurance of faith, having our hearts sprinkled from an evil conscience, and our bodies washed with pure water."

Through the finished work of Jesus, *His* Father is OUR Father. Thus we can truly say, *"Our Father, which art in heaven."* Galatians 4:6 tells us, "And *because* ye are sons, God hath sent forth the Spirit of His Son into your hearts, crying, Abba, Father." We are not God's *only begotten* Son, but we *are* sons of God: "Beloved, *NOW are we the sons of God,* and it doth not yet appear what we shall be: but we know that, when He shall appear, we shall be like Him; for we shall see Him as He is" (I John 3:2).

Since we are sons of God through the miracle of the new birth, "our fellowship is with the Father, and with His Son Jesus Christ" (I John 1:3).

Verse 14: *"I have given them thy Word; and the world hath hated them, because they are not of the world, even as I am not of the world."*

In verse 8 Jesus said, "I have given unto them the words which thou gavest me," and now He repeats, *"I have given them thy Word."* This goes much further than the expounding of Old Testament prophecies concerning Himself. Jesus was the perfect servant. Each morning He waited upon and looked to God for the words to give to His disciples that day, and He faithfully delivered to them every word the Father gave Him. His joy came by testimony of what His Father was, and now that testimony would be the joy of His disciples. Therefore He said, "I have given them thy Word."

"And the world hath hated them." The more fully surrendered we are and the more joy we display in our Christian living—not superficial joy, not emotionalism, but pure joy from the heart—the more the world will hate us; but we have God's promise that if we suffer with Him we will reign with Him. We should rejoice and be glad that we are counted *worthy* to suffer for His sake, worthy to be hated by the enemies of Jesus Christ because of our testimony. Paul wanted the Thessalonian Christians to "be counted worthy of the kingdom of God, *for which ye also suffer*" (II Thess. 1:5), and in verse 11 he said to them, "Wherefore also we pray always for you, that our God would count you *worthy of this calling,* and fulfil all the good pleasure of His goodness, and the work of faith with power."

Jesus Himself said, "Blessed are ye, when men shall revile you, and persecute you, and shall say all manner of evil against you falsely, *for my sake. Rejoice, and be exceeding glad: for great is your reward in heaven:* for so persecuted they the prophets which were before you" (Matt. 5:11,12).

In I John 2:15–17 we are commanded, *"Love not the world, neither the things that are in the world.* If any man love the world, the love of the Father is not in him. For all that is in the world, the lust of the flesh, and the lust of the eyes, and the pride of life, is not of the Father, but is of the world. And the world passeth away, and the lust thereof: but he that doeth the will of God abideth for ever!"

Those who are "of the world" are under the dominion of *the god of this world*, the prince of the power of the air—the devil. According to the Apostle Paul, *we* at one time followed the course of the world, we were by nature the children of wrath, our conversation was in the lust of the flesh, and we fulfilled the desires of the flesh. (Read Ephesians 2:1–10.) Since these characteristics are still true in the lives of *unbelievers,* it is only natural for them to hate believers because we are NOT of the world, we are not *conformed* to the world, we follow neither its policies nor its principles.

Also, the life of a truly born again, Spirit-filled believer condemns this world. *"By faith NOAH, being warned of God of things not seen as yet, moved with fear, prepared an ark to the saving of his house; by the which HE CONDEMNED THE WORLD, and became heir of the righteousness which is by faith"* (Heb. 11:7). Evil, ungodly men plot against believers and say all manner of ungodly things against them. The world *rejoices* when Christians suffer!

". . . I am not of the world." In I Corinthians 15:47,48 we read, "The first man (Adam) is of the earth, earthy: the second Man is the Lord from heaven. As is the earthy, such are they also that are earthy: and as is the heavenly, such are they also that are heavenly." The Lord Jesus Christ was never of this world, He was entirely separate from sin. All men are born sinners, but Jesus was sinless. *"For such an High Priest became us, who is HOLY, HARMLESS, UNDEFILED, SEPARATE FROM SINNERS, and made higher than the heavens"* (Heb. 7:26).

Jesus said to the Jews, "Ye are from beneath; *I am from above:* ye are of this world; *I am NOT of this world"* (John 8:23). Since the believer is in Christ and Christ is in the believer (Rom. 8:1; Col. 1:27), *believers* are not of this world. "If any man be in Christ, he is a new creature: old things are passed away; behold, all things are become new" (II Cor. 5:17).

Believers are partakers of the heavenly calling: "Wherefore, *holy brethren, partakers of the heavenly calling,* consider the Apostle and High Priest of our profession, Christ Jesus" (Heb. 3:1).

Believers are citizens of heaven: "For our conversation

is in heaven; from whence also we look for the Saviour, the Lord Jesus Christ" (Phil. 3:20).

Believers have an inheritance in heaven: "Blessed be the God and Father of our Lord Jesus Christ, which according to His abundant mercy hath begotten us again unto a lively hope by the resurrection of Jesus Christ from the dead, *to an inheritance incorruptible, and undefiled, and that fadeth not away, RESERVED IN HEAVEN FOR YOU,* who are kept by the power of God through faith unto salvation ready to be revealed in the last time" (I Pet. 1:3–5).

In view of these Scriptures, certainly there can be no doubt that we, *born again people,* are strangers and pilgrims while passing our sojourn on earth. This world is not our home. Like Abraham, we look for "a city which hath foundations, whose builder and maker is God" (Heb. 11:10).

I am so glad Jesus prayed for the safety and preservation of Christians in this world. I am so thankful for redemption through His precious blood, but I thank God that He lives to *keep* us day by day, to save us from this hostile, unfriendly world through which we travel on the way to our heavenly home!

David cried out, "They also that render evil for good are mine adversaries; because I follow the thing that good is" (Psalm 38:20).

John the Beloved wrote, "Marvel not, my brethren, if the world hate you" (I John 3:13).

But in spite of persecution from the world, in spite of the trials and tribulations believers are sure to face, Jesus did not ask that His people be removed from the world. He simply promised protection for them, as shown in our next verse.

Verse 15: *"I pray not that thou shouldest take them out of the world, but that thou shouldest keep them from the evil."*

Our Lord knew that the world in which He was leaving

the disciples would not change, it would not become better; yet knowing this, He made it clear that He was not asking for them to be taken *out* of the world. God could call Christians home to glory the moment they are saved, but if when they are persecuted He immediately *removed* them from the world, it would not be good for them—nor would it be good for the world.

Christians condemn the world through righteous living, and although wicked men may not read the Bible, *they read the lives of God's people;* and when we live blameless lives they take knowledge that we have been with Jesus. Therefore Jesus did not pray for the disciples to be taken out of the world, removed from persecution, trials, and tribulation. He prayed that God would keep them from evil, that they would not become *part* of the wicked world.

Beloved, even though we live in the midst of a wicked and perverse generation, *we have power to overcome.* Victory has already been provided for us if we will only trust and obey! "Whatsoever (whosoever) is born of God overcometh the world: *and this is the victory that overcometh the world, EVEN OUR FAITH*" (I John 5:4).

The Apostle Paul gives a warning and a promise in his letter to the Corinthian believers: "Wherefore let him that thinketh he standeth *take heed* lest he fall. There hath no temptation taken you but such as is common to man: but God is faithful, who will not suffer you to be tempted *above that ye are able; but will with the temptation also make a way to escape,* that ye may be able to bear it" (I Cor. 10:12,13).

To be sure we do not cherish tribulation, conflict, and persecution. It would be wonderful (in our way of thinking) to go to heaven without first undergoing persecution or heartache. But hear again the Apostle Paul:

"Therefore being justified by faith, we have peace with God through our Lord Jesus Christ: by whom also we have access by faith into this grace wherein we stand, and rejoice in hope of the glory of God. And not only so, but *we glory in tribulations also:* knowing that tribulation worketh patience; and patience, experience; and experience, hope: and hope maketh not ashamed; because the love of God is shed abroad in our hearts by the Holy Ghost which is given unto us" (Rom. 5:1–5).

If we did not suffer in this world, if we did not face persecution and trials, we would not appreciate Jesus half so much when we reach that land that is fairer than day: "For it became Him, for whom are all things, and by whom are all things, in bringing many sons unto glory, to make the Captain of their salvation perfect through sufferings" (Heb. 2:10).

God does not want His people to go into seclusion, shut themselves away in a monastery or some such place, and hide from the world. We are His representatives on earth and we *must* give out the Word and be witnesses for Him. The world needs the Gospel, and God has already promised victory in Jesus.

God's Word records the fact that three of the outstanding Old Testament saints prayed to be removed from this world —but God did not answer their prayers. When the Israelites, on their wilderness journey, complained and cried for meat to eat, *Moses* grew so wearied by their constant criticism and complaints that he prayed, "I am not able to bear all this people alone, because it is too heavy for me. And if thou deal thus with me, *kill me, I pray thee,* out of hand, if I have found favour in thy sight; and let me not see my wretchedness" (Num. 11:14,15).

Elijah prayed for death when he fled from the wrath of Jezebel after he had slain the prophets of Baal. He "went a day's journey into the wilderness, and came and sat down under a juniper tree: *and he requested for himself that he might die; and said, It is enough; now, O Lord, take away my life;* for I am not better than my fathers" (I Kings 19:4).

Jonah prayed that he might die. After he had obeyed the Lord and had preached repentance to Nineveh, the city repented, believed God, and was spared. This displeased

Jonah, and he prayed, "Therefore now, O Lord, *take, I beseech thee, my life from me;* for *it is better for me to die than to live!*" (Jonah 4:3).

It is not God's plan and purpose to take believers out of the world as soon as they are saved. We are in the world to bring glory and honor to the Lord Jesus Christ. In the sixth chapter of Hebrews, Paul speaks of "things that accompany salvation" (v. 9), and in verses 11 and 12 he said, "We desire that every one of you do shew the same *diligence* to the full assurance of hope unto the end: *THAT YE BE NOT SLOTHFUL, but followers of them who through faith and patience inherit the promises."*

Believers are not in this world to seek honor and glory for self. *We will be glorified by Jesus in the world to come.* God never saved *anyone* to sit down and do nothing! He has a ministry, a work of some kind, for each and every born again person, and we should not be anxious to receive our reward nor to leave this world until we have *completed* that work.

It is very important for us to realize that the God who *saves* us is also able to *keep* us. We are no more able to keep ourselves than we are able to save ourselves. *We are kept by the power of God* (I Pet. 1:5). In Genesis 20:6 God said to Abimelech, "I also withheld thee from sinning against me." In answer to Jeremiah's prayer for Israel God said, "I will make an everlasting covenant with them, that I will not turn away from them, to do them good; *but I will put my fear in their hearts, that they shall not depart from me*" (Jer. 32:40).

In Psalm 125:3 we read, "The rod of the wicked *shall not* rest upon the lot of the righteous; lest the righteous put forth their hands unto iniquity." And Psalm 23, beloved of all believers, promises that God will lead us "in the paths of righteousness for His name's sake" (v. 3).

Verse 16: *"They are not of the world, even as I am not of the world."*

Here is repetition of the words in verse 14. Jesus prayed these words twice—not because God did not hear Him the first time, but to emphasize and impress upon the hearts of the disciples the fact of their being IN the world but not OF it. God does not need to say anything but once in order to make it effective. Therefore when we find repetition in Scripture we should be sure we understand and profit by that repetition.

Since Jesus was praying especially for the preservation of the disciples as they traveled through a world in which they would find no comfort from evil men, it might be helpful and encouraging to point out the ways in which believers are *different* from the world:

First of all, we have a *different standing.* Unbelievers have their standing in *Adam;* born again believers are *in Christ by faith.* Unbelievers are under condemnation; believers are "accepted in the Beloved."

Believers have a *different nature*—divine nature. Unbelievers are in the flesh; therefore they cannot please God. Believers are in the Spirit, led by the Spirit to do the will of God.

Believers have a *different Master.* Jesus said to the Jews, "Ye are of your father the devil, *and the lusts of your father ye will do"* (John 8:44). Believers are children of God, and as dutiful sons of God we are subject to His will.

Believers have a *different aim* in life. We aim to please God, but unbelievers please themselves. We aim to glorify God; the unbeliever seeks glory for himself.

Believers have a *different citizenship.* Our citizenship is in heaven from whence we look for the Saviour. Unbelievers are of this earth, earthy; they are citizens of a world that lies in wickedness.

Believers live *different lives* because we are new creations in Christ Jesus. Old things are passed away, all things have become new. Unbelievers follow the "old man," the lust of the flesh. They do the deeds of the flesh because they are not sons of God.

Believers have a *different destiny.* Jesus said, "I go to prepare a place for you. . . I will come again, and receive you unto myself; *that where I am, there ye may be also*" (John 14:2,3). Unbelievers are destined for hell. All whose names are not found in the Lamb's book of life will be cast into the lake of fire (Rev. 20:15).

Verse 17: *"Sanctify them through thy truth: thy Word is truth."*

Jesus first asked for the protection and preservation of His disciples and their deliverance from the power of this world. Now He prays for their *sanctification,* that they might be made more holy. He was praying that they be led to higher ground, a higher degree of purity; and this was to be done through *"TRUTH."* Then, in order that we might know and understand what truth *is,* He said, *"Thy WORD is truth."*

To *sanctify* means "to set apart." The word can be used concerning a house, a vessel, an animal, and many other things. Jesus was praying for His disciples, and thus the meaning here would be that they might be cleansed thoroughly and entirely, and that they might live blameless lives.

The Apostle Paul sheds light on sanctification. Writing to the Christians at Thessalonica, he urged them to "Rejoice evermore. Pray without ceasing. In everything give thanks. . . . Quench not the Spirit. Despise not prophesyings. Prove all things; hold fast that which is good. Abstain from all appearance of evil. *AND THE VERY GOD OF PEACE SANCTIFY YOU WHOLLY; and I pray God your whole SPIRIT and SOUL and BODY be preserved BLAMELESS unto the coming of our Lord Jesus Christ*" (II Thess. 5:16–23).

Notice that Paul said "w-h-o-l-l-y," meaning *completely.* The believer is sanctified *positionally* the split second he is born again, when he is translated from the kingdom of Satan into the kingdom of God. But he is sanctified *pro-*

gressively as he feeds upon the milk, bread, and meat of the Word—in other words, as he grows in grace and becomes more dedicated, more fully surrendered to the will of God. *Positional sanctification* is instantaneous; *progressive sanctification* will never end until we see Jesus. Our Lord was praying here for His people to increase in holiness and practical godliness as they lived for Him day by day in a hostile world. He was praying, "Separate my people from sin day by day by making them more and more spiritually minded, more and more dedicated to the will of God."

This verse teaches the extreme importance of practical godliness in daily living. There are those who are sound—even cautious—concerning *doctrine,* but they are not subject to the mind of Christ and therefore they do not live lives of practical godliness. Jesus wants us to follow in His steps, thereby becoming more and more like Him day by day. We should *daily* pray for a more dedicated, Spirit-filled, Christ-controlled life.

Consider this solemn fact, fellow Christian: We possess *ALL of Christ* the split second we are born again—but He does not necessarily possess *all of US!* He comes into the *inner man* with the miracle of the new birth, but what about the *body?* We are commanded to present our bodies "a living sacrifice, holy, acceptable unto God, which is (our) *reasonable service*" (Rom. 12:1).

Romans 6:11—13 tells us, "Likewise reckon ye also yourselves to be *dead* indeed unto sin, but alive unto God through Jesus Christ our Lord. *Let not sin therefore reign in your mortal body,* that ye should obey it in the lusts thereof. *Neither yield ye your members as instruments of unrighteousness unto sin: but yield yourselves unto God,* as those that are alive from the dead, and your members as instruments of righteousness unto God." Whatsoever we do should be done to the glory of God, and sound doctrine *apart from practical godliness* is indeed poor testimony for pure Christianity!

The difference between justification and sanctification

is also pointed out here. You will notice that Jesus did not pray for the *justification* of the disciples. They were *already* justified. He prayed for their sanctification. We are justified by faith (Rom. 5:1), and justification is a perfect and complete work, never to be repeated. When we are justified by faith in the finished work of Jesus, we are justified *entirely*—not in part. Justification is imputed to us by Christ; it is perfect and complete the moment we are saved, *as complete as it can ever be.* There are no *degrees* of justification.

On the other hand, *sanctification* is an *inward work wrought in our hearts by the Holy Spirit* as we feed on the Word of God and walk in the light of the Scriptures. Therefore, as long as we remain in this life our sanctification will continue; we will grow in grace and advance in spiritual matters until we are taken to be with Jesus in the clouds in the air at the Rapture.

Some believe the erroneous doctrine of *imputed* sanctification, but such doctrine is not found in the Word of God. *Sanctification is not imputed.* If it were, why did Jesus *pray* for the sanctification of the disciples? Sanctification is by and through the Word of God. As we read and hear the Word, the Holy Spirit causes *the mighty truths* of the Word to bear more forcibly on our hearts and minds, and as we walk in the *light* of the Word we grow more holy day by day—a holiness that will never cease to grow. *This* is "progressive sanctification."

In our present verse Jesus points out the importance of reading, studying, and appropriating the Word of God. We should study the Word, we should attend services where the Word is preached and taught, and we should avail ourselves of the teaching in good commentaries compiled by God-fearing men, for these, too, will help us to understand the Word and grow in grace. It is true that every born again believer has the Holy Spirit in his heart; but God calls and anoints men as chosen vessels to expound the Word, and we need to study and profit by what such men have written as God has given them light and leadership.

Sanctification is not "a second work of grace," as some believe and teach. It is a *continual working* of grace in the heart of the believer as he studies and feeds upon the Word of God. Christ was praying here for men who were already born again and sanctified *positionally.*

We must be careful to rightly divide the Word of God, and therefore it is important for us to realize that sanctification does *not* mean *eradication of the carnal nature.* One verse will prove this:

In verse 19 of this chapter Jesus said, "For their sakes I sanctify myself." Since Jesus was sinless, absolutely devoid of the sinful nature, the meaning here could only be, *"I set myself apart* for their sakes."

In Jude, verse 1, we read of believers being *"sanctified by God the Father,"* and in Hebrews 10:10 we read that "we are *sanctified through the offering of the body of Jesus Christ* once for all." In II Thessalonians 2:13 and in I Peter 1:2 we read of believers being sanctified *"of the Spirit."*

In verse 15 of our present chapter, Jesus prayed, "Keep them from the evil." Here, He prays, "Sanctify them through thy truth." The former ("Keep them from evil") is secured and guaranteed by the latter ("Sanctify them through thy truth"). As long as we are in this tabernacle of flesh, we will be prone to stumble and make mistakes; but in I John 2:1,2 we read, "My little children, these things write I unto you, *that ye sin NOT. And if any man sin, we have an Advocate with the Father, Jesus Christ the righteous:* and He is the propitiation for our sins: and not for our's only, but also for the sins of the whole world." In I John 1:9 God promises, "If we *confess* our sins, He is faithful and just to forgive us our sins, and to cleanse us from all unrighteousness."

"Thy WORD is truth." Beloved, the Bible does not *"contain"* truth; *it IS truth!* The Bible does not *"contain"* the Word of God; *it IS the Word of God.* The Bible is the pure, unadulterated TRUTH, for God is its Author *and God*

cannot lie (Tit. 1:2; Heb. 6:18).

In Mark 4:24 Jesus warned, *"Take heed what ye hear:* with what measure ye mete, it shall be measured to you: and unto you that hear shall more be given." We do indeed need to be careful what we hear and to whom we listen, because we will one day give an account to God for what we hear and how we hear it. This is made very clear in John 12:46–48. Jesus said, "I am come a light into the world, that whosoever believeth on me should not abide in darkness. And if any man hear my words, and believe not, I judge him not: for I came not to judge the world, but to save the world. He that rejecteth me, and receiveth not my words, hath one that judgeth him: *the Word that I have spoken, the same shall judge him in the last day."*

Verse 18: *"As thou hast sent me into the world, even so have I also sent them into the world."*

Keep in mind the fact that Jesus was praying this prayer *audibly* in the presence of His disciples. He therefore prayed in this manner: "Father, I am asking for the day-by-day sanctification of my disciples because of their position here on earth. As you sent *me,* I send them; and I pray for their increased sanctification, that they may follow in my steps, that they may be lights in a dark world as they give testimony to your saving grace. Father, just as I have lived a holy, righteous life, separate from the world, so must *they* live if they are to carry on the work I am leaving them to do in this present evil world." Believers are God's witnesses in this world, and if the testimony of a witness is to be effective, his character must be blameless and above reproach. It was because of this that Jesus prayed especially for the sanctification of His disciples.

"As thou hast sent me into the world, even so have I also sent them into the world."

In chapter 20, verse 21 of our present study, Jesus said to His disciples, "Peace be unto you: as my Father hath sent me, even so send I you." And in I John 4:17 we read,

"Herein is our love made perfect, that we may have boldness in the day of judgment: because *as HE is, so are we in this world.*"

Jesus came to this world to declare and show forth the Father and His glories; He came to seek and to save that which was lost; He came as the compassionate, tender, longsuffering Saviour. Therefore if we would follow in His steps *WE must have the same characteristics.* We must have a burden for the fields that are white unto harvest, with laborers so few. We are His witnesses, His instruments; we are to tell the world about the Saviour—and since Christ was full of grace and truth, we also must be full of grace and truth. How? We are full of *grace* when we possess Christ and *He fully possesses us.* We are full of *truth* when we study and appropriate *the Word.*

Verse 19: *"And for their sakes I sanctify myself, that they also might be sanctified through the truth."*

This is one of those verses we may read over and over and over again, and then confess that man will never be able to fully probe and understand its depth! Certainly the Lord Jesus was not speaking of sanctification from the standpoint of becoming *holy, pure, and undefiled,* for He had been thus from the beginning. I believe what He was saying to the heavenly Father in the presence of His disciples was this: "I sanctify (consecrate and dedicate) myself, Father, as your great High Priest. I offer *myself* as a sacrifice in order that my disciples may be sanctified by the truth of the Word; that they may be holy, blameless witnesses for me here on earth. I want my people to be sanctified, holy, and blameless, as well as being redeemed and justified. Therefore, I offer my one supreme sacrifice—not only to redeem and justify my people, but also to *sanctify* them."

Titus 2:14 tells us that Christ "gave Himself for us, that He might redeem us from all iniquity, and purify unto Himself a peculiar people, zealous of good works."

Ephesians 5:25,26 tell us that Christ "loved the Church,

and gave Himself for it; *that He might sanctify and cleanse it with the washing of water by the Word.*"

I Peter 2:24 tells us that Christ "His own self bare our sins in His own body on the tree, that we, *being dead to sins, should live unto righteousness:* by whose stripes (we) were healed."

In His declaration of personal sanctification Jesus called to our attention the fact that He freely and voluntarily made His atoning sacrifice; there was no compulsion—He did it willingly. He laid His life down *"for their sakes,"* and it was for their sakes (and ours) that He sanctified Himself.

To me, the *deeper* meaning here applies to Christ—the glorified MAN—set apart on high at the right hand of the Majesty. It is the MAN, not the Spirit, who sits at the right hand of God today. Thus seated at the right hand of the Majesty *as a glorified Man,* He is the object of the believer's love and worship. Today Jesus is set apart from *all* men—and from things in heaven, things in earth, things under the earth. His name is above every name. He is set apart as *the heavenly Man,* high above all heavens, glorified above all glory.

By Christ's death we are saved from the penalty of sin, redeemed from eternal damnation. He died to redeem us; He ever lives to deliver us; and we are kept through His power because He lives to make intercession for us.

Verse 20: *"Neither pray I for these alone, but for them also which shall believe on me through their word."*

Having already prayed on behalf of the eleven disciples, Jesus now prays for the entire Church, *for ALL born again believers.* His prayer here is for all who will believe on Him through the preaching of the Word, even down to this present moment. We must remember that the disciples were the first to give out the message of grace and meet the enemy "head on." It is true that all Christians need to be kept by the power of God (for we certainly cannot keep ourselves). We need preservation and sanctification; but these eleven men stood in *special* need of these things for which Jesus prayed. They were the first to face a hostile, unfriendly world—a world that rejected and crucified their Saviour, a world that seemed determined to stamp out the new Christianity.

Notice that Jesus said, *"Them also which shall believe on me through their word."* They would, of course, give out the Word of God, and it is the WORD that brings salvation. Paul declared that the Gospel of Christ (*the Word*) "is the power of God unto salvation to every one that believeth" (Rom. 1:16). We are saved by God's grace (Eph. 2:8), but grace becomes ours by *faith;* and "faith cometh by hearing, and hearing by the Word of God" (Rom. 10:17). I repeat what I have already said several times in these studies: *It is impossible to be saved without first hearing the Word of God.*

It always refreshes my spirit and encourages my heart when I remember that Jesus prayed for me. He said, "Neither pray I for these (the disciples) alone, but for them also which *shall believe* on me." I put *my* name there. Jesus prayed for me individually, He prayed for the entire Church made up of all believers from Pentecost until the Rapture.

There are *seven things* in this prayer that are particularly interesting, things Jesus asked our heavenly Father to do for believers:

He prayed for our *preservation:* "Holy Father, keep through thine own name those whom thou hast given me" (v. 11).

He prayed for our *joy:* "That they might have my joy fulfilled in themselves" (v. 13).

He prayed for our *protection:* "That thou shouldest keep them from the evil (one)" (v. 15).

He prayed for our *sanctification:* "Sanctify them through thy truth: thy Word is truth" (v. 17).

He prayed for our *unification:* "That they all may be one; as thou, Father, art in me, and I in thee, that they also may be one in us" (v. 21).

He prayed that we might *be with Him in glory:* "I will that they also, whom thou hast given me, be with me where I am" (v. 24).

He prayed that we might *behold His glory:* "That they may behold my glory, which thou hast given me" (v. 24). And what a day that will be, when we behold His glory in that celestial city!

Jesus made these seven petitions on behalf of believers because believers are the Father's love-gift to the Son (v. 9). In verses 9 and 10 He prayed for God to sanctify and keep believers because "they are thine"—that is, believers belong to the heavenly Father, we are His children.

Throughout this intercessory prayer, please notice the relationship of believers to the world:

We are given to the Lord Jesus Christ OUT of the world (v. 6).

We are left IN the world (v. 11).

But we are not OF the world (v. 14).

All truly born again believers, those who live godly in Christ Jesus, will be hated by the world (v. 14).

Believers are kept from the evil of the world (v. 15), because greater is He that is in US than he that is in the world (I John 4:4).

Believers are sent forth INTO the world to witness and testify, to give out the Gospel message (v. 18).

True believers, united in the oneness of God the Father and God the Son, will glorify Jesus here in this world (v. 23).

The prayer of Jesus recorded here will become more and more blessed and precious to us if we will remember the circumstances under which He prayed at this particular time. He had been walking with His disciples for more than three years, He had faithfully completed the work the Father sent Him to do, and His earthly ministry was rapidly drawing to a close. Only a small group had believed on Him; the *masses* rejected Him and demanded His death. Now He was nearing Calvary, and shortly He would die there between two thieves. The faith of His disciples had already been tried and put to a severe test. He had told them He must soon leave them and return to His Father, and because this troubled and perplexed them He had explained to them that "except a corn of wheat fall into the ground and die, it abideth alone: but if it die, it bringeth forth much fruit" (John 12:24). Jesus was that "corn of wheat."

But He knew the promise of God. His supreme sacrifice had been foreordained before the foundation of the world was laid, and He knew victory was assured. Therefore, although He did not *look forward* to the cross in that He enjoyed it, He saw the glory on the other side. It was in the very shadow of Calvary, then, that He prayed this intercessory prayer; and surely, in the days of turmoil and tribulation that followed, the disciples often had occasion to remember the words of Jesus recorded here.

Verse 21: *"That they all may be one; as thou, Father, art in me, and I in thee, that they also may be one in us: that the world may believe that thou hast sent me."*

It would have been easier for the *eleven* to be one than for the Church today, because the Church has grown; and the greater the number, the more difficult it is to be one in mind, spirit, and purpose. Jesus was praying here that all who make up the Church may be of one mind, one heart, one practice, one doctrine, joined together in oneness even as Father, Son, and Holy Spirit are one. When believers are of one mind and in one accord the ungodly will take note that we are altogether new creations in Christ Jesus, citizens of another world, strangers and pilgrims on earth.

Certainly the unity between Father, Son, and Holy Spirit will never be *literally obtained* by believers; but we must *strive* after such unity. Oh, yes—there *can* be unity. The secret of such unity is, as Jesus said, "that they may be one in us." Born again believers are in Christ and Christ is in the believer; and as we are one in Him we can have unity one with another.

I believe the deeper meaning here refers to the unity in

the New Testament Church—unity between Jew, Gentile, and all classes. We are ALL one, the middle wall of partition has been broken down. In Ephesians 2:11–18 Paul wrote:

"Wherefore remember, that ye being in time past Gentiles in the flesh, who are called Uncircumcision by that which is called the Circumcision in the flesh made by hands; that at that time ye were without Christ, being aliens from the commonwealth of Israel, and strangers from the covenants of promise, having no hope, and without God in the world: but now in Christ Jesus ye who sometimes were far off are made nigh by the blood of Christ.

"*For He is our peace, who hath made both one, AND HATH BROKEN DOWN THE MIDDLE WALL OF PARTITION BETWEEN US;* having abolished in His flesh the enmity, even the law of commandments contained in ordinances; for to make in Himself of twain *one new man,* so making peace; and that He might reconcile both unto God *in ONE BODY* by the cross, having slain the enmity thereby: and came and preached peace to you which were afar off, and to them that were nigh. For through Him we both have access *by one Spirit* unto the Father."

"That the world may believe that thou hast sent me." This is the primary reason for believers' being in unity and harmony. Jesus said, "By this shall all men know that ye are my disciples, if ye have love one to another" (John 13:35). When Christians dwell together in unity, peace, and brotherly love the world takes knowledge that we have been with Jesus and that we are "different"; but when church people quarrel, bicker among themselves and stand divided, the world looks on with scorn and declares that unbelievers are "just as good" as church members. When unsaved people see dedicated, consecrated, Spirit-filled people dwelling together in love and unity, they recognize the fact that God is in the midst of such unity. I have said many times in my meetings that it is not the bootleggers and gangsters who hinder the cause of Christ. *It is born again church*

members who are poor advertisements for Jesus because of the lives they live, the places they go, and the spirit they demonstrate in their daily activities!

Four times in this prayer Jesus mentions unity among believers. (Note verses 11, 21, 22, and 23.) Surely, it must be important. I suggest again that He had in mind the division that had existed between Jews and Gentiles, and now He sits at the right hand of God to make intercession for all. He is calling out a people who will be "in Himself of twain one new man, so making peace" (Eph. 2:15).

Verse 22: *"And the glory which thou gavest me I have given them; that they may be one, even as we are one."*

Here is repeated our Lord's desire for unity among His people. He declared (in order that believers may be one) "I give them the glory which God the Eternal Father gave me." Many outstanding Bible commentators are puzzled and offer varied opinions as to the exact meaning of *"the glory which thou gavest me."* In view of the last part of the verse, it seems to me that Jesus is speaking here of *the giving of the Spirit* at Pentecost. In Ephesians 4:3 Paul speaks of "the unity of the Spirit," and I Peter 4:14 speaks of "the Spirit of glory." Then to the believers in Corinth, Paul wrote:

"Not that we are sufficient of ourselves to think any thing as of ourselves; but our sufficiency is of God; who also hath made us able ministers of the New Testament; not of the letter, but of the Spirit: for the letter killeth, but the Spirit giveth life. But if the ministration of death, written and engraven in stones, was glorious, so that the children of Israel could not stedfastly behold the face of Moses for the glory of his countenance; which glory was to be done away: how shall not the ministration of the Spirit be rather glorious? For if the ministration of condemnation be glory, much more doth the ministration of righteousness exceed in glory. For even that which was made glorious had no glory in this respect, by reason of the glory that excelleth. For if that which is done away was glorious, much more that which remaineth is glorious" (II Cor. 3:5–11).

All believers are possessors of the Holy Spirit (Rom. 8:9). We are justified (born of the Spirit) when we believe in the finished work of Jesus (Rom. 5:1; John 3:5). We also know that "whom He justified, them He also glorified" (Rom. 8:30). Please notice that the Scripture does not say that we WILL BE glorified at some future date, but "them He also *glorified"—past tense.* That is, the future glorification of the born again believer is as certain as if it were already accomplished! When we see Him we will be like Him (I John 3:2).

This is not man's opinion: it is the clear, understandable *Word of God.* We are saved by God's grace, and grace becomes ours by faith. We are *justified* by faith, we *walk* by faith, and *whatsoever is NOT of faith is sin.* Hebrews 11:1 defines faith as "the substance of things hoped for, the evidence of things not seen." It is our spiritual birthright to enjoy assurance of redemption and victory—*and more:* it is also our spiritual birthright to enjoy the assurance of glorification. Hear the Apostle Paul again:

"Ye are not in the flesh, but in the Spirit, if so be that the Spirit of God dwell in you. Now if any man have not the Spirit of Christ, he is none of His. And if Christ be in you, the body is dead because of sin; but the Spirit is life because of righteousness. But if the Spirit of Him that raised up Jesus from the dead dwell in you, *He that raised up Christ from the dead SHALL ALSO QUICKEN YOUR MORTAL BODIES by His Spirit that dwelleth in you"* (Rom. 8:9–11).

The union between Jesus and the believer produces the glory we enjoy here and the glory we WILL enjoy in its fulness even like unto Him, because when we SEE Him we will be like Him.

Verse 23: *"I in them, and thou in me, that they may be made perfect in one; and that the world may know that thou hast sent me, and hast loved them, as thou hast loved me."*

Verses 21 and 22 spoke of the unity and glorification of believers—unity on earth, and glorification in its fulness when Jesus returns for His Church. Now in our present verse He continues:

"I in them . . . ." In Colossians 1:27 we read, "Christ in you, the hope of glory."

"And thou in me." In John 10:30 Jesus said, "I and my Father are one." Then in II Corinthians 5:19 we are told that God was in Christ, reconciling the world unto Himself.

"That they may be made perfect in one." This includes not only the eleven, but ALL born again believers. The inner man is made perfect instantaneously at the new birth: ". . . That which is born of the Spirit is spirit" (John 3:6); and certainly the part of man that is born of the Holy Spirit is perfect. But when a person becomes a believer, he has two natures. He is a new man—but he lives in a tabernacle of flesh. That is the reason Paul said, "Let him that thinketh he standeth take heed lest he fall" (I Cor. 10:12). But there is victory; we are more than conquerors through Christ (I Cor. 10:13; Rom. 8:31–39). This perfection will reach its fulness when Jesus comes for the Church. Then, not only will we be perfect in the *inner man,* we will also have a perfect *body* just like the glorified body of Jesus. Paul speaks of the time when we all "come *in the unity of the faith,* and of the knowledge of the Son of God, *UNTO A PERFECT MAN, unto the measure of the stature of the fulness of Christ!"* (Eph. 4:13).

We know that when the Church is presented to the Lord Jesus Christ it will be "a glorious Church, not having spot, or wrinkle, or any such thing; but that it should be holy and without blemish" (Eph. 5:27).

In Hebrews 11:40 Paul speaks of the Old Testament saints: "God having provided some better thing for us, *that they without us should not be made PERFECT."*

When the Church is complete and caught up to meet

Jesus in the clouds in the air, it will be a *perfect* Church without spot or blemish of any kind. Then will be *perfect oneness,* and we will dwell in that glorious, Pearly White City that Jesus is now preparing for His bride. "When Christ, who is our life, shall appear, *then shall ye also appear with Him in glory"* (Col. 3:4).

Paul wrote to the Thessalonians of the time "when He shall come to be glorified in His saints, and to be admired in all them that believe . . ." (II Thess. 1:10).

"And hast loved them as thou hast loved me." There are not enough words in all the languages of all the world to touch the hem of the garment when it comes to explaining the depth of this statement! The reason God loves US as He loves JESUS is because of Christ's finished work in our behalf. All that we enjoy in salvation, all its fruits and benefits, are because of the merit in the life, death, burial, and resurrection of Jesus. God saves us for Christ's sake (Eph. 4:32). God "hath made us accepted in the Beloved" (Eph. 1:6). "For we are His workmanship, created in Christ Jesus unto good works, which God hath before ordained that we should walk in them" (Eph. 2:10).

We are redeemed, pardoned, justified, sanctified, made righteous, and *glorified* in and through the finished work of the Lord Jesus Christ. God the Father loved Jesus as His image—"the brightness of His glory, and the express image of His person" (Heb. 1:3). But now listen to these words concerning *believers:* "Seeing that ye have put off the old man with his deeds; and have put on the new man, which is renewed in knowledge AFTER THE IMAGE OF HIM THAT CREATED HIM" (Col. 3:9,10).

God loved Jesus as His only begotten Son; He loves US as "dear children" (Eph. 5:1). In Jeremiah 31:3 we read, "The Lord hath appeared of old unto me, saying, Yea, *I have loved thee with an everlasting love . . . ."* God the Father loved Jesus with an "everlasting love," and He loves us with the same kind of love. In John 13:1 we are told that "having loved His own which were in the world, He loved them unto the end"; and in Malachi 3:6 we read, *"I AM THE LORD, I CHANGE NOT."*

What assurance and comfort these tremendous truths bring to the children of God, hated and persecuted by a wicked world! What comfort it is to know that God the Father loves *us* even as He loved His only begotten Son.

It might be well to remind our readers that the Church for whose unity Jesus so earnestly prayed is not the *visible, local church.* It is the Church of the living God (Acts 20: 28). The Church for which He prayed is the Church of which Paul speaks in Ephesians 5:25–32:

"Husbands, love your wives, even as Christ also loved the Church, and gave Himself for it; that He might sanctify and cleanse it with the washing of water by the Word, that He might present it to Himself a glorious Church, not having spot, or wrinkle, or any such thing; but that it should be holy and without blemish. So ought men to love their wives as their own bodies. He that loveth his wife loveth himself. For no man ever yet hated his own flesh; but nourisheth and cherisheth it, even as the Lord the Church: For we are members of His body, of His flesh, and of His bones. For this cause shall a man leave his father and mother, and shall be joined unto his wife, and they two shall be one flesh. *This is a great mystery: BUT I SPEAK CONCERNING CHRIST AND THE CHURCH."*

Jesus was not praying that believers be united in church *discipline,* church *forms,* or church *government;* He was not praying for a "world church" in that all denominations come together and agree on a common form of government and worship. He was praying for *unity of heart and will,* true Bible doctrine, and true Christian practice. He was praying for ALL believers, that we be so fully surrendered, dedicated, and consecrated that we will be one *in mind, in heart, in will, in purpose,* united in such a way that ungodly men will be forced to confess that Jesus was Messiah and that He IS the Saviour, loving His people, saving them, and living to make intercession for them!

Verse 24: *"Father, I will that they also, whom thou hast given me, be with me where I am; that they may behold my glory, which thou hast given me: for thou lovedst me before the foundation of the world."*

Here Jesus makes the fourth and last request in His prayer of intercession on behalf of the disciples. He prayed for their *preservation,* He prayed for their *sanctification,* He prayed for their *unity,* and now He prays *that they may be with Him in glory,* that they may share with Him IN that glory.

"I will that they be with me where I am." Since Jesus was one with the Father, the Father's will was *His* will; and because of His finished work, because of His accomplishment through His death, burial, and resurrection, He had a perfect right to pray "I *will.*" He had purchased His disciples at the tremendous price of His blood, and they were His as His own purchased possession. Therefore His "I will" was founded on acknowledged, divine right. (Please refer to our discussion of verse 4.)

Our Lord's prayer that we be with Him where He is gives us assurance of our eternal dwelling place as born again believers. To the thief on the cross Jesus said, "To day shalt thou be with me in Paradise" (Luke 23:43). Paul assured the Thessalonian believers, "The Lord Himself shall descend from heaven with a shout, with the voice of the archangel, and with the trump of God: *and the dead in Christ shall rise first: Then we which are alive and remain shall be caught up together with them in the clouds, to meet the Lord in the air: AND SO SHALL WE EVER BE WITH THE LORD.* Wherefore comfort one another with these words" (I Thess. 4:16–18).

It did not please God to reveal to us the full nature of our future state. To the believers in Corinth Paul said, "I knew a man in Christ above fourteen years ago, (whether in the body, I cannot tell; or whether out of the body, I cannot tell: God knoweth;) such an one caught up to the third heaven. . . How that he was caught up into Paradise, and heard unspeakable words, which it is not lawful for a man to utter" (II Cor. 12:2,4). It is against God's law that the full nature of our eternal estate be revealed to us now—nor would our finite, limited minds be able to comprehend it; but it is "joy unspeakable and full of glory" to know that *where HE is, there we will be also.* When the Church is complete, we will be caught up to meet Jesus in the clouds in the air, "and so shall we ever be with the Lord." That will be perfect peace, perfect joy.

"That they may behold my glory, which thou hast given me." This does not mean that we will stand and gaze upon the glory of Christ as we would stand and behold a beautiful sight on earth. To behold His glory here means *participating* in His glory, *sharing* and *enjoying* His glory with Him.

The glory and honor of Jesus is the nearest and dearest thing to God's heart. The glory Jesus has in this world is in the believers, the redeemed ones; and because the glory of Jesus and the glory of the redeemed cannot be separated, we show forth His glory and praise when we live a life that is blameless and above reproach. So Jesus prayed to the heavenly Father, "Father, these are thine. Show forth my honor, my glory, and my praises here on earth in them, because if they should perish, my honor and glory on earth would perish with them."

When Jesus said "the glory which thou hast given me" He was undoubtedly speaking here of a very special glory which God the Eternal Father appointed to Christ in the eternal, everlasting covenant, as a reward for His finished work here on earth: "Wherefore God also hath highly exalted Him, and given Him a name which is above every name: that at the name of Jesus every knee should bow, of things in heaven, and things in earth, and things under the earth; and that every tongue should confess that Jesus Christ is Lord, to the glory of God the Father" (Phil. 2:9–11).

"For thou lovedst me before the foundation of the world."

This statement points out the glory of which Christ was speaking here. The glory in that eternal day is glory which was prepared for Him from all eternity before the world was, glory that is from everlasting to everlasting. We are redeemed with the precious blood of Christ, "foreordained before the foundation of the world" (I Pet. 1:20). It was foreordained that the Lamb would shed His blood and lay His life down; therefore *the glory that we will share with Him* throughout eternity was *also* foreordained. I readily admit that this is entirely too deep for our minds to understand. *"Such knowledge is too wonderful for me; it is high, I cannot attain unto it"* (Psalm 139:6).

Verse 25: *"O righteous Father, the world hath not known thee: but I have known thee, and these have known that thou hast sent me."*

This is the only place where Jesus addressed God as *"Righteous Father."* No doubt He used the term to point out the strong contrast between God's righteousness and the unrighteousness of the world—the world which was made by Him and yet knew Him not (John 1:10).

"I have known thee." Yes, even in His body of humiliation and in the midst of all the ungodliness and wickedness in the world where "the lust of the eye, the lust of the flesh, and the pride of life" held pre-eminence, Jesus did always those things that pleased the heavenly Father.

"And these have known that thou hast sent me." This little band of men, though weak in faith, perplexed about many things and troubled in spirit, had known God through knowing God's Son, and they knew and confessed that God the Father had sent Jesus into the world on a divine mission.

Verse 26: *"And I have declared unto them thy name, and will declare it: that the love wherewith thou hast loved me may be in them, and I in them."*

Here Jesus sums up what He had done (and was still

doing) for His little company of believers. He had made God known to them. He had declared God's name, God's character, God's attributes—and even after His ascension He would *continue* to declare this glorious message through the Holy Spirit. In Proverbs 1:23 we read, "I will pour out my Spirit unto you, I will make known my words unto you." The Holy Spirit came on the Day of Pentecost, and through ministers who preach the truth He is continually making known the Gospel message to any and all who will listen.

"That the love wherewith thou hast loved me may be in them, and I in them." Here is seen the Son's desire that the Father's love dwell in the hearts of His disciples, and that He *Himself* might dwell in their hearts. We read in I John 2:28, "And now, little children, *abide in Him*. . . ."

Jesus wants the Father's love to permeate the heart of every believer. He wants us to abide in Him—dedicated, consecrated fully; and so He prayed, "Father, it is my desire that my disciples may know and feel the love wherewith thou hast loved me, and that I may ever dwell supremely in their hearts by faith in pure, dedicated living."

To the Ephesians the Apostle Paul expressed his desire that Christ might dwell in their hearts by faith, and that they would be "rooted and grounded in love" (Eph. 3:17).

To the Romans he said, "Hope maketh not ashamed; because the love of God is shed abroad in our hearts by the Holy Ghost which is given unto us" (Rom. 5:5).

As Jesus brings this prayer to a close it is interesting to note that "LOVE"—not "faith" or "glory"—is the last word. It reminds us of the words of the Apostle Paul in I Corinthians 13:13: "And now abideth faith, hope, love (charity), these three; *but the greatest of these is LOVE* (charity)."

In verse 23 of our present chapter, Jesus said, "I in them, and thou in me, that they may be made perfect in one." The love of God the Father dwells in believers through the Lord Jesus Christ—"Christ in you, the hope of glory" (Col. 1:27). Believers are IN Christ (Rom. 8:1), "hid with Christ in God" (Col. 3:3), and "the love of God is shed abroad in our hearts by the Holy Ghost" (Rom. 5:5).

After His resurrection, Jesus continued to make known the name of God during the forty days He remained on earth before His ascension, and *after* He ascended He continued to make known the name of God through the Holy Spirit as the apostles preached the Word. He is *still* making known His name today by the ministry of the Spirit through the preaching of the Word of God by men called and anointed by the Holy Spirit to preach the truth; and this will continue until Jesus comes to receive His own.

When the *heart* is controlled by the Holy Spirit and filled with the love of God, the *life* will also be controlled by the love of God and we will love one another fervently, with a pure heart. Thus we will manifest to this wicked world the life and character of the Lord Jesus Christ who indwells us. Such a life will bring glory and honor to God the Father and Jesus our Saviour. This is the kind of life that will reap a rich reward in that great day when Jesus rewards His servants for faithful stewardship.

Fellow believer, we, too, should pray for the four things Jesus asked for His disciples:

Preservation,

Sanctification,

Unity,

And finally, *glory with Jesus* in that glorious morning of Rapture and resurrection!

CHAPTER XVIII

1. When Jesus had spoken these words, he went forth with his disciples over the brook Cedron, where was a garden, into the which he
entered, and his disciples.
2. And Judas also, which betrayed him, knew the place: for Jesus
ofttimes resorted thither with his disciples.
3. Judas then, having received a band of men and officers from the
chief priests and Pharisees, cometh thither with lanterns and torches
and weapons.
4. Jesus therefore, knowing all things that should come upon him,
went forth, and said unto them, Whom seek ye?
5. They answered him, Jesus of Nazareth. Jesus saith unto them,
I am he. And Judas also, which betrayed him, stood with them.
6. As soon then as he had said unto them, I am he, they went
backward, and fell to the ground.
7. Then asked he them again, Whom seek ye? And they said, Jesus
of Nazareth.
8. Jesus answered, I have told you that I am he: if therefore ye
seek me, let these go their way:
9. That the saying might be fulfilled, which he spake, Of them
which thou gavest me have I lost none.
10. Then Simon Peter having a sword drew it, and smote the high
priest's servant, and cut off his right ear. The servant's name was
Malchus.
11. Then said Jesus unto Peter, Put up thy sword into the sheath:
the cup which my Father hath given me, shall I not drink it?
12. Then the band and the captain and officers of the Jews took
Jesus, and bound him,
13. And led him away to Annas first; for he was father in law to
Caiaphas, which was the high priest that same year.
14. Now Caiaphas was he, which gave counsel to the Jews, that it
was expedient that one man should die for the people.
15. And Simon Peter followed Jesus, and so did another disciple:
that disciple was known unto the high priest, and went in with Jesus
into the palace of the high priest.
16. But Peter stood at the door without. Then went out that other
disciple, which was known unto the high priest, and spake unto her

that kept the door, and brought in Peter.

17. Then saith the damsel that kept the door unto Peter, Art not thou also one of this man's disciples? He saith, I am not.

18. And the servants and officers stood there, who had made a fire of coals; for it was cold: and they warmed themselves: and Peter stood with them, and warmed himself.

19. The high priest then asked Jesus of his disciples, and of his doctrine.

20. Jesus answered him, I spake openly to the world; I ever taught in the synagogue, and in the temple, whither the Jews always resort; and in secret have I said nothing.

21. Why askest thou me? ask them which heard me, what I have said unto them: behold, they know what I said.

22. And when he had thus spoken, one of the officers which stood by struck Jesus with the palm of his hand, saying, Answerest thou the high priest so?

23. Jesus answered him, If I have spoken evil, bear witness of the evil: but if well, why smitest thou me?

24. Now Annas had sent him bound unto Caiaphas the high priest.

25. And Simon Peter stood and warmed himself. They said therefore unto him, Art not thou also one of his disciples? He denied it, and said, I am not.

26. One of the servants of the high priest, being his kinsman whose ear Peter cut off, saith, Did not I see thee in the garden with him?

27. Peter then denied again: and immediately the cock crew.

28. Then led they Jesus from Caiaphas unto the hall of judgment: and it was early; and they themselves went not into the judgment hall, lest they should be defiled; but that they might eat the passover.

29. Pilate then went out unto them, and said, What accusation bring ye against this man?

30. They answered and said unto him, If he were not a malefactor, we would not have delivered him up unto thee.

31. Then said Pilate unto them, Take ye him, and judge him according to your law. The Jews therefore said unto him, It is not lawful for us to put any man to death:

32. That the saying of Jesus might be fulfilled, which he spake, signifying what death he should die.

33. Then Pilate entered into the judgment hall again, and called Jesus, and said unto him, Art thou the King of the Jews?

34. Jesus answered him, Sayest thou this thing of thyself, or did others tell it thee of me?

35. Pilate answered, Am I a Jew? Thine own nation and the chief priests have delivered thee unto me: what hast thou done?

36. Jesus answered, My kingdom is not of this world: if my king-

dom were of this world, then would my servants fight, that I should not be delivered to the Jews: but now is my kingdom not from hence.

37. Pilate therefore said unto him, Art thou a king then? Jesus answered, Thou sayest that I am a king. To this end was I born, and for this cause came I into the world, that I should bear witness unto the truth. Every one that is of the truth heareth my voice.

38. Pilate saith unto him, What is truth? And when he had said this, he went out again unto the Jews, and saith unto them, I find in him no fault at all.

39. But ye have a custom, that I should release unto you one at the passover: will ye therefore that I release unto you the King of the Jews?

40. Then cried they all again, saying, Not this man, but Barabbas. Now Barabbas was a robber.

In this chapter John begins his account of the sufferings and crucifixion of our Lord. This and the following chapters present the closing days of Christ's earthly ministry. Here we pass quickly from His prayer of intercession to His trial and crucifixion.

We will find that John gives a full account of the crucifixion, recording many interesting details not given by Matthew, Mark, and Luke. However, the four Gospels, all inspired of God, give a full account of the Lord's earthly ministry when they are read in harmony with each other.

Jesus Arrives at Gethsemane

Verse 1: *"When Jesus had spoken these words, He went forth with His disciples over the brook Cedron, where was a garden, into the which He entered, and His disciples."*

"When Jesus had spoken these words . . . ." This refers to the things He had taught them in chapters 15 and 16, as well as His intercessory prayer as recorded in chapter 17. In the Old Testament economy, the office of the priest was to *teach* the people, *pray* for them, and offer their sacrifices. Jesus had been teaching, He had just prayed for His disciples (and for all believers), and He was now ready to offer the supreme sacrifice—the one sacrifice that would satisfy God's holiness and righteousness thus making it

possible for God to be just, "and the Justifier of him which believeth in Jesus" (Rom. 3:26).

"He went forth with His disciples over the brook Cedron." In the introductory remarks at the beginning of chapter 17 we considered the fact that the Scripture does not tell us *where* the intercessory prayer was offered, and I stated that it was my opinion that this took place just before Jesus and His disciples crossed over the brook Cedron. *Wherever* He was when He prayed the prayer recorded in chapter 17, when the prayer was finished our Lord and His little band of disciples *"went forth"* from that place and crossed over Cedron into the Garden of Gethsemane.

The brook Cedron is located on the east side of Jerusalem. This is the same brook called *Kidron* in the Old Testament, and the Hebrew word means literally "winter torrent." In the summer the brook was dry; and then when the fall and winter rains came, it became a *torrent.*

David crossed this same little stream when he fled from Jerusalem because of Absalom's rebellion: "And all the country wept with a loud voice, and all the people passed over: the king also himself passed over the brook Kidron, and all the people passed over, toward the way of the wilderness" (II Sam. 15:23).

It was by this same brook that *Asa* burned his mother's idol: "Concerning Maachah the mother of Asa the king, he removed her from being queen, because she had made an idol in a grove: and Asa cut down her idol, and stamped it, and burnt it at the brook Kidron" (II Chron. 15:16).

It was into the brook Kidron that *Josiah* cast the dust of the idolatrous altars he destroyed: "And the altars that were on the top of the upper chamber of Ahaz, which the kings of Judah had made, and the altars which Manasseh had made in the two courts of the house of the Lord, did the king beat down, and brake them down from thence, and cast the dust of them into the brook Kidron" (II Kings 23:12).

Some Bible scholars believe that Jesus left the city of Jerusalem by the same route over which the scapegoat was driven out annually when it was sent into the wilderness on the Day of Atonement. This would present a logical comparison, since Jesus was on His way to Calvary to make atonement through the shedding of His blood.

He went forth with His disciples, crossed the brook Cedron, *"where was a garden, into the which He entered, and His disciples."* There is no doubt in my mind that this was the Garden of Gethsemane. We do not know what *kind* of garden it was, but very likely it was a garden of olive trees, and not a garden of beautiful flowers and shrubs as we think of gardens today. I visited this place when I was in Palestine, and I found it filled with olive trees. I was told that men who know about trees declare that some of the trees there today could easily have been there when Jesus used the garden as a place of prayer. (Having seen the *trunks* of these trees, I do not doubt their declaration!) This could have been a public garden, or it could have been privately owned. Be that as it may, we do know from the Scriptures that Jesus went there often to pray.

I find it interesting that Adam's fall took place in a garden—a magnificent garden planted by the hand of God; and in that garden were all kinds of trees "pleasant to the sight, and good for food; the tree of life also in the midst of the garden, and the tree of knowledge of good and evil. And a river went out of Eden to water the garden . . ." (Gen. 2:9,10). Yet in such a garden, *Adam sinned*—and through his disobedience all men died spiritually.

But thank God, four thousand years later, *Jesus* entered a garden; and there He met a personal devil, together with all the demons of hell. *These He conquered* and put to an open shame, "blotting out the handwriting of ordinances that was against us, which was contrary to us, and took it out of the way, nailing it to His cross; *and having spoiled principalities and powers, He made a shew of them openly, triumphing over them in it"* (Col. 2:14,15).

It was in a garden that sin originated here on earth, and thus began the disease that is sure spiritual death for man; but it was also in a garden that the blood of Jesus was shed (John 19:41)—the remedy for the disease that kills and damns. For some reason known only to God, *John* completely passes over Christ's agony in the garden; but we might point out the order of things here, since they are easily compiled from Matthew, Mark, and Luke:

First, Jesus and His disciples observed the last supper. He then gave the long discourse which we find in chapters 15 and 16 of John's Gospel, a discourse which only John records. Then in chapter 17 of our present study, Jesus prayed His intercessory prayer, and when that was finished He crossed with His disciples over the brook Cedron into the Garden of Gethsemane. There He met all the forces of spiritual wickedness and darkness. He prayed in such agony that His perspiration became "as it were great drops of blood falling down to the ground" (Luke 22:44).

It was here that Judas found Him when he came with soldiers to arrest Him. We do not know how much time elapsed between the arrival of Jesus in the garden and His betrayal and arrest later that night; it could have been several hours.

Why did Jesus leave the city and go into the garden after the last supper and His subsequent discourse and prayer? I believe this was in fulfillment of an Old Testament type—that is, in accord with the teaching concerning the Day of Atonement, the animal slain for the *sin*-offering (unlike the *burnt*-offering) was burned outside the camp. (Please study Leviticus 4:12–21; 16:27). In the same manner, the Lord Jesus, offering *Himself* for sin, "suffered without the gate," as declared in Hebrews 13:12:

"Wherefore Jesus also, that He might sanctify the people with His own blood, suffered without the gate." His atoning sufferings began in the Garden of Gethsemane, and when He had eaten supper and prayed, He went to the garden instead of remaining in the city.

There is another fulfillment of Old Testament type here: Jesus crossing the brook Cedron accompanied by His disciples parallels the account in II Samuel 15 where David was betrayed by his friend, Ahithophel. In bitter tears David, with his faithful followers, crossed this same brook centuries before—and Christ Jesus, who was born of the *lineage* of David, crossed it at the very time Judas was selling Him to His enemies for the price of an ordinary slave! (Study II Samuel 15, verses 23, 30, and 31.)

The Betrayal and Arrest

Verse 2: *"And Judas, also, which betrayed Him, knew the place: for Jesus ofttimes resorted thither with His disciples."*

It was not by accident that Jesus went into the Garden, nor that Judas found Him there. Verse 4 tells us that Jesus knew "all things that should come upon Him." He knew that He would be betrayed by Judas that night and that Judas would lead the soldiers to make the arrest. He went into the garden as a general would advance on a battlefield to meet the enemy. He knew exactly how and where Judas would betray Him; so instead of waiting for Judas to arrive at the garden and search for Him, He was there ready to face Judas and the band of soldiers when they arrived to take Him.

Judas knew where to find his Master, *"for Jesus ofttimes resorted thither with His disciples."* Gethsemane was His favorite place of prayer, especially during His last days on earth, and He frequently went into the garden with His disciples to pray. Luke 21:37 tells us that "in the day time He was teaching in the temple; and at night He went out, and abode in the mount that is called the mount of Olives." I doubt not that He spent the entire night in prayer on such occasions. In Luke 22:39 we read, "And He came out, and went, *as He was wont,* to the mount of Olives; and His disciples also followed Him."

It is interesting to notice that on previous occasions Jesus had escaped out of the hands of His enemies and avoided them because His hour had not arrived. In John 8:59, we are told that they took up stones "to cast at Him: but Jesus hid Himself, and went out of the temple, going through the midst of them, and so passed by." In John 12:36 we read that He "departed, and did hide Himself from them." But when that awaited "hour" came, He went to the place where He knew Judas would lead the officers and soldiers to arrest Him.

By going into the garden that night, Jesus gave a threefold testimony:

First, *He went to His death willingly and voluntarily.* He knew when He went into the garden that Judas would come there with the soldiers to arrest Him.

In the second place, *He made it convenient for His enemies to find Him.* Judas knew that the garden was our Lord's favorite place of prayer, he knew Jesus went there often, and he felt sure he would find Him there that night.

In the third place, *we see the hardness and cruelty of the heart of Judas.* He had undoubtedly been with Jesus on many occasions when the Saviour prayed and taught His disciples in the very place where Judas led the enemies of Jesus to arrest Him.

I think most of us have a favorite place of prayer. Of course we can pray anywhere, any time, under any circumstances; but when we are particularly burdened and can spend time alone in prayer, we have a favorite place where we go to be alone with God. I see the humanity of Jesus when I read here that He "ofttimes resorted thither" to pray.

How well do I remember the first days of my Christian experience! I lived on a farm, and out in the peach orchard I found a favorite spot under one certain peach tree where I went to talk to God. It was a quiet place where I was away from the disturbance and confusion of the world around me, and somehow God seemed a little nearer when I bowed there to meet Him in prayer. I repeat—we can pray anywhere; but I believe most Christians have one special place where they find communion with God a little sweeter than in any other place. This was true with our Saviour. *Gethsemane* was the place where He "ofttimes resorted" to pray.

Verse 3: *"Judas then, having received a band of men and officers from the chief priests and Pharisees, cometh thither with lanterns and torches and weapons."*

Anyone who will study the Gospels carefully will readily see that from the time of our Lord's arrest through the crucifixion, John passes over several points that are recorded by the other three Gospel writers—for example, we immediately notice that John does not mention Judas' bargaining with the chief priests to betray the Lord for thirty pieces of silver; but since the Scriptures are verbally inspired, we know the Holy Ghost gave John the part of the record he was to pen down for our edification, exhortation, and comfort. Why John did not mention everything given by Matthew, Mark, and Luke is not for us to know.

The *"band of men"* was a detachment of Roman soldiers whom Judas led to arrest Jesus, together with some of the servants of the chief priests and Pharisees. No doubt the religious leaders bargained with Pilate for the use of his soldiers on this occasion to arrest this most unusual Prisoner whom they intended to put to death at all costs.

Some Bible scholars believe that Judas led a "cohort" of soldiers, which would have been one-tenth of a legion and therefore would have embraced between four hundred and five hundred men. This could have been possible, since Matthew tells us that Judas came into the garden with "a great multitude" (Matt. 26:47).

The *"officers"* were the Jewish servants of the priests and the Pharisees. The Roman soldiers were connected to the garrison in the city of Jerusalem. Therefore both Gentiles and Jews were in the group that went to arrest Jesus.

Undoubtedly they were afraid the friends of Jesus might attempt to rescue Him, which could have been the reason for so large a company of men. Also, on other occasions when they had attempted to arrest Him, He had always escaped out of their hands. This time, they came with *"lanterns and torches and weapons,"* indicating that they meant to search until they found Him, and that they were *determined* to take Him.

But they need not have brought their many soldiers and officers, they need not have brought their lanterns, torches, and weapons. They did not need to search for Him. He was waiting for them and He voluntarily surrendered to them because His "hour" had come. Otherwise, they could not have laid hands on Him.

Verse 4: *"Jesus therefore knowing all things that should come upon Him, went forth, and said unto them, Whom seek ye?"*

"Knowing all things that should come upon Him . . . ." The foreknowledge of Christ was perfect; there were no "surprises" in His life.

In chapter 13, verse 3 we read, "Jesus knowing that the Father had given all things into His hands, and that He was come from God, and went to God." Notice the contrast between the subjects of the knowledge of Jesus in these two verses: In the previous verse He spoke of all things *given into* His hands; here He speaks of all things coming upon Him that would take all things *from* Him, even His life. He would be "cut off" (Dan. 9:26) and have nothing. In chapter 13 verse 3 Jesus was looking *beyond* His sufferings, beyond the cross, to the glory set before Him. In our present verse He was looking *directly to Calvary.*

Jesus suffered all the anguish, pain, woe, misery, and torment that sinners would suffer throughout eternity; and His suffering was made more terrible because of His *perfect foreknowledge* of those sufferings. I believe that from the early moments of His earthly life *He knew.* He saw the scourge, the crown of thorns, the whipping post, the old rugged cross, the wickedly cruel men who plucked the beard from His face. He knew the agonizing death that awaited Him at the end of life's journey on earth, He saw it every moment. Every time He walked through the meadows and saw a shepherd with his flock He knew that HE was the Lamb who would one day be offered in sacrifice for the sin of the world. Every sacrifice in the temple reminded Him that He was *the supreme sacrifice* whose blood would one day be shed for the remission of sin.

The fact that Jesus *"went forth"* does not mean that He left the garden. He simply came from the place where He had gone to pray, alone, while the disciples (Peter, James, and John) slept. Matthew 26:46 tells us that He came from His place of prayer, awakened the disciples, and said to them, "Rise, let us be going: *behold, he is at hand that doth betray me!*" He then *"went forth"* and said to Judas and those who were with him, *"Whom seek ye?"* He did not wait for Judas to point Him out nor for the soldiers to declare that they had come to arrest Him. *He* opened the conversation, as He did on other occasions. (See chapter 4, verse 7.)

"Whom seek ye?" The Holy Spirit here emphasizes Christ's willingness to lay His life down for sinners, His readiness to go forth and die the death the sinner *should* have died—even the death of the cross. Jesus *knew* why Judas and the company of soldiers and servants were there. Nevertheless, He approached them and asked the question so that He might formally surrender to them. The hour had arrived when He would be arrested, tried, and nailed to a cross, and He willingly stepped forward to meet the enemies who had come to arrest Him.

Verse 5: ***"They answered Him, Jesus of Nazareth. Jesus saith unto them, I am He. And Judas also, which betrayed Him, stood with them."***

Undoubtedly a goodly number of these men did not know Jesus by sight, for both Matthew and Mark tell us that Judas gave them a sign: "Whomsoever I shall kiss, that same is He" (Matt. 26:48; Mark 14:44). Evidently the sign had not yet been given when Jesus asked, "Whom seek ye?" They replied, *"Jesus of Nazareth."*

What Jesus said next must have startled them all, for He clearly made the bold confession, *"I AM HE!"* The personal pronoun "He" is not in the original Greek. It reads simply, "I AM." There is no doubt in my mind that Jesus spoke thus because He knew that the chief priests and Pharisees would remember what God said when Moses asked whom he should say sent him to the children of Israel in Egypt. "And God said unto Moses . . . Thus shalt thou say unto the children of Israel, *I AM hath sent me unto you*" (Ex. 3:14). Every Jew who knew the Old Testament Scriptures would recognize that title as belonging to Jehovah God, the God of Israel. Jesus wanted the chief priests and Pharisees to know that even in this dark hour He still proclaimed Himself *one with God*—God in flesh.

"And Judas also which betrayed Him stood with them." We know from this statement that as Judas stood there he was to again witness the divine power of Jesus, and in the demonstration of that power he would once more see proof that the Master with whom he had walked for three and one-half years was more than man—yes, that He was very God.

Verse 6: *"As soon then as He had said unto them, I am He, they went backward, and fell to the ground."*

Here is recorded a tremendous miracle. When Jesus said, *"I AM,"* the multitude of armed men *"went backward, and fell to the ground!"* The Roman soldiers knew little or nothing about Jesus, they *cared* nothing about Him, and certainly they had no cause to *fear* Him. Therefore it had to be *the power of the Word* that caused them to go backward and fall to the ground.

God spoke one day—*and the world came into existence!* (He could just as easily speak a word and *destroy* this world and everything in it.) It is not hard to believe that when Jesus declared, "I AM," the power of the Word flattened a multitude of armed men. For the last time before His crucifixion, Jesus exercised the divine power He had used on so many other occasions—the same power with which He calmed the waves and stilled the mighty wind. He spoke a word and demons came out of men and women alike. He spoke a word and the sick were healed, the dead came forth from the grave. He spoke—and the blind received their sight and lepers were made whole.

I believe that in performing this miracle He showed His disciples (and His enemies) that He was *surrendering* to be crucified. He was going to *lay His life down;* He was not going to die because He was being overpowered, taken by force, and could not *prevent* His death. He was going to the cross willingly, to suffer and pay the sin-debt. When Peter drew his sword and severed an ear from the high priest's servant, Jesus said to him, "Put up again thy sword into his place: for all they that take the sword shall perish with the sword. *Thinkest thou that I cannot now pray to my Father, and He shall presently give me more than twelve legions of angels?* But how then shall the Scriptures be fulfilled, that thus it must be?" (Matt. 26:52—54).

The Scriptures do not tell us how long these men lay prostrate on the ground—it could have been but momentarily, it could have been for several minutes. I personally believe they were struck to the ground and rendered helpless long enough for Jesus and His disciples to have escaped if they had *tried* to escape; but they did not. Yet even that mob could not have taken Jesus had He not been willing to go: "When the wicked, even mine enemies and my foes, came upon me to eat up my flesh, they stumbled and fell" (Psalm 27:2).

Beloved, think of this: If Jesus demonstrated such power when He was about to be *judged,* what power *will* He demonstrate when He comes to judge His enemies? And He IS coming in judgment some day! If He had this might and power on the verge of His crucifixion, what power will He display when He comes to reign in righteousness? That will be a glorious day indeed!

Verse 7: *"Then asked He them again, Whom seek ye? And they said, Jesus of Nazareth."*

Jesus repeated His question as if He wanted to test the effect of the miraculous power He had just exhibited before His enemies, but Judas and the others were so hardened, their hearts so calloused with unbelief and hatred, that as soon as they rose from the ground they proved by their actions that in spite of the miracle they had witnessed and in spite of the terror that must have gripped them, they were not ready to repent of their ungodliness and of their determination to put Him to death! Some of them should have recognized God in action—but they did not. I say reverently and humbly that even GOD cannot help one who is willingly ignorant and willingly blind!

The enemies of Jesus were entirely at His mercy here. John 19:11 tells us that no one could have any power at all against Jesus unless God the Father permitted it. Jesus said to Pilate, *"Thou couldest have no power at all against me, except it were given thee from above."* He could have walked away from them unmolested if He had chosen to do so.

What happened in the garden left all present without excuse. They should have recognized the true identity of Jesus. These Roman soldiers might never have seen Him before that night, but they witnessed the undeniable power of God when He spoke and the power of His words laid them flat on the ground, helpless. Therefore, in the day of judgment they will be without excuse! (In connection with this please study all of Psalm 27, all of Psalm 35, and all of Psalm 40. Read these passages and study them prayerfully.)

Verse 8: *"Jesus answered, I have told you that I am He: if therefore ye seek me, let these go their way."*

Here again Jesus displayed His tender care and thoughtfulness toward His weak, perplexed, frightened disciples. Even in this trying moment, facing the horrible hours ahead, He was not thinking of Himself. He was thinking of His disciples and of their safety. I am so thankful for our High Priest who can be "touched with the feeling of our infirmities," who was "in all points tempted like as we are, yet without sin." I am so glad for our invitation to "come boldly unto the throne of grace, that we may obtain mercy, and find grace to help in time of need" (Heb. 4:15,16).

In Hebrews 2:17 we read of our High Priest, "Wherefore in all things it behoved Him to be made like unto His brethren, that He might be a merciful and faithful High Priest in things pertaining to God, to make reconciliation for the sins of the people."

The protecting power of the Lord Jesus Christ is over all of His believing children. *"The angel of the Lord encampeth round about them that fear Him, and delivereth them"* (Psalm 34:7). This protecting power explains why Peter was not arrested when he cut off the ear of the high priest's servant. It also explains why John was not arrested when he stood by the cross with the mother of Jesus. It stands to reason that as vehemently as these men hated Jesus, they also hated the men who had followed Him faithfully throughout His public ministry; but the words of Jesus literally handcuffed His enemies and prevented them from arresting the disciples.

Verse 9: *"That the saying might be fulfilled, which He spake, Of them which thou gavest me have I lost none."*

Here was fulfillment of part of Christ's intercessory prayer: "Those that thou gavest me I have kept, and none of them is lost, but the son of perdition" (ch. 17, v. 12). This verse is a parenthetical comment to explain the episode recorded here. The statement has nothing to do with the *salvation* of the disciples, but with temporal death. Not one of His disciples had been destroyed physically, and certainly He was not speaking here of eternal life.

Judas had not at this time kissed the Lord nor said, "Hail, Master!" Although John does not record it, it was probably here that Judas stepped forward and betrayed Jesus with a kiss—and then they took Him.

Verse 10: *"Then Simon Peter having a sword drew it, and smote the high priest's servant, and cut off his right ear. The servant's name was Malchus."*

Weapons of the flesh cannot win spiritual battles. Here, as on several other occasions, Peter displayed more zeal than knowledge. He was over-confident, he acted in the flesh and in haste—and believers today are still following his example! In the Garden of Gethsemane Jesus had warned the disciples to watch and pray, lest they enter into temptation; but Peter slept while the Lord prayed. Had he stayed awake during the entire garden experience I doubt that he would have behaved as he did here and when he later denied the Lord.

This is a solemn warning to present day believers. We are in the flesh regardless of how spiritual we may be, and it is only as we walk in the Spirit that we do not *fulfill* the lusts of the flesh. The only way to overcome the flesh is to submit to the Spirit and walk as He leads. Peter was very bold here, but a few hours later he was very much a coward.

There is no doubt in my mind that Peter intended to *kill* Malchus—otherwise why did he aim at his head instead of aiming at his legs or arms? Possibly Malchus was the first of the mob to lay hands on Jesus, and Peter immediately came to the defense of his Lord; but the hand of divine power deflected his sword, and instead of severing Malchus' head from his shoulders, only his *ear* was removed. Luke 22:51 tells us that Jesus touched the ear and restored it. What man on earth had ever been able to demonstrate such power? No one standing in that company witnessing this great act of mercy and miraculous power had any excuse for not knowing that Jesus was very God in flesh, and His rejection by those who witnessed His power made the men who arrested Him even *more* guilty and their sin more terrible.

Had it not been for the mighty protecting power of the Lord Jesus Christ, this incident certainly could have ended in catastrophe. Think of all the soldiers and servants who had weapons! They could have pounced upon the eleven disciples and killed them all—and they probably would have done just that had not the power of God restrained them.

Peter did wrong in resisting authority. Spiritual battles are not fought with swords, clubs, or guns. *The Christian* battles the enemies of Christ with the sword of the Spirit, which is the Word of God. Hear the words of Paul, and appropriate them to your own heart and profit by them:

"Finally, my brethren, be strong in the Lord, and in the power of His might. Put on the whole armour of God, that ye may be able to stand against the wiles of the devil. For we wrestle not against flesh and blood, but against principalities, against powers, against the rulers of the darkness of this world, against spiritual wickedness in high places.

"Wherefore take unto you the whole armour of God, that ye may be able to withstand in the evil day, and having done all, to stand. Stand therefore, having your loins girt about with truth, and having on the breastplate of righteousness; and your feet shod with the preparation of the Gospel of peace; above all, taking the shield of faith, wherewith ye shall be able to quench all the fiery darts of the wicked. And take the helmet of salvation, and the sword of the Spirit, which is the Word of God: Praying always with all prayer and supplication in the Spirit, and watching thereunto with all perseverance and supplication for all saints" (Eph. 6:10–18).

Verse 11: *"Then said Jesus unto Peter, Put up thy sword*

into the sheath: the cup which my Father hath given me, shall I not drink it?"

Jesus had just declared Himself *"I AM."* He gave the word of command, and His enemies allowed the disciples to leave the garden unharmed; but in spite of His perfect supremacy as God in flesh, He now submits to the Father's will and takes from the Father's hand the awful cup of suffering, misery, and woe. He had never entertained the thought of NOT drinking this cup to its last bitter dregs. He who was sovereign humbled Himself and became the servant. He came into the world to serve, to save, *to lay His life down that WE might have life.*

"The cup which my Father hath given me, shall I not drink it?" In other words, Jesus said, "How *can* I do anything but drink the cup my Father gave me to drink?"

We find a similar statement from Jesus in chapter 12, verse 27: "Now is my soul troubled; and what shall I say? Father, save me from this hour: *but for this cause came I unto this hour!"* When He came to the brim of the cup of such bitterness as could never be described in the language of man, should He back away? No! He would drink it. He had come to do the Father's will, and the Father's will He would do!

Three "cups" are spoken of in the Scriptures:

In Psalm 116:13 we read of *"the cup of salvation."* The Psalmist said, "I will take the cup of salvation, and call upon the name of the Lord."

In Jeremiah 16:7 we read of *"the cup of consolation."* Jeremiah wrote, "Neither shall men tear themselves for them in mourning, to comfort them for the dead; neither shall men give them the cup of consolation to drink for their father or for their mother."

Then in Psalm 11:6 we read of *the cup of tribulation:* "Upon the wicked He shall rain snares, fire and brimstone, and an horrible tempest: this shall be the portion of their cup." Also concerning the cup of tribulation we read in Jeremiah 25:15, "For thus saith the Lord God of Israel unto me: Take *the wine cup of this fury* at my hand, and cause all the nations, to whom I send thee, to drink it!" And in Psalm 75:8 we read, "For *in the hand of the Lord there is a cup, and the wine is red;* it is full of mixture; and He poureth out of the same: but the dregs thereof, all the wicked of the earth shall wring them out, and drink them."

Jesus Brought Before the High Priest

Verses 12 and 13: *"Then the band and the captain and officers of the Jews took Jesus, and bound Him, and led Him away to Annas first; for he was father in law to Caiaphas, which was the high priest that same year."*

In this and the verses that follow, John the Beloved supplies details which are omitted by Matthew, Mark, and Luke. The other three Gospels tell us that Jesus was taken before *Caiaphas,* but John alone mentions His appearing first before Annas.

They "took Jesus and bound Him, and led Him away." As *the Son of God,* Jesus exposed the wickedness of all with whom He came in contact. As *the Son of man* He presented Himself humble and meek, even before His worst enemies, men who would have torn Him apart if they could have laid their hands on Him. Here, for the first time in His earthly ministry, we see the Lord Jesus in bondage. He submitted to His enemies to be dealt with at their will —to be bound, whipped, crowned with thorns, and crucified, suffering in the sinner's place.

Can you see Him, beloved? *the Lamb of God*—He who fed the hungry, healed the sick, opened the eyes of the blind, cleansed lepers, straightened withered limbs, restored the dead to life! Can you see Him as He is arrested as a common criminal, taken by wicked hands and bound, then led away to be brutally beaten, spit upon, ridiculed and jeered by the masses, and finally nailed to a cross? It was for you and for me that the dear Lamb of God endured these horrible things. He could have called twelve legions of angels to His defense; *all heaven* would have come to His rescue—but He was the only one who could pay the sin-debt, and He paid it willingly that we, through Him, might enjoy the glory that is eternally His.

Have you ever wondered why they *bound* Jesus? It could have been because Judas warned them to *"hold Him fast"* (Matt. 26:48). (Mark tells us that Judas instructed those to whom he betrayed the Lord that they should "take Him, and lead Him away *safely*"—Mark 14:44.)

But I believe the primary reason for Jesus' being bound at the time of His arrest was in order to fulfill types and prophecies in the Old Testament. The most outstanding type of Christ in His sufferings was *Isaac,* and when Abraham took Isaac to offer him in obedience to God's command, the first thing he did after laying the wood for the fire was to *bind* Isaac and place him on the altar. Read the full account in Genesis 22:1–14.

The same was true of animals offered. They were bound with cords: "God is the Lord, which hath shewed us light: bind the sacrifice with cords, even unto the horns of the altar" (Psalm 118:27).

There was, however, still another reason why they bound the Lord when they arrested Him: All men are born in sin; all unregenerated men are captives of sin and the devil, bound by sin's ties. Jesus was bound because He took our place. *OUR sins bound Him.* As our spotless substitute, He cried out, "For innumerable evils have compassed me about: mine iniquities (*our* iniquities which He bore—I Pet. 2:24; Isa. 53:5) have taken hold upon me, so that I am not able to look up; they are more than the hairs of mine head: therefore my heart faileth me" (Psalm 40:12). (Read all of Psalm 40, which speaks of Messiah, Jehovah's Servant, obedient unto death.) The Lord Jesus Christ, spotless Lamb of God, was *bound* that we, through His binding, might be *set free!*

"And led Him away to Annas first." The most probable explanation for this is that in the days of Jesus on earth

the high priest's office was not carried out as ordained of God; it was filled with utmost irregularity and disorder.

In the Old Testament economy the high priest was ordained of God and filled the office for a lifetime (Ex. 40:15; Num. 35:25). But in the days just preceding our Lord's ministry the high priest was *elected,* sometimes for a year, sometimes for a longer period. At the end of his allotted term he was removed from office and another priest was elected. *Lightfoot* tells us that the second temple stood only four hundred and twenty years, and during that time there were three hundred different high priests.

When Jesus was on earth there were probably several men still living who had served in the office of high priest. It seems that Annas, after being retired from the office, lived in the priest's palace with his son-in-law, Caiaphas, who was high priest that year, and our present Scripture indicates that he served as an assistant and advisor. The fact that he had formerly held the office and was older than Caiaphas probably explains why Jesus was taken before Annas prior to His being sent to Caiaphas. The close relationship between these two men and the fact that both were connected with the office of high priest at the same time is confirmed in Luke 3:2, which tells us that "*Annas and Caiaphas being the high priests,* the word of God came unto John the son of Zacharias in the wilderness." Also in Acts 4:6 we read, "*Annas the high priest, and Caiaphas,* and John, and Alexander, and as many as were of the kindred of the high priest, were gathered together at Jerusalem."

We see here the inconsistency of the Jews. They were sticklers for the Law of Moses, they declared themselves *keepers* of the law; but here, in regard to the office of the high priest, they were extremely *inconsistent* with the Law of Moses. Here we see their blindness and their willing ignorance.

The Jews did not have the power to decree a death sentence. But they brought Jesus before the high priest and the Sanhedrin where they could accuse Him of heresy and blasphemy, have Him convicted, and then turn Him over to the Roman government for the death sentence to be passed.

Verse 14: *"Now Caiaphas was he, which gave counsel to the Jews, that it was expedient that one man should die for the people."*

This verse is a parenthetical explanation peculiar to John and has reference to chapter 11, verses 49–52, where Caiaphas declared, "It is expedient for us, that one man should die for the people, and that the whole nation perish not." It was Caiaphas who made the motion that Jesus be put to death—not that He might die for the sins of the world, but that one should die that the people Israel should be delivered physically, not spiritually. What Caiaphas said was out of political consideration, for the Pharisees had just declared concerning Jesus, "If we let Him thus alone, all men will believe on Him: *and the Romans shall come and take away both our place and nation*" (ch. 11, v. 48).

The Sanhedrin, the "Supreme Court" of the Jews, had already reached a verdict before Jesus was even arrested and tried. They planned to put Him to death, and they intended carrying out what they had planned. Even though He was innocent, they meant to convict Him and nail Him to a cross. The sentence to be passed upon Him was already determined before the trial.

The trial of Jesus was the greatest farce ever to take place. There was nothing legal about it, there was no justice in it. The charges were false, false witnesses were hired to testify against Him, a verdict of "Guilty!" had been reached before court opened, and a sentence of death had been determined before the Prisoner was ever arrested!

It is refreshing to my heart to see how God has used the acts of wicked men—the Napoleons, the Hitlers, the Mussolinis and others—as His axes, hammers, crosses, swords, and guns to advance His work. Even though on the surface this all seems very cruel, God makes these things work for His glory and for the advancement of His Church. In Isaiah 10:5–16 we read:

"O Assyrian, *the rod of mine anger, and the staff in their hand is mine indignation. I will send him against an hypocritical nation, and against the people of my wrath will I give him a charge, to take the spoil, and to take the prey, and to tread them down like the mire of the streets.*

"Howbeit he meaneth not so, neither doth his heart think so; but it is in his heart to destroy and cut off nations not a few. For he saith, Are not my princes altogether kings? Is not Calno as Carchemish? Is not Hamath as Arpad? Is not Samaria as Damascus? As my hand hath found the kingdoms of the idols, and whose graven images did excel them of Jerusalem and of Samaria; shall I not, as I have done unto Samaria and her idols, so do to Jerusalem and her idols?

"Wherefore it shall come to pass, that when the Lord hath performed His whole work upon mount Zion and on Jerusalem, I will punish the fruit of the stout heart of the king of Assyria, and the glory of his high looks. For he saith, By the strength of my hand I have done it, and by my wisdom; for I am prudent: and I have removed the bounds of the people, and have robbed their treasures, and I have put down the inhabitants like a valiant man: and my hand hath found as a nest the riches of the people: and as one gathereth eggs that are left, have I gathered all the earth; and there was none that moved the wing, or opened the mouth, or peeped.

"Shall the axe boast itself against him that heweth therewith? or shall the saw magnify itself against him that shaketh it? as if the rod should shake itself against them that lift it up, or as if the staff should lift up itself, as if it were no wood.

"Therefore shall the Lord, the Lord of hosts, send among His fat ones leanness; and under His glory He shall kindle a burning like the burning of a fire."

Peter's Denial

Verse 15: *"And Simon Peter followed Jesus, and so did another disciple: that disciple was known unto the high priest, and went in with Jesus into the palace of the high priest."*

John does not mention the eleven disciples' leaving when Jesus was arrested. He tells of Peter's following Jesus, but unlike other writers he does not say that Peter followed "afar off." He simply says, *"Simon Peter followed Jesus, and so did another disciple."* (The "other disciple" is believed to have been John himself. See chapter 20, verses 2, 3, 4, and 8.)

Peter was anxious to know what they were going to do with Jesus, but he lacked the courage to stay near Him as a true disciple *should* have done. There is no doubt in my mind that Peter loved our Lord; he was ashamed to run away and hide and leave Him *completely*—but he was a spiritual coward, afraid to take a stand at a time when such loyalty could cost him his life. Peter had been self-confident when he should have been humble (John 13:37); he had slept when he should have prayed (Matt. 26:40), and he lacked the courage to take a stand for his Lord. Had Peter been humble instead of boastful, had he prayed instead of sleeping, he could have had the courage to walk with his Lord into the judgment hall, and he would not have denied Him.

The "other disciple" was *"known unto the high priest, and went in with Jesus into the palace of the high priest."* How this acquaintance between the high priest and John originated we do not know; there is no suggestion of it in the Scriptures. Every devout Jew went up to the city of Jerusalem at the time of great religious feasts, and it is not impossible that the high priest came to know John in that way. Also, John was probably one of John the Baptist's disciples (refer to our discussion of chapter 1, verses 35–37), and since Jerusalem and all Judaea went out to hear John the Baptist preach, the high priest could have met the beloved disciple at one of his riverside meetings.

But *however* these two came to know each other we read that this "other disciple" went with Jesus into the high priest's palace. I personally believe John stayed just as close to the Lord Jesus as they would *allow* him to stay.

Verse 16: *"But Peter stood at the door without. Then went out that other disciple, which was known unto the high priest, and spake unto her that kept the door, and brought in Peter."*

When they arrived at the house of the high priest, *"Peter stood at the door without."* Here is a little matter in the account of the fall of Peter which Matthew, Mark, and Luke do not mention. Undoubtedly Peter was having a terrific battle as he stood there. He loved the Lord, but he was a coward, afraid to acknowledge that love. It would have been far better for Peter had he *stayed* outside the door, or if he had run away with the others; but John, evidently well known in the household of Caiaphas, *"spake unto her that kept the door,"* and Peter was allowed to come on into the house.

Verse 17: *"Then saith the damsel that kept the door unto Peter, Art not thou also one of this Man's disciples? He saith, I am not."*

It was not a Roman soldier who challenged Peter, nor was it a Jewish officer with bayonet or sword. It was a young Jewish maiden! Thus did the providence of God humble Peter and strike a divine blow to his pride and self-esteem through the weaker vessel, a woman.

Whether this girl was just curious about Peter, whether she detected from his speech that he was a Galilean, or whether his countenance testified that he was fearful, somehow she concluded that Peter was a friend of the disciple who had gone in with Jesus, and therefore he, too, must be a follower of the Nazarene.

Satan was just as shrewd and cunning when he attacked Peter as he had been in the Garden of Eden when he tempted Eve. He did not boldly declare that God had *lied* to Adam and Eve. He simply *planted a doubt in her mind* by asking her a simple question—"*Hath* God said . . . ?" The damsel who kept the door in the house of Caiaphas did not ask Peter if he were a disciple of *Christ*; she simply asked, "Art thou not also one of *this Man's* disciples?" But her question frightened Peter, and he lied outright. He declared, *"I am NOT!"*

Verse 18: *"And the servants and officers stood there, who had made a fire of coals; for it was cold: and they warmed themselves: and Peter stood with them, and warmed himself."*

This verse is introductory to Peter's second and third denials in verses 25 and 27. A fire had been kindled in the outer court, and as the officers and chief priests stood around the fire warming themselves, Peter joined their company. It did not occur to him that it is better to freeze to death for Jesus than to stay comfortable by the devil's fire.

But Peter was cold spiritually as well as physically. The believer who, like Peter, follows Christ "afar off" will soon become very chilly in his soul, and as a matter of course he who is cold spiritually will seek out fleshly stimulants for warmth and comfort. The devil will always make it convenient for a backslider to warm himself by a fire kindled by the enemies of Jesus—the world, the flesh, and the devil.

"And Peter stood with them." In verse 5 the same thing was said of the traitor Judas—he stood with those who came to arrest Jesus. Peter was now keeping company with the same enemies of the Lord. He stood among them and warmed himself, associating with the very crowd that was demanding Jesus' death.

I believe Peter truly loved the Saviour, and undoubtedly as he held his hands to the fire and felt its warmth he longed to be near Jesus. His heart condemned him for his cowardice, and even though his hands and body were growing warm from the heat of the fire, he shivered in his soul! "Even in laughter the heart is sorrowful; and the end of that mirth is heaviness. The backslider in heart shall be filled with his own ways . . ." (Prov. 14:13,14).

The Greek word here translated *"a fire of coals"* is also used in John 21:9 where Jesus was roasting fish over "a fire of coals." These are the only two places in the New Testament where that particular word is used. It is extremely interesting to me that Peter *denied* the Lord by a fire of coals and it was by a fire of coals that Jesus gave him his commission to feed His lambs and His sheep. (Read chapter 21, verses 15–17.)

Like many Christians today, Peter was "with the crowd." He attempted to hide the fact that he was a disciple of Jesus by losing himself in the crowd around the fire. He tried to be comfortable and unconcerned in the midst of the enemies of Jesus—but he could not hide the fact that he was the Lord's disciple, and *neither can YOU!* If you are truly born again, the Holy Spirit dwells in your heart, and you cannot hide that fact.

Verse 19: *"The high priest then asked Jesus of His disciples, and of His doctrine."*

Here is the first judicial examination of our Lord. The high priest inquired concerning His *disciples*—who were they, how many disciples did He have, what position did they occupy in His work and in His plans?

He then questioned Jesus concerning His *doctrine.* What was included in His creed, what did He preach, what did He ask men to believe and do in order to be His followers? He was trying to get Jesus to make some admission by which He could be charged with heresy and blasphemy before the Sanhedrin, so that He could be officially condemned to death.

Instead of bringing a charge against Jesus and then calling witnesses to *prove* that charge, the high priest proceeded after the manner of the inquisition: *he asked questions in an attempt to ensnare his Prisoner.* In the first place, he had no legal right to question Jesus. The *Romans* were in power in Jerusalem at that time, and the priest was only the religious head of Israel. In the second place, the questions were asked in sarcasm and derision. The Lord's disciples had forsaken Him and fled, and the priest knew it. What he really asked Jesus was, "Where *are* your disciples? Why did you gather these men around you in the first place? What good are they to you? They deserted you when you most needed them."

If the priest had been sincere in his inquiry about the disciples he would have called them to testify on behalf of Jesus. John the Beloved was on hand, but the high priest did not call him to testify. And the reason for inquiring into the doctrine of Jesus was to ensnare Him and have some reason to condemn Him. (They finally accused Jesus of insurrection against the Roman government and blasphemy against the religion of the Jews.)

Verse 20: *"Jesus answered him, I spake openly to the world; I ever taught in the synagogue, and in the temple, whither the Jews always resort; and in secret have I said nothing."*

Jesus did not say that He had spoken openly *before* the world, but *TO* the world. His declaration that He had spoken *openly* was a direct rebuke to the high priest and those who were conspirators against Him. *He* had spoken openly—before the Jews and to the whole world; *but they had refused Him a trial in open court.* His message was for the world, not for one little group.

"I ever taught in the synagogue and in the temple." Here Jesus defends the truth, and truth never fears the light. Truth will stand. Jesus taught and preached in the established places of worship, which proved that He was not a separatist, nor was He proselyting. He honored the

synagogue because it was God's house of prayer. He came as God's Prophet and He entered God's house where the Jews went to worship. He preached and taught there, and there was no excuse for the high priest not knowing exactly *what* He had taught and what His doctrine was.

"In secret have I said nothing." This does not mean that Jesus did not privately instruct His disciples; but when He taught them in private He was simply amplifying and explaining more fully what He had preached in public. This is the Lord's own account of His ministry; therefore we know it is true. It shows that He was a public Teacher and kept back no part of His message from any class of the people. He had said nothing privately or secretly as if He had cause to be ashamed of it. Jesus was the Light of the world. He was Truth, He was God Incarnate. He did not speak in secret, He made no attempt to hide His doctrine, and on several occasions He plainly declared His purpose for coming into the world.

No doubt many of the chief priests and religious leaders in Israel remembered the words of Jehovah God recorded in Isaiah 45:19: "I have not spoken in secret, in a dark place of the earth: I said not unto the seed of Jacob, Seek ye me in vain: I the Lord speak righteousness, I declare things that are right."

Ministers of the Gospel today should walk openly and speak openly. We, too, have nothing to hide, and we certainly need not apologize for preaching the Word of God. The Apostle Paul declared, "Therefore seeing we have this ministry, as we have received mercy, we faint not; but have renounced the hidden things of dishonesty, not walking in craftiness, nor handling the Word of God deceitfully; but by manifestation of the truth commending ourselves to every man's conscience in the sight of God" (II Cor. 4:1,2).

It is most interesting that Jesus in His answer to the priest gave a brief outline of His *doctrine*—but He did not mention His *disciples.* He was the Good Shepherd, and He was protecting His sheep. *HE*, not the disciples, had come to lay His life down. Therefore He assumed all the responsibility and was willing to bear the punishment. What the disciples had done had nothing to do with what the chief priests were about to do to HIM.

"I ever taught in the synagogue, and in the temple." It is interesting that Jesus did not refuse to go into the synagogue and temple to teach even though corruption ran rampant in the Jewish religion. Four times in the Gospel of John we read of Jesus being in Jerusalem at the religious feasts, and each time He spoke in the temple. (These occasions are recorded in chapter 2:13; 5:1; 7:14; and 10:22.)

Verse 21: *"Why askest thou me? Ask them which heard me, what I have said unto them: behold, they know what I said."*

Here Jesus rebuked the priest concerning the gross injustice that was being heaped upon Him through the line of questioning he was following. Jesus asked him whether it was either reasonable or right to ask a prisoner to incriminate himself by supplying evidence which might be used against him. In essence, Jesus asked, "Why do you, the judge, seek information from me, your prisoner? Why ask ME about my disciples and my doctrine? Why not ask the people who heard me preach and teach? Ask *them* what I have said."

Verse 22: *"And when He had thus spoken, one of the officers which stood by struck Jesus with the palm of his hand, saying, Answerest thou the high priest so?"*

The literal Greek here reads, *"gave a blow on the face."* This could be the fulfillment of Micah 5:1: "Now gather thyself in troops, O daughter of troops: he hath laid siege against us: they shall smite the Judge of Israel with a rod upon the cheek."

Jesus had been bold in His reply to the priest, but even in His boldness He had been gentle and humble. In kindness He had answered questions that really did not deserve an answer—and what did He receive in return? A cowardly blow from one of His enemies, the first blow that was struck against the sacred body of our Lord and Saviour Jesus Christ. *It was not a Roman soldier* who struck Him; it was one of the Jews, His own people.

Verse 23: *"Jesus answered him, If I have spoken evil, bear witness of the evil; but if well, why smitest thou me?"*

Jesus answered the officer calmly and with dignity as He reproved him: "If what I have said is wicked, then bear witness to the wickedness of it in a just and orderly manner. But if I have spoken truth, what cause have you to strike me?"

Here Jesus showed that His great precepts of humility, dignity, and patience are to be practiced and lived, not just taught—not by outward show, but from the heart. If we are *angry* when we return good for evil, then we are no better than hypocrites. "A soft answer turneth away wrath: but grievous words stir up anger" (Prov. 15:1). We need to be firm, but we should speak softly and with humility. Throughout the indignity of His trial Jesus displayed no hot anger, no surging of the flesh. He showed no spirit of resentment. Rather, He *pitied* the poor, ignorant Jews who were demanding the death of their Messiah. Jesus manifested perfection in all things.

Contrast the reaction of Jesus here with the reaction of the Apostle Paul when the high priest Ananias commanded *him* to be smitten. Paul said, *"GOD shall smite THEE, thou whited wall!* for sittest thou to judge me *after* the law, and commandest me to be smitten *contrary* to the law?" Then the *spirit* of Paul triumphed over the flesh. His persecutors asked, "Revilest thou God's high priest?" and Paul replied, "I wist not, brethren, that he *was* the high priest: for it is written, Thou shalt not speak evil of the ruler of thy people." (Read the entire account in Acts 23:1—5.)

Here is seen the difference between the Lord Jesus Christ who was God in flesh, and the Apostle Paul—born again, fully dedicated, a spiritual giant—but with the frailties of the flesh. On no occasion did Jesus retract one single word He had spoken on earth. He spoke truth, and He had no need to retract it.

Verse 24: *"Now Annas had sent Him bound unto Caiaphas the high priest."*

Annas sent Jesus to Caiaphas, Caiaphas in turn questioned Him, but finding no reason to condemn Him sent Him to Pilate.

Verse 25: *"And Simon Peter stood and warmed himself. They said therefore unto him, Art not thou also one of His disciples? He denied it, and said, I am not."*

As Peter stood warming himself before the fire, the light from the glowing coals shining on his face, one of the men recognized him as one of the Lord's disciples and asked, *"Art not thou also one of His disciples?"* There are times when believers bring trials, tribulations, and persecutions on themselves when they go where they should not be—and such was Peter's predicament here. The only reason for a believer keeping company with unbelievers and the enemies of the Gospel should be to witness to them and win them for Christ, not sit comfortably with them by their own fire. Peter stopped to warm himself by the devil's fire—not to witness to these people (he lacked the courage for that), but to lose himself in the crowd *and appear as one of them!* He feared what might happen to him if it was discovered that he was one who had walked with Jesus. Perhaps, from his vantage point in the courtyard, he could hear the conversation between the high priest and Jesus. Perhaps he heard the priest inquire about the disciples, and he supposed that those who had closely followed Jesus would also be arrested soon and put to death along with their Master. Therefore he flatly denied that he knew the Lord.

Verse 26: *"One of the servants of the high priest, being*

his kinsman whose ear Peter cut off, saith, Did not I see thee in the garden with Him?"

Imagine Peter's inward reaction here! He had been seen in the garden with Jesus—and by one who was a relative of Malchus, whose ear Peter had severed from his head. Surely there would be no point in further denial of his association with the Christ! Could this be the same man who only a short while before had vowed, *"If I should DIE with thee, I will not deny thee in any wise!"* Was this the man who had said, "Although *all* shall be offended, *YET WILL NOT I"*? (Read Mark 14:26—31.) But in spite of his former protestations of love and faithfulness, and in spite of the fact that he had now been pointed out by one who had actually *seen* him among the disciples of Jesus, he did not change his denial, as we shall soon see.

Verse 27: *"Peter than denied again: and immediately the cock crew."*

If someone had suggested that Peter's weakest point was his cowardice, he would have resented it bitterly—and his friends would have resented it as well. Had he not displayed great bravery only a few hours before, when in the presence of a band of armed soldiers he had struck Malchus' ear from his head? Had he not always been the spokesman for the disciple band? And had he not recklessly and vehemently avowed his devotion to the Master? Yet the devil knows the weakness of every Christian, and it is in the weak places that he attacks. Had Peter been arrested, bound, and dragged into the judgment hall along with Jesus, he might have stood true; but under the circumstances, standing alone among the *enemies* of Jesus, the devil knew exactly where to attack, and Peter vowed that he had never known Jesus.

Believers can learn many lessons from the sad experience Peter had that day. Regardless of consecration and sincere dedication, the believer is weak and helpless within himself. Just a couple of hours before Peter profanely denied the Lord, he had partaken of the last supper, he had listened to the intercessory prayer, and above all, *he had been forewarned.* Jesus had clearly told him, "Simon, Simon, behold, Satan hath desired to have you, that he may sift you as wheat: but I have prayed for thee, that thy faith fail not . . ." (Luke 22:31,32). Yet, in spite of all these things which were to his advantage, Peter turned coward and denied his Lord.

It behooves us to realize that apart from the leadership of the Holy Spirit *we are no stronger than Peter was.* It is only as we are led by the Spirit that we are more than conquerors through Jesus Christ our Lord. We also need to be careful about our prayer life. Had Peter watched and prayed as the Lord instructed him in the Garden of Gethsemane, he would have found grace and help in his time of absolute need; but instead of praying, he took a nap! While Jesus prayed in such agony as to cause His perspiration to become "as it were great drops of blood," Peter slept. And what happened to him here should warn US not to be self-confident, careless in our prayers, or keep company with the Lord's enemies.

We can also profit from Peter's cowardice. He feared the men who had arrested Jesus lest he, too, be bound, tried, and condemned along with his Lord. "The fear of man bringeth a snare: but whoso putteth his trust in the Lord shall be safe" (Prov. 29:25). *Moses* was not afraid of *Pharaoh,* but rather, "he endured, as seeing Him who is invisible" (Heb. 11:27). God has promised never to leave us nor forsake us, *"so that we may boldly say, The Lord is my helper, and I WILL NOT FEAR WHAT MAN SHALL DO UNTO ME"* (Heb. 13:5,6).

When we study the record of Matthew, Mark, and Luke, we find that Peter's third denial was much louder and more emphatic than the first two had been. Matthew tells us that when for the *second* time someone said of Peter, "This fellow was also with Jesus of Nazareth," Peter *"denied with an OATH,* I do not know the Man!" Then after awhile

Peter's speech betrayed him and another said, "Surely thou also art one of them." This time, Matthew tells us that Peter began *"to curse and to swear,* saying, I know not the Man!" Then the cock crew, "and Peter remembered the word of Jesus, which said unto him, Before the cock crow, thou shalt deny me thrice. And he went out, and wept bitterly" (Matt. 26:69–75 in part).

Mark tells us that when the little maid said to Peter, "Thou also wast with Jesus of Nazareth," he denied it: "I know not, neither understand I what thou sayest." The second time he was accused of being one of the Lord's disciples he denied it again, and then someone said to him, "Surely thou art one of them: *for thou art a Galilaean, and thy speech agreeth thereto!"* At this point, Peter *"began to curse and to swear,* saying, I know not this Man of whom ye speak." And then the cock crew—and "Peter called to mind the word that Jesus said unto him, Before the cock crow twice, thou shalt deny me thrice. *And when he thought thereon, he wept"* (Mark 14:66–72 in part).

In *Luke's* account of Peter's denial of the Lord we read that when the maiden first pointed him out as having been with Jesus, he said, "Woman, *I know Him not!"* In a little while still another pointed him out and said, "Thou art also of them," and Peter replied, "Man, *I am not!"* Then in about an hour someone else said, "Of a truth, this fellow also was with Him: for he is a Galilaean." Then we read, "And Peter said, Man, I know not what thou sayest. And immediately, while he yet spake, the cock crew. *And the Lord turned, and looked upon Peter.* And Peter remembered the word of the Lord, how He had said unto him, Before the cock crow, thou shalt deny me thrice. *And Peter went out, and wept bitterly"* (Luke 22:54–62 in part).

John the Beloved does not mention the fact that Peter *swore* when he denied his Lord, nor does he tell us that Jesus *looked* at Peter when the cock crew, nor that Peter *"went out and wept"* in bitter repentance. Evidently, when the cock crew, Peter left the hall and no one made any attempt to detain him. John simply tells us that when Peter gave his third denial, *"immediately the cock crew."*

I was reared on the farm, and I know that there is nothing unusual about a rooster crowing at night or in early morning. It is entirely possible that no one else noticed the crowing of the cock that night as Jesus stood before the high priest. Only Peter heard it, and it must have sounded like thunder in his ears because it reminded him of his sin, and of the warning Jesus had previously given him.

Beloved, as long as we remain upon this earth, as long as we dwell in these tabernacles of flesh, the fall of Peter will be a profitable example to us, teaching us how great may be the fall of an outstanding, dedicated Christian who neglects to watch and pray, who depends upon his own strength instead of leaning on the everlasting arms of Jesus and depending on the power of God. You will notice that Peter's fall is recorded in *all four* of the Gospels, though not all give each detail in exactly the same way. And how thankful we should be that not only his *fall* is recorded, but we also have the record of the tender compassion of Jesus, His mercy in restoring a man who had blasphemed and declared that he had never known Him.

I would like to point out here that from the moment Peter denied the Lord the first time until he left the court in bitter tears of repentance was only *the space of about ONE HOUR!* and that is about the extent of backsliding that any blood-washed, genuinely born again believer can endure. People who say they have been in a backslidden condition for twenty or thirty years may be sincere in *believing* themselves to be backsliders, but actually they have never been born again. When one who knows the Lord Jesus in truth, in free and full pardon for sin, one who has fed from heaven's "joy unspeakable and full of glory" permits sin to come between him and his Lord, he cannot enjoy the husks of the world for very long. The most miserable person on earth is the genuine backslider—and those who can be happy and prosperous in sin have never been truly born again.

Jesus Before Pontius Pilate

Verse 28: *"Then led they Jesus from Caiaphas unto the hall of judgment: and it was early; and they themselves went not into the judgment hall, lest they should be defiled; but that they might eat the passover."*

Much that happened between the Lord's appearing before Annas and His arraignment before Pilate is not recorded by John. Verse 24 of this chapter told us that Annas sent Him *bound* unto Caiaphas; John then records Peter's three denials, and from there we find Jesus led to the hall of judgment to come before Pilate. All that transpired when He appeared before Caiaphas is not recorded by John the Beloved. We find that account in Matthew 26:57–68; 27:1,2; and in Mark 14:53 through 15:1. Luke records it in chapter 22 of his Gospel, verses 54 through the rest of that chapter.

Jesus was tried and condemned in the most fearful perversion of justice ever known. His examination before Caiaphas was a farce. Caiaphas had already passed sentence before he *questioned* Jesus. The spotless Lamb of God, He who came into the world to seek and to save that which was lost, stood before His enemies in handcuffs—tightly bound, perhaps even in leg-irons. He who was Judge of all the earth was standing before a fallen son of Adam to *be* judged! He who was Lord of glory, King of kings, God in flesh, was treated with foulest scorn and buffeted with the most horrible insults mortal man could devise. He who was every whit holy, the great I AM, was condemned to die as an impostor and a blasphemer. He who was Truth was condemned through the testimony of liars. He who is the resurrection and the life was sentenced to die the most cruel death ever known.

In Matthew 26:59,60 we read, "Now the chief priests, and elders, and all the council, sought false witness against

Jesus, to put Him to death; but found none: Yea, though many false witnesses came, yet found they none. At last came two false witnesses."

The Sanhedrin did not have the authority to invoke the death sentence; therefore they must bring some charge against Jesus when they brought Him before Pilate. The Roman governor would ask them, "What accusation bring ye against this Man?" and they must decide what that accusation would be. So they called in false witnesses. There were *scores* who could have—and no doubt would have—testified that Jesus had healed them, fed them, comforted them. *Hundreds* could have given witness to His miracles. But these people were not called to the witness stand. The religious leaders sought *false* witnesses who would lie against Him.

Under the Mosaic economy it was necessary that *two* witnesses testify against a person before he could be condemned: "At the mouth of two witnesses, or three witnesses, shall he that is worthy of death be put to death; but at the mouth of one witness he shall not be put to death" (Deut. 17:6). Deuteronomy 19:15 declares, "One witness shall not rise up against a man for any iniquity, or for any sin, in any sin that he sinneth: at the mouth of two witnesses, or at the mouth of three witnesses, shall the matter be established."

So two witnesses were finally found to testify against Jesus. They said, "This fellow said, I am able to destroy the temple of God, and to build it in three days" (Matt. 26:61). They were referring to the statement Jesus made in John 2:19 when He said, "Destroy this temple, and in three days I will raise it up"—but He was speaking of the temple of His *body,* not the temple in Jerusalem.

Caiaphas could not understand why Jesus did not reply to the accusation brought against Him, and he finally said, "I adjure thee *by the living God,* that thou tell us whether thou be the Christ, the Son of God" (Matt. 26:63).

Caiaphas meant that he was appointed to office by the

Lord God, under whose power we all are. But he heaped judgment upon his own head by his confession that he knew the living God and that he knew the high priest was appointed by God, a God who will not be mocked, a God who is truth. Yet *knowing this,* the high priest was attempting to condemn *the Son of God* through lying witnesses!

Then Jesus spoke; as an obedient Israelite He was *compelled* to speak, it was His *duty* to speak. This was according to the law, as found in Leviticus 5:1: "And if a soul sin, and hear the voice of swearing, and is a witness, whether he hath seen or known of it; if he do not utter it, then he shall bear his iniquity." In I Kings 22:16 we read, "And the king said unto him, How many times shall I adjure thee that thou tell me nothing but that which is true in the name of the Lord?"

Jesus was "made under the law" (Gal. 4:4), therefore He answered Caiaphas. He said, "Thou hast said: nevertheless I say unto you, Hereafter shall ye see the Son of man sitting on the right hand of power, and coming in the clouds of heaven" (Matt. 26:64).

The high priest's reaction to this was unique, to say the least: *"Then the high priest rent his clothes, saying, He hath spoken blasphemy; what further need have we of witnesses?* Behold, now ye have heard His blasphemy. What think ye?" And the people replied, *"He is guilty of death!"* (Matt. 26:65,66).

In Matthew 27:1,2 we read, "When the morning was come, all the chief priests and elders of the people took counsel against Jesus to put Him to death: and when they had bound Him, they led Him away, and delivered Him to Pontius Pilate the governor." This brings us up to the account given in our present verse in this chapter, where John tells us that Jesus was led from before Caiaphas unto the hall of judgment to appear before Pilate.

We might note that it was *morning,* according to Matthew 27:1, when Jesus was led to the judgment hall to stand before Pilate. He had been arrested *at night.* Therefore we know that His enemies had stayed up all night long in order to find—*and use*—lying witnesses against Him, to have some reason by which to condemn Him when they brought Him before Pilate. Their one desire now was to speedily obtain the governor's confirmation of the death sentence and then carry it out as swiftly as possible.

The Jews *"themselves went not into the judgment hall, lest they should be defiled; but that they might eat the Passover."* It may be asked, "How could the Jews eat the Passover at a time yet future, when Jesus and His disciples had eaten the Passover the night before?" You may rest assured that Jesus ate the Passover at the right time! Why then did the chief priests and rulers of the Jews eat the Passover *the next day*? Bible scholars have given various answers to this question; they do not agree.

The Passover was instituted in the twelfth chapter of Exodus. (Read the entire chapter.) God gave Israel specific instructions what to do, and when to kill the Passover lamb. The lamb was to be without spot or blemish, a male of the first year. It was to be taken from the sheep and goats and kept in a stall separate from all other animals until the fourteenth day of "Nisan"—(April, the first month of the Jewish year). On the fourteenth day of Nisan the lamb was to be slain in the evening (Ex. 12:6).

Then, the blood of the lamb was to be put "on the two side posts and on the upper door post of the houses, wherein they shall eat it" (Ex. 12:7).

The lamb was to be eaten that same night, *roasted,* and with unleavened bread and bitter herbs (Ex. 12:8).

Nothing was to remain until morning: "Ye shall let nothing of it remain until the morning; and that which remaineth of it until the morning ye shall burn with fire. And thus shall ye eat it; with your loins girded, your shoes on your feet, and your staff in your hand; and ye shall eat it in haste: it is the Lord's passover" (Ex. 12:10,11).

The Passover lamb was a type of Christ, "the Lamb of

God, which taketh away the sin of the world" (John 1:29). The blood applied to the door was God's guarantee of protection when the death angel passed through the land of Egypt: "And the blood shall be to you for a token upon the houses where ye are: and when I see the blood, I will pass over you, and the plague shall not be upon you to destroy you, when I smite the land of Egypt" (Ex. 12:13). (Please notice: *this was the blood of the passover lamb, NOTHING ADDED*!) So the blood of Jesus is our divine guarantee of protection: ". . . *the blood of Jesus Christ His Son cleanseth us from all sin*" (I John 1:7).

"By the which will we are sanctified through the offering of the body of Jesus Christ once for all. . . For by one offering He hath perfected for ever them that are sanctified" (Heb. 10:10,14).

The application of the blood in Egypt was a divine necessity for protection from the death of the firstborn. If the blood was not applied as God instructed, the firstborn would surely die! But the eating of the Passover feast was not a condition of safety; the Israelites did not *eat the Passover feast* until *after* the death angel had passed through the land of Egypt and the firstborn in every Egyptian home was slain; but even though they had not eaten the Passover feast, they were protected. Eating the Passover feast was a duty, it was a privilege, but it was not a divine condition of safety. (Study Exodus 12:34,39.)

In Exodus 12:12,24 we read, "For I will pass through the land of Egypt this night, and will smite all the firstborn in the land of Egypt, both man and beast; and against all the gods of Egypt I will execute judgment: I am the Lord. . . . And ye shall observe this thing for an ordinance to thee and to thy sons for ever."

The details of the later observances of the Passover differed from those of the Egyptian Passover—for instance, in Deuteronomy 16:5,6 the sacrifice could not be slain in the home, but only at a central sanctuary, and the feast of unleavened bread also became known as *Passover feast.* This feast was a type of Christ, "The Bread," and it lasted seven days (Ex. 23:15). The Passover feast typified the memorial supper instituted by Jesus (Matt. 26:26–28; I Cor. 11:23–26).

Most outstanding Bible scholars of the past believe that the eating of the Passover spoken of here in John's Gospel refers *not* to the slaying of the lamb on the fourteenth day of Nisan (like the Egyptian Passover), but to the Passover feast which lasted seven days *beginning* that night. (The Jewish day began at sundown–Matt. 26:17–20.) Jesus ate the Passover with His disciples that night, and the following seven days were observed as the *Passover week.*

This is the only reasonable explanation to me. I repeat: We know Jesus observed *the right day.* He fulfilled every jot and tittle of the law and the prophets (Matt. 5:17). He was the fulfillment of all the types, feasts, holy days, and rituals in the Old Testament. Therefore He kept Jehovah's day, and the only reasonable explanation as to the actions and words of the Jews in verse 28 is that they referred to the Passover *feast* which lasted seven days, and not to the *first day* when the lamb was slain.

The judgment hall was Roman property, and for a Jew to enter Gentile property would defile him, make him ceremonially unclean, and he would not have time to be cleansed before the Passover feast. Since every devout Jew was anxious to partake of the Passover, they went no further than the entrance to the judgment hall, and Pilate came out to them. No wonder Jesus said of these people, "O Jerusalem, Jerusalem, thou that killest the prophets, and stonest them which are sent unto thee, how often would I have gathered thy children together, even as a hen gathereth her chickens under her wings, and ye would not! Behold, your house is left unto you desolate. For I say unto you, Ye shall not see me henceforth, till ye shall say, Blessed is he that cometh in the name of the Lord" (Matt. 23:37–39).

These men, though painstakingly religious, no less than fanatics in regard to the Law of Moses, were making plans to execute the vilest act ever performed on the face of this earth—and yet they were afraid they would be *defiled!* There are thousands in churches today who are extremely "sanctimonious" outwardly, but have no sanctification of heart. They say much about form, ceremony, and ordinances, but they wear the mark of hypocrisy. They are careful about performing ceremonies, but they have no scruples whatsoever of neglecting matters that are more important. They are much concerned about the proper mode of baptism or where to put the tithe—but they have no concern about living a life that is spiritual and pleasing to God. *Religion* nailed Jesus to the cross so many centuries ago, and religion would nail Him to the cross *today* should He come to earth again! But when Christ comes into the *heart,* ritualism goes out. Christ and ritualism do not abide together.

Verse 29: *"Pilate then went out unto them, and said, What accusation bring ye against this man?"*

Pilate, hearing that the chief priests and elders had brought a prisoner into the courtyard before his palace and knowing that they would not *enter* the palace lest they be defiled, went out and spoke to them.

"What accusation bring ye against this Man?" In other words, "What crime has this Man committed?" Roman law made it impossible to judge or condemn a person without first hearing the charge or accusation against him.

Pilate undoubtedly knew that it was some *outstanding* prisoner or some matter of *grave importance* that required his attention, because Luke 23:1 tells us that "the whole multitude" including the entire Sanhedrin led Jesus into the court before the palace of the Roman governor. Pilate could not have been completely ignorant about what was going on, because the chief priests had secured a cohort of Roman soldiers only the night before, and certainly this could not have been accomplished without Pilate's knowledge and permission. This would have necessitated their explaining, at least partially, their need of the soldiers.

Roman law not only demanded that accusation be stated

against the prisoner before he could be tried; it also allowed the prisoner to testify for himself: "It is not the manner of the Romans to deliver any man to die, before that he which is accused have the accusers face to face, and have licence to answer for himself concerning the crime laid against him" (Acts 25:16). Thus spoke the Apostle Paul in appealing to Caesar during one of his imprisonments. In keeping with the dignity of his position, Pilate acted honorably in demanding the nature of the charge against Jesus.

Verse 30: *"They answered and said unto him, If He were not a malefactor, we would not have delivered Him up unto thee."*

The Jews knew they had no *evidence* by which to establish a legitimate accusation against Jesus, and they had hoped that Pilate would not ask such a question, that he would simply take their word for it since they were spiritual leaders in Israel. After all, he had allowed them to use his soldiers in arresting Jesus. Therefore they replied, *"If He were not a malefactor, we would not have delivered Him up unto thee."*

In other words, "Would you accuse *us* of arresting an innocent man? We are men of righteousness, men who are at the head of the Jewish religion. Do you think WE would bring an innocent man up for judgment? We have already tried the case and judged the Prisoner guilty. We are simply asking the necessary Roman sanction that He may be crucified."

Verse 31: *"Then said Pilate unto them, Take ye Him, and judge Him according to your law. The Jews therefore said unto him, It is not lawful for us to put any man to death."*

Pilate here indicated that he wanted nothing to do with the crucifixion of Jesus. Matthew tells us that Pilate's wife had *warned* him: "When he was set down on the judgment seat, his wife sent unto him, saying, *Have thou nothing to do with that just Man:* for I have suffered many things this day in a dream because of Him" (Matt. 27:19).

"Take ye Him, and judge Him according to your law." Pilate tried to shift all the responsibility to the chief priests and the Sanhedrin. He said in essence, "You do with your Prisoner what you want to do with Him. Go ahead and condemn Him and put Him to death according to your own law, but please do not trouble me with it." The Greek word here translated "judge" means much more than our conception of judging. It means *to condemn to death,* and according to Jewish law the only capital punishment they were allowed to inflict was death by stoning. But Jesus did not come into the world to be stoned. He came to die on a cross as it was foreordained before the world began.

Pilate proved to be a pitiable and miserable character. He was a Roman governor, but he was spineless. He knew Jesus was innocent, he knew "that for *envy* they had delivered Him" (Matt. 27:18). He also knew Jesus had not had a fair trial. But in spite of these facts he did not have moral courage to set Him free. He feared the displeasure of the Jews if he acquitted their Prisoner—and "the fear of man bringeth a snare" (Prov. 29:25).

There are some men like Pilate today. Some of them occupy high places, and their first desire is to please the people regardless of what they must do or not do to please them. Many who hold responsible positions in government or in the community try to please the public instead of doing what they know to be morally and spiritually right. This was the course Pilate followed on the day they led Jesus to Calvary.

In Luke 23:2 the Jews told Pilate, "We found this fellow perverting the nation, and forbidding to give tribute to Caesar, saying that He Himself is Christ a King." This was a very serious charge in the eyes of Rome, however untrue it was.

But Pilate's reasoning told him that the Jews and members of the Sanhedrin would not condemn a man to death if that man could (or would) free them from Roman rule. Therefore the case against Jesus would be a matter of religious difference and religious prejudice, rather than a matter of a political crime.

"It is not lawful for us to put any man to death." When the Jews said this, they defeated Pilate's attempt to put the case back in their hands and withdraw from it. We have already considered the fact that under Roman law it was impossible for the Jews to impose the death penalty. Only Rome had that authority.

By the Jews' own testimony here they declared the literal fulfillment of Jacob's prophecy in Genesis 49:10: "The sceptre shall not depart from Judah, nor a lawgiver from between his feet, until Shiloh come; and unto Him shall the gathering of the people be." Here before Pilate the Jews confessed that the sceptre *had* departed from Judah and they no longer had a law-giver of their own nation. They were under the rule of a foreign power, subjects of Rome.

Verse 32: *"That the saying of Jesus might be fulfilled, which He spake, signifying what death He should die."*

In chapter 3, verse 14, Jesus had declared, "As Moses lifted up the serpent in the wilderness, even so must the Son of man be lifted up." In chapter 12, verse 32, He said, "And I, if I be lifted up from the earth, will draw all men unto me." If the Jews had had authority to put Jesus to death they would have done so, but His death would have been by stoning; and as has been mentioned previously, He was foreordained to die on the cross, "lifted up."

When the Jews said, "It is not lawful for us to put anyone to death" they fulfilled the words Jesus had spoken to His disciples earlier in His ministry: "And Jesus going up to Jerusalem took the twelve disciples apart in the way, and said unto them, Behold, we go up to Jerusalem; and the Son of man shall be betrayed unto the chief priests and unto the scribes, and they shall condemn Him to death, and shall deliver Him to the Gentiles to mock, and to scourge, and to crucify Him: and the third day He shall rise again" (Matt. 20:17–19).

The trial of Jesus before Pilate is another example of the injustice meted out to Him—first by Annas, then by Caiaphas, and now by the Roman governor. Roman law required that the prisoner and his accusers be brought face to face in order that the prisoner might have opportunity to reply to the charges brought against him (Acts 23:27–29; 25:16). But Pilate denied Jesus this privilege. He examined Him as an enemy of Caesar—but it was the Jews, not the Romans, who had accused Him. If He had really opposed the authority and rights of the emperor, why had not the Roman authorities taken the initiative in arresting Him and demanding that He be tried for treason? Only Jews testified against Jesus; there were no Gentile witnesses.

Verse 33: *"Then Pilate entered into the judgment hall again, and called Jesus, and said unto Him, Art thou the King of the Jews?"*

Pilate must have been puzzled. Jesus was not wearing purple and fine linen. He had neither the clothes nor the *manner* of a monarch. He was humble, and certainly His *garments* were quite ordinary. Yet Pilate surely knew of the triumphal entry of Jesus into the Holy City only a few days before, when thousands cheered Him as King of kings and laid their clothes in the path of the little donkey on which He rode into the city; and if he knew, he surely remembered the masses who cheered Him, even though the *leaders* of Israel hated Him and were demanding His death. Pilate had heard of the sick who were healed and the dead who were raised by this Man, and seeing Him bound, helpless and seemingly hopeless, he asked, *"Art thou the King of the Jews?"*

Each of the four Gospel writers records this question. I do not doubt that secretly Pilate knew this was no ordinary man, and evidently he thought He *might be* a king. Therefore he *examined* Jesus as a king, he *sentenced* Him as a king, and he *crucified* Him as a king, "And set up over His head His accusation written, THIS IS JESUS THE KING OF THE JEWS" (Matt. 27:37).

I think what troubled Pilate most of all was that he did not know what *kind* of kingdom Jesus was to rule over, or whether that kingdom had the power to overthrow Roman rule. His question could have embraced both curiosity and contempt.

Verse 34: *"Jesus answered him, Sayest thou this thing of thyself, or did others tell it thee of me?"*

Jesus could not answer Pilate's question with "Yes" or "No." He WAS a King, He was KING of kings; but He was not a king in opposition to Caesar. He was not a king whose plans were to overthrow Rome. If He had said, "Yes, I am a king," Pilate in his unbelief and spiritual ignorance would have thought He had come to overthrow the government of Rome. On the other hand, if He said, "No, I am *not* a king," He would have denied the truth. I do not doubt that Pilate had heard of Jesus' instructions to "render unto Caesar the things which are Caesar's, and unto God the things that are God's" (Matt. 22:21; Mark 12:17; Luke 20:25). Surely the Roman governor had heard that Jesus withdrew and hid Himself when the multitude attempted to *force* Him to become King. The case was not between Jesus and Pilate, nor between Jesus and Rome. It was between Jesus and His own people, Israel. But Pilate was the man who would have the final word. He was the one who could say, "Crucify Him," or "Set Him free." So Jesus was pressing home to Pilate his individual responsibility as governor.

Verse 35: *"Pilate answered, Am I a Jew? Thine own nation and the chief priests have delivered thee unto me: what hast thou done?"*

Pilate evaded the question Jesus had just asked him, and in the question he asked here he denied his personal interest in the case and evaded his personal responsibility. He said, "I am not a Jew and I am not concerned about the Jewish religion. Your controversy is no concern of mine. What have you *done,* anyway, that your own people brought you before me and demanded your death?"

Verse 36: *"Jesus answered, My kingdom is not of this world; if my kingdom were of this world, then would my servants fight, that I should not be delivered to the Jews: but now is my kingdom not from hence."*

Pilate had asked, "Art thou the King of the Jews?" Jesus here began to answer that question: *"My kingdom is not of this world"*—that is, "My kingdom is not like yours, nor is it like *any* earthly kingdom. My kingdom is not defended with soldiers nor any of this world's arms. My kingdom was not begun by man, it did not come of man's power, wealth, or wisdom. It had its origin in heaven. *MY kingdom rules over the hearts and wills of men;* it does not depend upon taxes, armies, or weapons; it is not a kingdom to rise up and destroy Rome. I am not on trial today because I have rebelled against Roman authority, but because my own countrymen have rejected me as their Messiah."

The kingdom of the Lord Jesus Christ can get along without the powers of this world, but the kingdoms of this world cannot long get by without the power of Christ. Whether an individual, a family, or a kingdom, the person or power that ignores Christ is sure to fall. Daniel tells us that God "ruleth in the kingdom of men, and giveth it to whomsoever He will, and setteth up over it the basest of men" (Dan. 4:17). (Read also Daniel 4:25,32 and 2:20, 21.)

Every government on earth is responsible to God, and NO government can or will prosper very long without God's blessings. It may prosper and flourish for a season, but the government that forgets God is sure to fall. *Every* government should seek to promote charity, temperance, honesty, truth, and chastity among its subjects—and Christianity is the only thing that will produce these qualities. A government that does not promote Christianity is neither wise nor good. God will honor the nation that honors Him; but when the wicked are in power, the wrath of God is sure to fall sooner or later. America has become the greatest nation on earth because our forefathers were God-fearing men. Our constitution was drawn up with the Bible as its foundation, our first leaders were God-fearing men, and we still have a few such men in high places. America is a great nation because it has at least *recognized* God down through the years.

"If my kingdom were of this world, then would my servants fight, that I should not be delivered to the Jews." If Christ's kingdom were the kind of kingdom Pilate had in mind, if He were king over an earthly domain, then His disciples would have taken up arms to prevent His being arrested and crucified.

"But NOW is my kingdom not from hence." In verse 35 Pilate said to Jesus, *"Thine own nation* and the chief priests have delivered thee unto me." These words give full proof of the guilt of Israel. Through the testimony of Pilate (who represented the power of the world at that time) it was established that Israel had rejected their King, denied their Messiah, and sold their nation into the hands of another. "My kingdom is not of this world . . . my kingdom is not from hence" was not declared by the Lord Jesus until *after* Israel had rejected Him and demanded His death.

In this dispensation, Christ's kingdom is NOT an earthly kingdom; it is now in the hearts of those who believe on Him; but there is a day coming when He will return and reign on earth, and His kingdom will be *visible.* He will sit on the throne of David to reign, and the Church will reign with Him over the whole earth. The earth will then be full of His knowledge and glory as waters now cover the sea. There *will be* peace on earth, good will toward men—but only when He comes the second time. That is the blessed hope of the Church. We are looking for that glorious appearing of the great God and our Saviour Jesus Christ who is coming to reign in righteousness, and this earth will then be one great Garden of Eden!

Verse 37: *"Pilate therefore said unto Him, Art thou a king then? Jesus answered, Thou sayest that I am a king. To this end was I born, and for this cause came I into the world, that I should bear witness unto the truth. Every one that is of the truth heareth my voice."*

Pilate did not understand this. The prisoner who stood before him was composed, quiet, poised. He talked of His kingdom, declaring that it was not of this world. He then declared that there was a day coming when He *would* be King and His servants would reign with Him. These things were beyond Pilate's understanding. In verse 33 he had asked Jesus, "Art thou the King of the JEWS?" He did not ask that same question here; he simply asked, *"Art thou a KING, then?"* which suggests that Pilate was satisfied that Jesus would not attempt to overthrow his government, and he was a bit more interested now, not quite so scornful, perhaps more *curious* than interested.

"To this end was I born, and for this cause came I into the world, that I should bear witness unto the truth." If Pilate had had an open heart and an open mind surely he would have seen and recognized the truth, and would have confessed who Jesus was; but his heart and mind were closed against the truth. Jesus linked with His kingdom the fact that He was here to bear witness to the truth—He WAS Truth, He was indeed a KING, King of the Jews and King of glory; but He has a higher title than "king." *He was God in flesh.*

He was witness to the truth, He was preaching truth to Pilate that very moment, and that truth would have set Pilate free had he only received it.

"Every one that is of the truth heareth my voice." Only those who want to know the truth CAN know it. II Peter

3:5 speaks of those who are "willingly ignorant." Every person who has a desire in his heart to know Jesus will hear the truth *about* Jesus, and that truth is the Word of God (John 17:17). We are born again through the Word, the incorruptible seed (I Pet. 1:23). Pilate was standing in the very presence of Truth, he was listening to the Witness of the truth. To Pilate Jesus spoke words of truth that would have saved his soul had he only believed them.

Verse 38: *"Pilate saith unto Him, What is truth? And when he had said this, he went out again unto the Jews, and saith unto them, I find in Him no fault at all."*

"What is truth?" The question was not sincere; it was skeptical, sneering, cold. There were many sects, philosophies, schools, and religions in that day; some were Roman, some were Egyptian, some were Grecian—and no doubt Pilate had investigated all of them! Gallio, for instance, thought Christianity was simply "a question of words and names" (Acts 18:15). Pilate was undoubtedly skeptical of any and all religions. So he asked in scorn, "What IS truth?"

"And when he had said this, he went out again unto the Jews, and saith unto them, I find in Him no fault at all." Pilate was worried, uneasy. His *wife* had warned him to have nothing to do with the trial of Jesus, his conversation with the Nazarene had been more puzzling than incriminating, and he found nothing in his examination of the Prisoner to indicate that He was worthy of imprisonment or death. Personally, I believe the words of Jesus impressed Pilate much more deeply than he would admit. I am sure he recognized the Lord as more than an ordinary man, and I am doubly sure He knew Jesus was innocent; and since he found no fault in Him, he should have released Him promptly—but he did not obey the voice of his conscience. Instead, he tried to dodge the issue by reminding the Jews of their custom of releasing one prisoner at this season, and he asked them which prisoner they wanted

him to release at the present feast.

Verse 39: *"But ye have a custom, that I should release unto you one at the Passover: will ye therefore that I release unto you the King of the Jews?"*

John does not tell us much of what happened here, but Mark records the events clearly:

"Now at that feast (Pilate) released unto them one prisoner, whomsoever they desired. And there was one named Barabbas, which lay bound with them that had made insurrection with him, who had committed murder in the insurrection. And the multitude crying aloud began to desire (Pilate) to do as he had ever done unto them. But Pilate answered them, saying, Will ye that I release unto you the King of the Jews? For he knew that the chief priests had delivered Him for envy. But the chief priests moved the people, that he should rather release Barabbas unto them. And Pilate answered and said again unto them, What will ye then that I shall do unto Him whom ye call the King of the Jews? And they cried out again, Crucify Him! Then Pilate said unto them, Why, what evil hath He done? And they cried out the more exceedingly, Crucify Him! *And so Pilate, WILLING TO CONTENT THE PEOPLE, released Barabbas unto them, and delivered Jesus, when he had scourged Him, to be crucified"* (Mark 15:6–15).

Luke also gives events that took place at this part of the trial:

"Then said Pilate to the chief priests and to the people, I find no fault in this Man. And they were the more fierce, saying, He stirreth up the people, teaching throughout all Jewry, beginning from Galilee to this place. When Pilate heard of Galilee, he asked whether the Man were a Galilaean. And as soon as he knew that He belonged unto Herod's jurisdiction, he sent Him to Herod, who himself also was at Jerusalem at that time." Under Herod's questioning Jesus answered nothing, and all the while the chief priests and scribes were accusing Him. Therefore Herod and his "men of war" mocked Jesus, put a kingly robe on Him, and sent Him back to Pilate.

This time, Pilate said to the Jews, "Ye have brought this Man unto me, as one that perverteth the people: and, behold, I having examined Him before you, have found no fault in this Man touching those things whereof ye accuse Him: No, nor yet Herod: for I sent you to him; and, lo, nothing worthy of death is done unto Him. I will therefore chastise Him, and release Him. (For of necessity he must release one unto them at the feast.) And they cried out all at once, saying, Away with this Man, and release unto us Barabbas. . . And Pilate gave sentence that it should be as they required. *And he released unto them him that for sedition and murder was cast into prison, whom they had desired; but he delivered Jesus to their will*" (Luke 23:4–25 in part).

Here we see the real Pilate—cowardly, weak, double-minded. He knew Jesus was innocent, he knew that in justice He should be set free; but if Pilate offended the Jews there could be a riot which would bring him into disfavor with Caesar—and the Jews would certainly have seen to it that Caesar knew all about it, for in chapter 19, verse 12 of our present study they said, "If thou let this Man go, thou art not Caesar's friend: whosoever maketh himself a king speaketh against Caesar!"

It is entirely possible that Pilate hoped to be able to satisfy the Jews and yet set Jesus free. He was willing to condemn an innocent Man and sentence Him to death. Then if he could get the Jews to *release* Him at the Passover in accordance with their custom, *everybody* would be happy. But if he had such a scheme, it did not work.

"Ye have a custom . . . ." When this custom began we do not know, for there is no record of its beginning in either secular or sacred history; but Pilate immediately saw an opportunity to satisfy the Jews and ease his own conscience.

Mark 15:8 suggests that as soon as Pilate came out of his palace the crowd began to cry out that he grant them the privilege of choosing a prisoner to be released, as was the custom at this time. Pilate then asked, *"Will ye therefore that I release unto you the King of the Jews?"*

Verse 40: *"Then cried they all again, saying, Not this Man, but Barabbas. Now Barabbas was a robber."*

In the Greek, "cried" means literally *SHOUTED!* When Pilate suggested that they ask him to release Jesus, the Jews became enraged and shouted out, *"Not this Man, BUT BARABBAS!"*

"Barabbas was a robber." (The Greek word used here has the meaning of *"bandit."*) Barabbas was not just an ordinary petty thief. He was a wicked, ruthless killer who forcibly took what he wanted. Luke tells us that he was a murderer.

In *Matthew's* account of the trial we learn that it was the chief priests and elders who persuaded the multitude to ask for Barabbas and destroy Jesus; it was not the decision of the common people, arrived at without the help of their leaders. It was the decision of the rulers that the people should ask for Barabbas.

Matthew tells us that "when Pilate saw that he could prevail nothing, but that rather a tumult was made, *he took water, and washed his hands before the multitude, saying, I AM INNOCENT OF THE BLOOD OF THIS JUST PERSON: SEE YE TO IT! Then answered all the people, and said, HIS BLOOD BE ON US, AND ON OUR CHILDREN*" (Matt. 27:24,25).

The Jews made their decision that day, and *ever since* they asked for a robber and murderer instead of the Son of God the Jews have been robbed, murdered by the millions, persecuted in every corner of the earth. They have suffered *as a nation* as no other people have ever suffered. Time after time they have been brought under a blood bath. This they asked for when they said, "Let the blood of Jesus be upon us, and upon our children!"

There is a prophetic note here: *"Barabbas"* means "son

of the father"—but WHAT father? Surely this must point to the day when the Jews will accept Antichrist, the devil incarnate, when he sits in the temple and announces that he is God. (Read II Thessalonians 2:1–8.) The Antichrist will be the false messiah, but the Jews, having rejected their TRUE Messiah, will accept the impostor as God and worship him accordingly. In John 5:43 Jesus told His people, "I am come in my Father's name, and ye receive me not: if another shall come in his own name, him ye will receive."

We see in the action of the Jews that day just how hard-hearted and blood-thirsty unregenerate man can be! Nothing short of the bruised body and shed blood of Jesus would satisfy the Jews. Peter reminded them of this after the Day of Pentecost when he preached his second sermon. He said, "The God of Abraham, and of Isaac, and of Jacob, the God of our fathers, hath glorified His Son Jesus; *whom ye delivered up, and denied Him in the presence of Pilate, when he was determined to let Him go. But ye denied the Holy One and the Just, and desired a murderer to be granted unto you;* and killed the Prince of life, whom God hath raised from the dead; whereof we are witnesses" (Acts 3:13–15).

CHAPTER XIX

1. Then Pilate therefore took Jesus, and scourged him.

2. And the soldiers platted a crown of thorns, and put it on his head, and they put on him a purple robe,

3. And said, Hail, King of the Jews! and they smote him with their hands.

4. Pilate therefore went forth again, and saith unto them, Behold, I bring him forth to you, that ye may know that I find no fault in him.

5. Then came Jesus forth, wearing the crown of thorns, and the purple robe. And Pilate saith unto them, Behold the man!

6. When the chief priests therefore and officers saw him, they cried out, saying, Crucify him, crucify him. Pilate saith unto them, Take ye him, and crucify him: for I find no fault in him.

7. The Jews answered him, We have a law, and by our law he ought to die, because he made himself the Son of God.

8. When Pilate therefore heard that saying, he was the more afraid;

9. And went again into the judgment hall, and saith unto Jesus, Whence art thou? But Jesus gave him no answer.

10. Then saith Pilate unto him, Speakest thou not unto me? knowest thou not that I have power to crucify thee, and have power to release thee?

11. Jesus answered, Thou couldest have no power at all against me, except it were given thee from above: therefore he that delivered me unto thee hath the greater sin.

12. And from thenceforth Pilate sought to release him: but the Jews cried out, saying, If thou let this man go, thou art not Caesar's friend: whosoever maketh himself a king speaketh against Caesar.

13. When Pilate therefore heard that saying, he brought Jesus forth, and sat down in the judgment seat in a place that is called the Pavement, but in the Hebrew, Gabbatha.

14. And it was the preparation of the passover, and about the sixth hour: and he saith unto the Jews, Behold your King!

15. But they cried out, Away with him, away with him, crucify him. Pilate saith unto them, Shall I crucify your King? The chief priests answered, We have no king but Caesar.

16. Then delivered he him therefore unto them to be crucified. And

they took Jesus, and led him away.
17. And he bearing his cross went forth into a place called the
place of a skull, which is called in the Hebrew Golgotha:
18. Where they crucified him, and two other with him, on either
side one, and Jesus in the midst.
19. And Pilate wrote a title, and put it on the cross. And the writing was, JESUS OF NAZARETH THE KING OF THE JEWS.
20. This title then read many of the Jews: for the place where Jesus was crucified was nigh to the city: and it was written in Hebrew,
and Greek, and Latin.
21. Then said the chief priests of the Jews to Pilate, Write not,
The King of the Jews; but that he said, I am King of the Jews.
22. Pilate answered, What I have written I have written.
23. Then the soldiers, when they had crucified Jesus, took his garments, and made four parts, to every soldier a part; and also his coat:
now the coat was without seam, woven from the top throughout.
24. They said therefore among themselves, Let us not rend it, but
cast lots for it, whose it shall be: that the scripture might be fulfilled, which saith, They parted my raiment among them, and for my
vesture they did cast lots. These things therefore the soldiers did.
25. Now there stood by the cross of Jesus his mother, and his mother's sister, Mary the wife of Cleophas, and Mary Magdalene.
26. When Jesus therefore saw his mother, and the disciple standing
by, whom he loved, he saith unto his mother, Woman, behold thy son!
27. Then saith he to the disciple, Behold thy mother! And from
that hour that disciple took her unto his own home.
28. After this, Jesus knowing that all things were now accomplished,
that the scripture might be fulfilled, saith, I thirst.
29. Now there was set a vessel full of vinegar: and they filled a
spunge with vinegar, and put it upon hyssop, and put it to his mouth.
30. When Jesus therefore had received the vinegar, he said, It is
finished: and he bowed his head, and gave up the ghost.
31. The Jews therefore, because it was the preparation, that the
bodies should not remain upon the cross on the sabbath day, (for that
sabbath day was an high day,) besought Pilate that their legs might
be broken, and that they might be taken away.
32. Then came the soldiers, and brake the legs of the first, and of
the other which was crucified with him.
33. But when they came to Jesus, and saw that he was dead already, they brake not his legs:
34. But one of the soldiers with a spear pierced his side, and forthwith came there out blood and water.
35. And he that saw it bare record, and his record is true: and
he knoweth that he saith true, that ye might believe.

36. For these things were done, that the scripture should be fulfilled, A bone of him shall not be broken.
37. And again another scripture saith, They shall look on him whom they pierced.
38. And after this Joseph of Arimathaea, being a disciple of Jesus, but secretly for fear of the Jews, besought Pilate that he might take away the body of Jesus: and Pilate gave him leave. He came therefore, and took the body of Jesus.
39. And there came also Nicodemus, which at the first came to Jesus by night, and brought a mixture of myrrh and aloes, about an hundred pound weight.
40. Then took they the body of Jesus, and wound it in linen clothes with the spices, as the manner of the Jews is to bury.
41. Now in the place where he was crucified there was a garden; and in the garden a new sepulchre, wherein was never man yet laid.
42. There laid they Jesus therefore because of the Jews' preparation day; for the sepulchre was nigh at hand.

Nowhere else in all of the Bible do we find such striking, vivid demonstration of God's sovereignty as in the account of Pilate's treatment of the Lord Jesus Christ. God IS sovereign, He knows the end in the beginning. He knows everything *between* the beginning and the end, and our salvation was planned and foreordained of God before the foundation of the world (I Pet. 1:18–20). But the sovereignty of God has nothing to do with the free will of man—and Pilate was assured in his own heart that Jesus was innocent of any wrongdoing. The choice he made, therefore, was his own.

John records the fact that three times after Pilate examined Jesus, cross-examined Him, and examined Him again, he confessed: "I find no fault in Him" (ch. 18, v. 38; ch. 19, vv. 4,6). Luke 23:20 tells us that Pilate was "willing to release Jesus." Verse 22 of that same chapter tells us that Pilate said to the Jews, "I have found no cause of death in Him: I will therefore chastise Him, and let Him go." Then in Acts 3:13 we read that Pilate was *"determined to let Him go."* These Scriptures prove beyond any doubt that Pilate was personally convinced that Jesus had done nothing worthy of death.

Even though it was foreordained that Jesus should die on the cross, Pilate was not a machine or a puppet. When Jesus said to him, "Every one that is of the truth heareth my voice," He was appealing to Pilate's conscience; but the Roman ruler scornfully asked, "What IS truth?"—and then left the room without giving Jesus an opportunity to answer.

Pilate's *wife*—probably the best friend he ever had—sent him a warning: "When he was set down on the judgment seat, his wife sent unto him, saying, *Have thou nothing to do with that just Man: for I have suffered many things this day in a dream because of Him*" (Matt. 27:19).

Pilate tried to side-step the issue. In John 18:31 he said to the Jews, *"Take ye Him,* and judge Him according to *your* law." Then when he found that Jesus was a Galilaean and under Herod's jurisdiction, he sent Him to Herod "who himself was at Jerusalem at that time" (Luke 23:7). Thus he attempted to shift the responsibility from himself to Herod—but Herod returned the Prisoner to Pilate! In John 18:39, Pilate sought to persuade the Jews to have Jesus released instead of Barabbas, but again his strategy failed. Poor, frustrated Pilate! He finally called for a basin of water and washed his hands in the presence of the multitudes, attempting to wash the blood of Jesus from his hands and place the blame for the crucifixion on the heads of the Jews. Jesus was crucified according to the "determinate counsel and foreknowledge of God" (Acts 2:23).

Christ Before Pilate

Verse 1: *"Then Pilate therefore took Jesus, and scourged Him."*

Our English words do not even *suggest* the terrible suffering Jesus endured just before He went to the cross. Bible history tells us that prisoners under Roman rule were scourged before they were crucified, and many times they died under the scourge, never reaching the cross.

The Roman scourge was a wicked, cruel instrument of punishment. It was made of stout leather thongs attached to a heavy handle, and at the outer end of the thongs pieces of metal or jagged bone were tied. Prisoners who were scourged were often beaten beyond recognition, each blow of the scourge biting deep into the flesh of the victim—who had been stripped and his back laid bare to the scourge. We can well understand why Isaiah said of Jesus, "He hath no form nor comeliness; and when we shall see Him, there is no beauty that we should desire Him" (Isa. 53:2)—but thank God, *"with HIS stripes WE are healed!"* (Isa. 53:5).

It has been suggested that Jesus was probably scourged even more severely than other prisoners because Pilate hoped that when the Jews saw Him *after* the scourging they would be satisfied to set Him free. The Roman governor tried to please the Jews by ill treating Jesus as much as possible, at the same time hoping to ease his own guilty conscience by not putting Jesus to death. But in spite of the terrible scourging the Jews still demanded that He be nailed to a cross.

In I Peter 2:21—25 we read, "For even hereunto were ye called: because *Christ also suffered for us,* leaving us an example, that ye should follow His steps: who did no sin, neither was guile found in His mouth: Who, when He was reviled, reviled not again; when He suffered, He threatened not; but committed Himself to Him that judgeth righteously: *Who His own self bare our sins in His own body on the tree, that we, being dead to sins, should live unto righteousness: BY WHOSE STRIPES YE WERE HEALED.* For ye were as sheep going astray; but are now returned unto the Shepherd and Bishop of your souls."

Verses 2 and 3: *"And the soldiers platted a crown of thorns, and put it on His head, and they put on Him a purple robe, and said, Hail, King of the Jews! and they smote Him with their hands."*

According to Matthew 27:27, this took place in "the common hall," a room where the Roman soldiers spent their time, always ready to do anything the governor might call upon them to do. These men were experts in the art of torturing prisoners. What they did here was done in mockery, ridicule, and contempt. Jesus had announced that He was King of the Jews, but these ungodly men did not believe Him. Therefore after they scourged Him they made sport of Him by putting a crown of thorns on His head and putting a purple robe on Him.

There are not enough words in all the languages of all the world to adequately express the horrible torture, insults, and ridicule endured at the hands of His tormentors. They *"platted a crown of thorns, and put it on His head."* I have seen the thorn bushes with their long, sharp thorns, which are very common in Palestine. When I visited there a missionary who had spent more than thirty years in that country told me that the shepherds used them to build sheepfolds. The bushes were planted close together, and as they grew they made a wall so sharp and deadly that it would be impossible for man or beast to get through the fence without being cut to ribbons on the ugly, sharp thorns. It is believed to have been this kind of thorn bush from which the Roman soldiers fashioned the crown of thorns for Jesus. Then they pushed it down on His head until the blood ran from beneath the spikes.

I believe the crown of thorns was a token, declaring that Christ's kingdom was not of this world. When He was crowned with thorns He was crowned with that which is the curse of the earth, for when God cursed the earth He said, "Thorns also and thistles shall it bring forth to thee . . ." (Gen. 3:17,18). The crown of thorns on the Saviour's head presented a striking symbol of the terrible consequences of the fall of Adam, and of the curse being laid on the head of the spotless Lamb of God, the divine Substitute for sinners.

"And they put on Him a purple robe." This, too, was

done in mockery, to show the multitudes how ridiculous was the declaration that Jesus was a King. They chose a purple robe because emperors and rulers wore "purple and fine linen." Thus the jeering, mocking soldiers heaped *double* contempt upon our Lord. Undoubtedly this was the same robe that Herod and his men had put on our Lord. In Luke 23:11 we read that after Herod had questioned Jesus, he "with his men of war set Him at nought, and mocked Him, and arrayed Him in a gorgeous robe, and sent Him again to Pilate." Purple is a brilliant color, and there is no doubt that it caused Jesus to be very conspicuous as He was led through the streets from Herod's palace to the house of Pilate and when He was brought forth from Pilate's house, where a great multitude of Jews were waiting. But beloved, Jesus wore a robe of mockery, shame, and contempt *that WE might wear the robe of righteousness,* that WE might stand before God in that great resurrection morning dressed in robes pure and white!

In his unregenerate nature, man has always hated God. Jeremiah 17:9 declares, *"The heart is deceitful above all things, and desperately wicked: who can know it?"* Under inspiration of the Holy Spirit the Apostle Paul wrote, "Because the carnal mind is enmity against God: for it is not subject to the law of God, neither indeed *can* be. So then they that are in the flesh *cannot* please God" (Rom. 8:7,8).

Then in Romans 3:10–18 Paul gives a graphic description of unregenerate man—a sickening, horrible picture of human nature without Christ:

"As it is written, There is none righteous, no, not one: there is none that understandeth, there is none that seeketh after God. They are all gone out of the way, they are together become unprofitable; there is none that doeth good, no, not one.

"Their throat is an open sepulchre; with their tongues they have used deceit; the poison of asps is under their lips: whose mouth is full of cursing and bitterness: Their feet are swift to shed blood: Destruction and misery are in their ways: and the way of peace have they not known: There is no fear of God before their eyes!"

In the scourging and mocking of Jesus, these awful facts are clearly declared. Neither before nor since has the desperate wickedness of the unregenerate heart and the vileness of sin been so plainly set forth as when Jesus was delivered into the hands of ungodly men to be crucified at the request of the Jews. Here God Almighty withdrew all divine restraint, and human depravity displayed itself as never before! The hour had come when Jesus would pay the sin-debt and purchase redemption for poor, lost sinners, the hour when Satan would bruise the heel of Jesus as declared in Genesis 3:15.

Since Jesus was making atonement for sin, then sin must be revealed in all of its hideous ugliness and deadliness. Sin is lawlessness. I John 3:4 defines sin as "transgression of the law." Pilate set aside all the *principles* of law and decency when he turned Jesus over to a lawless mob to be crucified.

Sin is iniquity, iniquity is injustice, and there was no justice in what the Roman soldiers did to Jesus. He received every blow, every curse, every pain, and all the unspeakable anguish that should have fallen on US. We, as sinners, should have received all the agony of hell—and that is exactly what our Lord and Saviour endured that you and I might be spared that awful penalty for sin!

"Hail, King of the Jews!" Hear the mocking jeers of the Roman soldiers. Undoubtedly they believed the worst of Jesus—that He was illegitimate, impostor, false prophet. They heaped upon Him all the contempt of which they were capable before they finally crucified Him between two thieves! They scourged Him with a deadly Roman scourge, they crowned Him with a crown of thorns that tore His flesh, they robed Him in royal purple and mockingly hailed Him as King!

"And they smote Him with their hands." Isaiah 50:6 prophesies concerning the scourging of Jesus, even to the

smiting mentioned here: *"I gave my back to the smiters, and my cheeks to them that plucked off the hair: I hid not my face from shame and spitting!"*

Isaiah 53:2–5 also prophesies concerning this: ". . . He hath no form nor comeliness; and when we shall see Him, there is no beauty that we should desire Him. He is despised and rejected of men; a Man of sorrows, and acquainted with grief: and we hid as it were our faces from Him; He was despised, and we esteemed Him not. Surely He hath borne our griefs, and carried our sorrows: yet we did esteem Him stricken, smitten of God, and afflicted. *But He was wounded for OUR transgressions, He was bruised for OUR iniquities: the chastisement of our peace was upon Him; and with His stripes we are healed."*

Our frail, finite minds could never in this world grasp the full significance of what the blessed Son of God, sinless and without spot, suffered in our stead when He bore the chastisement of our peace and endured the stripes by which we are healed! Unless we could realize the terrible pain, anguish, misery, and woe of an everlasting hell that burns with fire and brimstone forever, we can never fully appreciate the cross. If we are to know, even in small measure, the sufficiency of the Saviour's substitution, we must realize that our sin deserves an eternity in hell, with every excruciating pain such an eternity could heap upon us! The Lord Jesus Christ was smitten on our behalf; His smiting is our salvation. He was smitten that we might go free.

Verse 4: *"Pilate therefore went forth again, and saith unto them, Behold, I bring Him forth to you, that ye may know that I find no fault in Him."*

"Therefore" points back to what was said in verses 1 through 3. His private conversation with Jesus convinced Pilate that the Prisoner was innocent, that He had done nothing amiss, and that there was *"no fault in Him."* Three times this shrewd politician confessed the faultlessness of

the Prisoner who stood before him. It is my belief that at this stage of the trial, Pilate fully intended to return Jesus to the Jews and have nothing more to do with the case; but as the trial progressed and the threats against his own political prestige grew more pronounced, he finally granted the Jews' request and sentenced Jesus to die on the cross.

It is unusual, it seems to me, that the declaration of our Lord's innocence was not made by one of His own, but by the godless Roman ruler! Such a statement would not have been so unusual if it had come from any one of His disciples, or from one of the five thousand hungry people He had fed with loaves and fishes, or from any of those whom He had healed. But instead, it came from the man whose death sentence gave the Jews permission to crucify their Messiah, our Lord and Saviour.

If I had opportunity to make *only one statement* to all the world, I think I would incorporate the words of Pilate in my statement and shout out to the whole world, *"I find no fault in JESUS!"* He did something for me that no one else could do—*He saved my soul.* He daily does something for me that no one else can do—*He keeps me* moment by moment. And not only did He redeem me from the *penalty* of sin—He saved me from the *power* of sin. He will, in the future, do something else for me that no one else can do—He is preparing a place for me, and He will come again to receive me unto Himself and will give me a glorified body just like His own glorious resurrection body (John 14:1–6; I John 3:1–3). Then I will be freed from the very *presence* of sin. Yes, it would give me a peculiar thrill to have opportunity to shout to the whole world, "I FIND NO FAULT IN JESUS!"

We need no Scriptures to *prove* the innocence and sinlessness of Jesus; as the Son of God, God Incarnate, He could not have been otherwise—but I would like for us to look at seven passages that *declare* His sinlessness and His perfection, even though we do not need proof of His divine character:

Matthew 27:4: After Judas realized what he had done, he cried out, *"I have sinned in that I have betrayed the innocent blood!"*

John 18:38: Pilate said to the Jews, *"I find in Him no fault at all."*

John 19:4: Pilate again declared to the Jews, "I bring Him forth to you, that ye may know that *I find no fault in Him."*

John 19:6: When the Jews continued to cry out, "Crucify Him!" Pilate said to them, "Take ye Him, and crucify Him: *for I find no fault in Him!"*

Luke 23:14,15: Pilate said to the Jews, "I, having examined Him before you, *have found no fault in this Man* touching those things whereof ye accuse Him: *No, nor yet Herod: for I sent you to him; and, lo, nothing worthy of death is done unto Him."*

Luke 23:41: From the cross the penitent thief cried out to his fellow criminal, dying on the opposite cross, "We receive the due reward of our deeds: *but this Man hath done nothing amiss!"*

Matthew 27:54: "Now when the centurion, and they that were with him, watching Jesus, saw the earthquake, and those things that were done, they feared greatly, saying, *Truly, this was THE SON OF GOD!"*

Verse 5: *"Then came Jesus forth, wearing the crown of thorns, and the purple robe. And Pilate saith unto them, Behold the Man!"*

The Greek word translated "forth" in this and the preceding verse literally means "outside, or without." It is the same Greek word used in Matthew 12:46 where we read, "While He yet talked to the people, behold His mother and His brethren stood *without,* desiring to speak with Him." It is the same Greek word used in Revelation 22:14,15: "Blessed are they that do His commandments, that they may have right to the tree of life, and may enter in through the gates into the city. For *without* are dogs, and sorcerers, and whoremongers, and murderers, and idolaters, and whosoever loveth and maketh a lie."

"Then came Jesus forth, wearing the crown of thorns, and the purple robe." Can you see Him as He stands there, meekly submitting to His enemies, a gazing-stock, an object of scorn? Wearing a purple robe of mockery, His back bleeding from the merciless scourging, and blood running down His face from the thorns that pierced His brow, the Lord of heaven and earth, the matchless King of glory, faced that howling, taunting mob—and He did it for US. "For ye know the grace of our Lord Jesus Christ, that, though He was rich, yet for your sakes He became poor, that ye through His poverty might be rich" (II Cor. 8:9).

"And Pilate saith unto them, BEHOLD THE MAN!" Some Bible scholars suggest that Pilate spoke these words in contempt—that is, "Behold the Man whom you accuse of making Himself a king! See what a helpless, contemptible creature He is?" Others suggest that he spoke from a heart of pity, as if to say to the Jews, "Look upon this poor, bleeding, defenseless Man whom you want me to crucify! Has He not been punished enough? Why can't you be satisfied with what I have done to Him?"

I am inclined to believe that Pilate spoke out of pity, being fully convinced of the Lord's innocence and seeking some way to avoid giving Him the death penalty. But he lacked the courage of his convictions; he was too much a coward and too fearful of losing favor with the Jews and with other Roman rulers.

Verse 6: *"When the chief priests therefore and officers saw Him, they cried out, saying, Crucify Him, crucify Him. Pilate saith unto them, Take ye Him, and crucify Him: for I find no fault in Him."*

Poor Pilate! The Jews would be satisfied with nothing less than seeing Jesus crucified. They beheld the Man who stood before them—a pitiful sight—but it did not touch their hearts. They were beyond feeling anything but hatred for

Him.

"They cried out, Crucify Him! Crucify Him!" You will notice it was the *chief priests* who led the cry demanding Christ's crucifixion, and the officers joined them, crying out for His blood—and of course the multitude followed the leaders. It was "religion" that nailed Jesus to the cross nearly two thousand years ago, and religion would nail Him to the cross today if He came into the world preaching the same message He preached then! The strongest enemies of Christianity today are the religious leaders in high places who deny the fundamentals of the faith and the verbal inspiration of the Scriptures.

"Take ye Him and crucify Him, for I find no fault in Him." In other words, Pilate said to the Jews, "If you want this innocent Person crucified, *you* take Him and nail Him to a cross!"

I sense here that Pilate felt disgust for the crowd who stood before him. He recognized their lawlessness, he knew they had no legitimate reason for crucifying Jesus, and "he knew that for envy they had delivered Him" (Matt. 27:18). (Mark 15:10 says that Pilate knew the *chief priests* had delivered Jesus for envy.) The Jews had already confessed that *they* could not lawfully put Jesus to death (John 18:31), and even though the Roman governor had examined and cross-examined Him and three times confessed that he found no fault in Him, the Jews continued to demand that he sentence Jesus to death—by *crucifixion.*

Verse 7: *"The Jews answered him, We have a law, and by our law He ought to die, because He made Himself the Son of God."*

The *political* accusation brought against Jesus had failed, so the chief priests now brought a *new* accusation against Him. He had done nothing against the Roman government, and Pilate refused to condemn Him on any political score; therefore the Jews accused Jesus of blasphemy. They said He had committed an offense against their law. They seemingly ignored Pilate's suggestion that *they* take Jesus and crucify Him, and since the Roman governor had refused to condemn the Prisoner as a political offender and an enemy of Rome, they now charged Him with blasphemy against God and against Jewish law. They said, *"He made Himself the Son of God"*—and according to Jewish law that made Him a blasphemer. Blasphemy was punishable by death.

When the Jews referred to their "law" they were probably thinking of Leviticus 24:16: "He that blasphemeth the name of the Lord, he shall surely be put to death, and all the congregation shall certainly stone him: as well the stranger, as he that is born in the land, when he blasphemeth the name of the Lord, shall be put to death." The Jews were demanding that Pilate put Jesus to death because He had *blasphemed their "law,"* and yet they did not themselves respect their law; for under Jewish law death was to be by *stoning*, but you will notice they did not ask that Jesus be stoned. They demanded that He be *crucified.* They were hypocrites here, just as they had been throughout the mock trial and condemnation of the Lord Jesus Christ.

The Jews brought *seven accusations* against the Lord Jesus Christ:

They accused Him of threatening *to destroy their temple:* "At the last came two false witnesses, and said, This fellow said, I am able to destroy the temple of God, and to build it in three days" (Matt. 26:60,61).

They accused Him of *being a malefactor:* "Pilate then went out unto them, and said, What accusation bring ye against this Man? They answered and said unto him, If He were not a malefactor, we would not have delivered Him up unto thee" (John 18:29,30).

They said *He perverted the nation:* "And they began to accuse Him, saying, We found this fellow perverting the nation . . ." (Luke 23:2).

They said He *opposed paying tribute to Caesar:* "We

found this fellow . . . forbidding to give tribute to Caesar, saying that He Himself is Christ a King" (Luke 23:2).

They accused Him of *stirring up the people*—which would, of course, bring about an uprising against Rome: "He stirreth up the people, teaching throughout all Jewry, beginning from Galilee to this place" (Luke 23:5).

They accused Him of *making Himself king:* "We found this fellow . . . saying that He Himself is Christ a King" (Luke 23:2).

They said He *made Himself the Son of God:* "Pilate saith unto them, Take ye Him, and crucify Him: for I find no fault in Him. The Jews answered him, We have a law, and by our law He ought to die, because He made Himself the Son of God" (John 19:6,7).

Verses 8 and 9: *"When Pilate therefore heard that saying, he was the more afraid; and went again into the judgment hall, and saith unto Jesus, Whence art thou? But Jesus gave him no answer."*

"When Pilate therefore heard that saying, he was the more afraid." There are various interpretations of Pilate's fear. Some suggest that he feared the Jews; others suggest that he was fearful of being unable to save Jesus from crucifixion. Still others believe that he was afraid of making the wrong decision—either by crucifying Jesus or by allowing Him to go free. I personally believe this statement emphasizes *"therefore,"* hence pointing back to the previous verse where the Jews declared, "He made Himself the *Son of God."* I believe this is what alarmed Pilate. That he was *"the MORE afraid"* indicates that he did not fear *at this moment only,* but that he had been afraid before this moment and now became even *more* afraid.

I believe Pilate was convinced from the beginning that Jesus was no ordinary man; I think he had fear in his heart, and as he learned more and more about the Prisoner, his fear gained in intensity. There can be no doubt that Pilate had seen *many* criminals condemned and put to death—

some guilty, some innocent and falsely accused; but he had never questioned another prisoner like *this Man.* Also, I doubt not that the solemn warning Pilate had received from his wife (Matt. 27:19) had impressed him deeply, and now the Jews were telling him that this unusual Person called Himself *"the Son of GOD."* No wonder Pilate was *"the more afraid!"*

"Whence art thou?" It is significant and noteworthy that Pilate did not ask, *"Whom* art thou?" Nor did he ask, *"Art thou* the Son of God?" He asked, *"WHENCE art thou?"* and it is evident that Pilate did not have the *human origin* of Jesus in mind. He had already sent Him to Herod as a Galilaean (Luke 23:5–7), and certainly he had heard of the miracles and works our Lord had done "throughout all Jewry." I am persuaded that his question was not asked of curiosity, but rather because he was "more afraid." He was perplexed and troubled; he simply could not understand all that was going on here. Perhaps he asked himself, "What if this Man IS from above? What if He IS a divine creature?" And with these questions turning over in his mind, Pilate led Jesus again into the judgment hall—undoubtedly hoping He might reveal something about Himself that would make it possible for the governor to take a definite stand and deliver Him out of the hands of the murderous mob waiting outside the palace. So he asked Him in private, "Whence art thou?"

"BUT JESUS GAVE HIM NO ANSWER!" Jesus had answered Pilate previously. This was the sixth question the governor had asked Him. In chapter 18 verse 33 he had asked, *"Art thou the King of the Jews?"* In chapter 18 verse 35 he had asked, *"Am I a Jew?"* and *"What hast thou done?"* In chapter 18 verse 37 he asked, *"Art thou a king then?"* and in chapter 18 verse 38 he asked, *"What is truth?"* To all of these questions Jesus gave an answer; but now when Pilate asks, "Whence art thou?" *He gave him no answer.*

The Lord's silence at this point proves that Pilate's question did not deserve an answer. He did not desire to know this for the sake of his own soul. If he had been sincere, desiring to know Jesus as his own personal Saviour, he would have received an answer, for Jesus never closed the door of salvation to anyone at any time. To me, His silence testified that He knew Pilate was seeking a way out of his dilemma, rather than seeking the way of salvation. He had already declared the Prisoner innocent, he had repeatedly declared that he found no fault in Him, and he had deliberately ignored the warning from his wife that he should have nothing to do with "that just Man." He had also asked "What is truth?"—but he had not waited for an answer. He had pushed aside his own conscience and ordered Jesus to be scourged, allowing Him to be humiliated and cruelly mistreated. Why then should Jesus tell him from whence He had come? Pilate's actions up to this point had forfeited any right to further revelation concerning this most unusual Prisoner. "He, that being often reproved hardeneth his neck, shall suddenly be destroyed, and that without remedy" (Prov. 29:1).

Verse 10: *"Then saith Pilate unto Him, Speakest thou not unto me? Knowest thou not that I have power to crucify thee, and have power to release thee?"*

Pilate was accustomed to prisoners falling down before him and begging, willing to do anything to receive his favor. The silence of this Man was a new experience for him, and he was both angered and surprised.

"Knowest thou not that I have power to crucify thee, and have power to release thee?" The Greek word here translated "power" could be rendered "authority or commission." Pilate boasted of his *power*—but he was cowardly, afraid of Caesar, afraid of the Jews, afraid to resist popular opinion. He wanted to please the Jews, he wanted to please Caesar, and at the same time he wanted to soothe his own conscience and shift responsibility for the crucifixion of Jesus. He *had* power to release Jesus, but he was

afraid to *exercise* that power. He was, however, trying to impress upon the Prisoner the idea that it was foolish to refuse to answer his questions.

Verse 11: *"Jesus answered, Thou couldest have no power at all against me except it were given thee from above: therefore he that delivered me unto thee hath the greater sin."*

Jesus could have paralyzed Pilate's tongue when he spoke those arrogant, haughty words in verse 10. He could have stopped his wicked heart from beating, thus plunging him into hell that very moment; but He used none of His divine powers against him. He calmly replied, *"Thou couldest have no power AT ALL against me, except it were given thee FROM ABOVE."*

In His reply, Jesus glorified the Father's name, rebuked Pilate, and at the same time gave official testimony of His own identity and His relationship to God the Father. He acknowledged Pilate's power—but not in the way Pilate expected it to be acknowledged. Jesus referred to power that comes from above, power that is limited according to God's pleasure and not according to man's desire.

In other words, whatever Pilate did to Jesus would be permitted by the power of Almighty God, for He alone is absolute and sovereign. Pilate would be less apt to understand this power, and thus less guilty than the Jews who knew that all power is from God. In Deuteronomy 32:39–42 God declared: "See now that I, even I, am He, and there is no god with me: I kill, and I make alive; I wound, and I heal: neither is there any that can deliver out of my hand. For I lift up my hand to heaven, and say, I live for ever. If I whet my glittering sword, and mine hand take hold on judgment; I will render vengeance to mine enemies, and will reward them that hate me. I will make mine arrows drunk with blood, and my sword shall devour flesh; and that with the blood of the slain and of the captives, from the beginning of revenges upon the enemy."

Pilate and the Jews were but instruments in the hands of Almighty God, and His power could have annihilated them in a split second; but since it was foreordained before the foundation of the world that the spotless, sinless Lamb of God would pay the price and purchase redemption for sinners, God allowed the Jews and Pilate to have their way with Jesus at the time appointed in His eternal plan.

Jesus acknowledged Pilate's authority just as He recognized the civil courts in His day. He respected the law, even to the very end of His earthly life. He did not deny the power of Rome over the Jews, but He *did* insist that even *that* power came from above.

Under inspiration the Apostle Paul wrote, "Let every soul be subject unto the higher powers. For there IS no power but of God: the powers that be are *ordained* of God" (Rom. 13:1); and in Proverbs 8:15,16 we read, "By me kings reign, and princes decree justice. By me princes rule, and nobles, even all the judges of the earth."

"He that delivered me unto thee hath the greater sin." In Luke 22:22 Jesus said, "Truly the Son of man goeth, as it was determined: but *woe unto that man by whom He is betrayed!"* God's foreordained counsels (I Pet. 1:18–20) do not abolish the sin and guilt of men who *execute* His counsel. This fact is plainly revealed in the passage just given from Luke.

In Romans 9:17–24 we read: "For the Scripture saith unto Pharaoh, Even for this same purpose have I raised thee up, that I might shew my power in thee, and that my name might be declared throughout all the earth. Therefore hath He mercy on whom He will have mercy, and whom He will He hardeneth. Thou wilt say then unto me, Why doth He yet find fault? For who hath resisted His will? Nay but, O man, who art thou that repliest against God? Shall the thing formed say to Him that formed it, Why hast thou made me thus? Hath not the potter power over the clay, of the same lump to make one vessel unto honour, and another unto dishonour? What if God, willing to shew His wrath, and to make His power known, endured with much longsuffering the vessels of wrath fitted to destruction: and that He might make known the riches of His glory on the vessels of mercy, which He had afore prepared unto glory, even us, whom He hath called, not of the Jews only, but also of the Gentiles?"

Jesus meekly bowed to Pilate's authority—at the same time declaring that such authority was permitted only by Jehovah God. In the statement He made here, however, He declared Himself the Judge of men as He apportioned and compared the guilt of the Roman governor and the guilt of the Jews who had *delivered* Him to Pilate. In this, He maintained His divinity and His divine dignity to the end.

Jesus clearly taught here the degrees of sin and guilt. Yes, there will be degrees of punishment in the lake of fire. God's Word plainly declares, "That servant, which knew his Lord's will, and prepared not himself, neither did according to His will, shall be beaten with many stripes. But he that knew not, and did commit things worthy of stripes, shall be beaten with few stripes. For unto whomsoever much is given, of him shall be much required: and to whom men have committed much, of him they will ask the more" (Luke 12:47,48).

Verse 11 records the last words Jesus spoke during His mock trial. From here to the cross, He fulfilled the prophecy of Isaiah 53:7: ". . . He is brought as a lamb to the slaughter, *and as a sheep before her shearers is dumb, so He openeth not His mouth.*"

Verse 12: *"And from thenceforth Pilate sought to release Him: but the Jews cried out, saying, If thou let this Man go, thou art not Caesar's friend: whosoever maketh himself a king speaketh against Caesar."*

Throughout the trial Pilate had displayed no desire to put Jesus to death, but *now* he puts forth a *stronger* effort to save Him from the cross. *"From thenceforth Pilate sought to release Him.*" Evidently Pilate left Jesus in the judgment hall and returned to the mob of Jews outside, to plead with them to let him release Jesus; but the Holy Spirit did not see fit to give us the words he spoke at that time. He must have made a very earnest appeal to them, for this time their demand for the crucifixion of Jesus carried a *threat* against Pilate himself: *"If thou let this Man go, thou art not Caesar's friend!"*

Poor Pilate! What the Jews said to him amounted to this: "It matters not your *personal* feelings toward this Man Jesus, it matters not your personal feelings about US—but you had better consider the feelings of the *emperor!* This Man has declared that He is a King, and any person who claims to be a king is speaking against Caesar. Therefore, if you let Him go free, you are not Caesar's friend—and you know what that would mean to your political standing."

Yes, Pilate knew what Caesar's displeasure would mean to him as governor. It was by Caesar that he had been appointed, and while he knew the Jews had neither love nor respect for Caesar, he also knew that they would waste no time in sending word to Rome that the governor had neglected the best interest of the emperor—and Pilate would be in great trouble, trouble that would put an end to his political career.

Verse 13: *"When Pilate therefore heard that saying, he brought Jesus forth, and sat down in the judgment seat in a place that is called the Pavement, but in the Hebrew, Gabbatha."*

When Caesar was brought into the picture, Pilate knew he must give way to the demands of the Jews and condemn his innocent Prisoner to death. If he allowed Jesus to go free, the emperor would be notified that his governor had released a Prisoner who claimed kingship, and such action could be considered treason against the Roman government if Caesar chose to interpret it in that light. So Pilate brought his Prisoner out, and then took his place *"in the judgment seat in a place that is called the Pavement, but in the Hebrew, Gabbatha."* This was outside the palace in the courtyard, in the paved area adjacent to the palace. Bible antiquity tells us that "the judgment seat" in the Roman provinces in that day was the place where justice was administered. It was in the open air, and the judge sat on a tribunal on raised ground which was covered with marble. What John means is that the *same* place which in Greek was called *"Pavement"* was called in the Hebrew *"Gabbatha."* (The Greek word *"Pavement"* means *marble,* and the Hebrew word *"Gabbatha"* means *a raised place;* thus from the two words we have the form and material of the place of the judgment seat.)

Pilate had failed in his efforts to deliver Jesus. He would no longer oppose the Jews, because that would entail self-sacrifice. Poor, spineless Pilate! One of the greatest cowards of all history, he took his seat publicly on the judgment seat and pronounced the sentence of death by crucifixion, the sentence that would nail the Son of God to a Roman cross.

The Final Rejection

Verse 14: *"And it was the preparation of the Passover, and about the sixth hour: and he saith unto the Jews, Behold your King!"*

"The preparation of the Passover" does not mean that this was the hour for preparing *the Passover meal.* This was the day *preceding* the great Sabbath of the *Passover week,* and it was known among the Jews as "the preparation," the day when they prepared for the Passover Sabbath, which was a "high day" (v. 31).

The *time* stated in this verse—(*"about the sixth hour"*)—has confused many people. It has been suggested that there is a conflict between this statement and that in Mark

15:25 where we read, "It was the *third* hour, and they crucified Him." However, there IS no discrepancy between these two statements: *Mark* spoke of the hour when Jesus was literally *nailed to the cross;* John was speaking not of the time of day but of the preparation of the *Passover.* The meaning is, "It was the preparation of the Passover, and about the sixth hour after the preparation began."

Why is such minute detail recorded concerning the hour of preparation and the hour of crucifixion? I believe the Holy Spirit gave us this record in order that we might compare the two. For six hours the Jews had been working untiringly in preparation for the approaching Sabbath—and during the *next* six hours Jesus finished His great work, the work which will bring the people Israel into that eternal rest of which the Sabbath is a picture (Heb. 4:9).

"Behold your King!" Words of mockery, no doubt; but they were words of truth because Jesus *was* their King. How sad that they did not recognize Him!

Verse 15: *"But they cried out, Away with Him! Away with Him! Crucify Him! Pilate saith unto them, Shall I crucify your King? The chief priests answered, We have no king but Caesar!"*

Because of God's *great love,* the death of Jesus was decreed before the foundation of the world was laid; and now, because of such *great hatred,* sinners were demanding His death!

Two prophecies were fulfilled here:

Isaiah 49:7: "Thus saith the Lord, the Redeemer of Israel, and His Holy One, to Him whom man despiseth, to Him whom the nation abhorreth, to a servant of rulers, Kings shall see and arise, princes also shall worship, because of the Lord that is faithful, and the Holy One of Israel, and He shall choose thee."

Isaiah 53:3: "He is despised and rejected of men; a man of sorrows, and acquainted with grief: and we hid as it were our faces from Him; He was despised, and we esteemed Him not."

"Pilate saith unto them, *Shall I crucify your King?*" Whether this question was asked in mockery or in compassion I do not know, but it was the last time Pilate gave the Jews opportunity to release—or crucify—their Messiah, and their reply brought shame upon the Jewish nation for centuries to come:

"The chief priests answered, WE HAVE NO KING BUT CAESAR!" What shame, that the people Israel should cry out, "No king but *Caesar.*" And they have been under that verdict since that hour. Since the hour when they crucified their King and released Barabbas, Israel has been "without a king, and without a prince, and without a sacrifice . . ." (Hos. 3:4).

Verse 16: *"Then delivered he Him therefore unto them to be crucified. And they took Jesus, and led Him away."*

Here is recorded the conclusion of the most unjust, most cruel trial ever held! Acts 8:33 tells us, "In His humiliation His judgment was taken away: and who shall declare His generation? for His life is taken from the earth."

"And Pilate gave sentence that it should be as they required" (Luke 23:24). Pilate formally surrendered Jesus to the chief priests and the religious leaders and gave permission to put Him to death by crucifixion.

The word *"delivered"* is very important here, because Jesus was delivered *for our offences:* "He that spared not His own Son, but delivered Him up for us all, how shall He not with Him also freely give us all things?" (Rom. 8:32). He was "delivered for our offences, and was raised again for our justification" (Rom. 4:25). Christ was delivered to death, that all who believe in His shed blood may be delivered from eternal death and set free from the condemnation of sin. He took our place.

"And they took Jesus and led Him away." There was no delay between the condemnation and the crucifixion of Jesus; He went directly from judgment to execution. I do

not believe the chief priests themselves actually laid hands on Him and led Him away, but they were the responsible persons and agents in having Jesus crucified. Judgment was no sooner pronounced, than with all possible haste the prosecutors set about to execute the sentence. Possibly they were afraid Pilate might change his mind or that there might be an uproar among the common people. They had had a hard time getting the decision they wanted from Pilate, and they did not mean to take a chance on having that decision reversed or set aside.

Verse 17: *"And He bearing His cross went forth into a place called the place of a skull, which is called in the Hebrew Golgotha."*

The enemies of Jesus lost no time in carrying out the sentence of crucifixion. They took Him immediately from judgment to Golgotha.

Every detail of the sufferings of Jesus was set forth in some prophecy or type. For instance, in Leviticus 16:27 we read, "And the bullock for the sin-offering, and the goat for the sin-offering, whose blood was brought in to make atonement in the holy place, shall one carry forth without the camp; and they shall burn in the fire their skins, and their flesh, and their dung."

Jesus bearing His cross and going forth was beautifully foreshadowed in Genesis 22:6 when Abraham took the wood for the burnt-offering "and laid it upon Isaac his son; and he took the fire in his hand, and a knife; and they went both of them together."

Jesus going forth out of Jerusalem exemplified Paul's teaching in Hebrews 13:12,13: "Wherefore Jesus also, that He might sanctify the people with His own blood, suffered without the gate. Let us go forth therefore unto Him without the camp, bearing His reproach."

At this point in our Lord's last hours before His death, the other Gospels supply details not given by John. In Matthew 27:32 we are told that "as they came out, they found a man of Cyrene, Simon by name: him they compelled to bear His cross." The fact that this man was *compelled* to carry the cross indicates that there was not one person in all the multitude who had compassion for Jesus—even those who had claimed to be His friends lacked the courage to volunteer to carry His cross.

They *"went forth into a place called the place of a skull, which is called in the Hebrew Golgotha."* The expression "in the Hebrew" is used in verse 13 of this chapter in connection with the crucifixion of Jesus, and the same term is used in John 5:2 where by the pool of Bethesda Jesus in mercy healed a man who had been paralyzed for many years. In contrast, at Golgotha we see the brutality of His enemies. At Bethesda He had shown mercy, compassion, and tenderness; but at Golgotha His enemies had *NO mercy, NO compassion.* They delighted in the cruelty heaped upon Him.

Verse 18: *"Where they crucified Him, and two other with Him, on either side one, and Jesus in the midst."*

This verse records the fulfillment of at least two Old Testament prophecies:

First of all, it fulfills the declaration of *the manner* in which our Lord was to die. A thousand years before Jesus went to Calvary, the Psalmist declared, "Dogs have compassed me: the assembly of the wicked have inclosed me: they pierced my hands and my feet" (Psalm 22:16). This particular fulfillment of prophecy is indeed noteworthy. It was the custom of the Jews to put people to death by *stoning,* not by crucifixion. Pilate could have instructed them to stone Jesus, but *not one word* of God's prophecy could fail—not even prophecy concerning the death of His Son for the remission of sin. Therefore Pilate released Jesus to the Jews to be put to death by crucifixion, the Roman method of execution; and even under Roman rule it was used for only the vilest, most hardened criminals.

The second prophecy fulfilled here was declared in Isaiah

53:12: "Therefore will I divide Him a portion with the great, and He shall divide the spoil with the strong; because He hath poured out His soul unto death: and He was numbered with the transgressors; and He bare the sin of many, and made intercession for the transgressors." Crucified between two thieves, Jesus was thus *numbered with the transgressors,* the object of the Jews being to add insult to injury and heap final indignity upon Him. Little did they realize that they were fulfilling prophecy concerning their Messiah!

Someone may wonder why God allowed the Son of His love to be so outrageously and terribly mistreated. We need to realize that Almighty God allowed it because Jesus was taking the place of the sinner, and God gave us a true picture of what we deserved! Jesus took the place of shame, indignity, condemnation, and eternal torture because he was taking *our* place. The unspeakable agony that fell on Him should have fallen on US because of our sins. ALL have sinned and come short of the glory of God, there is none righteous—no, not one; and if Jesus had not taken our place we would all spend eternity in the lake of fire. Not one of us would escape!

So great was Christ's love for sinners that even in His dying hour, in the last moments of His great sacrifice, He snatched a brand from the burning, He plucked one from the pit and took him that day to Paradise:

"And one of the malefactors which were hanged railed on Him, saying, If thou be Christ, save thyself and us. But the other answering rebuked him, saying, Dost not thou fear God, seeing thou art in the same condemnation? And we indeed justly; for we receive the due reward of our deeds: but this Man hath done nothing amiss. And he said unto Jesus, Lord, remember me when thou comest into thy kingdom. *And Jesus said unto him, VERILY I SAY UNTO THEE, TO DAY SHALT THOU BE WITH ME IN PARADISE*" (Luke 23:39—43).

Verse 19: *"And Pilate wrote a title, and put it on the*

cross. And the writing was, JESUS OF NAZARETH THE KING OF THE JEWS."

Pilate's reason for placing this inscription over the cross of Jesus is something we can never know for sure. Perhaps he did it out of anger and vexation at the Jews. Perhaps his intention was solely to annoy and insult them. Perhaps Pilate really believed that Jesus WAS King of the Jews. But whatever his motive, the overruling hand of God so ordered matters that even on the cross our Lord was labeled "King." He *came* to be a King, and although not acknowledged by His subjects, He lived, died, and rose again as King of kings and Lord of lords.

A careful reader of the Gospels will not fail to observe that each Gospel writer gives the inscription in a slightly different form. The versions do not *contradict* each other, but no two are worded exactly alike. The explanation is very simple when we consider that it was written in three different languages. The one common point is *"the King of the Jews"*—and that each writer says.

Verse 20: *"This title then read many of the Jews: for the place where Jesus was crucified was nigh to the city: and it was written in Hebrew, and Greek, and Latin."*

Notice that the Holy Spirit placed the Hebrew language first. This was the language of the Jews, the language of religion in that day. *Greek* was the language of science, philosophy, and culture; it was used by the learned people. *Latin* was the language of law, the language used by the Romans. Therefore, all who gathered around the cross of Jesus could read Pilate's inscription in their own tongue; and in the realms of religion, science, and law Christ was—and still is—*King.* He is *the final revelation of the true God,* "the brightness of His glory, and the express image of His person" (Heb. 1:3). He said to Philip, "He that hath seen me hath seen the Father" (John 14:9).

Jesus is *the force of all true science.* "He is before all things, and *by Him* all things consist" (Col. 1:17).

He is *the true Law Giver and the true Law Administrator.* He is "the *end* of the law for righteousness to every one that believeth" (Rom. 10:4). Paul tells us in Romans 8:2–4, "The law of the Spirit of life in Christ Jesus hath made me free from the law of sin and death. For what the law could not do, in that it was weak through the flesh, God sending His own Son in the likeness of sinful flesh, and for sin, condemned sin in the flesh: that *the righteousness of the law* might be fulfilled in us, who walk not after the flesh, but after the Spirit."

Verse 21: *"Then said the chief priests of the Jews to Pilate, Write not, The King of the Jews; but that He said, I am King of the Jews."*

This is the only place in the Scriptures where the religious rulers are referred to as *"the chief priests of the JEWS."* They were no longer *God's* priests; they had rejected their Messiah, and God set Judaism aside. Jesus was near that moment when He would cry out, "It is finished!" That was the end of Judaism and the beginning of the day of God's marvelous grace. The veil in the temple was rent in twain from top to bottom when Jesus died on the cross, and by that one Offering the holy of holies was opened to *all.* Jesus had conquered the world, the flesh, and the devil; He was soon to conquer death, hell, and the grave . . . "whom God hath raised up, having loosed the pains of death: because it was not possible that He should be holden of it" (Acts 2:24). Therefore when Jesus said, "It is finished," it WAS finished even though He was not yet risen from the dead. He had *promised* to rise again, and that promise made His resurrection as sure as if it were already accomplished.

"Write not, The King of the Jews; but that He SAID, I am King of the Jews." Pilate's inscription over the cross of Jesus was taken as an insult; it was a blow to the pride of the chief priests and religious leaders among the Jews. By announcing that Jesus was King of the Jews, Pilate was

also announcing that the Jews were in the process of *crucifying* their King as a common criminal. Therefore they requested him to change the inscription so that those who read it would think Jesus was an impostor, one who simply *claimed* to be their King.

Verse 22: *"Pilate answered, What I have written I have written."*

I *must* speak a good word for Pilate here. He could be firm when it suited him to be so—and here he exhibited more courage than some religious leaders do today! Personally, I believe he was convinced that Jesus was not of this world. Assuredly he knew beyond doubt that this was not an ordinary person, and even though he lacked the courage to set Him free when he knew He was innocent, he boldly and emphatically refused to change the title he had placed on the cross of Jesus. Pilate's heart was wicked and unbelieving, but he respected Jesus—and he held the Jews in bitter contempt because he knew they had testified falsely against Jesus.

Verse 23: *"Then the soldiers, when they had crucified Jesus, took His garments, and made four parts, to every soldier a part; and also His coat: now the coat was without seam, woven from the top throughout."*

"When they had crucified Jesus" does not mean that the crucifixion events were over and Jesus was dead, but rather that the soldiers had finished their bloody work of nailing Him to the cross and raising the cross to its place between the two thieves. Having nailed Jesus to the cross and put Pilate's inscription over His head, the soldiers set about to divide His garments among themselves.

They *"took His garments, and made four parts, to every soldier a part."* This was a customary practice in that day—the garments of the person executed were given to the executioner. In this case, they were given to the four Roman soldiers who carried out Pilate's orders in putting Jesus to death. They had a legal right to claim His clothes. He had been stripped (probably down to a loin-cloth) before He was nailed to the cross.

What shame our blessed Lord must have endured as He hung there, His tortured body exposed to the gaze of the ungodly multitudes! He who was the very soul of kindness, graciousness, and modesty was now brazenly exposed to the gaze of the taunting, reviling, wicked men who had demanded His death. This is set forth in Psalm 22:16–18, where we read, *"Dogs have compassed me: the assembly of the wicked have inclosed me: they pierced my hands and my feet. I MAY TELL ALL MY BONES: THEY LOOK AND STARE UPON ME. They part my garments among them, and cast lots upon my vesture!"*

While the crowds mocked and jeered, the soldiers divided what few clothes Jesus had. (I am sure they were not many, for He who was rightful Heir to the riches of heaven was the poorest of men while He dwelt on earth.)

"And also His coat: now the coat was without seam, woven from the top throughout." When the soldiers came to the *coat* of Jesus (probably intending to rend it into four pieces, dividing it between themselves), they realized that this was the most unusual garment they had ever seen! It had no seams; it was woven "throughout," in one piece.

I have always wondered who *made* that coat for Jesus. Was it His *mother*, weaving love and devotion into each thread? Perhaps *Martha* made it, she who was so concerned for her Master's comfort and well-being. Or it could have been made by Mary Magdalene, out of whom Jesus cast seven devils. The Scripture gives no hint of who made the coat, and of course if God had wanted us to know, He would have revealed it in His Word—but one thing we know for certain: *some dear soul* spent many, many hours of loving labor in designing and weaving such a garment, a coat without a seam, "woven from the top throughout." Surely each thread was fashioned by hands dedicated unreservedly to Him for whom the coat was made.

I like to think of this garment as standing for *the conduct and character* of our Lord. It was His outer garment, its one piece denoting *unity,* speaking of the unbroken perfection of His ways.

In the Scriptures, a coat or robe speaks of righteousness. Isaiah 61:10 says, "I will greatly rejoice in the Lord, my soul shall be joyful in my God; for *He hath clothed me with the garments of salvation,* He hath covered me with *the robe of righteousness,* as a bridegroom decketh himself with ornaments, and as a bride adorneth herself with her jewels."

When the *prodigal son* returned home, "the father said to his servants, *Bring forth the best robe, and put it on him;* and put a ring on his hand, and shoes on his feet" (Luke 15:22).

When Adam and Eve sinned they saw their nakedness, and they fashioned aprons of fig leaves to cover themselves; but God condemned their self-made covering and clothed them with "coats of skins" (Gen. 3:21). Sinful Adam was clothed by Almighty God; but *the sins of the sons of Adam UNCLOTHED God's Son.* The *first* Adam, in Eden, was clothed by God; the *last* Adam, the Sinless One, was unclothed by wicked men and nailed to a cross, that WE might be clothed with the righteousness of God. Yes, when we believe on the Lord Jesus Christ and trust Him as our Saviour, God puts heaven's *best robe* on us: *He clothes us with the robe of righteousness,* the righteousness of His only begotten Son!

Verse 24: *"They said therefore among themselves, Let us not rend it, but cast lots for it, whose it shall be: that the Scripture might be fulfilled, which saith, They parted my raiment among them, and for my vesture they did cast lots. These things therefore the soldiers did."*

Here, as previously mentioned, is the fulfillment of Psalm 22:18—a prophecy spoken a thousand years before it literally happened on Calvary. The soldiers recognized the Lord's coat as an unusual and very serviceable garment, and rather than tear it apart they agreed to cast lots for it; and in so doing they unknowingly supplied evidence of the truth of the Word of God. Without either knowledge or intent they added to the great cloud of witnesses who testify and prove that the Bible is the unalterable, undeniable, forever final Word of God, verbally inspired.

Yes, God was in control, directing each and every detail of the happenings around the cross. No word of His can ever fail. All the prophecies concerning Christ's first coming were literally fulfilled, the prophecies concerning His death and resurrection were literally fulfilled, and the prophecies of His second coming will *also* be literally fulfilled in God's appointed time!

Verse 25: *"Now there stood by the cross of Jesus His mother, and His mother's sister, Mary the wife of Cleophas, and Mary Magdalene."*

All four Gospel writers treat the death of Jesus with fulness of detail. His birth, His baptism, and His temptation are described by *two* of the Gospel writers, but many of His miracles and discourses are found in only *one* Gospel. However, the supreme importance of His crucifixion is declared by the fact that His sufferings and death are recorded *in detail* by Matthew, Mark, Luke, and John.

The crucifixion of Jesus is the heart, soul, and bloodstream of Christianity. His death on the cross is the hub of the wheel of salvation, and all the spokes of the wheel proceed therefrom. If the crucifixion were removed from the Gospels, our Bible would become a book without a message, for the cross is the *origin* of the message of salvation, "and without shedding of blood is no remission" (Heb. 9:22). Without the sufferings of Jesus we would have no Saviour!

Each of the four Gospel writers presents the Lord Jesus Christ in his own individual manner:

Matthew wrote primarily for the Jews, and he therefore presents Christ as *the Son of David, King of Israel.* Everything in that Gospel contributes to this primary theme.

Mark shows the Lord Jesus Christ as *God's workman,* and his entire writing points directly to the Servant and His service.

Luke presents the Lord as *the Son of man* and spends much time pointing out His human perfections, with His sympathies directed toward mankind.

John the Beloved declares Jesus as *the Son of Almighty God,* God Incarnate, the Living Word. He dwells at length on the divine glories and the divine dignity and majesty of the Lord's person.

John gives no record of the agony of Jesus in Gethsemane, but *only* John tells us that when Jesus said, "I AM," those who had come to arrest Him fell backward to the ground. In this, John points to the deity of Jesus—the great "I AM," *God in flesh.*

Also, John does not give the details of what took place when Jesus appeared before Caiaphas, but he describes minutely the trial before Annas; and he is the only Gospel writer who records what Jesus said to Pilate concerning the Kingdom: "My kingdom is not of this world: if my kingdom were of this world, then would my servants fight, that I should not be delivered to the Jews: but now is my kingdom not from hence" (ch. 18, v. 36).

John is the only one who records the testimony that Jesus came into the world to bear witness unto the truth: "To this end was I born, and for this cause came I into the world, that I should bear witness unto the truth" (ch. 18, v. 37 in part).

Only John tells us of the Lord's declaration that Pilate could have no power against Him except it were given of God (ch. 19, v. 11). And now in our present passage John tells of this marvelous coat without seam, for which the soldiers gambled around the cross. None of the other Gospels give this interesting record.

In the verses to follow, John tells us that the legs of Jesus were not broken (v. 33), and that blood and water gushed from His pierced side (v. 34). The beloved disciple does not record the awful cry of Jesus, "My God! My God! Why hast thou forsaken me?" but it is he who gives the Lord's mighty cry of victory: "IT IS FINISHED!" John gave the information that Joseph and Nicodemus came with costly spices to anoint the body of Jesus, and begged Pilate for the body that they might bury it. The four Gospels, written by four different men under inspiration of the Holy Spirit, differing in content to some degree, when read in harmony with each other give clear and indisputable proof of the verbal inspiration of the Word of God.

"Now there stood by the cross of Jesus His mother." There were several groups around the cross that day. Calvary was so situated that many thousands could stand around "the place of a skull" within viewing distance of the three crosses. Thousands of Jews were there, satisfying their wicked hearts, thirsting for the blood of this Man whom they crucified as an impostor and a blasphemer. Roman soldiers were there—some of them were on duty, others no doubt were there out of curiosity.

But the Holy Spirit names another group—those who were there because of *love.* This little company was but five in number—but in the Bible, five is the number for *grace,* and it is used many times in the Scriptures. For instance, there were *five porches* at the pool of Bethesda, there were *five wise virgins,* and *five loaves* by which the multitudes were fed. In general, the groups around the cross of Jesus typified sinners—the total depravity of mankind; but these five people were trophies of God's saving grace.

First, there was Mary *the mother of Jesus.* Beyond any doubt she now realized the full import of the words spoken to her by Simeon in the temple thirty years before: ". . . Simeon blessed them, and said unto Mary His mother, Behold, this child is set for the fall and rising again of many in Israel; and for a sign which shall be spoken against: (YEA, A SWORD SHALL PIERCE THROUGH THY OWN SOUL ALSO,) that the thoughts of many hearts may be revealed" (Luke 2:34,35). Mary was now seeing these words fulfilled—what a horrible sight for a mother to look upon! Her Son had harmed no one. He had fed the hungry, healed the sick, opened the eyes of the blind, cleansed the lepers, made the lame to walk; but there is no mention of any of these people around the cross. Even the disciples, save "that disciple whom Jesus loved," had deserted Him and fled. The thousands whom He had fed, healed, blessed, and comforted had turned away—but *His mother* was there near Him, probably as near as she was allowed to go.

It was dangerous for Mary to be there, but she forgot all personal danger. Neither of the four Gospel writers records one word spoken by her during the time she stood by the cross. Evidently she suffered her grief in unbroken silence. Crowds mocked and sneered as they passed by the cross, wagging their heads and "shooting out the lip" (Psalm 22:7). Around the foot of the cross the Roman soldiers gambled for the Lord's garments. And in the midst of the mockery, scorn, and insults His mother stood—watching and hearing it all. We cannot know nor begin to imagine what went through the heart of Mary during those horrible hours, but we must confess that she was a strong woman. Most women would have displayed feminine weakness, fainting, crying out in uncontrollable weeping—but not Mary, the mother of Jesus.

The second woman named in the little group was Mary, wife of Cleophas. We know very little about this woman, the present verse simply stating that she was the wife of Cleophas and the sister of the mother of Jesus. But this one reference is sufficient to prove her loyalty to her Lord. She was present in that tragic hour when He needed friends most of all.

The third woman in the group was Mary Magdalene, out of whom Jesus had cast seven demons. It was to her that Jesus first appeared after His resurrection (John 20:11–18).

How significant that each of these women was named *Mary*—a name that means "bitterness." Who would doubt that their hearts were *filled* with bitterness, anguish, and misery as they witnessed the death of the Lamb of God?

The fourth woman standing near the cross that day was *John's* mother. She is not mentioned here, but Matthew tells us that she was there: "And many women were there . . . among which was Mary Magdalene, and Mary the mother of James and Joses, *and the mother of Zebedee's children*" (Matt. 27:55,56).

The fifth member of this little company was John himself, *"the disciple whom Jesus loved."* Insofar as the Word reveals to us, John was the only one of the disciples present when Jesus was dying on the cross.

Verse 26: *"When Jesus therefore saw His mother, and the disciple standing by, whom He loved, He saith unto His mother, Woman, behold thy son!"*

On the cross, Jesus was occupied with the greatest work ever performed—in heaven, in earth, or in all creation: *He was bearing in His own body the sins of all the world for all time and eternity!* This *no man* could possibly have done—nor can man fully appreciate it. It is impossible for mortal mind to conceive of the burden Jesus carried as He hung on the cross—yet in that awful hour when He was forsaken by man, soon to be forsaken by God Himself, *He did not forget His natural ties.* He saw His mother standing with John, the beloved disciple, and He honored her then just as He had honored Mary and His foster father Joseph when He was a lad (Luke 2:51). (Scripture does not tell us where *Joseph* was at this tragic time; some believe that he had died many years before.) But Mary was there, and Jesus honored her even in His darkest hour on earth.

"Woman, behold thy son." Twice in John's Gospel Jesus addressed Mary as "woman." In chapter 2, verse 4, when His mother told Him there was no wine at the wedding feast, He said to her, "Woman, what have I to do with thee? mine hour is not yet come." Here, speaking to her

from the cross, He again addresses her as "woman," but the term was not discourteous or disrespectful. In John 20:13, the angels at the open tomb said to Mary Magdalene, "*Woman,* why weepest thou?" In verse 15 of that same chapter *Jesus* asked her, "*Woman,* why weepest thou?" I believe Jesus had called Mary "Mother," but in death He put an end to all His natural relationships; and from Calvary on, even His mother was linked to Him only by a spiritual relationship. When Mary witnessed the death of Jesus on the cross she was seeing Him for the last time as her Son in the flesh. He would come from the tomb in a spiritual body, Saviour of the world, Lord of lords and King of kings.

All believers are united to Jesus by a closer bond than that of earthly ties. In II Corinthians 5:16 Paul declared, "Wherefore henceforth know we no man after the flesh: yea, though we have known Christ after the flesh, yet now henceforth know we Him no more."

Mary is not mentioned at all as having to do with the *resurrection* of Jesus, but she was present with the one hundred and twenty who waited in the upper room for the coming of the Holy Ghost. In Acts 1:14 we read, "These all continued with one accord in prayer and supplication, with the women, *and Mary the mother of Jesus,* and with His brethren."

In other words, Mary was one of those who waited—she was *with* them, not *over* them; she was not superior to them in any way. She was in the upper room to be endued with power to become an effective witness, and she received the instruction just as the others received it.

In His last moments on earth as the Son of man, Jesus assured His mother that she was not to finish her earthly pilgrimage alone. John would love and care for her just as He Himself had loved and cared for her—and certainly there is nothing in the Scripture to indicate that Jesus was ever anything but loving and considerate of His mother. As He closed His earthly life, therefore, He provided for her future by making her His living legacy to John, the beloved disciple.

Verse 27: *"Then saith He to the disciple, Behold thy mother! And from that hour that disciple took her unto his own home."*

In other words, Jesus said to John, "Regard *my* mother as *your* mother. Take her and care for her as you care for your own mother." *"And from that hour that disciple took her unto his own home."*

How marvelously are both our Lord's *divine* and *human* affections demonstrated here—very God, yet very man. As man, He remembered His mother and provided for her. As God, He is the head of the Church (Eph. 5:23), the head of the family of God.

Undoubtedly Mary's other children were not fitted or prepared to take care of her in later years. In Psalm 69:8 it was prophesied, "I am become a stranger unto my brethren, and an alien unto *my mother's children.*" Some teach that Mary *had* no other children, that only one child, JESUS, was born to her; otherwise He would not have committed her into *John's* keeping. Certainly Jesus was her *firstborn,* conceived of the Holy Ghost before Mary and Joseph were married; but according to Matthew 13:55,56, Mary *did* have other children: When Jesus was teaching in the synagogue "in His own country" the people asked, "Is not this the carpenter's son? Is not His mother called Mary? and *His brethren,* James, and Joses, and Simon, and Judas? And *His sisters,* are they not all with us?" But from the quotation just given from Psalm 69, we would assume that the other children of Mary had *denied* Jesus and refused to receive Him as Messiah (John 7:1—5). Therefore He gave His mother's keeping into the hands of one whom He knew loved Him and would remain faithful to the trust given him.

Also, in our present verse we find Scriptural proof that Mary the mother of Jesus was not intended to be honored as divine. God never meant for anyone to pray to Mary or worship her. She was a woman among other women, and common sense teaches that since Mary needed human care and Jesus committed her to the care of John the Beloved, she certainly could not care for, protect, or answer prayer for others! Even in the Annunciation, when Gabriel spoke with her about the birth of Jesus, he said to her, "Hail, thou that art highly favoured, the Lord is with thee: *blessed art thou AMONG women*" (Luke 1:28). You will notice that the angel said "among," not *over* or *above* other women. Mary was never intended to mediate between God and men: "For there is one God, *and ONE MEDIATOR between God and men, THE MAN CHRIST JESUS*" (I Tim. 2:5).

Verse 28: *"After this, Jesus knowing that all things were now accomplished, that the Scripture might be fulfilled, saith, I thirst."*

Read this verse again. Read it slowly, prayerfully, and analyze every word. Jesus knew *"that all things were now accomplished."* This is the fifth time He spoke from the cross. It was after three hours of darkness had engulfed the land. It was after God had literally turned His face away, withdrawing His countenance from Jesus. It was after He had suffered the fierceness of the outpoured wrath of a holy God, suffering for sinners, taking the sinner's place. Then at the close of those awful hours He cried out, "My moisture is turned into the drought of summer" (Psalm 32:4). In other words, "I THIRST!"

Jesus, knowing *all* things, knew that this was prophesied centuries before. In Lamentations 1:13 it was foretold, "He hath made me desolate and faint." But as terrible as the thirst of Jesus was, He did not cry out for water to ease His sufferings or moisten His parched lips. Since He had come into the world to do the will of God and to work God's works—and do it perfectly—He cried, "I thirst"—*not* to satisfy His thirst, but to satisfy His Father in heaven; for in death, as in life, He did always those things that pleased God.

Yes, the Creator of all streams, springs, rivers, and fountains of refreshing water knew the torment of thirst; it was one of the agonies attendant upon death by crucifixion. Here is proof of Christ's humanity—God, yet man—*not superhuman,* but "made like unto His brethren in all things," sin apart. He was not a *humanized GOD,* nor was He a *divine MAN.* He was God in the *beginning,* He was *with* God; but now He is forever man, the Man Christ Jesus, now seated at the right hand of God.

Yet when the Word became flesh, He did not cease to be God. He did not lay aside His divine attributes.

As man, *He became weary in body:* In Mark 4:38 He was asleep in the little ship, resting on a pillow, even as you and I; and a great storm arose, and the disciples awakened Him crying, "Master, carest thou not that we perish?" He rose and rebuked the storm, and brought peace to the troubled sea. He was "wearied with His journey" when He stopped to rest at Jacob's well where His conversation with the Samaritan woman took place (John 4:6—29).

As a man, *He became hungry:* "Now in the morning as He returned into the city, He hungered. And when He saw a fig tree in the way, He came to it, and found nothing thereon, but leaves only, and said unto it, Let no fruit grow on thee henceforward for ever. And presently the fig tree withered away" (Matt. 21:18,19).

As a man, *He shed tears of compassion* (John 11:35).

As a man, *He felt the need of prayer:* "And in the morning, rising up a great while before day, He went out, and departed into a solitary place, and there prayed" (Mark 1:35).

As a man, *Jesus rejoiced:* "In that hour Jesus rejoiced in spirit, and said, I thank thee, O Father, Lord of heaven and earth, that thou hast hid these things from the wise and prudent, and hast revealed them unto babes: even so, Father; for so it seemed good in thy sight" (Luke 10:21).

As a man, *He was troubled:* "When Jesus therefore saw

(Mary) weeping, and the Jews also weeping which came with her, He groaned in the spirit, and was troubled" (John 11:33).

Yet for all His qualities of humanity, *very man,* He never laid aside His deity. He was no less God because of His manhood.

Verse 29: *"Now there was set a vessel full of vinegar: and they filled a spunge with vinegar, and put it upon hyssop, and put it to His mouth."*

In Matthew 27:34, they offered Jesus vinegar mixed with gall. This He refused. But we must not confuse these two statements. *Vinegar and gall* was a mixture given to criminals to deaden the pain of crucifixion, and such was refused by our Lord. He suffered all the agony crucifixion could bring, and He accepted nothing to lessen the pain. His mind was clear and His memory unimpaired until the very moment He passed His spirit back to God.

But He did not refuse to drink of the vinegar. He accepted it in obedience to the heavenly Father's will. Someone—probably one of the Roman soldiers—filled a sponge with the vinegar and pressed it to the parched lips of Jesus, unaware that he was fulfilling prophecy spoken centuries before: "They gave me also gall for my meat; and in my thirst they gave me vinegar to drink" (Psalm 69:21).

The Greatest Word Ever Spoken On Earth

Verse 30: *"When Jesus therefore had received the vinegar, He said, It is finished: and He bowed His head, and gave up the ghost."*

In the Greek language, *"It is finished"* is only one word —*"TETELESTAI!"* It can be translated "It is *finished*... It is *accomplished* . . . It is *completed."* Therefore, when Jesus cried out "Tetelestai!" He was saying, "I have *completed* every detail of redemption. I have *accomplished* that for which I came into the world. I have fulfilled every jot and tittle of the law and the prophets. I have satisfied the righteousness, the holiness, and the purity of God. *I have FINISHED redemption's plan!* I am now ready to return to my heavenly Father."

There are several reasons why I say *"Tetelestai"* is the the greatest word ever spoken on earth:

1. It was spoken by *the greatest Person* who ever lived—the *only* Person in heaven, on earth, or in all creation who *could* have finished the work that had to be finished if God were to be just and yet justify the ungodly. Jesus came to earth on a singular mission—to do the will of the heavenly Father. He did not come to set an example, to found a great religion, nor to establish an earthly church. He came to pay the sin-debt, to make atonement for the soul. Only Jesus could completely satisfy the great heart of God. He fulfilled every wish, met every requirement, did all things always under all circumstances that pleased God (John 8:29). And when He came to the end of His earthly ministry He could say, *"Tetelestai! It is finished!"*

2. "Tetelestai" is the greatest word ever spoken because *it made known the greatest announcement ever proclaimed on earth.* You may ask, "Was not the *birth of Jesus* the greatest announcement?" No! because His birth, His life, the example He set, and all the miracles He performed could never have availed in the least where redemption is concerned. If Jesus had not been lifted up from the earth, there would have *been* no redemption (John 3:14; 12:32). The cross of Jesus was a divine imperative: no cross, no salvation! God could not acquit the wicked unless a sinless substitute was given, and the Son of God was the only One who could make that substitution.

"And almost all things are by the law purged with blood; *and without shedding of blood is no remission*" (Heb. 9:22). The crimson thread runs from the Garden of Eden through Revelation. All the blood of *animals* from Eden to Calvary pointed to the Lamb of God without spot or blemish. All forgiveness since Calvary is based on the finished work of Jesus. If He had not finished the work the Father sent Him to do, salvation would never have been a reality, for without His blood there is no cleansing, no forgiveness of sins.

In Isaiah 64:6 we are told, "We are all as an unclean thing, *and all our righteousnesses are as filthy rags;* and we all do fade as a leaf; and our iniquities, like the wind, have taken us away." But the Apostle Paul assures us that *Christ "is made unto us wisdom, and RIGHTEOUSNESS, and sanctification, and REDEMPTION"* (I Cor. 1:30).

We need to realize the truth of Galatians 2:20: "I am crucified with Christ: nevertheless I live; *yet not I, but Christ liveth in me:* and the life which I now live in the flesh I live by the faith of the Son of God, who loved me, and gave Himself for me!"

Romans 8:1 promises, "There is therefore *now no condemnation to them which are in Christ Jesus,* who walk not after the flesh, but after the Spirit," and Colossians 2:9,10 declares that the fulness of the Godhead rests in Christ, *and WE are "complete in HIM."* What *can* be added to completion?

"Jesus paid it all,
All to Him I owe;
Sin had left a crimson stain—
He washed it white as snow!"

3. "Tetelestai" is the greatest word ever spoken *because of its scope:* It concerns the greatest number of people ever affected by any other announcement—it reaches every mortal since Adam, and all who *will be* born between the present time and the consummation of all things. Through the centuries, announcements and proclamations have been made which affected many people, but never another that touches every person from the beginning of time to the end of the ages. From the other side of Calvary men of faith looked forward to the Lamb who hung on the tree, whose blood

was shed for the remission of sin; and from *this* side of Calvary believers look back to the blood of the Lamb without spot or blemish, He who laid His life down that we might have life. Calvary is the center of God's eternal program, and without the finished work of Jesus *not one soul* could ever be justified freely from all sin and stand before God without condemnation.

4. "Tetelestai" is the greatest word ever spoken *because it announced the greatest victory ever won.* Since the day Lucifer was cast out of heaven (Isa. 14:12–15; Ezek. 28: 11–15), he has waged ceaseless warfare against Almighty God. Satan is a created being, but God did not create him to be as he is now. He was created "*Lucifer,* son of the morning," "the anointed cherub that covereth." He was second only to the Trinity in power, and Ezekiel declares that he was "full of wisdom, and perfect in beauty," *perfect in all his ways* from the day he was created until iniquity was found in him. Personally, I believe Lucifer was an archangel, perhaps *chief* of the archangels. Jesus said, "I beheld Satan as lightning fall from heaven" (Luke 10:18); and from the moment he lost his place in God's economy he has tried to frustrate the purpose and program of God. But he has fought a losing battle, and when Jesus cried, "Tetelestai!" that cry meant total victory for Himself and absolute defeat to the kingdom of Satan. He is still operating, but he is a defeated being—and he *knows* it. In God's own good time, at the *appointed* time, Satan will be cast into the lake of fire that burns with brimstone, to be tormented forever and ever (Rev. 20:10).

Satan witnessed the miracle of the creation of man, and he was not long in seeking to destroy God's *purpose* in that creation. He tempted Eve to violate the one prohibition God had placed upon the couple. Eve yielded to temptation, she ate of the forbidden fruit, she gave to Adam and *he* ate, and through his disobedience to God's command, sin passed upon the entire human race.

In Genesis 3:15 God declared to Satan, "I will put enmity between thee and the woman, and between thy seed and her seed; it shall bruise thy head, and thou shalt bruise His heel"—and the very moment God declared enmity between the seed of the woman and the seed of the serpent, *the devil declared war* against the seed of the woman and set about to frustrate God's purpose.

It was then that Satan began his diabolical scheme for his unending program to corrupt and destroy the Seed that would bruise his head. His first move to accomplish this is recorded in the fourth chapter of Genesis. (Please read the entire chapter.) To Adam and Eve, two sons (Cain and Abel) were born. Undoubtedly Satan thought Abel was the Seed, or the line through which the Seed would come; and by working through Cain he succeeded in *murdering* Abel. But his efforts were to no avail, for in verse 25 of that chapter we read, "And Adam knew his wife again; and she bare a son, and called his name Seth: *For God,* said she, *hath appointed me ANOTHER SEED instead of Abel, whom Cain slew!*"

Satan's next attempt to stop the seed of the woman is recorded in Genesis chapter 6. In verse 2 of that chapter we read, "The sons of God saw the daughters of men that they were fair; and they took them wives of all which they chose." From the union between the sons of God and the daughters of men, giants were born—the Hebrew reads, "*monstrosities.*" Through this scheme of Satan, earth's inhabitants became so corrupt, the universal wickedness of man was so great, that the Lord repented of having *created* man. He said, "I will destroy man whom I have created from the face of the earth; both man, and beast, and the creeping thing, and the fowls of the air; for it repenteth me that I have made them" (Gen. 6:1–7 in part).

Again Satan's plan failed; for in Genesis 6:8 we read, "*BUT NOAH found grace in the eyes of the Lord.*" God instructed Noah to build an ark, and Noah obeyed God "to the saving of his house; by the which he condemned the world, and became heir of the righteousness which is by faith" (Heb. 11:7). We know, of course, that the ark was a type of Christ.

Time and time again Satan attempted to corrupt and destroy the promised Seed. Noah got drunk (Gen. 9:20,21); Abraham lied about Sarah, his wife (Gen. 12:10–20; 20: 1–11); the brothers of Joseph sold him into Egyptian slavery in an attempt to destroy him (Gen. 37:2–28). But God remembered Joseph just as He had remembered Noah and Abraham, and Satan's plans were frustrated again.

But he did not give up. At one time it seemed that he might even succeed in his efforts to destroy the Seed of the woman, for there was but *one little boy* left through whom the Seed could come. But God saw to it that this little boy was hidden and protected until a time when he could be safely placed on the throne. (Read the account in II Chronicles 22:10 through 23:11.) Through this child, the lineage continued until the promised Seed, Jesus, came into the world—but even then, the devil did not give up!

In the second chapter of Matthew we read that when Jesus was born in Bethlehem, wise men from the east came to Jerusalem, saying, "Where is He that is born King of the Jews? for we have seen His star in the east, and are come to worship Him." This troubled Herod the king, and he called the wise men to inquire of them *at what time* the star had appeared, and he instructed them to let him know when they had found the child so that he might worship Him, also. But hear this: *"BEING WARNED OF GOD IN A DREAM that they should not return to Herod, they departed into their own country another way!"*

Herod had not wanted to worship Jesus at all. He wanted to destroy Him. But God protected His Son, the Seed of the woman, the Saviour through whom the promised redemption would come. Herod was so enraged because the wise men had thwarted his plan that he "sent forth, and slew all the children that were in Bethlehem, and in all the coasts thereof, from two years old and under, according to the time which he had diligently enquired of the wise men."

But Herod had not reckoned on the surety of God's eternal plan. An angel appeared to Joseph in a dream, saying, "Arise, and take the young child and His mother, and flee into Egypt, and be thou there until I bring thee word: for Herod will seek the young child to destroy Him." So Joseph took Jesus and His mother *by night,* and "departed into Egypt: and was there until the death of Herod: that it might be fulfilled which was spoken of the Lord by the prophet, saying, Out of Egypt have I called my Son" (Matt. 2:1–18 in part).

Again and again and again Satan attempted to destroy Jesus, but all of his plans failed. Even after the Lord entered His public ministry, the Jews on occasion took up stones to stone Him (John 8:59; 10:31), but they could not cast the stones. He had not come into the world to be stoned; He came to be lifted up on a cross, *"that whosoever believeth in Him should not perish, but have eternal life"* (John 3:15).

On one occasion, as He taught in the synagogue at Nazareth, the people became so enraged that they "rose up, and thrust Him out of the city, and led Him unto the brow of the hill whereon their city was built, *that they might cast Him down headlong. BUT HE PASSING THROUGH THE MIDST OF THEM WENT HIS WAY"* (Luke 4:16–30).

There is no doubt in my mind that all hell was allied against Jesus in the Garden of Gethsemane as He prayed that night, and I believe the devil himself led the attack in an attempt to kill the Lamb of God before He could reach the cross with His eternal sacrifice. I believe that is why Jesus prayed in such agony that His perspiration "was as it were great drops of blood falling down to the ground" (Luke 22:44).

He *could* have died under the merciless flogging inflicted upon Him by the Roman soldiers just before the crucifixion. He *could* have died under the weight of the cross on the way to Golgotha. Certainly Satan did his utmost to destroy Him before He reached Calvary so that He would not be lifted up and draw men unto Himself (John 12:32).

But all hell could not prevail against the divine plan and program which foreordained that the spotless Son of God should die on the cross. He marched on to Calvary, and there He paid the supreme penalty for sin, according to the blueprint drawn up by the Holy Trinity before the foundation of the world was laid! And when Jesus cried out, "IT IS FINISHED!" *the greatest battle of the ages was won.*

On the cross two eternities met: Jesus reached out with one hand and took all the sins from Adam to Calvary; with the other hand He reached to the end of the ages and took all the future sins of mankind, nailing them all to His cross. Therefore it is no longer the *sin-question,* but the *SON-question: "What think ye of CHRIST? Whose Son is He?"* Beloved, the way you answer that question will determine where you spend eternity, for salvation depends upon believing in and receiving the finished work of Jesus on the cross. All who receive Him by faith become sons of God, born into God's family.

I repeat: "Tetelestai" is the greatest word ever spoken. It was spoken by *the greatest Person* who ever lived, it made known *the greatest announcement* ever proclaimed, an announcement that *affected more people* than any announcement before or since; and it *declared the greatest victory* ever won. I say with Paul, *"THANKS BE UNTO GOD FOR HIS UNSPEAKABLE GIFT!"* (II Cor. 9:15).

"And He bowed His head, and gave up the ghost." All through these studies I have stressed the fact that everything about Jesus was unique, and the order of His actions here is evidence of that uniqueness. *"He bowed His head"* suggests that until that moment He had held His head erect. Through His hours of unparalleled suffering on the cross He did not swoon. Even more unusual is the meaning of the Greek word used here, for it does not suggest that

the head of Jesus *fell forward,* but rather that He calmly, reverently, *BOWED His head.* No dying mortal has ever displayed such superb composure!

The Seven Sayings from the Cross

Jesus spoke seven times from the cross, and those seven sayings exhibit His perfection as the Word made flesh:

1. He spoke forgiveness for those who had nailed Him to the cross: "Father, forgive them; for they know not what they do" (Luke 23:34).

2. He spoke salvation to the penitent thief: "Verily, verily I say unto thee, To day shalt thou be with me in Paradise" (Luke 23:43).

3. He spoke love and devotion to and for His mother: *"Woman, behold thy son!* Then saith He to the disciple (John), *Behold thy mother!"* (vv. 26,27 this chapter).

4. He spoke words of anguish such as this world has never known or heard: "And about the ninth hour Jesus cried with a loud voice, saying, Eli, Eli, lama sabachthani? that is to say, My God, my God, why hast thou forsaken me?" (Matt. 27:46).

5. He spoke of His physical suffering: He said, *"I thirst"* (v. 28, this chapter).

6. He spoke the greatest word ever uttered, announcing the greatest victory ever won: *"Tetelestai!* It is finished!" (v. 30, this chapter).

7. He spoke words of contentment, of peace in His heart, knowing that He had finished His work on earth and had completely satisfied the heavenly Father. With confidence and contentment He could say, *"Father, into thy hands I commend my spirit"* (Luke 23:46). He literally *dismissed His spirit,* He *laid down His life* as He stated in John 10:15–18.

Not A Bone of Him Broken

Verse 31: *"The Jews therefore, because it was the preparation, that the bodies should not remain upon the cross on the sabbath day, (for that sabbath day was an high day,) besought Pilate that their legs might be broken, and that they might be taken away."*

"The Jews" here can only mean the chief priests, the rulers and religious leaders of Israel—the same men who had demanded that Pilate crucify Jesus.

"The preparation" refers to the day preceding the Passover Sabbath which was "an high day," a great day in the year; and unless something was done to hasten the death of Jesus, His body would remain on the cross until this "high day." The Jewish law would be broken (Deut. 21:22,23), and a dead body would hang throughout the Sabbath in full view of the temple.

So the Jews *"besought Pilate that their legs might be broken."* This was often done as a means of hastening death, for it was not unusual for criminals to hang on a cross for several days before death claimed them—and the Jews did not realize that regardless of anything they might do, Jesus would die at the very moment He was *appointed* to die.

Verse 32: *"Then came the soldiers, and brake the legs of the first, and of the other which was crucified with Him."*

It has been suggested that the two crosses of the thieves were set a bit forward in position, with the cross of Jesus between, arranged so that the sufferers could see each others faces. If the crosses were in a triangular position, with the two thieves forward, the soldiers would naturally begin with the crosses they came to first. This formation would perhaps account for the penitent thief being able to read the inscription over our Lord's head, proclaiming Him "King of the Jews."

The Greek word here translated *"brake"* means more

than our English word. It means to "shiver to pieces"— that is, with some instrument, probably a heavy hammer, the leg bones were literally *crushed* in order to hasten death.

We might also note here that the Roman soldiers again unconsciously fulfilled Scripture when they broke the legs of the penitent thief. Jesus had said to him, *"TO DAY shalt thou be with me in Paradise,"* and by hastening his death the soldiers made it possible for him to enter Paradise that very day just as Jesus had promised. Otherwise, he could have lingered for several days on the cross.

Verse 33: *"But when they came to Jesus, and saw that He was dead already, they brake not His legs."*

Here is further evidence that Jesus died a unique death. Nails in the hands and feet pierced no vital organ, and the victim of crucifixion bled very slowly; therefore death was long in coming. The fact that Jesus was dead after *only six hours* on the cross was not a natural thing to expect, and Pilate marvelled even to the extent of calling the centurion and inquiring about this extraordinary outcome of our Lord's crucifixion (Mark 15:44,45).

Also, the fact that Jesus *"was dead already"* testifies that no man took His life from Him. The Jews *demanded* His death—but they did not kill Him. Pilate *consented* to His death—but he did not kill Him. The Roman soldiers *nailed Him to the cross*—but they did not kill Him. *HE LAID HIS LIFE DOWN OF HIMSELF:* In John 10:17,18 Jesus declared, "Therefore doth my Father love me, because I lay down my life, that I might take it again. *No man taketh it from me, but I LAY IT DOWN OF MYSELF. I have power to lay it down, and I have power to take it again.* This commandment have I received of my Father."

Some skeptics today maintain that Jesus did not die. They say He simply *fainted* and then *revived* after He was placed in the tomb; but the Roman soldiers testify against this theory. These men knew their business, they had watched many people die. They would not have disregarded

Pilate's orders if they had not been absolutely sure that the Man on the middle cross was dead when they came to the cross to break His legs. Thus was prophecy again fulfilled by these unbelieving soldiers (see v. 36).

Verse 34: *"But one of the soldiers with a spear pierced His side, and forthwith came there out blood and water."*

Here is one of the greatest miracles recorded in all of the Word of God: Blood flowing from a dead body would have been miraculous, but *BLOOD AND WATER flowed from the pierced side of Jesus—flowed at the same time, yet separated!* This was witness that God has given us eternal life, and that life is in His only begotten Son:

"There are three that bear witness in earth, the Spirit, and the water, and the blood: and these three agree in one. If we receive the witness of men, the witness of God is greater: for this is the witness of God which He hath testified of His Son. He that believeth on the Son of God hath the witness in himself: he that believeth not God hath made Him a liar; because he believeth not the record that God gave of His Son. And this is the record, that God hath given to us eternal life, and this life is in His Son. He that hath the Son hath life; and he that hath not the Son of God hath not life" (I John 5:8–12).

Here the foundation of the Church was laid: The opened side of Jesus gave forth water and blood—water, *the living Word,* and blood, the crimson flow that *cleanses from all sin.* These two cannot be separated. It is the water, the Word, that brings saving faith: "Faith cometh by hearing, and hearing by the Word of God" (Rom. 10:17); and it is by the precious blood that we have remission of sins: ". . . without shedding of blood is no remission" (Heb. 9:22).

Verse 35: *"And he that saw it bare record, and his record is true: and he knoweth that he saith true, that ye might believe."*

This indicates that John was an eyewitness to all that

happened at the crucifixion, as he records it in this chapter. He also gives firsthand testimony in his first epistle: "This is He that came *by water and blood,* even Jesus Christ; not by water only, but by water and blood. And it is the Spirit that beareth witness, because the Spirit is truth" (I John 5:6).

Verse 36: *"For these things were done, that the Scripture should be fulfilled, A bone of Him shall not be broken."*

Here the beloved disciple quotes Psalm 34:20, words literally fulfilled at this time. God kept all the bones of His only begotten Son because it was prophesied centuries before, and God's Word cannot be altered or broken. Pilate ordered his soldiers to break the legs of the men on the three crosses—but *all* of the Roman soldiers together with *all of Caesar's legions* could not have broken one single bone in the body of Jesus, for God had ordained otherwise!

Also, that not a bone in the body of Jesus was broken was a fulfillment of type under Mosaic law: In Exodus 12:46 we read of the Passover lamb, "In one house shall it be eaten; thou shalt not carry forth ought of the flesh abroad out of the house; NEITHER SHALL YE BREAK A BONE THEREOF."

For fifteen centuries, Israel had observed the law of the Passover, but they had no idea of the meaning of the words in their law as applied here. If one bone in the body of Jesus had been broken, *the Word of God* would have been broken, and this could not be.

Verse 37: *"And again another Scripture saith, They shall look on Him whom they pierced."*

This has reference to the prophecy of Zechariah 12:10, prophecy which has been only partially fulfilled: "And I will pour upon the house of David, and upon the inhabitants of Jerusalem, the spirit of grace and of supplications: *and they shall look upon me whom they have pierced,* and they shall mourn for Him, as one mourneth for his only son, and shall be in bitterness for Him, as one that is in bitterness for his firstborn." This prophecy will have its complete fulfillment when Jesus comes the second time and stands on the Mount of Olives:

"And His feet shall stand in that day upon the Mount of Olives, which is before Jerusalem on the east, and the Mount of Olives shall cleave in the midst thereof toward the east and toward the west, and there shall be a very great valley; and half of the mountain shall remove toward the north, and half of it toward the south" (Zech. 14:4).

It is then that Israel will recognize Him by the scars in His hands and feet: "And one shall say unto Him, What are these wounds in thine hands? Then He shall answer, Those with which I was wounded in the house of my friends" (Zech. 13:6).

The Burial of Jesus

Verse 38: *"And after this Joseph of Arimathaea, being a disciple of Jesus, but secretly for fear of the Jews, besought Pilate that he might take away the body of Jesus: and Pilate gave him leave. He came therefore, and took the body of Jesus."*

God overrules all things that would hinder any detail of prophecy from being fulfilled. The Romans never allowed any victim of crucifixion to be placed in a sepulchre. It was against Roman law to bury a crucified criminal. Thus Jesus, being "numbered with the transgressors," would not receive the honor of a funeral; He would not be buried if Roman law were carried out. So the sovereignty of God is again brought out here, because when Joseph asked for the body of Jesus, Pilate granted his request.

This is the first time Joseph of Arimathaea is mentioned in the Scriptures; there is no record of his actions up to this time, nor do we hear of him *after* he placed the body of Jesus in his new tomb. He loved Jesus, but he had been a *secret* disciple *"for fear of the Jews."*

Here is testimony to the power of the cross: Joseph of Arimathaea had been weak in spiritual matters while Jesus lived, but here he risked his life by asking for the body of his Lord. He was asking for something which under Roman law would normally have been denied, and Pilate could have condemned him to death as one of the followers of Jesus. Yet he came forward openly—(Mark 15:43 says *"boldly"*)—and claimed the body of Jesus at a time when even the disciples had scattered and fled in terror.

Verse 39: *"And there came also Nicodemus, which at the first came to Jesus by night, and brought a mixture of myrrh and aloes, about an hundred pound weight."*

Nicodemus is mentioned three times in Scripture. He is mentioned the first time when he came to Jesus by night. The second time we read of him was when he defended Jesus before the Jewish council (John 7:50,51), and in our present verse he came with Joseph to request the body of Jesus and help with His burial. The Holy Spirit is careful each time Nicodemus is mentioned, to identify him—not only by name, but as the one who "came to Jesus by night." (I personally believe he was saved that night, but if he was not, then surely he was born again shortly thereafter.)

The service Nicodemus and Joseph of Arimathaea rendered to Jesus in His burial will never be forgotten. Their names are recorded here, and wherever this Gospel is preached those names will be called by ministers of the Gospel. Any service rendered to Christ, even if it be but a cup of cold water given in His name, will never be overlooked nor go unrewarded.

Nicodemus brought with him *"a mixture of myrrh and aloes"*—spices with which to anoint the Lord's body for burial. These must have cost quite a sum of money, for they were of *"about an hundred pound weight"*—and that, dear friend, is a lot of spices!

All of the Gospel writers name Joseph of Arimathaea as

a leader in this transaction, and each of them mentions something about him:

Matthew tells us that he was a rich man: "When the even was come, there came a rich man of Arimathaea, named Joseph, who also himself was Jesus' disciple" (Matt. 27:57).

Mark describes him as "an honourable counsellor, which also waited for the kingdom of God" (Mark 15:43).

Luke tells us that he was "a counsellor . . . a good man, and a just: (The same had not consented to the counsel and deed of them;) he was of Arimathaea, a city of the Jews: who also himself waited for the kingdom of God" (Luke 23:50,51).

Then in our present passage *John the Beloved* brings him before us as "a disciple of Jesus, but secretly for fear of the Jews," until at this time Joseph stepped forward and openly claimed the body of Jesus for burial.

From the Scriptures we know that Nicodemus and Joseph of Arimathaea were not the only outstanding Jews who were secret disciples of our Lord, for John 12:42 plainly declares that "among the chief rulers also *many believed on Him; but because of the Pharisees they did not confess Him, lest they should be put out of the synagogue.*" Nicodemus and Joseph had the courage to step out and honor Jesus when to do so meant risking their very lives.

Verse 40: *"Then took they the body of Jesus, and wound it in linen clothes with the spices, as the manner of the Jews is to bury."*

Note the precise manner of the preparation of the body of Jesus for burial:

He was not laid in a coffin or vault as we bury our loved ones today. His body was wrapped in linen cloths spread with sweet spices—probably in powdered form. Mark 15:46 tells us that Joseph "bought *fine* (expensive) *linen,* and took Him down, and wrapped Him in the linen, and laid Him in a sepulchre *which was hewn out of a rock . . . .*"

Verse 41: *"Now in the place where He was crucified there was a garden; and in the garden a new sepulchre, wherein was never man yet laid."*

It was in a garden that the first Adam sinned, and through his sin death moved upon all mankind. Here in another garden, the last Adam paid the sin-debt and provided the incorruptible seed that brings the new birth and life eternal.

Jesus was placed in *"a new sepulchre, wherein was never man yet laid,"* and Matthew 27:60 tells us that the tomb was Joseph's own. From His birth through His death, Jesus owned nothing of this world's goods. He was born in a borrowed manger, He borrowed a boat from which to preach, He borrowed a little boy's lunch with which to feed five thousand guests, He rode into Jerusalem on a borrowed donkey, and now in death he lay in a borrowed tomb. In II Corinthians 8:9 the Apostle Paul says, "Ye know the grace of our Lord Jesus Christ, that, though He was rich, *yet for your sakes He became poor, that ye through His poverty might be rich!"*

Verse 42: *"There laid they Jesus therefore because of the Jews' preparation day; for the sepulchre was nigh at hand."*

The Jewish day began at six in the evening and lasted from sundown to sundown. When we consider that Jesus gave up the ghost at three in the afternoon, we realize that there were only three hours left before the Passover Sabbath for Joseph and Nicodemus to take His body from the cross, prepare it for burial, and place it in the tomb. The fact that *"the sepulchre was nigh at hand"* was certainly to their advantage. How completely God looks after every detail of His plan and program!

I have often wondered if John the Beloved did not have a hand in helping with the burial of Jesus. It would have been a heavy task for only two men, for Jesus was a full grown man, and the addition of a hundred pounds of spices would have placed a tremendous burden on them. It seems so reasonable that the disciple whom Jesus loved, having stayed near the cross during the hours of the crucifixion, would also have remained to help with the burial; but the Scripture does not tell us whether he did or not.

So He who had been *born* of a virgin was placed in a virgin tomb, to remain for three days and then come forth as He had promised, for it was impossible for death to hold Him. Thus, "what the law could not do, in that it was weak through the flesh, God sending His own Son in the likeness of sinful flesh, and for sin, condemned sin in the flesh: that the righteousness of the law might be fulfilled in us, who walk not after the flesh, but after the Spirit" (Rom. 8:3,4).

"For the law having a shadow of good things to come, and not the very image of the things, can never with those sacrifices which they offered year by year continually make the comers thereunto perfect. For then would they not have ceased to be offered? because that the worshippers once purged should have had no more conscience of sins. But in those sacrifices there is a remembrance again made of sins every year. For it is not possible that the blood of bulls and of goats should take away sins.

"Wherefore when He cometh into the world, He saith, Sacrifice and offering thou wouldest not, but a body hast thou prepared me: In burnt-offerings and sacrifices for sin thou hast had no pleasure. Then said I, Lo, I come (in the volume of the book it is written of me,) to do thy will, O God. Above when He said, Sacrifice and offering and burnt-offerings and offering for sin thou wouldest not, neither hadst pleasure therein; which are offered by the law; then said He, Lo, I come to do thy will, O God. He taketh away the first, that He may establish the second. By the which will we are sanctified through the offering of the body of Jesus Christ ONCE FOR ALL" (Heb. 10:1–10).

"It is finished! TETELESTAI!"

CHAPTER XX

1. The first day of the week cometh Mary Magdalene early, when it was yet dark, unto the sepulchre, and seeth the stone taken away from the sepulchre.

2. Then she runneth, and cometh to Simon Peter, and to the other disciple, whom Jesus loved, and saith unto them, They have taken away the Lord out of the sepulchre, and we know not where they have laid him.

3. Peter therefore went forth, and that other disciple, and came to the sepulchre.

4. So they ran both together: and the other disciple did outrun Peter, and came first to the sepulchre.

5. And he stooping down, and looking in, saw the linen clothes lying; yet went he not in.

6. Then cometh Simon Peter following him, and went into the sepulchre, and seeth the linen clothes lie,

7. And the napkin, that was about his head, not lying with the linen clothes, but wrapped together in a place by itself.

8. Then went in also that other disciple, which came first to the sepulchre, and he saw, and believed.

9. For as yet they knew not the scripture, that he must rise again from the dead.

10. Then the disciples went away again unto their own home.

11. But Mary stood without at the sepulchre weeping: and as she wept, she stooped down, and looked into the sepulchre,

12. And seeth two angels in white sitting, the one at the head, and the other at the feet, where the body of Jesus had lain.

13. And they say unto her, Woman, why weepest thou? She saith unto them, Because they have taken away my Lord, and I know not where they have laid him.

14. And when she had thus said, she turned herself back, and saw Jesus standing, and knew not that it was Jesus.

15. Jesus saith unto her, Woman, why weepest thou? whom seekest thou? She, supposing him to be the gardener, saith unto him, Sir, if thou have borne him hence, tell me where thou hast laid him, and I will take him away.

16. Jesus saith unto her, Mary. She turned herself, and saith unto

him, Rabboni; which is to say, Master.

17. Jesus saith unto her, Touch me not; for I am not yet ascended to my Father: but go to my brethren, and say unto them, I ascend unto my Father, and your Father; and to my God, and your God.

18. Mary Magdalene came and told the disciples that she had seen the Lord, and that he had spoken these things unto her.

19. Then the same day at evening, being the first day of the week, when the doors were shut where the disciples were assembled for fear of the Jews, came Jesus and stood in the midst, and saith unto them, Peace be unto you.

20. And when he had so said, he shewed unto them his hands and his side. Then were the disciples glad, when they saw the Lord.

21. Then said Jesus to them again, Peace be unto you: as my Father hath sent me, even so send I you.

22. And when he had said this, he breathed on them, and saith unto them, Receive ye the Holy Ghost:

23. Whose soever sins ye remit, they are remitted unto them; and whose soever sins ye retain, they are retained.

24. But Thomas, one of the twelve, called Didymus, was not with them when Jesus came.

25. The other disciples therefore said unto him, We have seen the Lord. But he said unto them, Except I shall see in his hands the print of the nails, and put my finger into the print of the nails, and thrust my hand into his side, I will not believe.

26. And after eight days again his disciples were within, and Thomas with them: then came Jesus, the doors being shut, and stood in the midst, and said, Peace be unto you.

27. Then saith he to Thomas, Reach hither thy finger, and behold my hands; and reach hither thy hand, and thrust it into my side: and be not faithless, but believing.

28. And Thomas answered and said unto him, My Lord and my God.

29. Jesus saith unto him, Thomas, because thou hast seen me, thou hast believed: blessed are they that have not seen, and yet have believed.

30. And many other signs truly did Jesus in the presence of his disciples, which are not written in this book:

31. But these are written, that ye might believe that Jesus is the Christ, the Son of God; and that believing ye might have life through his name.

The Bodily Resurrection of Jesus

The resurrection of Jesus was first declared in Genesis

3:15, and throughout the Old Testament we find many more prophecies of His coming, prophecies of His sufferings, His death, and His resurrection. God had declared to Satan, "It (the seed of the woman) shall bruise thy head, and thou shalt bruise His heel." In order that this be true and Satan's head be bruised, the resurrection was a divine imperative. Satan was to bruise the heel of Jesus—and he did just that on Calvary; but before the beginning of the Millennium Jesus will personally put Satan in the pit "and shut him up, and set a seal upon him, that he should deceive the nations no more, till *the thousand years* should be fulfilled." Then at the beginning of the eternal ages He will put Satan into the lake of fire and brimstone, where he will be "tormented day and night *for ever and ever*" (Rev. 20:1—10).

The Old Testament sets forth many types of our Lord's sufferings, death, and resurrection. The *ark* was a type of Jesus conquering the world, the flesh, the devil, death, hell, and the grave—it passed through the waters of judgment and came to rest upon the cleansed earth: ". . . Once the longsuffering of God waited in the days of Noah, while the ark was a preparing, wherein few, that is, eight souls were saved by water. The like figure whereunto even baptism doth also now save us (not the putting away of the filth of the flesh, but the answer of a good conscience toward God,) by the resurrection of Jesus Christ" (I Pet. 3:20,21).

Abraham's offering of Isaac was a perfect figure of the death, burial, and resurrection of Jesus. When Isaac asked, "Where is the lamb for a burnt-offering?" Abraham replied, *"God will provide Himself a lamb* for a burnt-offering." Then as Abraham took the knife in hand to slay Isaac, an angel spoke to him and said, "Lay not thine hand upon the lad, neither do thou any thing unto him. . . And Abraham lifted up his eyes, and looked, and behold behind him *a ram caught in a thicket* by his horns: and Abraham went and took the ram, and offered him up for a burnt-offering in the stead of his son" (Gen. 22:1–14).

The Apostle Paul spoke of this in Hebrews 11:17–19: "By faith Abraham, when he was tried, offered up Isaac: and he that had received the promises offered up his only begotten son. Of whom it was said, That in Isaac shall thy seed be called: *Accounting that God was able to raise him up, even from the dead; from whence also he received him IN A FIGURE.*"

The children of Israel crossed over the Red Sea on dry ground *three days* after they had slain the Paschal lamb—a type of believers being raised and caught up to be with Jesus in the clouds in the air.

Jonah's three days and three nights in the belly of the whale is certainly a type of our Lord's three days and three nights in the heart of the earth.

In Psalm 16:9–11 we read, "Therefore my heart is glad, and my glory rejoiceth: my flesh also shall rest in hope. *For thou wilt not leave my soul in hell; neither wilt thou suffer thine Holy One to see corruption. Thou wilt shew me the path of life:* in thy presence is fulness of joy; at thy right hand there are pleasures for evermore!"

No minister on earth believes in the shed blood of Jesus more than I do, and probably no minister has preached more often on that subject than I have—for *without* the shedding of blood there can be no remission of sin; but it is just as necessary that we preach *the resurrection,* because if Jesus had not risen bodily from the dead, there could be no hope for us. Paul expresses the importance of the resurrection in his letter to the Corinthian church:

"Now if Christ be preached that He rose from the dead, how say some among you that there is no resurrection of the dead? But if there be no resurrection of the dead, then is Christ not risen: and if Christ be not risen, then is our preaching vain, and your faith is also vain. Yea, and we are found false witnesses of God; because we have testified of God that He raised up Christ: whom He raised not up, if so be that the dead rise not.

"For if the dead rise not, then is not Christ raised: and if Christ be not raised, your faith is vain; ye are yet in your sins. Then they also which are fallen asleep in Christ are perished. If in this life only we have hope in Christ, WE ARE OF ALL MEN MOST MISERABLE" (I Cor. 15:12–19).

It is not enough to preach Calvary alone, for we cannot separate the death and the resurrection of Jesus. In I Corinthians 15:1–4 Paul defines the Gospel:

"Moreover, brethren, I declare unto you the Gospel which I preached unto you, which also ye have received, and wherein ye stand; by which also ye are saved, if ye keep in memory what I preached unto you, unless ye have believed in vain. For I delivered unto you first of all that which I also received, how that *Christ DIED for our sins* according to the Scriptures; and that *He was BURIED,* and that *HE ROSE AGAIN the third day* according to the Scriptures."

Jesus was "delivered for our offences, and was raised again for our justification" (Rom. 4:25). If He had remained in the tomb we would have no salvation, no justification.

It was because the apostles were witnesses of His resurrection that they spoke with such boldness:

The resurrection was the heart of the message Peter gave on the Day of Pentecost: "Ye men of Israel, hear these words: Jesus of Nazareth, a man approved of God among you by miracles and wonders and signs, which God did by Him in the midst of you, as ye yourselves also know: Him, being delivered by the determinate counsel and foreknowledge of God, ye have taken, and by wicked hands have crucified and slain: *whom God hath raised up, having loosed the pains of death: because it was not possible that He should be holden of it.*

"For David speaketh concerning Him, I foresaw the Lord always before my face, for He is on my right hand, that I should not be moved: Therefore did my heart rejoice, and my tongue was glad; moreover also my flesh shall rest in hope: because *thou wilt not leave my soul in hell, neither wilt thou suffer thine Holy One to see corruption.* Thou hast made known to me the ways of life; thou shalt make me full of joy with thy countenance.

"Men and brethren, let me freely speak unto you of the patriarch David, that he is both dead and buried, and his sepulchre is with us unto this day. Therefore being a prophet, and knowing that God had sworn with an oath to him, that of the fruit of his loins, according to the flesh, *He would raise up Christ to sit on his throne;* he seeing this before *spake of the resurrection of Christ,* that His soul was not left in hell, neither His flesh did see corruption. This Jesus hath God raised up, whereof we all are witnesses" (Acts 2:22–32).

Peter and John preached the resurrection after the healing of the lame man at the temple gate:

"As the lame man which was healed held Peter and John, all the people ran together unto them in the porch which is called Solomon's, greatly wondering. And when Peter saw it, he answered unto the people,

"Ye men of Israel, why marvel ye at this? or why look ye so earnestly on us, as though by our own power or holiness we had made this man to walk? The God of Abraham, and of Isaac, and of Jacob, the God of our fathers, hath glorified His Son Jesus; whom ye delivered up, and denied Him in the presence of Pilate, when he was determined to let Him go.

"But ye denied the Holy One and the Just, and desired a murderer to be granted unto you; and killed the Prince of life, WHOM GOD HATH RAISED FROM THE DEAD; WHEREOF WE ARE WITNESSES. And His name through faith in His name hath made this man strong, whom ye see and know: yea, the faith which is by Him hath given him this perfect soundness in the presence of you all" (Acts 3:11–16).

When the apostles were called before the Sanhedrin they preached the resurrection: "Then Peter, filled with the

Holy Ghost, said unto them, Ye rulers of the people, and elders of Israel, if we this day be examined of the good deed done to the impotent man, by what means he is made whole; be it known unto you all, and to all the people of Israel, that by the name of Jesus Christ of Nazareth, whom ye crucified, whom GOD RAISED FROM THE DEAD, even by Him doth this man stand here before you whole. This is the stone which was set at nought of you builders, which is become the head of the corner. Neither is there salvation in any other: for there is none other name under heaven given among men, whereby we must be saved" (Acts 4:8–12).

They preached the resurrection when the rulers of Israel commanded them not to speak in the name of Jesus. They answered, "We ought to obey God rather than men. *The God of our fathers RAISED UP JESUS, whom ye slew and hanged on a tree* . . . and we are His witnesses of these things . . . ." (Acts 5:17–33 gives the account in full.)

When Peter went to the house of Cornelius with the message of *"salvation by grace through faith,"* he preached the resurrection of Jesus. (Please read Acts chapter 10.)

When Paul preached in the synagogue in Antioch, he preached the resurrection, quoting from Psalm 16:10 and stating that *"He, whom God raised again, saw no corruption"* (Acts 13:37).

No one witnessed the actual resurrection itself, but in this chapter of John's Gospel we find the record of several of the appearances of Jesus to His disciples and others after He rose from the grave. God did not allow human eye to witness this greatest event of all history, both sacred and secular; nor did He allow mortal eyes to gaze upon Jesus during His moments of deepest agony while He hung on the cross. God spread darkness over all the earth during this most horrible time of His Son's suffering, agony such as the mind of man could not understand or the words of man adequately explain.

Blackness veiled the Christ while He made His atonement

on the cross. God did not allow mortal man to gaze upon His infinite work in the death of His Son. Man witnessed the wicked, cruel way in which Jesus was treated during the mockery of His trial; man witnessed the horrible fact of the crucifixion and the flight of the disciples as they deserted their Lord and sought safety for themselves; but when God laid on His only begotten Son *the iniquity of us all,* when God made His soul an offering for our sin, He blacked out the universe and did not permit the eyes of man to behold His part in the death of Jesus. God alone bore witness to that horrible sight, He alone felt the full impact of that terrible moment.

I realize that it is impossible for us to comprehend that Jesus the Lamb was actually smitten by God the Father; but God demanded a perfect substitute, and what God demanded, *only GOD could provide:*

"For all have sinned, and come short of the glory of God; being justified freely by His grace through the redemption that is in Christ Jesus: *Whom GOD hath set forth to be a propitiation through faith in His blood,* to declare His righteousness for the remission of sins that are past, through the forbearance of God; to declare, I say, at this time His righteousness: that He might be just, and the justifier of him which believeth in Jesus" (Rom. 3:23–26). It was GOD who "set forth" His Son.

It was in the shedding of the precious blood of the Lamb of God that the *essence* of the atonement was exhibited on the cross, and *without* the shedding of His blood the atonement could never have been. God was the *Exhibitor,* the Lamb was the *Exhibit;* and His shed blood was the essence of the atonement.

"God commendeth His love toward us, in that, while we were yet sinners, Christ died for us" (Rom. 5:8). The Gospel of the marvelous grace of God is a glorious fact about a most glorious act: *the God of grace commended His love toward us*—and in His love *He associates Himself* with the horrible death of Christ on the cross for sinners.

In this we see a striking contrast: It is possible that MAN would sacrifice himself for a *good* man, but *GOD sacrificed Himself for BAD men*—strengthless, ungodly sinners who were His enemies.

"For what the law could not do, in that it was weak through the flesh, God sending His own Son in the *likeness* of sinful flesh, and for sin, condemned sin in the flesh" (Rom. 8:3). Christ's *atonement* explains His *Incarnation*—that is, the Incarnation took place in order that the sin of the world might be put away by the offering of the body of Jesus Christ *once,* for all, forever, never to be repeated. By His *one offering* He satisfied God forever.

God's very nature—His holiness and His righteousness—demands that He condemn sin, and this He did in a specific way: *He judged CHRIST, His only begotten Son, for US.* The Lord Jesus took a body of flesh, thus identifying Himself with the believer's sin. *HE did no sin,* but God made Him to be sin (not a sinner) *for US:* "For He hath made Him to be sin for us, who knew no sin; that we might be made the righteousness of God in Him" (II Cor. 5:21).

Jesus gave Himself, an offering for sin, in order that all who believe in His shed blood and finished work may be set free from the *penalty* and the *power* of sin. Christ answered to God for man's sin, He judged sin in His own body on the cross. Therefore, when we believe on Him and put our trust in His shed blood and finished work, we are made "the righteousness of God in HIM." He was made a curse *that WE might be delivered* from the curse of sin: "Christ hath redeemed us from the curse of the law, being made a curse for us: for it is written, Cursed is every one that hangeth on a tree" (Gal. 3:13).

God will not acquit the wicked (Nah. 1:3). In Deuteronomy 13:6—10 He instructed Moses not to spare *the idolater,* but to put him to death. God's warning concerning idolaters is repeated in Deuteronomy 29:18—28.

God did not spare *Saul* when he disobeyed the instructions in I Samuel 15:3—9 and failed to destroy Agag, king of the Amalekites. He kept back the goodly cattle and spared the king; therefore God took his kingdom from him: "And Samuel said unto Saul, I will not return with thee: for thou hast rejected the word of the Lord, and the Lord hath rejected thee from being king over Israel. . . The Lord hath rent the kingdom of Israel from thee this day, and hath given it to a neighbour of thine, that is better than thou" (I Sam. 15:26,28).

God did not spare *Pharaoh* when the Egyptian king dared to rebel against Him. "He cast upon them the fierceness of His anger, wrath, and indignation, and trouble, by sending evil angels among them. He made a way to His anger; He spared not their soul from death, but gave their life over to the pestilence; and smote all the firstborn in Egypt . . ." (Psalm 78:49–51). Read the entire account in Exodus, chapters 5 through 14.

God did not spare *the angels who sinned,* "but cast them down to hell, and delivered them into chains of darkness, to be reserved unto judgment" (II Pet. 2:4).

He did not spare *the people of Noah's day.* Peter tells us that God "spared not the old world, but saved Noah the eighth person, a preacher of righteousness, bringing in the flood upon the world of the ungodly" (II Pet. 2:5). The entire account is given in Genesis, chapters 6 and 7.

God did not spare *Israel* from being cut off from the blessing they would have received had they believed Him. Because of their unbelief they were judged. "Because of unbelief they were broken off, and thou standest by faith. Be not high minded, but fear: *For if God spared not the NATURAL BRANCHES, take heed lest He also spare not thee*" (Rom. 11:20,21).

Above all, *God did not spare HIMSELF:* "He that spared not His own Son, but delivered Him up for us all, how shall He not with Him also freely give us all things?" (Rom. 8:32).

Isaiah also declared, "Who hath believed our report? and to whom is the arm of the Lord revealed? For He shall grow up before Him as a tender plant, and as a root out of a dry ground: He hath no form nor comeliness; and when we shall see Him, there is no beauty that we should desire Him. He is despised and rejected of men; a Man of sorrows, and acquainted with grief: and we hid as it were our faces from Him; He was despised, and we esteemed Him not. *Surely He hath borne our griefs, and carried our sorrows: yet we did esteem Him stricken, SMITTEN OF GOD, AND AFFLICTED*" (Isa. 53:1–4).

"And without controversy great is the mystery of godliness: God was manifest in the flesh, justified in the Spirit, seen of angels, preached unto the Gentiles, believed on in the world, received up into glory" (I Tim. 3:16).

If WE were to be spared, God could not spare *Jesus.* But now it is a glorious fact that anyone who will believe on Jesus, trust in His shed blood and finished work, can be spared for the sake of ONE—Jesus, the spotless Lamb of God. Because HE was bruised by Jehovah, because HE was "smitten of God," WE can be spared through faith in HIM:

"As many as received Him, to them gave He power to become the sons of God, even to them that believe on His name: which were born, not of blood, nor of the will of the flesh, nor of the will of man, *BUT OF GOD*" (John 1:12,13).

All three Persons of the Trinity operated in connection with the Incarnation (Heb. 10:5; Phil. 2:7; Luke 1:35).

All three Persons of the Trinity were active in the atonement (Isa. 53:6–10; Eph. 5:2; Heb. 9:14).

In like manner, Father, Son, and Holy Ghost operated in connection with *the bodily resurrection* of Jesus (Rom. 6:4; 8:11; John 10:17).

And just as God the Father, God the Son, and God the Holy Spirit were all active in the Incarnation, the atonement, and the bodily resurrection, so do all three Persons of the Godhead operate together as having to do with our salvation.

Verse 1: *"The first day of the week cometh Mary Mag-*

dalene early, when it was yet dark, unto the sepulchre, and seeth the stone taken away from the sepulchre."

The resurrected Lord made eleven appearances between His resurrection and His ascension:

1. He appeared to Mary Magdalene when she was alone (Mark 16:9; John 20:14).
2. He appeared to certain women returning from the sepulchre (Matt. 28:8–10).
3. He appeared to Simon Peter when he was alone (Luke 24:34).
4. He appeared to two disciples on the road to Emmaus (Luke 24:13–16).
5. He appeared to the disciples assembled at Jerusalem, but Thomas was not present with them (John 20:19–24).
6. He appeared to them again a week later when Thomas was present (John 20:26).
7. He appeared to seven of the disciples who were fishing at the Sea of Galilee (John 21:1,2).
8. He appeared to the eleven apostles (and possibly others) on a mountain in Galilee (Matt. 28:16–20).
9. He appeared to more than five hundred brethren at one time (I Cor. 15:6).
10. He appeared to James when he was alone (I Cor. 15:7).
11. Just before His ascension He appeared to all of the apostles (and possibly others) on the Mount of Olives.

It was then that they beheld Him as He was taken up "and a cloud received Him out of their sight" (Acts 1:1–12).

"*The first day of the week cometh Mary Magdalene early . . . .*" John and Mark both make it clear that Mary Magdalene was alone when Jesus appeared to her (Mark 16:9; John 20:11–15). Matthew tells us that Mary Magdalene and "the other Mary" came to the sepulchre together, that they saw an angel and heard the announcement that Jesus had risen (Matt. 28:1–7). They ran to bring the tidings of the resurrection to the disciples, Jesus met them on the way and both of the women saw Him at the same time. Is there a *contradiction* here? How can these two accounts be reconciled?

After carefully studying all the accounts given concerning the appearances of Jesus between His resurrection and His ascension, we conclude that Mary Magdalene and "the other Mary" were not alone at the sepulchre the morning of the resurrection. (Read Mark 16:1, Luke 23:55,56 and 24:1; compare these passages with Matthew 28:1, and it becomes clear that several women were with the two Marys.)

When they came near to the sepulchre, the women saw the open tomb, the stone having been rolled away. It came to the mind of Mary Magdalene that the body of Jesus had been stolen or taken away, and without a moment's hesitation she ran to Peter and John to tell them the news. This record we find in verses 1 and 2 of our present chapter.

Then while Mary Magdalene was gone from the sepulchre, the other women who were with her went up to the tomb and found the body of Jesus gone. They saw the angels and were told that Jesus had risen; and they were commanded to go and tell His disciples. They left the tomb to carry the news of the resurrection, some going in one direction, some in another.

While they were gone, Mary Magdalene *returned* to the sepulchre with Peter and John shortly after the other women had left the tomb. It stands to reason that Peter and John could outrun Mary, and therefore they arrived at the tomb ahead of her. They saw that it was empty, and they went away, leaving Mary standing by the tomb, weeping. She then saw the angels. Immediately thereafter she saw the Lord Himself, and He spoke to her as recorded in verse 17 of this chapter: "Jesus saith unto her, Touch me not; for I am not yet ascended to my Father: but go to my brethren, and say unto them, I ascend unto my Father, and your Father; and to my God, and your God."

In the meantime, the other women were carrying the resurrection message to other disciples in various parts of the city. Mary (wife of Cleophas) and Salome were on their way when Jesus met them—no doubt very shortly after

He had appeared to Mary Magdalene. The other women did not see Him, but gave the message of His resurrection to other disciples in the Jerusalem area, as they had been instructed to do.

Shortly after this, Jesus appeared to Peter, who had already returned to the grave a second time when he heard Mary Magdalene's report that she had talked with Jesus.

That same day, Jesus joined the two disciples on the way to Emmaus, they having left Jerusalem after Joanna and the women with her had reported seeing the angels, finding the open tomb, and receiving the message that Jesus had risen from the dead.

It was in the evening of that same day that Jesus appeared to the apostles and others who were with them, Thomas not being present at that time.

John simply tells us that Mary Magdalene came to the tomb *early* (even before daylight) and saw the stone taken away from the door of the tomb. Matthew gives a little more on this than John does. In Matthew 28:2–4 we read, "And, behold, there was a great earthquake: for the angel of the Lord descended from heaven, and came and rolled back the stone from the door, and sat upon it. His countenance was like lightning, and his raiment white as snow: and for fear of him the keepers did shake, and became as dead men."

The stone that had lain over the door of the tomb was a huge stone; it probably weighed several thousand pounds—and here we learn that it was rolled away by an angel. Christ could easily have removed the stone Himself, or He could have come out of the grave without its even *being* moved. When *Lazarus* was called from the tomb, human hands removed the stone from the door of his sepulchre, as Jesus commanded them; but the stone from the tomb of Jesus was removed by *heavenly* hands, by order of Almighty God. In all things Jesus must have pre-eminence.

Verse 2: *"Then she runneth, and cometh to Simon Peter,*

and to the other disciple, whom Jesus loved, and saith unto them, They have taken away the Lord out of the sepulchre, and we know not where they have laid Him."

Various Bible scholars have given various reasons why Mary sought Peter and John. These two disciples seemed nearer to the Lord Jesus than the others; *John* was "the beloved disciple," and we are plainly told that he and Peter were in the trio of favored witnesses on the Mount of Transfiguration (Matt. 17:1–8). Jesus also took these same three disciples further into the Garden of Gethsemane when He went there to pray just before His arrest and trial: "Then cometh Jesus with them unto a place called Gethsemane, and saith unto the disciples, Sit ye here, while I go and pray yonder. And He took with Him Peter and the two sons of Zebedee, and began to be sorrowful and very heavy" (Matt. 26:36,37).

Even after the arrest of Jesus, Peter and John stayed close by. It is true that Peter followed "afar off," and that he grievously backslid before the trial had gone very far; but at least he was there while the others were hiding somewhere. *Only John* witnessed Peter's backsliding—and he probably witnessed the bitter tears of repentance after Jesus turned and looked at Peter. I like to think that a close and beautiful friendship existed between John and Peter. Their nearness to the Lord was logically the reason Mary ran to find *them* instead of some of the other disciples when she found the stone rolled away from the door of the tomb where Jesus had been laid.

"They have taken away the Lord out of the sepulchre, and we know not where they have laid Him!" Mary loved the Lord Jesus with all of her heart, but she was walking by sight, not by faith. When she saw that the stone had been removed from the door of His tomb she immediately concluded that someone had stolen His body. It did not once occur to her that He was alive and had walked out of the tomb as He had declared He would do. It could be that Mary had not actually heard Jesus make the assertion

that He would rise again on the third day, but surely she had heard it from others, if not from Jesus Himself. She did not have the completed, written Word as we have it today, where we can look back and see Calvary and the resurrection as an accomplished fact. Missing the body of her Lord, Mary had no idea where He was, and her one thought was that someone had stolen Him away.

Verse 3: *"Peter therefore went forth, and that other disciple, and came to the sepulchre."*

When Mary told them the stone had been taken away and the body of Jesus was gone, Peter and John hastened to the sepulchre to see for themselves what these things meant. Also, under the Mosaic law, *a woman* was not eligible to bear witness. A truth was declared "at the mouth of two or more witnesses"—*but those witnesses must be MEN.* So here we have two acceptable witnesses—Peter and John—to testify to the empty tomb.

Verse 4: *"So they ran both together: and the other disciple did outrun Peter, and came first to the sepulchre."*

The fact that they *ran* is evidence of their excitement and anxiety, and John outran Peter. It has been suggested that this happened because Peter had a guilty conscience on account of his denial of Jesus just before the crucifixion, but this does not seem logical. Had he still felt guilty because he had earlier denied the Lord, he would not have gone to the sepulchre *at all*—and certainly he would not have gone *running.* Also, if he had had a guilty conscience he would not have *entered* the sepulchre, as verse 6 tells us he did. The more reasonable conclusion would be that John outran Peter because he was much the younger of the two.

But whatever the reason, the fact that John *outran* Peter does not necessarily mean that he *loved* Jesus any more than Peter did. Many saints of God today cannot run at all; they are on hospital beds and in wheelchairs. Devotion to Jesus is not measured by bodily exercise, but by what we do for Him in the right spirit in spreading the Gospel and winning souls.

Verse 5: *"And he stooping down, and looking in, saw the linen clothes lying; yet went he not in."*

There have been many suggestions as to why John did not enter the sepulchre when he arrived and found it empty. He did enter a bit later (v. 8), therefore it was not according to the suggestion of some that he would be ceremonially defiled. I would think that since John was the younger of the two men, if there was any real reason why he hesitated in entering the tomb it was because Peter was older than he, and out of respect for the older man he graciously waited and allowed Peter to enter the tomb first. Also, as previously pointed out, it was necessary that *two* witnesses testify in order to establish a point of truth.

We are told here that John *stooped down* to look into the tomb. In that day, many sepulchres were caves. This particular one was hewn out of the side of a rock hill, and in the back of the tomb was a place hewn out for the body to be laid to rest. I have seen the tomb in the garden near Calvary which is believed to be the tomb where the body of Jesus was laid, and I saw the place carved out where the body was laid. It would be *necessary* to stoop down in order to look into such a sepulchre to see if a body were still in the small place carved out for it.

When John looked in he saw the linen clothes in which the body of Jesus had been wrapped. The Greek language suggests that the graveclothes had not been disturbed, but were lying in perfect order exactly as they had been when they held the body of Jesus. The sight of them satisfied John, for he then knew that no enemy had stolen the body of his Lord. He at once understood that a miracle had taken place.

Verses 6 and 7: *"Then cometh Simon Peter following him, and went into the sepulchre, and seeth the linen clothes lie, and the napkin, that was about His head, not lying with the linen clothes, but wrapped together in a place by itself."*

John had come to the tomb, he had seen the stone rolled away, but he had stopped at the doorway to look inside; he did not enter. Then came Peter close behind him—and I do not imagine that he even *paused* at the door. It would have been in keeping with his temperament and his impulsive nature to go right on into the sepulchre. Salvation by grace changes the heart, but the basic temperament of a person is not altered by grace. Peter was always impulsive in both speech and actions. I can easily imagine that in his excitement he did not stop until he was inside the tomb and saw the graveclothes lying there.

Greek authorities tell us that there are two different words used in this passage to express *seeing.* John saw *at a glance*—in other words, he glanced into the tomb, and what he saw convinced him that a miracle had happened. But Peter *looked as a spectator.* He examined the surroundings, carefully checked everything, and then he, too, was convinced of a miracle. A quick glance satisfied John, but Peter had to do some observing before he was satisfied. Each man behaved in his own characteristic fashion—which should teach us that we need to make allowance for wide varieties in the individual character of born again, God-fearing believers today.

What Peter and John saw was clear evidence of an orderly transaction. The linen clothes were in place, the napkin that had been around the head of Jesus lay in a place by itself, separate from the linen clothes. There were no signs of haste. Certainly *thieves* would not have taken time or trouble to roll the napkin up and put it in one place, and arrange the linen clothes neatly in another place. If the body had been stolen, the thieves would have taken clothes and all.

Verse 8: *"Then went in also that other disciple, which came first to the sepulchre, and he saw, and believed."*

Perhaps John heard Peter exclaim from within the tomb, or perhaps Peter called to him from within. At any rate, John then entered the empty tomb. I think John realized the fact of the Lord's resurrection, and the statement *"he saw and believed"* applies to that realization rather than to believing unto salvation. It does not mean that John had not been converted until this time, for certainly we know he was a devout believer and had walked with Jesus throughout His earthly ministry. What he believed here was that Jesus had risen from the grave, and it could be that John was *the first* to grasp this marvelous truth. He was not believing *unto salvation,* but unto *the bodily resurrection of Jesus.*

Verse 9: *"For as yet they knew not the Scripture, that He must rise again from the dead."*

The literal Greek here reads, "as yet they had not known." The meaning is simply that up until this time Peter and John, like the other disciples and followers of Jesus, had not yet fully understood the meaning of the words of Jesus when He had told them that He would rise again from the dead.

Just what *"Scripture"* is referred to here is not stated. I believe it refers to the Old Testament teaching, both in type and in typical events in the Old Testament economy, which pointed to the Lamb of God, smitten and raised again from the dead. It could point to *the entire account* of the coming Lamb, from Genesis 3:15 until He came in the fulness of time (Gal. 4:4).

Notice the statement, *"that He MUST rise again from the dead."* This is to be taken literally. It was a divine necessity that Jesus rise from the dead in order to purchase our redemption and complete the work the Father had sent Him to do. *He must DIE*—but He must also *rise again* in order to become our substitute that we might be saved from sin.

The disciples and those who followed Jesus might have

momentarily forgotten His words concerning His resurrection on the third day, but His *enemies* had not forgotten. The chief priests and Pharisees came to Pilate and said, "*Sir, we remember that that deceiver said, while He was yet alive, After three days I will rise again.* Command therefore that the sepulchre be made sure until the third day, lest His disciples come by night, and steal Him away, and say unto the people, He is risen from the dead: so the last error shall be worse than the first. Pilate said unto them, Ye have a watch: go your way, make it as sure as ye can. *So they went, and made the sepulchre sure, sealing the stone, and setting a watch*" (Matt. 27:62–66). But all the forces of Satan could not prevail against the foreordained plan and program of Almighty God. Jesus rose the third day as promised, and because HE lives, WE live!

Verse 10: "*Then the disciples went away again unto their own home.*"

The tomb was empty, the body of Jesus was gone. The graveclothes were there just as He had lain in them, but the body of the Lord had risen. Convinced of this, Peter and John saw no reason to tarry longer at the empty sepulchre. So they returned to their own homes, knowing now that Jesus had done exactly what He had promised to do.

Verses 11 and 12: "*But Mary stood without at the sepulchre weeping: and as she wept, she stooped down, and looked into the sepulchre, and seeth two angels in white sitting, the one at the head, and the other at the feet, where the body of Jesus had lain.*"

Why was Mary still at the tomb? Why did she not leave when Peter and John left? The Scripture does not tell us why she lingered there alone after the others had gone, but I believe she stayed near the tomb simply *because she was a woman.* Woman is a special creation of God. He created the earth and all things therein, He made man and let him name all the animals; but in all creation

Adam found no one to be his helpmate. God saw the loneliness of man, He saw that man's life was not complete, and He created woman to be his companion and helpmate. Woman has a greater capacity for love and appreciation than man has. Jesus had cast seven devils out of Mary Magdalene, and she appreciated and loved Him so much that she was reluctant to leave the last place where she had known Him to be, even though she now thought someone had stolen His body away. Her actions were those of typical womanhood, while Peter and John behaved in a perfectly masculine way.

Consider the contrast even today between man and woman: When a loved one is lowered into the grave, most of the time the men walk away from the graveside, while the mother or wife must often be helped or carried away. Since it is woman's nature to love more deeply than man, she *suffers* more deeply in sorrow at the loss of a loved one. Mary had a longing in her heart that would not be satisfied and she could not leave the place where her Lord had been laid. The fact that His body was gone did not satisfy her. In spite of the fact that the tomb was empty and the graveclothes lying neatly in place, she was not satisfied that Jesus had literally *risen* from the dead. In her uncertainty she lingered by the tomb, and burdened with grief, *she wept.*

"And as she wept, she stooped down, and looked into the sepulchre." It would be difficult to imagine *why* Mary looked inside the tomb. Surely Peter and John had told her what they had found inside, surely she knew the sepulchre was empty. But her heart was hard to convince. Perhaps because of some last, tiny ray of hope, perhaps because she knew not what else to do, she stooped and looked inside the open, empty tomb—and she saw a wondrous sight!

She saw *"two angels in white sitting, the one at the head, and the other at the feet, where the body of Jesus had lain."* Apparently these heavenly beings had come and gone, and then returned—in an invisible, supernatural, and unexplainable way (insofar as the human mind is concerned). Peter and John did not see them when *they* went into the tomb, but when Mary looked inside after the two disciples had gone, she not only *saw* the angels, she *talked* with them.

These angels were dressed *"in white,"* the symbol of purity, perfection, sinlessness, free from all defilement and stain. White was the color of Christ's raiment when He was transfigured (Matt. 17:2), and white will be worn by the redeemed in glory (Rev. 3:4; 7:9; 19:7,8).

It is interesting to notice the *position* of the two angels in the tomb: One sat at the head, and the other at the feet, of the place where Jesus had lain. I believe God placed them thus to guard the body of the Lamb while He lay in the tomb. In Psalm 91:11 we read, "He shall give His angels charge over thee . . . ."

Angels are not born; they are God's *created beings.* They are God's servants, ministers to the heirs of salvation (Heb. 1:14). They appear instantaneously, supernaturally, as God commissions them. Wherever a believer walks, angels are in attendance. We cannot *see* them, but we know they are present with us because God's Word declares it: "The angel of the Lord encampeth round about them that fear Him, and delivereth them" (Psalm 34:7).

An angel announced to the virgin Mary that she would be the mother of God's only Son (Luke 1:26–38). Angels announced the birth of Jesus (Luke 2:8–14). Angels ministered to Him when He met a personal devil on the Mount of Temptation (Matt. 4:11). An angel came to strengthen Him when He prayed in the Garden of Gethsemane (Luke 22:43). And here in our present chapter, angels announce *His resurrection.*

Verse 13: *"And they say unto her, Woman, why weepest thou? She saith unto them, Because they have taken away my Lord, and I know not where they have laid Him."*

The angels spoke gently to Mary—they knew why she

wept, but they asked the question to stir up her mind and make her think seriously. They wanted her to answer for herself whether or not she really had any *reason* for weeping. Jesus had clearly declared that He would rise the third day, and having found the tomb empty Mary should have realized what had happened and then she would have rejoiced instead of mourning. But she could think of only one thing: the body of her Lord was missing from His tomb, and she had no idea where it had been taken. The spiritual significance of the empty tomb did not break through to her troubled mind. She was thinking only in terms of the natural. She knew her Lord had been dead when He was taken from the cross. She knew He had been prepared for burial and placed in this sepulchre. And now she had come with sweet spices to anoint His body (Mark 16:1) only to find Him gone! She answered the angels in almost the same words she had used in speaking to Peter and John:

"They have taken away my Lord, and I know not where they have laid Him!" To Peter and John she had said, "THE Lord," and here she said, "MY Lord." But in both instances she said, "*They* have taken away His body," and she had no idea of whom she was speaking, she did not know to whom "*they*" applied.

The fact that Mary was unperturbed by the angels indicates the depth of her grief. She showed no surprise at their presence although she undoubtedly recognized them as heavenly creatures. They did not disturb her line of thought, she did not fear them. She could think only in terms of what had happened to the body of her Lord.

Verse 14: *"And when she had thus said, she turned herself back, and saw Jesus standing, and knew not that it was Jesus."*

So concerned was Mary about the body of Jesus that she turned her back on the two heavenly creatures in whose presence she was standing. Even angels held no attraction or particular interest for her.

"She turned herself back, and saw Jesus standing." Such devotion as Mary's is never overlooked by the Lord Jesus Christ. It was to her that He first appeared, it was to her that He first spoke. Her love for Him had compelled her to linger by the tomb after Peter and John had gone, and that love was rewarded. She was the first to see the resurrected Christ, she was the first to hear Him speak.

But she *"knew not that it was Jesus."* It has been suggested that Mary failed to recognize Jesus because her eyes were filled with tears—but I disagree. If that were true, she would not have recognized the angels in the sepulchre. I believe she failed to recognize Jesus because her eyes were *"holden."* I believe God prevented her recognition of Jesus at that moment. When Jesus joined the two disciples as they traveled to Emmaus later that same day, they did not recognize Him because *"their eyes were holden* that they should not know Him" (Luke 24:16).

I believe the body of Jesus at that moment when Mary first saw Him was different from the body which had been laid in the tomb, different from the body with which He returned when the disciples fell at His feet and held Him. At this moment, He had just come from the tomb, He had not ascended to the heavenly Father—and Mary was seeking the body of her Lord as it had been when He was laid in the tomb. But we are to know Him no more after the flesh (II Cor. 5:16). Since His resurrection we are to know Him as head of the new creation that is the New Testament Church. It would have been a small thing indeed for Jesus, Creator of heaven and earth and all things that therein are, to assume an appearance that Mary would not have recognized. It would have been equally easy for Him to cause her eyes to be unable to distinguish His identity.

Verse 15: *"Jesus saith unto her, Woman, why weepest thou? Whom seekest thou? She, supposing Him to be the gardener, saith unto Him, Sir, if thou have borne Him hence, tell me where thou hast laid Him, and I will take Him away."*

"Why weepest thou? Whom seekest thou?" Jesus spoke very tenderly to Mary—and yet in His words we note a gentle rebuke. He knew why she was weeping, He knew whom she sought; but He asked her the questions in order to arrest her attention. She could think of nothing at that moment except the fact that she could not find the body of the One whom she so loved, and Jesus could not get the living message across to her until He caused her to stop and think. In questioning her, He was gently reminding her that He had clearly said He would lay His life down and that He would take it again—but she had forgotten, or else she did not understand the meaning of what He had said. Her mind remained concentrated on finding the missing body of her Lord.

"Sir, if thou have borne Him hence, tell me where thou hast laid Him, and I will take Him away!" Three times here Mary referred to Jesus as "Him," not bothering to tell this Man (whom she supposed to be the gardener) the name of Him whom she sought. Evidently she supposed that every one in the entire countryside knew whom she sought.

We might also notice that Mary did not consider that she, a woman, would be unable to lift the body of a man and remove it to any place! She was so absorbed with her one thought that she boldly said, "Tell me where thou hast laid Him, *and I will take Him away!"*

Verse 16: *"Jesus saith unto her, Mary. She turned herself, and saith unto Him, Rabboni; which is to say, Master."*

When Jesus spoke to Mary in the previous verse, He called her "woman." Now He uses her *name.* When He addressed her as "woman" He spoke as *God,* but when He said *"Mary"* He was speaking as her Redeemer and Saviour.

In John 10:4 and 27 we read, "When He putteth forth His own sheep, He goeth before them, and the sheep follow

Him: *for they know His voice. . .* My sheep hear my voice, and *I know them,* and they follow me." Jesus called Mary "woman" to let her know that He was God—exalted above every creature and every human relationship; but He called her "Mary" as one of His own whom He loved. God said to Moses, *"I know thee by name,* and thou hast also found grace in my sight" (Ex. 33:12b).

"But now thus saith the Lord that created thee, O Jacob, and He that formed thee, O Israel, Fear not: *for I have redeemed thee, I have called thee by thy name; thou art mine"* (Isa. 43:1).

"She turned herself, and saith unto Him, Rabboni; which is to say, Master." Yes, not only does the Shepherd know His sheep by name, but the sheep know the voice of the Shepherd. Mary responded to the voice of Jesus: the moment He spoke, she cried out, *"Master!"* True repentance is not "turning around," because to turn *around* is to face again in the same direction. True repentance is turning "face *about."* The sinner is dead in trespasses and sin; to be born again is to turn to life, *to Jesus,* turning away from the world, the flesh, and the devil. Mary turned *face about.* She was looking toward the place of death, but when Jesus called her she turned to Him and called Him "Master."

Verse 17: *"Jesus saith unto her, Touch me not; for I am not yet ascended to my Father: but go to my brethren, and say unto them, I ascend unto my Father, and your Father; and to my God, and your God."*

The declaration in this verse will never be fully understood until we see Jesus in that heavenly Bible class and He explains to us exactly what He meant when He said, *"Touch me not."* Certainly He did not say it because it would have been sinful or wrong for Mary to touch His risen body, for only a short time later He allowed the other women who had been at the tomb to touch Him: "And as they went to tell His disciples, behold, Jesus met them, saying, All hail. *And they came and held Him by the feet, and worshipped Him*" (Matt. 28:9). It was only a week after He said to Mary, "Touch me *not*" that He said to Thomas, "Reach hither thy finger, and behold my hands; and reach hither thy hand, and thrust it into my side: and be not faithless, but believing" (John 20:27). So certainly it would not have been *wrong* for Mary to touch Him.

According to Liddell and Scott's *Lexicon,* the Greek word here translated *"touch"* means "to fasten one's self to, to cling to, hang on by, lay hold on, or grasp," and that is what Jesus could not allow Mary to do at that point.

"For I am not yet ascended to my Father." Undoubtedly when Mary recognized Jesus she fell at His feet and for joy was about to throw her arms around Him. In adoration and worship she would have kissed His feet as did the woman in Luke 7:36–50. But Jesus knew what Mary was about to do, and He forbade her to touch Him *because He had not yet ascended to His heavenly Father.*

On the day Mary was commanded "Touch me not," God's High Priest waved a sheaf of firstfruits before Jehovah while He (*Himself* the firstfruits from the dead) would be fulfilling the type in presenting Himself before Jehovah God. "But now is Christ risen from the dead, and become the firstfruits of them that slept" (I Cor. 15:20). Jesus was the firstfruits, and He came to fulfill every type in the Old Testament economy:

"And the Lord spake unto Moses, saying, Speak unto the children of Israel, and say unto them, When ye be come into the land which I give unto you, and shall reap the harvest thereof, then ye shall bring a sheaf of the firstfruits of your harvest unto the priest: and he shall wave the sheaf before the Lord, to be accepted for you: on the morrow after the sabbath the priest shall wave it" (Lev. 23:9–11).

Matthew, Mark, and Luke do not record the admonition of Jesus, "Touch me not." But John presents Jesus as *very God in flesh,* and since He was to leave this earth and return to the Father as our great High Priest, Mary was not to become attached to His body, *the visible Man* walking on earth. Believers are to know Him as the head and foundation of the New Testament Church, head of the new relationship between God and man, "for we are members of His body, of His flesh, and of His bones" (Eph. 5:30).

"Go to my brethren, and say unto them, I ascend unto my Father, and your Father; and to my God, and your God." Mary was honored in that Jesus commissioned her to be the first to be a witness to His resurrection, carrying the news to others. Others had seen the empty tomb—*but Mary had seen JESUS!* A woman had anointed Him for His burial (John 12:1–7), and a woman was the first person to whom He revealed Himself in His resurrection glory. God highly honored holy, dedicated women in bringing salvation down to man, and He honors and uses dedicated women today in the ministry of soul-winning service in this Dispensation of Grace.

This is the first time Jesus spoke of His followers as *"brethren."* In John 12:24 He had said to them, "Except a corn of wheat fall into the ground and die, it abideth alone: but if it die, it bringeth forth much fruit." The *"corn of wheat"* was Jesus, and as He came back from the grave He became the firstfruits of the resurrection, *"the firstborn among many brethren"* (Rom. 8:29). How wonderful that Christ is not ashamed to call us "brethren" (Heb. 2:11).

"I ascend unto my Father and your Father; and to my God, and your God." Born again believers are brought into the same position *Jesus* has with the heavenly Father. We sit together in heavenly places with Jesus (Eph. 2:6); we are hid with Christ in God (Col. 3:3).

When Jesus laid His life down for us He *detached* Himself from us in the bodily sense, and we are now attached to Him in the spiritual realm. We are not to cling to Him in His earthly form; we are rather to trust in Him from the spiritual standpoint. *Positionally* we are with Him in heaven even now, and one day He will call us to meet Him in the clouds in the air. And in the first resurrection we will be made like Him (I Thess. 4:13–18; I John 3:1–3).

Jesus did not say to Mary, "Go tell my disciples that I have *risen.*" He said, "Go tell them that *I ASCEND.*" He wanted them to understand that He had not come back from the grave to remain with them on earth. In John 16:7 He had explained to them that it was expedient for Him to go away, otherwise the Comforter would not come. And now He instructs Mary to tell them that He is about to ascend into the heavens to take His place at the right hand of the Father as their representative and High Priest.

In Matthew 28:10 Jesus told the women, "Go tell my brethren that they go into Galilee, and there shall they see me," but He did not name an earthly place of meeting when He gave Mary *her* message to the disciples. He simply sent them word that He was going to ascend to the Father.

God's preachers preach many times on Calvary, we preach many times on the resurrection; but I fear most of us do not give sufficient time and importance to the *ascension* of Christ. If He had lived a perfect life on earth (but had missed Calvary) His perfect life could not have saved us. If He had died, but had remained in the grave, His death could not have saved us. He died for our sins "according to the Scriptures," but His sinless life plus His sacrificial death could not have saved us if He had not risen from the dead. Even if He had risen, *but remained upon this earth,* His ministry for us would have been incomplete because *He ascended to make intercession for us!*

"Who is he that condemneth? *It is CHRIST that died,* yea rather, that is risen again, who is even at the right hand of God, *who also maketh intercession for us*" (Rom. 8:34).

"God, who at sundry times and in divers manners spake in time past unto the fathers by the prophets, hath in these last days spoken unto us by His Son, whom He hath appointed heir of all things, by whom also He made the worlds; who being the brightness of His glory, and the express image of His Person, and upholding all things by the word of His power, *when He had by Himself purged our sins, SAT DOWN ON THE RIGHT HAND OF THE MAJESTY ON HIGH*" (Heb. 1:1–3).

The virgin birth, the sinless life, the death, resurrection, and ascension of the spotless Lamb of God—and now His intercession as the Man Christ Jesus, our High Priest—are great fundamental facts that should be preached in unity, never separated.

"Wherefore in all things it behoved Him to be made like unto His brethren, that He might be a merciful and faithful high priest in things pertaining to God, to make reconciliation for the sins of the people" (Heb. 2:17).

"For we have not an high priest which cannot be touched with the feeling of our infirmities; but was in all points tempted like as we are, yet without sin. Let us therefore come boldly unto the throne of grace, that we may obtain mercy, and find grace to help in time of need" (Heb. 4: 15,16).

"For there is one God, and one Mediator between God and men, the Man Christ Jesus" (I Tim. 2:5).

Verse 18: *"Mary Magdalene came and told the disciples that she had seen the Lord, and that He had spoken these things unto her."*

Mary was not offended by the Lord's reproof concerning her touching Him. Like a devoted, obedient servant, she did as He commanded her and immediately went in search of the disciples to tell them she had *seen* the Lord, and that He had sent them a message by her.

I like to think that Mary went to Peter's house first of all, and that she delivered her message first to Peter and John. I am sure she told the good news to all with whom she came in contact, and I believe she *ran,* not wasting one moment in getting out the good news of the resurrection. But Mark 16:10,11 gives the record of the effect her message had on the disciples:

"And she went and told them that had been with Him, as they mourned and wept. And they, when they had heard that He was alive, and had been seen of her, BELIEVED NOT!"

Jesus Appears to the Disciples; Thomas Not Present

Verse 19: *"Then the same day at evening, being the first day of the week, when the doors were shut where the disciples were assembled for fear of the Jews, came Jesus and stood in the midst, and saith unto them, Peace be unto you."*

"The same day at evening"—i. e., the evening of the resurrection day—*"the first day of the week . . . the disciples were assembled."* On this day the disciples were assembled together, apart from the world, to pray and discuss the things Mary had told them. After the resurrection the disciples *always* met on the first day of the week, the day following the Jewish Sabbath. This is the Lord's Day, our Sunday. "Sabbath" is not a word to be used in this Day of Grace, for there is no such thing as a Christian "Sabbath."

The first Sabbath was the day of *God's* rest—*NOT man's rest,* because man had not done anything from which TO rest. In Genesis 2:1—3 we read, *"Thus the heavens and the earth were finished, and all the host of them. And on the seventh day God ended His work which He had made; AND HE RESTED ON THE SEVENTH DAY FROM ALL HIS WORK WHICH HE HAD MADE. And God blessed the seventh day, and sanctified it: because that in it He had rested from all His work which God created and made."* The Hebrew reads literally, "He *sabbathed* on the seventh day." The word "sabbath" means *rest,* to cease from all work. God had finished creation so He "sabbathed" on the seventh day. God rested—but not because He was tired: "Hast thou not known? hast thou not heard, that *the everlasting God, the Lord, the Creator of the ends of the earth, fainteth not, NEITHER IS WEARY?* There is no searching of His understanding" (Isa. 40:28).

The Sabbath was given to Israel (and ONLY to Israel) as an ordinance and a command—*but it was given only AFTER the first Passover lamb was slain.* The death of the Passover lamb was a symbol of the death of the Lamb of God: ". . . For even Christ our Passover is sacrificed for us: therefore let us keep the feast, not with old leaven, neither with the leaven of malice and wickedness; *BUT WITH THE UNLEAVENED BREAD OF SINCERITY AND TRUTH*" (I Cor. 5:7,8).

The Sabbath was first made known to Israel in the gathering of the manna: "And Moses said, Eat that to day; for to day is a sabbath unto the Lord: to day ye shall not find it in the field. *Six days ye shall gather it; but on the seventh day, which is the sabbath, in it there shall be none*" (Ex. 16:25,26). The manna was the bread from heaven which sustained the life of Israel in their wilderness journey. *Jesus* is "the Bread of Life," and whosoever shall eat of that Bread shall never hunger and shall never die. Jesus Himself declared, "I am the living bread which came down from heaven: if any man eat of this bread, he shall live for ever: and the bread that I will give is my flesh, which I will give for the life of the world. . . Verily, verily, I say unto you, Except ye eat the flesh of the Son of man, and drink His blood, ye have no life in you. Whoso eateth my flesh, and drinketh my blood, hath eternal life; and I will raise him up at the last day" (John 6:51—54). Please study the entire passage of John 6:30—59.

The Sabbath which was revealed to the children of Israel by and through the manna was both symbolic and prophetic: It declared that God would again find rest in man—but *this time* the Man would meet all the requirements of God. In a body made like unto the first man, Adam, He would satisfy all the demands of divine righteousness through sinless living; and then by laying down His life and taking it again He would become *eternally the Redeemer of sinners*—justification to all who would believe in Him, propitiation for the sins of mankind, Mediator between God and men.

At Mount Sinai, the Sabbath that was first revealed in the gathering of the manna was made part of the Ten Commandments. It was given as the fourth commandment and became law to the nation Israel:

"Remember the sabbath day, to keep it holy. Six days shalt thou labour, and do all thy work: but the seventh day is the sabbath of the Lord thy God: in it thou shalt not do any work, thou, nor thy son, nor thy daughter, thy manservant, nor thy maidservant, nor thy cattle, nor thy stranger that is within thy gates" (Ex. 20:8—10).

The Sabbath was given *to Israel* as a perpetual sign between the children of Israel and Jehovah God, to set them apart from all other people and nations: "Wherefore the children of Israel shall keep the sabbath, to observe the sabbath throughout their generations, for a perpetual covenant. *It is a sign between me and the children of Israel* for ever: for in six days the Lord made heaven and earth, and on the seventh day He rested, and was refreshed" (Ex. 31:16,17).

Not only were the Israelites commanded to *keep* the Sabbath, but if any of them broke it they suffered the penalty of death: "Six days may work be done; but in the seventh is the sabbath of rest, holy to the Lord: *whosoever doeth any work in the sabbath day, he shall surely be put to death"* (Ex. 31:15).

Numbers 15:33—36 records what happened to one man who was caught *gathering sticks* on the Sabbath:

"And they that found him gathering sticks brought him unto Moses and Aaron, and unto all the congregation. And they put him in ward, because it was not declared what should be done to him. *And the Lord said unto Moses, The man shall be surely put to death: all the congregation shall stone him with stones without the camp.* And all the congregation brought him without the camp, and stoned him with stones, and he died; as the Lord commanded Moses."

God gave the Sabbath day to Israel, He imposed the death penalty upon those who broke His command, and that penalty has never been modified, revised, or done away with. The death penalty for breaking the Sabbath is just as much a part of the law as *the Sabbath day itself* is part of the law, and the Sabbath is as much a part of the law today as it was the day God commanded it to be *made* law unto Israel. God has not changed His mind about the law, the Sabbath, or sin; but *"God was in Christ, reconciling the world unto Himself,* not imputing their trespasses unto them; and hath committed unto us the word of reconciliation" (II Cor. 5:19).

Therefore, "What the law could not do, in that it was weak through the flesh, God sending His own Son in the likeness of sinful flesh, and for sin, condemned sin in the flesh: *that the righteousness of the law might be fulfilled in us* . . ." (Rom. 8:3,4). Thus we see that *"Christ is the END of the law for righteousness TO EVERY ONE THAT BELIEVETH"* (Rom. 10:4).

The law was given *specifically to Israel;* Gentiles have *never* been under the law: "For when the Gentiles, *which have not the law,* do by nature the things contained in the law, these, *having not the law,* are a law unto themselves" (Rom. 2:14).

"For sin shall not have dominion over you: *for ye are not under the law, but under grace"* (Rom. 6:14).

"Therefore if any man be in Christ, he is a new creature: old things are passed away; behold, all things are become new" (II Cor. 5:17).

"But ye are not in the flesh, but in the Spirit, if so be that the Spirit of God dwell in you. Now if any man have not the Spirit of Christ, he is none of His. And if Christ be in you, the body is dead because of sin; but the Spirit is life because of righteousness" (Rom. 8:9,10).

Believers today have no more to do with the Jewish Sabbath than life has to do with death ("for the letter killeth, but the Spirit giveth life"—II Cor. 3:6b). Christ is indeed "*the end of the law* for righteousness" to every believer. Therefore Christians today worship on the first day of the week, the Lord's Day, the day Jesus rose from the dead.

Matthew tells us that Mary Magdalene and "the other Mary" came to the sepulchre "in the end of the sabbath, as it began to dawn toward *the first day of the week*" (Matt. 28:1).

Mark tells us that when the Sabbath was past, Mary Magdalene and Mary the mother of James came to the tomb "very early in the morning *the first day of the week*" (Mark 16:1,2).

Luke declares, "Now *upon the first day of the week,* very early in the morning, they came unto the sepulchre . . ." (Luke 24:1).

And finally, *John* tells us that on "*the first day of the week* cometh Mary Magdalene early, when it was yet dark . . ." (John 20:1).

The "*first day of the week*" as mentioned in this chapter was the dawn of a new day, the day of the empty tomb, the day of the risen Christ who is *the end of the law* to those who believe.

In Leviticus 23:9—11 we read, "And the Lord spake unto Moses, saying, Speak unto the children of Israel, and say unto them, When ye be come into the land which I give unto you, and shall reap the harvest thereof, then ye shall bring a sheaf of the firstfruits of your harvest unto the priest: and he shall wave the sheaf before the Lord, to be accepted for you: *on the morrow AFTER the sabbath* the priest shall wave it."

"The morrow after the Sabbath" was certainly the first day of the week, the beginning of a *new* week—and Jesus fulfilled the type: *He rose from the dead on the first day of the week* as a fulfillment of that sheaf of firstfruits: "Now is Christ risen from the dead, and become the *firstfruits* of them that slept" (I Cor. 15:20).

More than a thousand years before the birthday of the Church, Christ (speaking by the Spirit through David) announced the first day of the week as the Lord's Day: "The Stone which the builders refused is become the head stone of the corner. This is the Lord's doing; it is marvellous in our eyes. *This is the day which the Lord hath made;* we will rejoice and be glad in it" (Psalm 118:22–24).

The first members of the New Testament Church worshipped on the first day of the week—*the Lord's Day,* not the Jewish Sabbath: "And *upon the first day of the week,* when the disciples came together to break bread, Paul preached unto them, ready to depart on the morrow; and continued his speech until midnight" (Acts 20:7).

Jesus rose from the dead on the first day of the week, and during the forty days He spent on earth *after* the resurrection He did not meet with His disciples even *once* on the Sabbath: He always met with them on the first day of the week. It was on the first day of the week that He broke bread with them, it was on the first day of the week that He gave them the great commission to spread the Gospel—and on the fortieth day after His resurrection He ascended back to heaven to take His seat at the right hand of the Father as High Priest of His Church (Acts 1:3–9).

It was on the first day of the week that He revealed Himself to John the Beloved in exile on Patmos (Rev. 1:10). On the first day of the week He gave John the message to the seven churches in Asia. On the first day of the week He gave John the Revelation—the capstone of the pyramid of the Bible.

In all of the epistles, as well as in The Revelation, the first day of the week stands out from all other days as THE day given to believers in this Dispensation of Grace. There is not one place in the New Testament where Jesus commanded His apostles (or other believers) to keep the Sabbath. The Christian is to keep *every* day holy unto the

Lord, but in this Day of Grace we are to assemble and *bring our offerings into the house of God* on the *first day of the week* (I Cor. 16:2).

It is true that the Apostle Paul often taught in the synagogue on the Jewish Sabbath, but he went there to speak to the Jews, and that was the day they came together for worship. The Sabbath was the day on which Paul had opportunity to deliver the message of grace to his own people whom he so longed to see saved. Romans 9:1–3 expresses the length to which Paul was willing to go to see Israel brought to Christ:

"I say the truth in Christ, I lie not, my conscience also bearing me witness in the Holy Ghost, that I have great heaviness and continual sorrow in my heart. *For I could wish that myself were accursed from Christ for my brethren, my kinsmen according to the flesh!*" Paul would have been willing to be *lost himself* in order to see Israel saved, and it was for that reason that he went to the synagogue on the Jewish Sabbath to proclaim the Gospel to them.

"Then the same day at evening, being the first day of the week, WHEN THE DOORS WERE SHUT . . . came Jesus and stood in the midst." John is the only Gospel writer who tells us that the doors were shut where the disciples had assembled. They had barred the door because of their fear of the Jews, lest they be put to death as followers of Jesus; but He had conquered the world, the flesh, the devil, death, hell, and the grave, and bars on a door could not keep HIM out. He entered the room without opening the door or removing the bars. In Acts 12:5–11 an *angel* opened the prison gates and set Peter free; but Jesus did not *need* an angel to open the door—He entered the room with the door *closed.* Glorious truth! *We* will one day have a body just like the resurrection body of Jesus (I John 3:2; I Cor. 15:42–44).

Consider the Lord's greeting to His disciples on this first meeting after His resurrection. Peter had profanely denied Him during His trial, and *all* of the disciples had forsaken Him and fled (although John later returned and was present at the crucifixion). How would Jesus be *expected* to greet these poor, weak followers? Would He demand reasons for their actions? Would He reprimand and criticize them? God's Word plainly tells us to reprove, rebuke, and exhort (Tit. 2:15; II Tim. 4:2)—and *there is a time* to name sin, cry aloud, and spare not. But Jesus was the Master Preacher; He knew exactly what to say and when to say it. My own heart is encouraged by His words as He greeted His disciples for the first time since coming from the tomb. No reproof, no reprimand, no reminder of their weakness and failure, but the gentle greeting, *"Peace be unto you!"*

The angels' message at His birth was "Peace on earth, good will toward men." He is the Prince of Peace, and one day He will bring *lasting* peace to this troubled world. *There will BE no peace* as long as Satan holds sway; but when Jesus puts him in the pit and sets a seal on him, there will be peace on earth and good will among men. King Jesus will sit on the throne of His father David, and the knowledge of the Lord will cover the earth as the waters now cover the sea. Even though we do not have "peace on *earth*" today, we *can* have peace in our hearts, because Jesus said, "Peace I leave with you, *my peace* I give unto you" (John 14:27). In John 16:33 He said, "These things I have spoken unto you, that *in me* ye might have peace."

Verse 20: *"And when He had so said, He shewed unto them His hands and His side. Then were the disciples glad, when they saw the Lord."*

I am sure we could not measure the disciples' astonishment when Jesus appeared in their midst while the doors and windows of the room were barred. He showed them His hands and His wounded side, to convince them that He was indeed the same Person with whom they had walked for three and one-half years, *the same Jesus*, but now in His incorruptible body. He was a Man—not a spirit, not an angel, but a MAN, the same Man who now sits at the right hand of God in heaven (I Tim. 2:5).

Luke tells us that Jesus said to the astonished disciples, "Behold *my hands and my feet,* that it is I myself: handle me, and see; for a spirit hath not flesh and bones, as ye see me have" (Luke 24:39). *John* especially mentions His pierced *side*: "And when He had so said, He shewed unto them His hands *and His side.*" There is a special reason why John spoke of the Lord's wounded side. The beloved disciple presented Jesus as *God in flesh, the only begotten SON of God.* He is the fulfillment of type—*the ark.* He is *our ark,* and *the door was in the SIDE of the ark.* The side of Jesus was opened that we may enter by faith in His shed blood and finished work.

"Then were the disciples glad when they saw the Lord!" Surely no words could describe the feelings of these men when they realized that they were actually in the presence of their risen Lord. Their fears subsided, their hearts were filled with hope, and they received *peace.* Jesus had kept His promise to return from the grave: "Ye now therefore have sorrow: but *I will see you again, and your heart shall rejoice, and your joy no man taketh from you*" (John 16:22).

When I read this passage I think, *"What will WE do when we first see Jesus?"* Can you imagine what we will do when we first see His face, when we first stand in His presence?

Luke gives a wonderful account of this appearing of Jesus, and I think it would be well worth our time to study the passage from Luke's Gospel, along with our present verse:

"And as they thus spake, Jesus Himself stood in the midst of them, and saith unto them, Peace be unto you. *But they were terrified and affrighted, and supposed that they had seen a spirit.*" (Notice that "spirit" here is not capitalized. In other words, the disciples thought they were seeing a *ghost.*)

"And He said unto them, *Why* are ye troubled? and why

do thoughts arise in your hearts? Behold my hands and my feet, that it is I myself: handle me, and see; for a spirit hath not *flesh and bones,* as ye see me have." (The life of the flesh is in the blood, according to Leviticus 17:11, and Jesus had given His blood for the salvation of sinners. He had presented the blood to the heavenly Father and then returned to earth to appear in the presence of the disciples in *a body of flesh and bones*—no blood—a body incorruptible.)

"And when He had thus spoken, He shewed them His hands and His feet. And while they yet believed not for joy, and wondered, He said unto them, Have ye here any meat? And they gave Him a piece of a broiled fish, and of an honeycomb. And He took it, and did eat before them.

"And He said unto them, These are the words which I spake unto you, while I was yet with you, that all things must be fulfilled, which were written in the law of Moses, and in the prophets, and in the psalms, concerning me. Then opened He their understanding, that they might understand the Scriptures" (Luke 24:36—45).

Jesus not only invited the disciples to *handle* Him and see that He was not a ghost or a spirit-being, *He also asked for food.* They gave Him broiled fish and honeycomb and He ate in their presence, thus giving further proof that He was a real Man.

Some may ask if *we* will eat in heaven. We will have a body like the resurrection body of Jesus; *He* ate broiled fish and honeycomb, and this would indicate that *we* can eat if we so desire—but it will not be necessary that we eat in order to sustain life. For example, in Revelation 22:1,2 we read, "He shewed me a pure river of water of life, clear as crystal, proceeding out of the throne of God and of the Lamb. In the midst of the street of it, and on either side of the river, was there *the tree of life, WHICH BARE TWELVE MANNER OF FRUITS, and yielded her fruit every month:* and the leaves of the tree were for the healing of the nations." There will be an abundance of fruit, the tree will bear a harvest each month—and if no one *eats* in the eternal home of the redeemed there will certainly be a lot of fruit going to waste!

Verse 21: *"Then said Jesus to them again, Peace be unto you: as my Father hath sent me, even so send I you."*

When Jesus greeted the disciples with "Peace be unto you" He knew they were terrified and astonished beyond measure, and He spoke peace to their hearts and minds in order that they might recognize Him as a Man and not as a ghost being. The *second* time He spoke peace to them He did so because He was sending them into an unfriendly world.

In His intercessory prayer, Jesus said to the heavenly Father, "As thou hast sent me into the world, even so have I also sent them into the world. . . Neither pray I for these alone, but for them also which shall believe on me through their word" (John 17:18,20).

It is wonderful to know that Jesus spoke peace to His disciples before He sent them into an unfriendly, hostile world—but He was not speaking to them alone. He was speaking *to all believers* throughout this Day of Grace. Even now He speaks peace to the hearts of His children before He commands them to go and witness to an unbelieving world.

We look to Him for peace and strength. Through Him we not only have *peace WITH God,* we also have within our hearts *the peace OF God:*

"Therefore being justified by faith, *we have peace WITH God through our Lord Jesus Christ*" (Rom. 5:1).

"And *the peace OF God,* which passeth all understanding, shall keep your hearts and minds through Christ Jesus" (Phil. 4:7).

Peace *with* God and the peace *of* God are divine necessities for effective service, and without them we will have no desire to lead *others* into the peace of God. We will find no joy in winning souls. As sons of God, believers are also *sons of peace,* but we are not to harbor peace in our hearts and fail to share it with others. We are the *messengers of peace* and we possess the *only* true message of peace. We need to deliver that message to a hostile world. Jesus came into the world to declare God the Father (John 1:18); He sends US into the world to declare the peace of God that comes into the heart by faith in the finished work of God's Son on Calvary—*and apart from Calvary there IS no peace for the human heart!*

Verse 22: *"And when He had said this, He breathed on them, and saith unto them, Receive ye the Holy Ghost."*

"He breathed on them" is a singular statement; it stands completely alone in the New Testament. There is no other record of the Lord Jesus "breathing" on anyone, and the same Greek word is not used anywhere else.

What is meant by the declaration that Jesus *breathed on the disciples?* Man was *created* from the dust of the ground; God "breathed into his nostrils the breath of life; and man became a living soul" (Gen. 2:7). I believe the Word of God is teaching here that the only possible way for the *natural* man to become a new creation in Christ Jesus is *through the life-giving power of the Holy Spirit.* Until we are born of the Spirit we are not saved, and certainly we are not commissioned to be witnesses.

I am not suggesting that the disciples were not believers until after Jesus breathed on them. *They were believers*—but they were believers under the old economy. Jesus had told them earlier that the Holy Spirit would not only be *with* them, but would be *IN* them, and this is the beginning of life eternal. He said to Nicodemus, "Except a man be born of water *and of the Spirit,* he cannot enter into the kingdom of God" (John 3:5). In John 6:44 He declared, "No man can come to me, except the Father which hath sent me draw him . . . ."—and in John 6:63 He said, *"It is the Spirit that quickeneth;* the flesh profiteth nothing: the words that I speak unto you, they are spirit, and they are life."

In Romans 8:1,2 the Apostle Paul tells us, "There is therefore now no condemnation to them which are in Christ Jesus, who walk not after the flesh, *but after the Spirit.* For the law of the Spirit of life in Christ Jesus hath made me free from the law of sin and death."

It is the Spirit that quickens and makes us alive, it is the Spirit that makes us new creations in Christ Jesus: "Ye are not in the flesh, but in the Spirit, if so be that the Spirit of God dwell in you. Now if any man have not the Spirit of Christ, he is none of His" (Rom. 8:9). Ephesians 4:30 warns, *"Grieve not the holy Spirit of God, whereby ye are sealed unto the day of redemption!"*

Paul tells us that "the first man Adam was made *a living soul;* the last Adam (the Lord Jesus Christ) was made *a quickening spirit"* (I Cor. 15:45). In Genesis 2:7 God the Eternal Father breathed into the nostrils of Adam and he became a living soul. In our present verse *Jesus* breathed on the apostles and they became new creations in Christ Jesus (II Cor. 5:17). In Ezekiel 37:9,10, the Holy Spirit breathes upon Israel and the dry bones come alive; and in Isaiah 11:4 we are told that one day God will destroy the wicked *"with the breath of His lips."*

Galatians 4:1–7 also sheds light on our present verse:

"Now I say, That the heir, as long as he is a child, differeth nothing from a servant, though he be lord of all; but is under tutors and governors until the time appointed of the father.

"Even so we, when we were children, were in bondage under the elements of the world: But when the fulness of the time was come, God sent forth His Son, made of a woman, made under the law, *to redeem them that were under the law,* that we might receive the adoption of sons.

"And because ye are sons, God hath sent forth the Spirit of His Son into your hearts, crying, Abba, Father. *Wherefore thou art no more a servant, but a son; and if a son, then an heir of God through Christ."*

The disciples were born from above *before* Jesus said, "Receive ye the Holy Spirit." They were children of God, *but they were still under the Mosaic economy.* Now they are no longer servants, but sons—heirs of God and joint-heirs with Christ.

The disciples were different men after Jesus breathed on them and said, "Receive ye the Holy Ghost." If we study the last chapter in each of the Gospels, and the first chapter of Acts, we will find proof that their unbelief, their weaknesses, their confusion, and their perplexities were gone. When they stood with Jesus on the Mount of Olives while He instructed them concerning Pentecost, when He began to rise and a cloud received Him out of their sight, they were not the weak, perplexed, unbelieving disciples they had been when they left the tomb after the crucifixion. In Luke 24:51—53 we read, "And it came to pass, while He blessed them, He was parted from them, and carried up into heaven. *And they worshipped Him, and RETURNED TO JERUSALEM WITH GREAT JOY: and were continually in the temple praising and blessing God. Amen!"* The joy that flooded their hearts was the joy the Holy Spirit had put within them: "For the kingdom of God is not meat and drink; but righteousness, and peace, and joy in the Holy Ghost" (Rom. 14:17).

On the Day of Pentecost the disciples were *baptized* in the Holy Ghost, and this baptism placed them in the New Testament Church and endued them with power to become effective witnesses; but fifty days *before* Pentecost the Holy Spirit indwelt them and remained in their hearts. Jesus had conferred upon them light and knowledge of divine truth which up to that time they had not possessed. They loved their Lord, they were happy in His presence; but they were sadly ignorant concerning His true purpose in coming into the world and they were ignorant concerning *the necessity for His death* and *the surety of His resurrection.* But when He breathed on them He bestowed upon them the Spirit of knowledge and understanding. *Light* was the first thing made in the creation (Gen. 1:3), and *light in the heart* is the beginning of true salvation. The entrance of the Word brings light (Psalm 119:130).

Verse 23: *"Whose soever sins ye remit, they are remitted unto them; and whose soever sins ye retain, they are retained."*

This verse of Scripture has been misunderstood, abused, and misused down through the centuries. One group uses it to confer upon their priests the power to forgive sins, but *no man* has ever had that power. *Only JESUS can forgive sins.* (Please read Luke 5:17–26.)

To be able to understand our present verse we must know to whom the Lord was speaking, and we must consider *the time* when these words were spoken. To whom WAS Jesus speaking here? Was He speaking to the apostles in particular, to disciples in general, to *all* ministers? If the words were meant *for ALL disciples,* they certainly cannot confer on any *particular* group (ministers, priests, or evangelists) the power to forgive sins. Such a belief is not only *unreasonable,* it is without any Scriptural grounds. On the other hand, if Jesus was speaking only to the ten apostles who were in the room with Him, then those today who claim the power to forgive sins are even *more* in error, because the apostles were not priests at that time, nor did they ever *become* priests.

If Jesus conferred upon the disciples the power to forgive sins, and if that power was to be handed down to others, why do we not find this mentioned in the Epistles? There is not one word in Acts, in any of the Epistles, or in The Revelation pertaining to any *mortal* remitting or retaining sins. There is no mention in the Church Epistles (Romans through Thessalonians), nor in the Pastoral Epistles (Timothy through Philemon) of a priest-class (or persons) to whom power had been handed down to remit sins. The New Testament does not even *mention* the priesthood in the Church. We *have* a great High Priest—Jesus, who sits at the right hand of the Father—and *in Him all believers are kings and priests* in the spiritual sense:

"Ye are a chosen generation, a royal priesthood, an holy nation, a peculiar people; that ye should shew forth the praises of Him who hath called you out of darkness into His marvellous light" (I Pet. 2:9).

Regardless of whether the words of our present verse were spoken to disciples in general or to the apostles exclusively, the statement contains no grounds whatsoever on which priests can claim the power to forgive sins or hear confession from sinners.

Now *what about the TIME these words were spoken*—in what dispensation or *period* of time was the statement made? It was certainly before the *Church* was born, for the Church was born on the Day of Pentecost. These words were spoken during the transition period, and they were spoken to the apostles *who were men in a category all their own.* Since the Apostle Paul passed from earth to heaven there have been no other apostles. There are none *today.* Believers? *Yes.* Ministers? *Yes.* Evangelists? *Yes.* Apostles? *NO!* They were men endowed with special power to perform miracles, and no man since Paul has wrought such miracles. The apostles were never meant to have successors. God did not call and ordain apostles in the New Testament Church. Pastors, teachers, missionaries, evangelists, but no apostles.

When Jesus comes again and offers the Kingdom to Israel, there will again be men with supernatural power working great miracles: "And I will give power unto my two witnesses, and they shall prophesy a thousand two hundred and threescore days, clothed in sackcloth. . . These have power to shut heaven, that it rain not in the days of their prophecy: and have power over waters to turn them to blood, and to smite the earth with all plagues, as often as they will" (Rev. 11:3,6).

The words of Jesus in this twenty-third verse are given in conjunction with the words in verse 22—that is, He breathed on the disciples and they received the Holy Spirit. He did not set up an ecclesiastical office, He did not say, "I now make you *priests.*" Whatever He meant the disciples to understand, He certainly did not suggest to them that He had given them an office which they were to hand down to others—nor did they claim this right. Not one of the apostles at any time said to any person, "I hereby forgive your sins." The only confession that brings remission of sins in this Dispensation of Grace is our confession to God in the name of Jesus. John tells us, "If we *confess* our sins, He (JESUS) is faithful and just to forgive us our sins, and to cleanse us from all unrighteousness" (I John 1:9). When a believer sins, *JESUS* (not a priest, pastor, or evangelist) *is the propitiation:* "He is the propitiation for our sins: and not for our's only, but also for the sins of the whole world" (I John 2:2).

I must confess that I do not fully comprehend the meaning of the words of Jesus here, but I do know that in the strictest sense, the *commission and office* of the apostles had to do with that particular period of time, and was confined to them and to the Apostle Paul.

The apostles possessed ministerial qualifications that were peculiar to them and them alone. These qualifications they could not (and did not) transmit to others:

They confirmed their teaching by miracles.

Some of them were inspired by the Holy Ghost to write down portions of the New Testament.

They had power to discern spirits as in the case of Peter's dealing with Ananias and Sapphira (Acts 5:1–11).

They declared the Gospel without error, preaching with infallible accuracy. They made not a single mistake in their interpretations.

In all of these qualifications they stood alone; they had no successors. The apostles were specially qualified for a particular period of time and for the special work they had to do. *Their office was one which began and ended with them.*

The apostles could not have the power to forgive sins—nor did they *claim* to have such power. That is a special prerogative of God. In the house of Cornelius Peter declared, "To Him give all the prophets witness, that *through HIS NAME whosoever believeth in HIM shall receive remission of sins*" (Acts 10:43).

Paul preached, "Be it known unto you therefore, men and brethren, that *through this Man* (Jesus) *is preached unto you the forgiveness of sins: and by HIM all that believe are justified from all things, from which ye could not be justified by the law of Moses*" (Acts 13:38,39).

Paul declared to the Corinthian believers, "To whom ye forgive any thing, I forgive also: for if I forgave any thing, to whom I forgave it, for your sakes forgave I it *in the Person of CHRIST*" (II Cor. 2:10).

It is true that the apostles possessed unique authority and power, but they did not hand this authority and power down to anyone.

I believe the words in our present verse must mean nothing more than that the apostles *had the AUTHORITY to DECLARE* those who had been forgiven and those who had not been forgiven, just as the Jewish priest had authority to pronounce those who were clean and those who were unclean in the cases of leprosy.

The uniqueness of the apostles' preaching and authority was that these men did not have the written Word as we have it today; *they SPOKE by inspiration,* and (including the Apostle Paul) they were the last to speak the inspired Word. Since John the Beloved penned down *The Revelation,* there has been no man to speak or write under divine inspiration as the apostles did. When they spoke, they were speaking words given to them by the Holy Spirit. When they said, "*Repent, believe, and your sins are forgiven,*" their words carried *authority* because they were speaking *inspired* words, words which you and I now *read.* They spoke with authority, and now God's ministers read and preach what they said with *the same authority.*

The only man who speaks with authority about sins forgiven (or any other spiritual matter) is the man who gives forth God's Word. Jesus declared, "He that rejecteth me, and receiveth not my words, hath one that judgeth him: the Word that I have spoken, the same shall judge him in the last day" (John 12:48). Now "that which is perfect" is come (I Cor. 13:10), and ministers are commanded to "preach the Word" (II Tim. 4:2)—and when we preach the Word we speak with authority.

The only way the apostles *remitted* sins was by the preaching of the Gospel of the grace of God, and they had the authority to declare that all who believed on Jesus and repented in His name were remitted of sins and given eternal life (Acts 10:43). The only way the apostles *retained* men's sins was by announcing the wrath of God upon all who refused to hear the Gospel of grace and believe on Jesus. Just before He ascended, Jesus said to the apostles, "Thus it is written, and thus it behoved Christ to suffer, and to rise from the dead the third day: and *that repentance and remission of sins should be preached IN HIS NAME among all nations,* beginning at Jerusalem. And ye are witnesses of these things" (Luke 24:46—48).

In the light of the Scriptures, let us not ascribe to ministers a power that God has given only to His Son. To regard a minister or priest as a mediator between God and the soul of an individual, to confess sins privately to him and receive from him private absolution from sin is a doctrine entirely foreign to the Word of God. It is a man-made system—deadly and blasphemous!

Verse 24: *"But Thomas, one of the twelve, called Didymus, was not with them when Jesus came."*

We do not know much about Thomas, but he seemed to be a person who lived in fear, gloom, and despondency. When Jesus told His disciples that Lazarus was dead and that He was going into Bethany, Thomas said, "Let us also go, *that we may die with Him*" (John 11:16). Here he evidenced little faith in the ability and power of Jesus to take care of him regardless of circumstances.

When Jesus said, "Whither I go ye know, and the way ye know," Thomas said, "Lord, we *know not* whither thou goest; and how can we know the *way*?" (John 14:4,5). It is from these accounts that we must draw our picture of the character and nature of Thomas.

The Word of God does not tell us *why* Thomas was not with the other apostles on the night when Jesus first appeared to them, but *whatever* his reason for being absent he missed a blessing and lived in suspense through the entire week following. It is noteworthy that the other disciples did not rebuke him for his absence that night. When he joined their company they simply told him, *"We have seen the Lord!"*

Verse 25: *"The other disciples therefore said unto him, We have seen the Lord. But he said unto them, Except I shall see in His hands the prints of the nails, and put my finger into the print of the nails, and thrust my hand into His side, I will not believe."*

This is the only place in the New Testament where *nails* are mentioned. The Romans did not always nail their victims to the cross; sometimes they *bound* them there—but nails were driven through the hands and feet of Jesus in fulfillment of Psalm 22:16: "For dogs have compassed me: the assembly of the wicked have inclosed me: *they pierced my hands and my feet.*"

"The other disciples therefore said unto (Thomas), *We have seen the Lord.*" We are not told where the other disciples were when they spoke these words to Thomas—nor do we know *when* they were spoken. *I believe* it was on the same evening Jesus first appeared to them. Probably Thomas came in shortly after Jesus had gone from the upper room. I can imagine that all ten of the others cried out with joy that they had seen Jesus.

But Thomas promptly replied that unless he *personally*

saw Him, and unless he touched the nailprints and thrust his hand into the Lord's wounded side, *he would not believe.* How sad! All of the other apostles had seen Jesus, but Thomas refused to believe the testimony of these tried and true friends with whom he had fellowshipped for more than three years. This was a sacred occasion, and Thomas sinned grievously—for he not only refused to believe the *resurrection* message, he refused to believe that his brethren were telling the truth.

I am sure that Thomas' faith in Jesus as the Messiah was just as strong as the faith of the other apostles, but neither he nor the others fully understood the crucifixion and the resurrection. Also, the *Jews* believed in spirits and in the appearance of angels as messengers from God, and since Thomas was a Jew he probably thought the other apostles had seen a spirit or the ghost of Jesus.

This was what happened when *Peter* was imprisoned by Herod. He was sleeping between two guards, bound with two chains; but the angel of the Lord came and set him free. Peter went at once to the home of John Mark, where the Christians were having prayermeeting, and a little maid answered his knock on the door. She ran to tell the others that Peter was there, but "they said unto her, Thou art mad. But she constantly affirmed that it was even so. Then said they, *It is his angel.* But Peter continued knocking: and when they had opened the door, and saw him, they were astonished." (Acts 12:5–17 gives the account in full.)

I am certain Thomas believed that the ten apostles had seen *something,* but had they seen *the body of Jesus?* No, he could not believe that—unless he could touch that body and see it with his own eyes. I am not excusing or defending Thomas—we could not wholly excuse him anyway, because he had heard Jesus speak many times concerning the resurrection which was to occur three days after His crucifixion, and he had witnessed the resurrection of *Lazarus.* Surely if Jesus could raise a man who had been dead for four days, He could Himself come back from the dead!

Jesus Appears to the Disciples; Thomas Present

Verse 26: *"And after eight days again His disciples were within, and Thomas with them: then came Jesus, the doors being shut, and stood in the midst, and said, Peace be unto you."*

This was probably the same house and the same room where the disciples were assembled when Jesus appeared to them the *first* time—and again *the doors were shut.* Someone might ask why the disciples were still afraid, still meeting behind closed doors eight days after the Lord's resurrection. We must not forget that the rulers in Israel had accused the disciples of *stealing* the body of Jesus (Matt. 28:11–15), and therefore they found it necessary to take every precaution for their own safety. Thus they met behind closed doors.

But even while the doors were bolted, suddenly Jesus appeared in the midst of the disciples and brought the same gracious greeting: *"Peace be unto you."*

Verse 27: *"Then saith He to Thomas, Reach hither thy finger, and behold my hands; and reach hither thy hand, and thrust it into my side: and be not faithless, but believing."*

Jesus knew what Thomas had said; no one had told Him, for none of the disciples had seen Him since eight days before—but in His omniscience He knew the declaration Thomas had made. Yet He dealt gently with the unbelieving disciple. He invited him to touch the scars in His hands and side and see for himself that He was not a ghost or a spirit.

When Jesus invited Thomas to put his finger in the scars and thrust his hand into His side, He pointed out that which is the only ground for true peace. Jesus purchased peace on Calvary, and apart from the scars in His hands and side there could BE no true peace.

I believe this verse answers the question, "Will WE see the scars in the hands and feet and side of Jesus when we meet Him in glory?" I believe we *will!* Jesus was in His resurrection body when He invited Thomas to examine the scars. The bodies of the saints who sleep in the dust will be raised incorruptible—*resurrected,* not re-created—and we will know as we are known. I will know my children and my children will know me. The Apostle Paul declared, "Now we see through a glass, darkly; but then face to face: now I know in part; *but then shall I know even as also I am known*" (I Cor. 13:12).

I believe Zechariah 13:6 is further proof of this: "And one shall say unto Him, What are these wounds in thine hands? Then He shall answer, Those with which I was wounded in the house of my friends."

Paul tells us that the body will be sown in corruption, raised in incorruption . . . sown in dishonour, raised in glory . . . sown in weakness, raised in power . . . sown a natural body, raised a spiritual body (I Cor. 15:42—44). Jesus was in His resurrection body when the *disciples* recognized Him, and I find nothing in the Scriptures to indicate that *we* will be unable to see the nailprints in His hands and feet and the wound in His side, just as Thomas did.

"Be not faithless, but believing." In this admonition Jesus gently rebuked Thomas and at the same time chastised him for his declaration of unbelief. *Doubt* was the besetting sin of Thomas—and I am afraid many of us today are guilty of that same sin. We should pray consistently and study the Word daily, that our faith be increased. God honors faith, and "without faith it is impossible to please Him" (Heb. 11:6).

Verse 28: *"And Thomas answered and said unto Him, My Lord and my God."*

"Doubting Thomas" was instantly transformed into a

devout worshipper! There was no longer any room in his heart for unbelief. He did not need to place his fingers in the scars in the hands of his Lord nor thrust his hand into His wounded side. He had vowed that he would not believe unless he did this, but he changed his mind when he saw Jesus and heard Him speak. He believed *without* touching the Lord. (This is evident in verse 29.)

"My Lord and my God!" This statement is not found anywhere else in the Gospels; there is no other place where anyone called Jesus *"God."* Even though he had doubted and his faith was weak, after his doubting was satisfied Thomas gave the strongest testimony to the deity of Christ ever to come from the lips of mortal man up to that moment. Thomas had now received the Holy Spirit, as had the other ten disciples, because "no man can say that Jesus is the Lord, but *by the Holy Ghost*" (I Cor. 12:3).

The fact that Jesus *allowed* Thomas to call Him *"God"* is further proof of His deity. When *Peter* entered the house of Cornelius, that devout man fell down at Peter's feet to worship him, "But Peter took him up, saying, Stand up; *I myself also am a man*" (Acts 10:25,26).

The same thing happened to Paul and Barnabas in the city of Lystra. The people wanted to make a sacrifice to them and worship them, but Paul and Barnabas said, "Sirs, why do ye these things? *We also are men of like passions with you,* and preach unto you that ye should turn from these vanities unto the living God . . ." (Acts 14:11–18).

John the Beloved fell down to worship the angel (Rev. 22:8,9); but the angel said to him, *"See thou do it not:* for I am thy fellowservant, and of thy brethren the prophets, and of them which keep the sayings of this book: *worship God."*

But when Thomas said, *"My Lord and my God,"* Jesus did not rebuke him. He *accepted* such worship because Thomas had spoken the truth. *Jesus IS Lord and GOD.* His deity is the hub of the wheel of truths which are the foundation of Christianity. If Jesus had not been very God in flesh, then His atonement, His priesthood, *His entire work of redemption,* would have been worthless and blasphemous. His deity is taught throughout the Word of God with evidence that all hell cannot destroy or overthrow.

Verse 29: *"Jesus saith unto him, Thomas, because thou hast seen me, thou hast believed: blessed are they that have not seen, and yet have believed."*

Here is a warning to those who seek signs and feelings. Jesus accepted Thomas' confession, "My Lord and my God"—but He also reminded him that he had believed because of what he *saw.* There is greater blessing in just *believing GOD.* "For what saith the Scripture? *Abraham BELIEVED GOD,* and it was counted unto him for righteousness" (Rom. 4:3). Those who honor God most are those who believe Him without signs or "feelings." I thank God that we are not saved by *feelings;* feelings vary—but the grace of God never changes: *"Jesus Christ the same yesterday, and to day, and for ever"* (Heb. 13:8).

Under inspiration Peter wrote: "Blessed be the God and Father of our Lord Jesus Christ, which according to His abundant mercy hath begotten us again unto a lively (living) hope by the resurrection of Jesus Christ from the dead, to an inheritance incorruptible, and undefiled, and that fadeth not away, reserved in heaven for you, who are kept by the power of God through faith unto salvation ready to be revealed in the last time. Wherein ye greatly rejoice, though now for a season, if need be, ye are in heaviness through manifold temptations: that the trial of your *faith,* being much more precious than of gold that perisheth, though it be tried with fire, might be found unto praise and honour and glory at the appearing of *Jesus Christ: WHOM HAVING NOT SEEN, ye love; in whom, though now YE SEE HIM NOT, yet believing, ye rejoice with joy unspeakable and full of glory: receiving the end of your FAITH, even the salvation of your souls"* (I Pet. 1:3—9).

According to these words penned down by Peter, the joy

salvation brings is *unspeakable.* And *Paul* speaks of "the *peace* of God, which *passeth all understanding"* (Phil. 4:7). It is impossible to describe the joy and peace that come to the heart when we believe on the Lord Jesus Christ. We are not *saved* by feelings, sight, or signs; we do not *live* by feelings, sight, or signs. *We are saved BY GRACE, THROUGH FAITH, we are KEPT by the power of God through faith, and "whatsoever is NOT of faith is SIN!"* (Rom. 14:23).

We have never seen Jesus in the flesh—but we know He lived, died, rose again, and that He is now seated in glory at the right hand of the Majesty. We know these truths by the testimony of the Word of God, for *God cannot lie:* "Wherein God, willing more abundantly to shew unto the heirs of promise *the immutability of His counsel,* confirmed it by an oath: That by two *immutable* things, in which it was *IMPOSSIBLE FOR GOD TO LIE, we might have a strong consolation,* who have fled for refuge to lay hold upon the hope set before us" (Heb. 6:17,18).

In Titus 1:2 Paul also speaks of the *"hope of eternal life, which God, THAT CANNOT LIE, promised before the world began."*

We also know these Scriptural truths because Jesus abides in the heart of every believer: "Hereby we *know* that we are of the truth, and shall assure our hearts before Him. For if our heart condemn us, God is greater than our heart, and knoweth all things. *Beloved, if our heart condemn us not, then have we confidence toward God"* (I John 3:19—21).

Faith which rests solely upon the Word of God, without sight, signs, wonders, feelings, thrill, or chills, is that which Christ declares blessed! The ugliest and most insulting sin mortal man can commit against a holy God is *the sin of UNBELIEF:*

"He that believeth on the Son of God hath the witness in himself: *he that believeth NOT God HATH MADE HIM A LIAR;* because he believeth not the record that God gave of His Son" (I John 5:10).

The Key to the Gospel of John

Verses 30 and 31: *"And many other signs truly did Jesus in the presence of His disciples, which are not written in this book: But these are written, that ye might believe that Jesus is the Christ, the Son of God; and that believing ye might have life through His name."*

Every book in the Bible has a key. Sometimes the key is found by the front door, sometimes we find it by the back door; but in each book there is a key verse (or verses) which explain the primary doctrinal truths set forth in that particular book. For example, in I John, the key hangs by the front door: "And these things write we unto you, *that your joy may be full*" (I John 1:4). John's first epistle is known as *"the JOY book."*

The key to *The Revelation* also hangs by the front door: "Write the things *which thou hast seen,* and the things *which are,* and the things *which shall be hereafter*" (Rev. 1:19).

But in the Gospel of John the key is near the close of the book; these last two verses in chapter 20 unlock the "salvation Gospel" for us.

"And many other signs truly did Jesus . . . which are not written in this book." There is no way of knowing how many miracles Jesus did in the course of His public ministry. The *last verse* of John's Gospel declares that He did so many things "which, if they should be written every one . . . *even the world itself* could not contain the books that should be written"—and I accept that verse literally! I believe if all the things Jesus did and all the things He said had been written down, the world truly could not contain the books that would of necessity have been written.

John made it clear that there were many things which he did not write. For example, there are other signs which declare *the bodily resurrection of Jesus* which are recorded by others, but which John did not pen down:

In Luke 24 we read of Jesus' joining the two disciples

on their way to Emmaus, "but their eyes were holden that they should not know Him" (v. 16). In that same chapter Luke tells of the Lord's eating of broiled fish and honeycomb (vv. 41–43), and in verse 45 of that chapter we read, "Then opened He their understanding, that they might understand the Scriptures."

Matthew 28:18–20 records the Great Commission: "And Jesus came and spake unto them, saying, All power is given unto me in heaven and in earth. Go ye therefore, and teach all nations, baptizing them in the name of the Father, and of the Son, and of the Holy Ghost: Teaching them to observe all things whatsoever I have commanded you: and, lo, I am with you alway, even unto the end of the world. Amen."

Yes, there are other books that enlighten us concerning different phases of the Lord's ministry—even His death, burial, and resurrection—that John did not record; but he explained, *"These are written, that ye might believe that Jesus is the Christ, the Son of God; and that believing ye might have life through His name."* Thus the Holy Spirit gives the *reason* for the resurrection signs recorded by John the Beloved. They were not written just to furnish historical information on the *facts* of the resurrection of Jesus; they were written *that we might BELIEVE on Him,* and in believing, have life eternal.

Since the Gospel of John is "the salvation book," *believing God* is emphasized here as nowhere else in the entire Word of God:

The *object* of saving faith is God in the Person of His only begotten Son, the Lord Jesus Christ: "Believe on Him whom God hath sent" (John 6:29; 14:1).

The *warrant* of saving faith is God in the authority of His Word—the Word that was in the beginning *with* God, the Word that *was* God: "They believed the Scripture" (John 2:22; 4:50).

The *call* of saving faith is Christ in His substitutionary work on the cross—He willingly laid His life down, no man took it from Him. He *gave* His life "that all men through Him might believe" (John 1:7; 3:16–18).

The *result* of saving faith is salvation. We are saved by God's *grace* (Eph. 2:8,9). The *grace* of God brings *salvation* (Tit. 2:11), but *faith* brings grace (Rom. 3:22–24). It is *faith* that makes us sons (John 1:12). Through *faith,* condemnation is removed (John 3:18). Through *faith,* complete satisfaction is ours, and we become a blessing to others (John 7:37,38). *True faith* produces works that glorify God (John 14:12), and faith that *does NOT* produce works that glorify God is *dead* faith (James 2:26).

The *power* of saving faith removes darkness: "I am come a light into the world, that whosoever believeth on me should not abide in darkness" (John 12:46). We have been delivered "from the power of darkness," and have been "translated" into the kingdom of God's dear Son—the kingdom of light (Col. 1:13).

The *confession* of saving faith is, "We believe and are sure that thou art that Christ, the Son of the living God" (John 6:69). "Whosoever believeth that Jesus is the Christ is born of God: and every one that loveth Him that begat loveth him also that is begotten of Him" (I John 5:1). "If thou shalt confess with thy mouth the Lord Jesus, and shalt believe in thine heart that God hath raised Him from the dead, thou shalt be saved" (Rom. 10:9).

Lack of faith (unbelief) has damned every person who cries out for a drop of water in hell today. It is not *s-i-n-s* (plural) that damn the soul; it is *S-I-N* (singular). Jesus came to take away *"the SIN of the world"*—unbelief (John 1:29). "He that BELIEVETH NOT is condemned" (John 3:18).

What must one do to be lost? Gamble? Drink? Lie? Cheat, steal, or murder? NO! I repeat: *"He that BELIEVETH NOT is condemned ALREADY."* Every soul that spends eternity in the lake of fire will be there because of *unbelief.* God's Word makes this very clear: *"HE THAT BELIEVETH NOT SHALL BE DAMNED"* (Mark 16:16b).

"He that believeth on the Son hath everlasting life: and *he that BELIEVETH NOT the Son shall not see life; but THE WRATH OF GOD ABIDETH ON HIM*" (John 3:36).

The Greek word for *"believe"* occurs ninety-nine times in the Gospel of John. The word is *pisteuo,* derived from *pistis,* which comes from a primary verb, *peitho,* meaning "to convince by argument, by analogy; to pacify or conciliate by other fair means; passively to assent to evidence; to rely by inward certainty."

The same word is also used in other places in the Bible:

In Acts 5:40 it is translated *"agreed."*

In I John 3:19 it is translated *"assure."*

In Acts 17:4 it is translated *"believe."*

In II Thessalonians 3:4 it is translated *"confidence."*

In Galatians 3:1 it is translated *"obey."*

In Romans 8:38 it is translated *"persuaded."*

In Philippians 2:24 it is translated *"trust."*

And in Acts 23:21 it is rendered *"yield."*

In the Gospel of John we find many references to the *practical outcome* of true saving faith. True faith *always* confesses Jesus, and the practical outcome of saving faith produces *satisfaction WITH Jesus:* "Jesus said unto them, I am the bread of life: he that cometh to me shall never hunger; and he that believeth on me shall never thirst" (John 6:35).

The practical outcome of saving faith manifests itself in works that glorify God: "Verily, verily, I say unto you, He that believeth on me, the works that I do shall he do also; and greater works than these shall he do; because I go unto my Father" (John 14:12).

The practical outcome of saving faith is walking in the steps of Jesus: "I am come a light into the world, that whosoever believeth on me should not abide in darkness" (John 12:46).

The practical outcome of true saving faith is the blessing of eternal life, and *we KNOW that we have eternal life:* "He that believeth on the Son of God HATH THE WIT-

NESS IN HIMSELF: he that believeth not God hath made Him a liar; because he believeth not the record that God gave of His Son. And this is the record, that God hath given to us eternal life, AND THIS LIFE IS IN HIS SON. He that hath the Son hath life; and he that hath not the Son of God hath not life. These things have I written unto you that believe on the name of the Son of God; THAT YE MAY KNOW THAT YE HAVE ETERNAL LIFE, and that ye may believe on the name of the Son of God" (I John 5:10–13). Those who maintain that we cannot *know* that we are born again have simply never been saved, for there is no such thing as salvation apart from assurance!

Beloved, have YOU believed on the Lord Jesus Christ for salvation? or did you just "join a church" where you were voted into membership and baptized in water?

The Philippian jailer asked Paul and Silas, "Sirs, *what must I do to be saved?*" They replied, "Believe on the Lord Jesus Christ, and thou shalt be saved, and thy house." "And they spake unto him the word of the Lord, and to all that were in his house. And he took them the same hour of the night, and washed their stripes; and was baptized, he and all his, straightway. And when he had brought them into his house, he set meat before them, *and rejoiced,* believing in God with all his house" (Acts 16: 30–34).

If you are not saved, if you do not KNOW you are saved, then I invite you to "believe on the Lord Jesus Christ," and *whoever* you are, *whatever* you are, you will be saved—and you will KNOW you are saved, and you, too, can rejoice!

CHAPTER XXI

1. After these things Jesus shewed himself again to the disciples at the sea of Tiberias; and on this wise shewed he himself.

2. There were together Simon Peter, and Thomas called Didymus, and Nathanael of Cana in Galilee, and the sons of Zebedee, and two other of his disciples.

3. Simon Peter saith unto them, I go a fishing. They say unto him, We also go with thee. They went forth, and entered into a ship immediately; and that night they caught nothing.

4. But when the morning was now come, Jesus stood on the shore: but the disciples knew not that it was Jesus.

5. Then Jesus saith unto them, Children, have ye any meat? They answered him, No.

6. And he said unto them, Cast the net on the right side of the ship, and ye shall find. They cast therefore, and now they were not able to draw it for the multitude of fishes.

7. Therefore that disciple whom Jesus loved saith unto Peter, It is the Lord. Now when Simon Peter heard that it was the Lord, he girt his fisher's coat unto him, (for he was naked,) and did cast himself into the sea.

8. And the other disciples came in a little ship; (for they were not far from land, but as it were two hundred cubits,) dragging the net with fishes.

9. As soon then as they were come to land, they saw a fire of coals there, and fish laid thereon, and bread.

10. Jesus saith unto them, Bring of the fish which ye have now caught.

11. Simon Peter went up, and drew the net to land full of great fishes, an hundred and fifty and three: and for all there were so many, yet was not the net broken.

12. Jesus saith unto them, Come and dine. And none of the disciples durst ask him, Who art thou? knowing that it was the Lord.

13. Jesus then cometh, and taketh bread, and giveth them, and fish likewise.

14. This is now the third time that Jesus shewed himself to his disciples, after that he was risen from the dead.

15. So when they had dined, Jesus saith to Simon Peter, Simon,

son of Jonas, lovest thou me more than these? He saith unto him, Yea, Lord; thou knowest that I love thee. He saith unto him, Feed my lambs.

16. He saith to him again the second time, Simon, son of Jonas, lovest thou me? He saith unto him, Yea, Lord; thou knowest that I love thee. He saith unto him, Feed my sheep.

17. He saith unto him the third time, Simon, son of Jonas, lovest thou me? Peter was grieved because he said unto him the third time, Lovest thou me? And he said unto him, Lord, thou knowest all things; thou knowest that I love thee. Jesus saith unto him, Feed my sheep.

18. Verily, verily, I say unto thee, When thou wast young, thou girdedst thyself, and walkedst whither thou wouldest: but when thou shalt be old, thou shalt stretch forth thy hands, and another shall gird thee, and carry thee whither thou wouldest not.

19. This spake he, signifying by what death he should glorify God. And when he had spoken this, he saith unto him, Follow me.

20. Then Peter, turning about, seeth the disciple whom Jesus loved following; which also leaned on his breast at supper, and said, Lord, which is he that betrayeth thee?

21. Peter seeing him saith to Jesus, Lord, and what shall this man do?

22. Jesus saith unto him, If I will that he tarry till I come, what is that to thee? follow thou me.

23. Then went this saying abroad among the brethren, that that disciple should not die: yet Jesus said not unto him, He shall not die; but, If I will that he tarry till I come, what is that to thee?

24. This is the disciple which testifieth of these things, and wrote these things: and we know that his testimony is true.

25. And there are also many other things which Jesus did, the which, if they should be written every one, I suppose that even the world itself could not contain the books that should be written. Amen.

The *opening* verses of John's Gospel are in the nature of a *prologue,* and this closing chapter provides the *epilogue.* In chapter 1, the Holy Spirit clearly teaches that Christ was *"in the beginning"* with the Father, in the bosom of the Father, and that He came forth *from* the Father *to declare the Father* and purchase redemption for poor, hell-deserving sinners. Chapter 1 exhibits the eternal life of Christ *before* He was manifested in flesh in the world. In this last chapter we see *the spiritual sway of Christ IN the world,* even though He is now in heaven seated at the right hand of the Father. The Man Christ Jesus *in a body* sits at the right hand of the Majesty on high—but He also *abides in the heart of every believer* in the Person of the Holy Spirit. "If any man have not the Spirit of Christ, he is none of His" (Rom. 8:9).

In this chapter we see the disciples on the Sea of Galilee, the Lord Jesus no longer with them but directing from the shore. This points to the fact that believers today are in the world, and though our Lord no longer is with us in body, He directs us from the right hand of the Father in heaven. He leads us, directs us, provides for our every need, and He has promised *never* to leave us nor forsake us (Heb. 13:5).

Also in this closing chapter of John's Gospel, Jesus assures us that He will come again to receive us unto Himself, and until His return He charges us, *"Feed my lambs . . . Feed my sheep."*

In this chapter we will see the barrenness of serving in the flesh and following self-will. Peter said, "I go a fishing," and the other disciples immediately declared, "We will go with you." God did not tell Peter to go fishing, nor did the Holy Spirit lead the other disciples to go with him. They were following self-will and human leadership. They toiled in the energy of the flesh, therefore they labored in vain; but when Jesus appeared on the shore and gave them directions, they *followed* His directions and were blessed abundantly—their net was *filled* with fish! Jesus still graciously provides for His own, but we must trust Him for leadership and follow His directions if we are to have *abundant* blessing, the kind of blessing He wants to give.

In this final chapter, Jesus also points out that the only *right motive* for Christian stewardship is *LOVE TO CHRIST.* Whatsoever we do should be done for His glory and because we love Him, not because of personal ambition or desire for self-glory.

It is in these closing verses that Jesus points out His

power to appoint the time and the manner of the *death* of born again believers; and finally, He assures us that He will come again. Christians are not to look for death, but for *life*—"for that blessed hope, and the glorious appearing of the great God and our Saviour Jesus Christ" (Tit. 2:13).

The miracle recorded in this last chapter is the only recorded miracle wrought by Jesus after His resurrection (other than, of course, His miraculous *appearances*), and it is not found anywhere else in the Gospels.

Verse 1: *"After these things Jesus shewed Himself again to the disciples at the sea of Tiberias; and on this wise shewed He Himself."*

"After these things" speaks of the things recorded in the previous chapter where Jesus appeared to the disciples on two occasions. Up to this point His appearances were to assure the disciples that He was *the same Jesus* with whom they had walked and served for more than three years; but *now* He speaks words great with prophetic significance as having to do with the future relationship between Him and His disciples.

"Jesus shewed Himself again to the disciples." This automatically brings up the question, Where was Jesus during the time He was *not* seen by the disciples, when He did not manifest or show Himself? It is evident that He was not with the disciples *all* of the time during the forty days between His resurrection and His ascension. He visited them on several occasions, but He was not with them all day, every day. (I am speaking, of course, of *the Man,* Christ Jesus, the *resurrected Man* who is now seated at the right hand of the Majesty.) *As GOD He is everywhere;* but where was He *as Man* when He was not seen by the disciples during His forty days on earth after His resurrection? The Bible does not tell us where He was. We do know that He appeared to His disciples throughout the forty-day interval: ". . . He shewed Himself alive after His passion by many infallible proofs, being seen of them

forty days, and speaking of the things pertaining to the kingdom of God" (Acts 1:3). Between the time of His resurrection and His ascension He was visible and invisible; He appeared suddenly and then *disappeared* as He had come—but where He went we are not told. It pleased God to reveal only this much to us, and we will accept it as divine truth and not fret about where Jesus was during the time the disciples did not see Him.

The *Sea of Tiberias* where Jesus showed Himself at this time is also called the *Sea of Galilee,* and is also sometimes referred to as the *Lake of Gennesaret.* It is a body of fresh water approximately twelve miles long and six and three-quarter miles wide, through which the river Jordan flows. It lies 655 feet below the level of the Mediterranean Sea.

This Sea of Tiberias (or, the Sea of Galilee) holds interest for every Christian, because many of the mightiest miracles wrought by Jesus during His earthly ministry were performed near its shores. For instance, it was here that Jesus walked on the water and came to His disciples in the midst of a storm (Matt. 14:22–34).

It was here that Jesus on another occasion stilled the wind and the waves by simply speaking a word (Matt. 8:23–27).

It was on the Sea of Galilee that He granted some of His disciples a miraculous catch of fish, so many that the net broke (Luke 5:1–6).

It was from the waters of the Sea of Galilee that Peter caught the fish which held in its mouth the money to pay taxes for Peter and Jesus (Matt. 17:24–27).

It was near here that Jesus fed the five thousand with five loaves and two fishes (Matt. 14:15–21).

It was here that Jesus cast a legion of demons out of the man of Gadara, causing the demons to enter into a herd of swine, "and the herd ran violently down a steep place into the lake, and were choked." As a result of this miracle, the inhabitants of that area besought Jesus to depart from their country (Luke 8:26–39).

The towns of Chorazin, Bethesda, Bethsaida, and Capernaum all were located near the Sea of Galilee, and it was in these towns that Jesus did some of His mightiest works. During the three and one-half years of the Lord's public ministry there was no other place where He wrought so many miracles and did so many outstanding works as in the district around the Sea of Galilee, here referred to as "the Sea of Tiberias."

It was not by accident that Jesus appeared to His disciples in this familiar area, and when they recognized Him as He stood on the shore, *surely* they were reminded of all the mighty miracles they had witnessed there before His crucifixion. Perhaps they remembered that He had *called them* from their fishing boats and their nets along these shores more than three years before, inviting them to follow Him and become "fishers of men." And it was here that He would give them their last instructions before He ascended back to the Father.

"On this wise shewed He Himself" lets us know that each little detail of this account is important and that we are to read the ensuing verses with special care, giving undivided attention to what is recorded in them.

Verse 2: *"There were together Simon Peter, and Thomas called Didymus, and Nathanael of Cana in Galilee, and the sons of Zebedee, and two other of His disciples."*

Christ appeared here before seven disciples. *Seven* is God's number for perfection, and since seven witnesses saw Jesus they could provide undeniable evidence of what transpired at that time. Seven witnesses saw Him, ate the breakfast He prepared for them, and heard His words.

We are not told *why only seven* of the disciples were present here. It seems reasonable that the entire company of eleven had gone into Galilee when the Passover feast ended, as the Lord had commanded them to do (Matt. 28:10), but we are not told why only these seven were present at this particular time.

We are already well acquainted with Peter and Thomas. Of Nathanael we know little. We read of him in John 1:45–51 where Philip found him and brought him to Jesus, and this present verse tells us that his home was in *Cana,* where Jesus wrought His first miracle by turning water into wine at a wedding.

The *"sons of Zebedee"* were fishermen before Jesus called them, and in Matthew 10:2 we read of "James the son of Zebedee, and John his brother." So James and John were among the seven present on this memorable morning when Jesus met them on the shore of the Sea of Galilee.

John then mentions *"two other of His disciples,"* but he does not name them.

Verse 3: *"Simon Peter saith unto them, I go a fishing. They say unto him, We also go with thee. They went forth, and entered into a ship immediately; and that night they caught nothing."*

"I go a fishing." As was characteristic of Peter, it was he who took the initiative and led the way back to the fishing boat. He was a natural leader, and whether for good or bad he went all the way. When he followed the Lord he followed wholeheartedly, and when he *denied* Him his denial was emphatic, even confirmed with an oath.

We can imagine that at this time the disciples were restless, uncertain, not knowing where to turn or what to do. They did not take time to pray for God's leadership—perhaps at that point in their ministry they did not know exactly *how* to pray effectively. While the Lord had been with them in person they had had no need to pray, and now without His guidance they knew not what to do. Then self-willed Peter declared, "I go a fishing," and the others were immediately ready to follow him.

Here we plainly see that wrong decisions in leadership will have an adverse effect on those who follow. Leaders in the church should always give time to prayer, and be sure of the direction of the Holy Spirit, lest in taking the wrong step they lead others astray.

There is nothing wrong with *fishing.* It is an honorable way to earn a living, and in Peter's day it was a very *usual* way of providing a livelihood. But these men were fishing for fish when they should have been fishing for souls, and that is what brought about their complete failure. They had been professional fishermen before Jesus called them to follow Him; they knew the waters of the Sea of Galilee, for they had fished there before they had left their nets to follow Jesus. Therefore, the fact that they caught nothing throughout an entire night of labor at their net proves that they were not in the will of God. Jesus had plainly told them, *"Without ME ye can do nothing"* (John 15:5).

Greek authorities tell us that *"a boat"* reads literally *"THE boat,"* which suggests that some of these fishermen—possibly Peter—had not disposed of their fishing equipment when they left the nets to follow Jesus. This could account for the boat being available to Jesus when the multitudes pressed about Him so that "He went into a ship, and sat; and the whole multitude stood on the shore" (Matt. 13:2); and it could also account for the fact that the boat was at their disposal when the seven disciples decided to go fishing and *"entered into a ship immediately, AND THAT NIGHT THEY CAUGHT NOTHING!"*

Verse 4: *"But when the morning was now come, Jesus stood on the shore: but the disciples knew not that it was Jesus."*

"When the morning was now come . . . ." There is little or no twilight in Palestine. When the sun disappears in the evening it is suddenly *dark,* and when the sun rises in the morning it rises quickly, bringing sudden daylight.

"Jesus stood on the shore!" I like to think that our Lord appeared suddenly here, just like He appeared when the disciples were assembled in the upper room with the doors shut. In His risen body He came and then departed, appearing and disappearing according to His own will; and

since He was in His glorified body on the morning spoken of here, it seems to me that He would *not* have come casually walking along the shore.

"The disciples knew not that it was Jesus." The disciples had returned to their old profession, their minds were at that moment occupied with bodily needs, and they were not expecting to see the risen Lord. Like Mary Magdalene, they did not recognize Him, they were not aware of His presence. I wonder how often *we* are in His presence and yet do not recognize Him? He promised never to leave us nor forsake us, and He is a very present help in time of trouble. May God help us to be aware of His blessed presence moment by moment each day!

Verse 5: *"Then Jesus saith unto them, Children, have ye any meat? They answered Him, No."*

The Greek word translated *"children"* is a familiar, friendly mode of address, as we would say "boys" or "lads" when addressing a group of young men. Jesus spoke warmly to them.

"Have ye any meat?" Jesus *knew* the disciples had no meat, He knew they had labored all night in vain. He asked the question to alert their minds and begin a conversation with them, in like manner as He had asked the Samaritan woman for a drink of water at Jacob's well (John 4:7).

"Meat" as used in the Greek meant *anything edible.* When *we* think of meat we think of some kind of flesh—beef, pork, fowl; but in our text it meant anything that was good to eat, anything good for nourishment. Actually, Jesus was asking for a confession from them, an admission that they had not caught even one little fish.

"They answered Him, No." They had toiled all night without taking one fish. Such is the reward of self-willed service! The results of such service will always be barren, empty, and vain. Jesus said, "If any man serve me, let him *follow ME*" (John 12:26a)—and *Paul* tells us, "There-

fore, my beloved brethren, be ye stedfast, unmoveable, always abounding in the work of the Lord, forasmuch as ye know that *your labour is not in vain IN THE LORD*" (I Cor. 15:58).

Christ-Directed Service Brings Results

Verse 6: *"And He said unto them, Cast the net on the right side of the ship, and ye shall find. They cast therefore, and now they were not able to draw it for the multitude of fishes."*

We might well imagine that the disciples were disappointed, discouraged, and most assuredly they were tired and hungry. Then the Person on the shore called out to them, *"Cast the net on the right side of the ship"*—and they instantly obeyed, without question and without argument. Perhaps the authority in the Lord's voice impelled them to obey, or maybe they were now beginning to realize that the Stranger on the shore was not a stranger after all.

"They cast therefore, and now they were not able to draw it for the multitude of fishes." Surely the disciples must have been reminded of another occasion (recorded by Luke) when they had labored all night without a catch. Luke tells us that the fishermen had, on that occasion, gone out of their boats and were washing their nets after a night of fruitless toil. Jesus entered into Peter's boat and sat down and taught the people who were on the shore. Then He said to Peter, "Launch out into the deep, and let down your nets for a draught." Peter replied, "We have toiled all the night, and have taken nothing: nevertheless at thy Word I will let down the net." And "when they had this done, they inclosed a great multitude of fishes: *and their net brake*" (Luke 5:1–6). But notice: Jesus said, "Let down your NETS (plural)." Peter replied, "I will let down the NET (singular)." Of course, when Peter let down ONE net instead of letting down all the nets, the multitude of fishes broke the net. Had he let down all of the nets as

Jesus had instructed him to do, he would have saved all of the miraculous draught of fishes, as well as avoiding breaking the net.

On this present occasion, however, they obeyed the Lord without question, and they caught a multitude of fish—so many that they were not able to immediately draw in the net. When we obey the Lord and seek His will for our lives we will be successful in the undertaking He assigns us to do. It may be in the business world, it may be in the ministry, fishing for the souls of men; but *wherever* He leads, if we follow His leadership and trust Him for the outcome, we can count on blessing and outstanding results.

Jesus had said to the disciples, "Come ye after me, and *I will MAKE you* to become fishers of men" (Mark 1:17). Success in God's ministry is not determined by eloquence, education, or dynamic personality, *but by the power of GOD* in the life of the minister. No man can come to Jesus unless the Father, through the Holy Spirit, draws him (John 6:44), and ministers cannot hope to reach men for Jesus unless the Holy Spirit *leads.*

Jesus declared, *"All power is given unto me in heaven and in earth"* (Matt. 28:18), and we know that in keeping His commandments *"there is GREAT REWARD"* (Psalm 19:11).

Verse 7: *"Therefore that disciple whom Jesus loved saith unto Peter, It is the Lord. Now when Simon Peter heard that it was the Lord, he girt his fisher's coat unto him, (for he was naked,) and did cast himself into the sea."*

John the Beloved was the first of the seven disciples to recognize Jesus. Because of his deep devotion to his Lord he had keener perception, and certainly the miraculous draught of fishes convinced him that the Man on the shore *could be* no one but Jesus. Turning to Peter he exclaimed, *"It is the Lord!"* and Peter behaved in his usual, impulsive manner: he *"girt his fisher's coat unto him . . . and did cast himself into the sea."* The boat was too slow for Peter;

he must reach his Lord as quickly as possible—and with no thought for the consequences or the wisdom of what he was doing, he sprang into the water and either swam or waded to shore, leaving the others to bring in the net full of fish and take care of other responsibilities.

The Greek word here translated *"fisher's coat"* is found only in this one passage. We are told that fishermen laid this outer garment aside when they were fishing or lowering the nets. It covered the upper part of the body, and when we read that Peter was "naked" that does not necessarily mean that he had on no clothes at all. The upper part of his body was naked, for he had removed his fisher's coat while toiling over the nets. But even though only part of his body was exposed, evidently he felt the need to cover himself in the presence of the Lord. It was perfectly *natural and in order* for him to remove his outer garment while handling the nets, but since God clothed Adam and Eve, He expects man (created in His own image) to wear clothes.

Verse 8: *"And the other disciples came in a little ship; (for they were not far from land, but as it were two hundred cubits,) dragging the net with fishes."*

The other disciples did not plunge into the water and swim or wade to shore as Peter did. They took time to land the net with its miraculous draught of fishes and then brought the boat to shore—but did that mean that they loved Jesus any less than Peter did? I think not. They remained in the ship to care for their catch and pull the fish safely to shore; they were faithful in taking care of what the Lord had given them from the standpoint of the needs of this life. Had they been as impulsive as Peter was, they would have lost what the Lord had so miraculously placed in their hands. We must admire Peter's zeal in his devotion to Jesus, but we must equally admire the others who stayed with the boat to save the net and the fishes.

Nothing is said about Peter's *reaching* Jesus before the

other disciples did, nor is there any record of what was said or what transpired between Peter and Jesus when they met on the shore.

Verse 9: *"As soon then as they were come to land, they saw a fire of coals there, and fish laid thereon, and bread."*

We know from the history given in the books of Moses concerning the Israelites' journey from Egypt to Canaan, that God furnished food for them in the wilderness. Was it any great wonder, then, that Jesus should have miraculously prepared breakfast for His weary disciples here on the shore of the Sea of Galilee? The fire, the fish, the prepared bread—all of these were created by Him. He *willed* it, and it was done—food for the physical needs of His followers. Jesus knew these men, He knew their faith was weak—but in His omniscience He also knew that they would grow stronger, that they would faithfully carry on His work on earth after He ascended back to the Father, and He sustained them and provided for their needs even in this hour when they had followed their own will instead of seeking HIS will.

It is God's good pleasure to bless His children and supply their every need. "For the Lord God is a sun and shield: the Lord will give grace and glory: *no good thing will He withhold from them that walk uprightly*" (Psalm 84:11). David declared, "I have been young, and now am old; yet have I not seen the righteous forsaken, nor his seed begging bread" (Psalm 37:25). He will provide our temporal needs as well as our spiritual needs if we will only allow Him to do so. Jesus promised, "Seek ye first the kingdom of God, and His righteousness; *and all these things shall be added unto you*"(Matt. 6:33).

The Greek word translated *"fire of coals"* is found in only two places in the New Testament—here, and in John 18:18 where the enemies of Jesus "made a fire of coals; for it was cold: and they warmed themselves: *and Peter stood with them, and warmed himself.*" It was by *that* fire of coals that Peter backslid, and now by "a fire of coals" kindled by Jesus he is to be given his commission: *"Feed my lambs . . . Feed my sheep."*

Certainly the Creator of all things could have provided bread and fish *without* kindling a fire, but I believe He made the fire to remind Peter of the night he had denied his Lord.

Verse 10: *"Jesus saith unto them, Bring of the fish which ye have now caught."*

Here Jesus called on the disciples to *produce proof* that in casting the net according to His command, their labor had not been in vain. Thus He was teaching them that the secret of success is to listen to His Word, receive it, obey it, and follow His command. The only message today that will draw men to Jesus is the Word of God. The Word brings saving faith, *apart* from the Word there can BE no true faith in the finished work of Jesus, and *without faith in His finished work there can be no salvation.* "Faith cometh by hearing, and hearing by the Word of God" (Rom. 10:17). It is honorable to labor with our hands, to earn a livelihood by honest toil; but if God has called us to labor with the Gospel net and fish for men, we must obey. It would be sinful to do otherwise.

Verse 11: *"Simon Peter went up, and drew the net to land full of great fishes, an hundred and fifty and three: and for all there were so many, yet was not the net broken."*

Surely this verse does not suggest that Peter, *by himself,* drew the net to land. Verse 6 told us that the disciples were not able to draw in the net because of the "multitude of fishes," and our present verse tells us that they were "*great* fishes." Therefore one man, even one as physically strong as Peter evidently was, would have found it impossible to land such a catch singlehanded. It would seem more reasonable that he joined the other disciples and together they pulled the net ashore.

Two miracles are here: first, the large catch of fish after a night of empty toiling; and then, in spite of the multitude of *"great fishes"* the net was not broken, all of which was the result of obedience to the command of Jesus. When we follow the Word of God we, too, can be assured of success and there will be no sad mistakes. To follow our *own* will is to invite failure.

There is no scriptural explanation of why the net contained *"an hundred and fifty and three"* fish, nor why the *number* of fish was named. There have been many suggestions and much speculation about it, but had the Holy Spirit wanted us to *know* why there were one hundred and fifty-three fish He would have told us. Perhaps the disciples knew; perhaps this was a lesson for them alone. It seems to me that this is one of the places to apply Deuteronomy 29:29: *"The secret things belong unto the Lord our God . . . ."*

We are not told what the disciples *did* with their miraculous catch of fish. If I were speculating on this I would suppose that they took them into the city and sold them. This seems reasonable, for surely they needed the money, and Jesus never encouraged wastefulness. At the feeding of the five thousand, when the meal was ended He said to the disciples, "Gather up the fragments that remain, *that nothing be lost*" (John 6:12). And of those "fragments" they gathered twelve baskets full, one for each of the twelve. Therefore we know that whatever disposal was made of the fish on this particular occasion, they were not wasted.

Jesus Will Supply Our Needs Today

Verse 12: *"Jesus saith unto them, Come and dine. And none of the disciples durst ask Him, Who art thou? knowing that it was the Lord."*

In keeping with the theme of the "salvation Gospel," the invitation *"Come"* is found in it three times:

In the early days of the Lord's ministry, when the Jordan

valley was a place of much activity with great crowds going out to hear John the Baptist, we read this account of the *first* invitation:

"Again the next day after John stood, and two of his disciples; and looking upon Jesus as He walked, he saith, Behold the Lamb of God! And the two disciples heard him speak, and they followed Jesus. Then Jesus turned, and saw them following, and saith unto them, What seek ye? They said unto Him, Rabbi, (which is to say, being interpreted, Master,) where dwellest thou? He saith unto them, *COME AND SEE.* They came and saw where He dwelt, and abode with Him that day . . ." (John 1:35–39). One of those disciples was Andrew, and after spending the day with Jesus he was never the same again.

The *second* invitation is found in John 7:37,38:

"In the last day, that great day of the feast, Jesus stood and cried, saying, If any man thirst, *let him COME UNTO ME, and drink.* He that believeth on me, as the Scripture hath said, out of his belly shall flow rivers of living water." Jesus was speaking here of *living* water. He is the water of life, and the thirsty soul can find satisfaction in drinking freely of that water. When we drink of the living water, it flows through us as a *river* of water, blessing others.

The *third* invitation is found in our present passage. The disciples had toiled at their nets all night without catching any fish; they were tired, discouraged, defeated. Jesus turned their defeat into glorious victory with His simple invitation, *"COME AND DINE."* Here is seen God's provision for His own, through His divine power, and His invitation is the same today:

To those who *doubt,* He invites, *"Come and SEE."*

To all who *thirst,* He invites, *"Come and DRINK."*

All who hunger for the bread of life are invited, *"Come and DINE."*

Christ is able to make Himself known to us today, He is able to satisfy our thirst and our hunger, He is able to supply our every need—but we must seek first His kingdom if we hope for Him to do these things for us. We must live in His Word, seeking His divine will and direction in all that we do. He will save us, sustain us, supply our needs—both spiritual and physical—and will go with us "even unto the end."

The Lord's actions in providing breakfast for His weary disciples showed His tender compassion for their physical needs and their discouraged minds. Even though He was in His resurrection body, He *knew* their needs, and in tenderness and love He supplied those needs. Yes, in His risen, glorified body He was the same loving, compassionate, all-sufficient Person as when He walked with the disciples before His crucifixion; and His Word plainly tells us that *even today* He can be *"touched with the feeling of our infirmities,"* because He was *"in all points tempted like as we are,* yet without sin" (Heb. 4:15).

"And none of the disciples durst ask Him, Who art thou?" The disciples stood in awe and amazement at the sight of Jesus and the food He had prepared for them, but they did not ask, "Who art thou?" because they were fully satisfied that it was the Lord. Undoubtedly their minds were filled with reverence for this One who appeared and disappeared at will in a supernatural manner. It does not seem unreasonable to suppose that Jesus had provided for His disciples on many occasions before the crucifixion, but this particular occasion was no ordinary thing for them. And He says to us today, "Behold, I stand at the door, and knock: if any man hear my voice, and open the door, *I will come in to him, and will sup with him, and he with me*" (Rev. 3:20).

Verse 13: *"Jesus then cometh, and taketh bread, and giveth them, and fish likewise."*

The shore of the Sea of Galilee was familiar territory to these men; they had been there with Jesus many times before—and now as He ate and drank in their presence and served them the meal He had prepared for them, how could they ever *doubt* again? His actions and His words made it clear that they were to *continue* to look to Him to supply their needs, just as they had depended on Him during His earthly ministry. Though in His resurrection body, He still knew their needs, He could still *supply* those needs, and He wanted them to understand that they were to look to Him for provision and sustenance even after He ascended back to the Father.

(The record does not *tell* us that Jesus ate with His disciples on this occasion, but it seems that He *would* have done so, although it was not necessary for Him to eat in order to sustain His strength. It would seem a natural thing for Him to eat in their company, as He had eaten broiled fish and honeycomb in the upper room.)

In Genesis 18, where Abraham entertained angels, we read, "Let a little water, I pray you, be fetched, and wash your feet, and rest yourselves under the tree: and I will fetch a morsel of bread, and comfort ye your hearts; after that ye shall pass on: for therefore are ye come to your servant. And they said, So do, as thou hast said.

"And Abraham hastened into the tent unto Sarah, and said, Make ready quickly three measures of fine meal, knead it, and make cakes upon the hearth. And Abraham ran unto the herd, and fetcht a calf tender and good, and gave it unto a young man; and he hasted to dress it. *And he took butter, and milk, and the calf which he had dressed, and set it before them; and he stood by them under the tree, AND THEY DID EAT*" (vv. 4–8). It is not unreasonable, then, to suppose that the Lord, in His resurrected body, dined with His disciples that day on the shore of the Sea of Galilee.

It was customary for Jesus to give thanks before a meal. In John 6:11, where He fed the five thousand, we read that He "took the loaves; and *when He had given thanks*, He distributed to the disciples, and the disciples to them that were set down; *and likewise of the fishes . . . .*" But we notice in our present passage that He did not give thanks before the meal.

When He fed the five thousand, He was acting as *perfect MAN*—the servant ministering to the needs of others. *As the Man Christ Jesus* He gave thanks to God for what God had given them on that occasion. Here on the shore, breakfasting with His disciples, He did not give thanks because He was glorified, He was in His resurrection body, and He would have them recognize Him now, not only as Jesus, *Saviour,* but also as *Lord of their lives, GOD in flesh.* When He fed the five thousand, His *humanity* was more prominent. Here, even though He was (and still is) concerned about the physical needs of His disciples, He was crowned with glory and honor, the glorified Christ.

In Luke 12:37, speaking of His second coming, He said, "Blessed are those servants, whom the Lord when He cometh shall find watching: Verily I say unto you, that *He shall gird Himself, and make them to sit down to meat, and will come forth and serve them!*" Yes, He will give His children "to eat of the tree of life, which is in the midst of the paradise of God," and He will feed them with "the hidden manna" (Rev. 2:7,17).

Verse 14: *"This is now the third time that Jesus shewed Himself to His disciples, after that He was risen from the dead."*

There has been much discussion concerning mention of *"the third time."* This of course was *not* the third time Jesus had been *seen* after His resurrection. He had been seen on various occasions by different people. He appeared to Mary Magdalene, He appeared to Joanna and the other women. He appeared to Simon Peter, and to the two disciples on the way to Emmaus. He made *two* appearances in the upper room with the disciples—once when Thomas was not there, once when Thomas was present.

The meaning in this verse must be that *this was the third time He had appeared where a number of His disciples were gathered together.* The first five appearances were on the same day He rose from the dead, and His sixth appearance was a week *after* the resurrection. All of those appearances are recorded in the previous chapter.

These first fourteen verses in the last chapter of John's Gospel constitute an unusual passage of Scripture, given to us to convey great spiritual truths under the figures of the boat, the net, the fish, the fire. These are truths for this Dispensation of Grace as we look forward to the coming of the Lord in the Rapture. In these accounts are spiritual lessons the Lord would have us learn.

First of all, this remarkable appearance of Jesus to His disciples reminds us of the primary duty of ministers of the Gospel (and of the entire Church) during this Dispensation of Grace. Believers are to be *"fishers of men."* Jesus told His disciples, *"Without ME ye can do nothing."* This was proved to them when they decided *of themselves* to go fishing, and then fished all night without results. Their barren efforts were then contrasted against *the multitude of fish* that filled their net when they cast it according to the Lord's direction.

Today, as then, the minister of God can do nothing without Jesus, without the leadership of the Holy Spirit. It is the good pleasure of Jesus to give success to His preachers and to all of His faithful servants, it is His joy to see His work grow and flourish; but when we make our own plans and choose our own ways, *God cannot bless us.* It is only as we follow His leadership that He can abundantly bless believers today. We are "fishers of men," yes—*but we must use the Gospel net!*

The breakfast Jesus prepared for His disciples that day also suggests *the great marriage feast of the Lamb,* when Jesus comes for His bride, the New Testament Church:

"Let us be glad and rejoice, and give honour to Him: for the marriage of the Lamb is come, and His wife hath made herself ready. And to her was granted that she should be arrayed in fine linen, clean and white: for the fine linen is the righteousness of saints. And he saith unto me, Write,

Blessed are they which are called unto the marriage supper of the Lamb. And he saith unto me, These are the true sayings of God" (Rev. 19:7–9).

I believe the sudden appearance of Jesus *at a dark hour in the lives of His disciples* points to the Rapture of the Church. These men were experienced fishermen; fishing had been their full time occupation until Jesus called them to leave their nets and follow Him. But they seemed to have lost their ability to make good at their old trade, and it had been a dark night for them. Then Jesus appeared—and everything suddenly changed from darkness to light, from sadness to joy and glory! I believe the Rapture of the Church is near at hand, the night is far spent, and the Lord's coming is imminent. We will soon hear the trumpet that will call us to meet Jesus in the air:

"For the Lord Himself shall descend from heaven with a shout, with the voice of the archangel, and with the trump of God: and the dead in Christ shall rise first: Then we which are alive and remain shall be caught up together with them in the clouds, to meet the Lord in the air: and so shall we ever be with the Lord" (I Thess. 4:16,17).

The Only Acceptable Motive for Service

Verse 15: *"So when they had dined, Jesus saith to Simon Peter, Simon, son of Jonas, lovest thou me more than these? He saith unto Him, Yea, Lord; thou knowest that I love thee. He saith unto him, Feed my lambs."*

Before Peter's fall, Jesus had warned him that Satan would put him to the test: He said to Peter, "Simon, Simon, behold, Satan hath desired to have you, that he may sift you as wheat: But I have prayed for thee, that thy faith fail not: and when thou art converted, strengthen thy brethren." To this warning Peter replied, "Lord, I am ready to go with thee, both into prison, and to death" (Luke 22:31–33).

You will notice that Jesus did not pray that Peter would

not *fall.* In His omnipotence He could have *kept* him from falling. What He prayed for was that Peter's *faith* fail not. It was necessary that Peter be taught a lesson concerning the true condition of his heart. He needed to learn the worthlessness of self-confidence and the truth of Proverbs 16:18: *"Pride goeth before destruction, and an haughty spirit before a fall."* It took Satan's "sifting" to humble Peter's spirit and place his confidence in the Saviour rather than in himself.

It is a happy day in the life of any believer when he realizes that he is no match for the devil. The Lord Jesus Christ is the only Person who ever defeated Satan on his own ground (Matt. 4:1–11). Sometimes even a dedicated believer must undergo a sad experience in his life before he recognizes his own weakness. Even the Apostle Paul, one of God's spiritual giants, declared, "Most gladly therefore will I rather glory in my infirmities, *that the power of Christ may rest upon me.* Therefore I take pleasure in infirmities, in reproaches, in necessities, in persecutions, in distresses for Christ's sake: *FOR WHEN I AM WEAK, THEN AM I STRONG*" (II Cor. 12:9,10). Self-confidence is a characteristic of the flesh.

God *leads* us, He does not *drive.* He is the Good Shepherd, and He leads as a good shepherd should; but when the sheep refuse to follow, they fall into snares and must suffer the consequences. When we are disobedient, God chastens us because He loves us:

"For whom the Lord loveth He chasteneth, and scourgeth every son whom He receiveth. If ye endure chastening, God dealeth with you as with sons; for what son is he whom the father chasteneth not? But if ye be *without* chastisement, whereof all are partakers, then are ye bastards, and not sons. . . Now no chastening for the present seemeth to be joyous, but grievous: nevertheless afterward it yieldeth the peaceable fruit of righteousness unto them which are exercised thereby" (Heb. 12:6–11). In connection with this, it would be well to read the entire twelfth chapter of

Hebrews.

I am so glad that Jesus not only prayed for Peter and the other disciples, but for all believers—including you and me. In John 17:20 we read, "Neither pray I for these alone, *but for them also which shall believe on me* through their word." To realize the full truth of this verse, put *your name* in it—thus: "Neither pray I for these alone, but for John Brown (or Mary Green, or whatever *your* name may be) which shall believe on me."

Believers are more than conquerors through Christ, but *only* through Him (Rom. 8:37). The eighth chapter of Romans is one of my favorite chapters in all of the Word of God—it *begins* in Christ and it *ends* in Christ, and so does the Christian life. In Romans 8:1 we read, "There is therefore now no condemnation *to them which are IN Christ Jesus,* who walk not after the flesh, but after the Spirit"—and in the last verse of the chapter we read that neither "height, nor depth, nor any other creature, shall be able to separate us from the love of God, *which is IN Christ Jesus our Lord!"*

Christ IN US is our assurance of victory. He is the conqueror of the world, the flesh, the devil, death, hell, and the grave.

"Jesus saith to Simon Peter, Simon, son of Jonas, lovest thou me more than these?" Here began a conversation deeply interesting in character and extremely important in its message. We need to pray for the Holy Spirit to open our hearts and minds that we may be able to comprehend the message recorded here for our instruction and edification.

Why did Jesus speak *directly to Peter?* I believe it was because none of the other disciples had *claimed as much* as Peter claimed the day before the crucifixion. No other disciple had boasted so confidently that he would never turn back and forsake his Lord. Peter boasted that he would go with Him to prison or to death—yet when the testing time came, no other disciple proved so unstable and so weak in the dark hours just before Jesus was crucified.

Jesus could have called Peter aside and spoken privately with him instead of speaking before six witnesses; but we reap what we sow, and Peter had *denied* Jesus before witnesses—before the Lord's *enemies!* It is true that Peter had wept tears of repentance and Jesus had forgiven him; but he must be instructed so that this same failure would not happen again. Three times Peter denied Jesus before witnesses, so three times he must be asked, "Lovest thou me?" And he must *answer* before witnesses. Thus did Jesus remind him of his fall, his pride, his overconfidence, his lack of prayer, and his trust in his own strength.

Yes, Peter had been forgiven—but he had *not* been fully restored to his position as a trusted minister of the Gospel and a fisher of men. This was what Jesus set about to do in the presence of the other six disciples, because in His omniscience He knew the possibility that some of the others might later claim that because of Peter's weakness and backsliding he was not *fitted* to be a minister of the Gospel. By restoring him to full fellowship and authority, Jesus precluded any such possibility. After this conversation, certainly no one dared say that Peter did not have the same authority accorded the other disciples. They could not say that he had forfeited his right to full apostleship. Jesus publicly questioned him, publicly forgave him, and *publicly commissioned him* to do the work of an apostle, along with the others of the disciple band.

By speaking directly to Peter, Jesus also pointed out to him the primary qualification of a disciple and minister—not the type of person who was ready to fight with the sword on provocation, not loud and boisterous, filled with impulsive zeal apart from love. A true minister of the Gospel must be longsuffering, patient, gentle, loving. His first aim should be to love as Jesus loved, to serve as Jesus served, and to recognize the fields white unto harvest with laborers so few. In love and tenderness he should go after the lost, bring them into the fold, and after they become members of the flock he should feed the lambs and watch after the sheep. Peter was in the school of God here, and Christ taught him great lessons of truth that *we* also need to learn. (In connection with this, please read I Corinthians, chapter 13, where Paul deals with the Christian graces.)

You will notice that Jesus did not ask, "Peter, do you believe me to be *the Son of God?*" He did not ask, "Peter, have you been *born again?*" He asked a very simple, heart-searching question: "Peter, *lovest thou ME?*" The right answer to this question would take care of the other questions He might have asked.

The phrasing of the question—"Lovest thou me *more than these?*"—has brought many questions and suggestions as to what Jesus meant by "more than these." It seems to me that since Peter had *boasted* more than any of the other disciples and then had *failed* more miserably than any of the others, Jesus was asking him, "Peter, as you look back to Calvary in the light of all that has happened, *do you REALLY love me more than these others do?* Have you been *more faithful* than they?" Thus was He showing Peter his place among the other apostles. Was he serving because of his deep love for the Lord? or was he serving impulsively, with zeal but without knowledge? Paul advised young Timothy, "The servant of the Lord *must not strive; but be gentle unto all men, apt to teach, patient, in meekness instructing those that oppose themselves;* if God peradventure will give them repentance to the acknowledging of the truth" (II Tim. 2:24,25).

"Yea, Lord, thou knowest that I love thee." Peter knew that Jesus knew what was in his heart. He remembered the night he had denied his Lord, and in sincere humility he answered, "Lord, you know all of my faults and weaknesses, you know my lack of faith; but in spite of that knowledge, you also know that I love you!" I would not be surprised if Peter honestly wondered, "*Do* John and the others love Him as much as I do? Could they *possibly* love Him *more?*"

As Peter publicly confessed his love for Jesus, now Jesus publicly commissioned him for his future ministry, giving him a chance to *prove* his professed love: *"Feed my lambs!"* The Word is the bread of life. Paul speaks of the "meat" of the Word (I Cor. 3:2), and *Peter* speaks of "the sincere *milk* of the Word" (I Pet. 2:2). When Jesus said, "Feed my lambs" He meant for Peter to be a faithful minister of the Word, feeding the flock, caring for the weaker ones and watching over them.

Sometimes we do more eternal good by feeding the weak, humble, insignificant members of the church than in trying to help some who feel that they are already full grown and need no help. For example, there are some Christians who will *readily* accept a place as teacher of an adult Bible class in Sunday school, but if they are called upon to teach a class of *beginners,* they *refuse.* Feeding "lambs" is a place of tremendous service. Jesus wanted Peter to understand that he could not prove his love for Him by taking pre-eminence, seeking high places, or attempting to rise above others. Love to Christ is demonstrated and proved in loving, humble service.

Peter never forgot this lesson, for later, in his first epistle, he wrote to the Church, "The elders which are among you I exhort, who am also an elder, and a witness of the sufferings of Christ, and also a partaker of the glory that shall be revealed: *Feed the flock of God which is among you, taking the oversight thereof, not by constraint, but willingly; not for filthy lucre, but of a ready mind; neither as being lords over God's heritage, but being ensamples to the flock.* And when the Chief Shepherd shall appear, ye shall receive a crown of glory that fadeth not away" (I Pet. 5:1–4).

What a change the grace of God wrought in Peter! and how far-reaching was his vision as he *grew* in grace and in the knowledge of his Lord and Saviour, Jesus Christ. His conversation with Jesus that morning by the Sea of Galilee bore fruit an hundredfold or more.

Verse 16: *"He saith to him again the second time,*

Simon, son of Jonas, lovest thou me? He saith unto Him, Yea, Lord; thou knowest that I love thee. He saith unto him, Feed my sheep."

This verse is similar (but not identical) to the preceding one. We note that Jesus did not ask here, "Lovest thou me *more than these?*" Also, here the commission is "Feed my *sheep,*" instead of "Feed my *lambs.*" By "sheep" Jesus undoubtedly meant the members of the flock who were more advanced in the faith and in their Christian experience. But both lambs and sheep demand attention from a faithful minister.

"Yea, Lord, thou knowest that I love thee." Greek scholars tell us that there are *two* Greek words, one of which is much stronger than the other, which are rendered "love" in this passage. To be true to the Greek, one of these words should be translated *"love"* and the other should be rendered *"affection."* In both verses (15 and 16) *Jesus* used the stronger word correctly translated "love"; but when Peter answered, he used the *weaker* word which should be translated "affection"—i. e., "Lord, thou knowest that I *have affection* for thee." Peter did not speak boastfully here as he did when he had declared that he would never forsake his Lord. It is evident that he did not feel so confident about his love after making such a sad mistake the night of the Lord's arrest.

Some declare that Peter held supremacy over the other apostles, but such doctrine is not of the Scriptures. Peter never exercised supremacy over *any* of the other apostles, but *being sent BY them, he obeyed:* "Now when the apostles which were at Jerusalem heard that Samaria had received the Word of God, *they sent unto them Peter and John"* (Acts 8:14). We have the record of one instance where Paul *openly rebuked* Peter, and Peter held his peace. For the full account read Galatians 2:11–18. It was Peter's nature to be impulsive, and he was often spokesman for the group, often taking the initiative—but this did not result in his supremacy over the others.

Verse 17: *"He saith unto him the third time, Simon, son of Jonas, lovest thou me? Peter was grieved because He said unto him the third time, Lovest thou me? And he said unto Him, Lord, thou knowest all things; thou knowest that I love thee. Jesus saith unto him, Feed my sheep."*

For the third time the question was asked, *"Simon, son of Jonas, lovest thou me?"* And then we notice, *"Peter was grieved"* because Jesus had again repeated the question which had twice been answered in the affirmative. Peter *answered* for the third time, but he used stronger language here, for he appealed to the omniscience of Jesus more strongly than before. He said, *"Lord, thou knowest ALL things!"*

Peter here confessed that certainly Jesus was God in flesh, for *only GOD knows "ALL things."*

In all three of these verses we notice Jesus said, *"MY lambs . . . MY sheep."* The lambs and the sheep were HIS, not Peter's. Some ministers today need to learn that the flock is God's, not theirs. They appoint themselves "lords over God's heritage" instead of taking their rightful place as under-shepherds. They become "boss" of the church and run it as if they owned it. Such is not in accordance with the instruction Jesus gave Peter.

"Feed my sheep." There are two Greek words translated *"feed."* One means "to provide food and pasture," and is used in verses 15 and 17. The other word means not only to provide food, but also "to lead and direct, to do the work of a shepherd." A good shepherd not only *feeds* his flock, he also leads them around the pitfalls and dangers, and protects them from wolves that may enter the fold in sheep's clothing. Feeding is part of the shepherd's responsibility, but there is more to being a good shepherd than just providing pasture for the flock.

These verses contain truth that needs to be learned and obeyed by the Church in this Dispensation of Grace. Jesus asked Peter, *"Lovest thou me?"* Love to Christ is the most important grace any Christian can possess, and certainly it is the most important grace *a minister* can have! It matters not how zealous one may be, how well trained and well educated, nor how eloquent his speech; his service will be worth little to the kingdom of God unless he possesses that greatest of all graces—*LOVE.* I refer you again to the thirteenth chapter of I Corinthians, where Paul closes his dissertation with these words: "And now abideth faith, hope, charity (LOVE), these three: *BUT THE GREATEST OF THESE IS LOVE!*" A believer may be lacking in many ways, he may not have the training and education he needs, he may not have such talent as many others have; but if his heart is overflowing with love for Jesus, he can win souls and bring glory to God, thus assuring a full reward in heaven.

Love *begets* love. *GOD is love.* God loved us and sent the Son of His love to die for us. Jesus did not ask Peter, "Are you well educated?" He did not ask, "Are you eloquent of speech?" He did not ask, "Are you accomplished in the social graces?" No, He simply asked, *"Peter, do you LOVE me?"* If we love Jesus as we should, we will love the lost enough to go out into the highways and hedges and win them for HIM!

I do not doubt that after his restoration, Peter loved Jesus more deeply than ever, and when he became an old man he remembered that day on the shore of the Sea of Galilee when Jesus had asked three times for an avowal of love, and then had commissioned him to feed the sheep and the lambs of the flock of God. Those memories were precious to Peter, and "precious" became a word to be used freely in his epistles, penned under inspiration of the Holy Ghost. To him, no message was quite as precious as that of the shed blood of the Lamb without spot or blemish.

In I Peter 1:18,19 he wrote: "Forasmuch as ye know that ye were not redeemed with corruptible things, as silver and gold, from your vain conversation received by tradition from your fathers; *but with the PRECIOUS blood of Christ,* as of a lamb without blemish and without spot."

In I Peter 2:6,7 he wrote, "Wherefore also it is contained in the Scripture, Behold, I lay in Sion *a chief corner stone, elect, PRECIOUS:* and he that believeth on Him shall not be confounded. *Unto you therefore which believe He is PRECIOUS:* but unto them which be disobedient, the Stone which the builders disallowed, the same is made the head of the corner."

This does not sound like the man who, on the night before the crucifixion, cursed and three times declared, "I do not know the Nazarene. I have never met Him; He is no friend of mine!" After that experience on the shore of the Sea of Galilee, Peter found shelter from the storms of life behind the Cornerstone, Jesus. In the Stone he found strength, and to him the Chief Cornerstone was "*precious.*" Peter had indeed been "confounded" the night he denied Jesus, but after this lesson in humility he was confounded no more!

Peter's second epistle opens with this salutation: "Simon Peter, a servant and an apostle of Jesus Christ, *to them that have obtained like PRECIOUS faith* with us through the righteousness of God and our Saviour, Jesus Christ."

Peter grew in grace after the Sea of Galilee experience. He realized that the Gospel intrusted to him included much more than reconciliation to God, redemption from sin, and salvation from hell. It is wonderful to be saved by God's grace and reconciled to God by the power of the cross; but reconciliation and redemption are only the beginning—*not the end*—of our salvation. Jesus commanded Peter, "Feed my lambs . . . Feed my sheep"—and those who would feed others must first be fed. That day, Peter began to feed on the living Word, the milk, the bread, the strong meat, and he was then able to feed others.

Saving grace becomes ours instantly when we exercise faith in the finished work of Jesus, but as long as we live on earth we can grow in grace and our Christian experience can expand. We should declare with the Apostle Paul,

"Brethren, I count not myself to have apprehended: *but this one thing I do, forgetting those things which are behind, and reaching forth unto those things which are before, I press toward the mark for the prize of the high calling of God in Christ Jesus*" (Phil. 3:13,14).

It was Peter who declared, "According as His divine power hath given unto us all things that pertain unto life and godliness, through the knowledge of Him that hath called us to glory and virtue: Whereby are given unto us *exceeding GREAT AND PRECIOUS promises:* that by these ye might be partakers of the divine nature, having escaped the corruption that is in the world through lust" (II Pet. 1:3,4).

The record contained in the Gospels concerning the Apostle Peter shows us that the blood of Jesus Christ and the Spirit of the living God can lift even a poor, faltering, faithless one and place him above his failures and weaknesses, making him an instrument of blessing to countless thousands who need to know the Gospel message of the *precious blood* of Christ, the *precious Cornerstone,* the *precious faith,* and the *precious promises!*

The Time and Manner of Peter's Death Foretold

Verses 18 and 19: *"Verily, verily, I say unto thee, When thou wast young, thou girdedst thyself, and walkedst whither thou wouldest: but when thou shalt be old, thou shalt stretch forth thy hands, and another shall gird thee, and carry thee whither thou wouldest not. This spake He, signifying by what death he should glorify God. And when He had spoken this, He saith unto him, Follow me."*

Here is the last of the double "verilies" so familiar to John's Gospel, and the words were addressed to Peter. In Luke 22:33 Peter had declared that he was ready to follow Jesus to prison—*or to death.* Here Jesus assured him that this, the highest honor that could come to a saint, would be granted him; for his feeding of the flock of God would ultimately bring him to martyrdom. He would be forced to stretch forth his hands, he would be bound, and he would be carried where he would not have gone willingly—to prison and to death.

The Scriptures do not describe the actual *death* of Peter, but Bible history and antiquity bear out the prophecy of Jesus here. We are told by historians that Peter met death by crucifixion, and when his executioners were ready to nail him to the cross he requested that he be crucified head downward, declaring that he was not worthy to die as his Lord had died.

I believe Peter *meant* what he said when he declared, "Lord, I am ready to go with you to prison or to death." He *was* willing to give his life for Jesus, but the flesh was weak—weaker than Peter realized. Then as he grew in grace and became strong in the Lord, he counted it an honor to die a martyr's death for the glory of the Lamb of God and for the sake of the Gospel. Feeding the lambs and the sheep would not bring him *earthly* praise and reward. On the contrary, it would bring suffering, persecution, imprisonment, and death. And it happened just as Jesus said it would.

"When thou wast young" does not necessarily mean that Peter was an old man at that time. Jesus was simply pointing out that when Peter was a lad or a much younger man, he walked where he chose to walk. The statement was simply to remind Peter that as a young man he had had freedom and independence—a young fisherman, living an adventurous, free life on the Sea of Galilee.

"When thou shalt be old" at least assured Peter that he had a good many years of ministry ahead of him. There would be times of tribulation and trouble, and in the end he would face a martyr's death for the sake of the Gospel; but in the meantime he would serve his Lord in the *ministry* of the Gospel, a service that would reach to old age.

"Thou shalt stretch forth thine hand and another shall gird thee, and carry thee where thou wouldest not." This

points to the time when Peter would be arrested, imprisoned, the executioner would command him to stretch forth his hands, and he would be bound and led away to be martyred. This does not mean that Peter would *resist* his death. It means that he would be taken where he would not ordinarily or willingly go. Jesus did not promise His disciples an easy life. In this instance He assured Peter of the consequences of his ministry, the cost of his faithful feeding of the lambs and the sheep.

No believer *enjoys* suffering. Jesus did not enjoy Calvary. He endured the cross, despising the shame, for the joy that was set before Him (Heb. 12:2). For the Christian, we count it a privilege to be able to share with Christ, for we know if we suffer with Him we will also reign with Him (Rom. 8:17; II Tim. 2:12). Christians do not long to die, they do not enjoy the thought of dying; but the truly born again person is not *afraid* to die.

There is a vast difference between being afraid to die and being anxious to die. I trust I shall be living when the Rapture takes place, I hope to be one of those who can shout, "O death, where is thy sting? O grave, where is thy victory?" There will be folks living when the Rapture occurs, and the saints will be changed instantly, "in the twinkling of an eye," and caught up to meet Jesus in the clouds in the air (I Cor. 15:51–55). I long to be among those who hear the trump of God and the call that will take us to meet Jesus in the air. I repeat, I am not anxious to die, I want to live as long as God will let me live; but I am not *afraid* to die: "There is no fear in love; but *perfect love casteth out fear:* because fear hath torment. He that feareth is not made perfect in love" (I John 4:18). *Jesus in the heart* is perfect love!

Believers may groan, but they will not grumble if they are filled with the love of God, controlled and led by the Holy Spirit. Paul and Silas were in jail at Philippi, they had been beaten, they were locked in the innermost cell with their feet held fast in the stocks; but at midnight they prayed and sang praises to God. Read the account in the sixteenth chapter of Acts.

There is no way of knowing what the commentators might have made of what Jesus said to Peter here if the Holy Spirit had omitted verse 19! The statement *"what death"* in the Greek reads "what *kind* of death." Verse 18 described the death Peter would die, and Bible authorities agree that it describes death by crucifixion.

I am so thankful for verse 19 because it teaches clearly and unmistakably that a believer can *glorify God* in death as well as in life. Today God is calling upon us to *live* for Him; He wants our bodies a living sacrifice (Rom. 12:1)—but if the day comes when we must seal our testimony with our blood, then we certainly can glorify God in death.

Church historians tell us that the martyrs in the days of "Bloody Mary" and other cruel rulers glorified God much more by death than by life. When a saint of God walks to the stake and with head held high testifies of the peace and joy in his heart and dies with a smile on his face, he gives a testimony that agnostics, atheists, and murderers will not forget.

When Jesus said to Peter, *"Follow me,"* I believe He meant not only for Peter to follow him *that very moment,* but also meant for him to follow Him throughout life. The breakfast meeting was ended and Jesus commanded Peter to leave the boats and the nets and come along with Him, to follow Him not only that day, but throughout the apostle's life and ministry, from that day forward.

Jesus is just the same today. He says to all of us, "Come to me . . . Learn of me . . . Follow me": "Come unto me, all ye that labour and are heavy laden, and I will give you rest. Take my yoke upon you, and learn of me; for I am meek and lowly in heart: and ye shall find rest unto your souls. For my yoke is easy, and my burden is light" (Matt. 11:28–30).

Verses 20 and 21: *"Then Peter, turning about, seeth the disciple whom Jesus loved following; which also leaned on*

His breast at supper, and said, Lord, which is he that betrayeth thee? Peter seeing him saith to Jesus, Lord, and what shall this man do?"

Peter's nature was marked by three characteristics: First, he was *impulsive*—I doubt that his fellow disciples ever knew what to expect from him next. Second, he was *inquisitive.* Third, he was *temperamental*—he could be extremely happy one moment, and extremely sad the next.

The seaside breakfast was ended, but the disciples still lingered in the company of Jesus. It was wonderful to be in His presence, to be assured that He had risen. Peter had been given his commission—"Feed my lambs . . . Feed my sheep . . . Follow me." Suddenly Peter looked at John ("the disciple whom Jesus loved") and asked, *"Lord, what shall THIS man do?"* In other words, "Lord, you have instructed *me* as to what *I* am going to do, even to the manner of my death. *Now what about John?* What is going to happen to *him?* What are *his* duties to be?"

One of Peter's greatest weaknesses was looking at others, thinking of others, and trying to please others. He was more concerned about John and what John was going to do than he was about the commission he himself had just received. The Lord's rebuke was gentle, but it was nonetheless a rebuke as He answered Peter's question.

Verse 22: *"Jesus saith unto him, If I will that he tarry till I come, what is that to thee? Follow thou me."*

In other words, "Peter, if I am your Lord and if you are to do my will by feeding my lambs and my sheep, if you are to be my under-shepherd, *you must keep your eyes on ME*—not on John or on other people. What happens to John is not your business."

Verse 20 tells us that Peter *turned about* and saw John following. If Peter had kept his eyes forward instead of turning to look behind him he would not have been prompted to ask the question that brought a rebuke from Jesus. He had just commanded Peter, *"Follow me,"* and if Peter had kept his face forward, following Jesus, he would not have had a chance to be curious about *John.*

A saint of God should never look back. If we are where God would have us, if we are doing what He calls us to do, then our command is to do it well; and if we give our best to the ministry God has given us, we will have a full reward at the end of life's journey—and no time to be curious or critical about what others are doing! God deals with *individuals,* He *calls* individuals, and each believer has his own ministry. Each believer is God's steward, and if we do what He *bids* us do we will be so busy we will not have time to ask questions about the ministry or stewardship of our fellow Christians.

In the last chapter of the prophecy God gave to Daniel, we read, "I heard, but I understood not: then said I, *O my Lord, what shall be the end of these things?* And He said, *Go thy way, Daniel: for the words are closed up and sealed till the time of the end. . . But go thou thy way till the end be: for thou shalt rest, and stand in thy lot at the end of the days*" (Dan. 12:8,9,13). Daniel did not understand all that he had written, but God assured him that in due time the words *would be* understood, and Daniel need not concern himself about it. If as individual believers we would look to the Lord, obey Him, walk in His steps and seek His will for our own lives, we would be happy and blessed of the Lord—and we would not fret about others.

Jesus *knew* what would happen to John. He knew John would be exiled to Patmos because of his testimony, and that he would spend many lonely days in exile; but what good would it have done to reveal this to *Peter?* It would only have saddened him; and Jesus knew Peter would have enough disappointments and persecutions, trials and tribulations, without trying to bear *John's* burdens too. It was for Peter's good that he not know what was to happen to John.

Have you ever stopped to thank God that He does not

let us know what tomorrow holds? If He should reveal our tomorrows we would never have a moment of complete satisfaction and peace! God knows each of our tomorrows until the day He calls us home; but I am glad we *live* by faith, *walk* by faith, and moment by moment we are kept in His love.

Verse 23: *"Then went this saying abroad among the brethren, that that disciple should not die: yet Jesus said not unto him, He shall not die; but, If I will that he tarry till I come, what is that to thee?"*

As a result of what Jesus said to Peter here, the first ecclesiastical tradition was born. It became a common saying in that day among believers that John would never die, he would live until Jesus came to earth a second time. Probably some thought John would be translated as Enoch and Elijah were, and others thought that he would live until Jesus actually returned to set up the kingdom. But John makes it very clear that Jesus meant no such thing. He did not say John would live until He returned, nor did He say that John would not die. He said, "*IF* I will that he tarry till I come . . . ."

We see here how easily tradition can begin, how easily the truth can be twisted and misunderstood. We need add no supposition to the Word of God. We need to read it word for word, line upon line, and let it say what it says without adding what we think or suppose. The Word of God is our Textbook, it is Truth, and we dare not deviate from it.

Removing one little word—"*IF*"—would make the Lord's statement read, "*I will* that he tarry till I come." Thus we see that by taking out a word or adding a word, the *message* of the Word can be distorted and wrecked. The other disciples heard what Jesus said to Peter, and evidently one of them, in repeating the conversation, either repeated it *incorrectly* or those who *heard* the account repeated it incorrectly, and the saying became common throughout the countryside that *John would not die.*

Verse 24: *"This is the disciple which testifieth of these things, and wrote these things: and we know that his testimony is true."*

In keeping with his customary humility, John does not give his name but refers to himself as *"the disciple which testifieth of these things."* He wrote as the Holy Ghost gave him words, and he testifies here that he told the truth as the Holy Spirit inspired him to write. He declares that the testimony of this book can be trusted because every word in it is true.

Verse 25: *"And there are also many other things which Jesus did, the which, if they should be written every one, I suppose that even the world itself could not contain the books that should be written. Amen."*

I believe what this verse declares, *literally.* No one will ever know in this life how many miracles Jesus worked, how many things He did, and how many words He spoke that are not recorded in any book—and if all those things *had* been written, the account would fill so many volumes that the whole world could not contain them!

For instance, in the Gospel of Matthew we read: "And Jesus went about all Galilee, teaching in their synagogues, and preaching the Gospel of the kingdom, and healing all manner of sickness and all manner of disease among the people. And His fame went throughout all Syria: and they brought unto Him all sick people that were taken with divers diseases and torments, and those which were possessed with devils, and those which were lunatick, and those that had the palsy; and He healed them. And there followed Him great multitudes of people from Galilee, and from Decapolis, and from Jerusalem, and from Judaea, and from beyond Jordan" (Matt. 4:23–25).

In this short passage alone, notice the miracles, the healings, the sermons preached, which are not recorded except in simple statement that Jesus did these things.

When John the Baptist sent disciples to ask Jesus, "Art thou He that should come, or do we look for another?" Jesus replied, "Go and shew John again those things which ye do hear and see: The blind receive their sight, and the lame walk, the lepers are cleansed, and the deaf hear, the dead are raised up, and the poor have the Gospel preached to them" (Matt. 11:2–5). Again, no details are given—just a simple statement of fact concerning the intense activity that followed wherever Jesus went.

If we had the detailed report of every miracle Jesus wrought, this world would indeed be filled and running over with books. But thank God for the Gospel of John, the Gospel that tells us that God loved us and gave Jesus to die for us. Thank God for the Gospel that tells us to *hear* His Word, *believe* His Word, and salvation is ours. In this "salvation Gospel" we learn that Jesus is the Water of life, the Bread of life, the Light of the world, the Way, the Truth, and the Life!

This does not mean that the unrecorded things Jesus did were not important. He never spoke an idle word, He never did anything that was insignificant or trifling. But those who do not believe the things that are written in the four Gospels—Matthew, Mark, Luke, and John—would not believe if they had a world full of books about Jesus and His ministry and mission here on earth!

When the rich man lifted up his eyes in hell and begged Abraham to send Lazarus to warn his five brothers not to come to that awful place, Abraham replied, "They have Moses and the prophets; let them hear them." The rich man said, "If one went unto them from the dead, they will repent." But Abraham said, *"If they hear not Moses and the prophets, neither will they be persuaded, THOUGH ONE ROSE FROM THE DEAD"* (Luke 16:27–31).

How I thank God for the Gospel of John. I have preached more sermons from this Gospel than from any other one book in the entire Bible, I have seen more people born again at the climax of messages delivered from this Gospel than from any other book in the Bible, and I shall continue to use its message as long as God leaves me on earth to preach His Word! All that we need to know in order to be born again and become a child of God is found in the Gospel of John.

Truly, "And without controversy great is the mystery of godliness: God was manifest in the flesh, justified in the Spirit, seen of angels, preached unto the Gentiles, believed on in the world, received up into glory" (I Tim. 3:16). The Incarnation was a divine imperative if God were to be just and yet justify the ungodly. It is the pre-existent Personality as the only begotten of the Father who must always define and defend the character of the Incarnation as the definite act of Jehovah God and not at all the act of man. Man had nothing to do with the Incarnation. The Word makes it plain that *woman* cannot conceive a personality even in the natural realm: "For he (Levi) was *yet in the loins of his FATHER* (Abraham) when Melchisedec met him" (Heb. 7:10).

Sinful man could not beget sinless human nature, and that which was born of Mary was sinless human nature, nature that could be produced only by and through the interfering, miraculous act of Almighty God. And as Jehovah God, the Eternal Father, overshadowed Mary in the Person of the Holy Ghost, she conceived in her womb and brought forth her firstborn Son clothed with the created humanity produced by God Himself.

Only God could provide what God demanded to make atonement for sin. If atonement was to be made, then a *sinless* one must die; but *God cannot* die, He is from everlasting to everlasting. Therefore the one to be sacrificed to atone for sin must have *human* nature, but *sinless* human nature; and only a holy, sinless God could produce such nature. Therefore for a substitute to suffer death, to make atonement, and taste death for every man, God must become incarnate.

As the Son of God and God the Eternal Son, Jesus was in the beginning with the Father from all eternity. Because of the Son's place and His function in the Godhead, He was the only Person OF the Godhead who could become incarnate. Therefore Jesus was God manifested in flesh, and in Him we see the Word incarnate. As God in flesh, Jesus went to the cross, offered His perfect humanity, *THE sacrifice for sin, offered once, for all, forever.*

What was it that satisfied God? Was it the miracles Jesus wrought while He was on earth? Jesus declared, "I do always those things that please (the Father)" (John 8:29). Was *this* what satisfied God? Was it the horrible suffering Jesus endured in the Garden of Gethsemane when His perspiration became as drops of blood? Was it His horrible suffering when He cried out, "My God! My God! Why hast thou forsaken me?" No, it was none of these things that satisfied the holiness, righteousness, and perfection of God. *It was the infinite value of THE INFINITE PERSONALITY of the only begotten Son! It was THE PERSON who offered the sacrifice. It was JESUS.*

And He who made the atonement for sin is coming again for us in that glorious morning of the first resurrection when the dead in Christ shall be raised and the living saints will be caught up together with them to meet the Lord in the clouds in the air. He is the *firstbegotten:* "And again, when He bringeth in the firstbegotten into the world, He saith, And let all the angels of God worship Him" (Heb. 1:6).

This blessed Gospel of John tells us all of these things, and makes them clear. Christ died to redeem us, He lives to make intercession for us. Only ONE Christian life began in Bethlehem of Judaea and ended at the cross, and that life was Jesus. Every other Christian life begins at the cross, and one day we will meet Jesus in the clouds in the air and after the Tribulation period we will return to the earth with Him to reign for one thousand glorious years!

Dear reader, are YOU born again? Are YOU truly saved

by God's grace through faith in the finished work of Jesus? As I bring this commentary to a close I bow my head and humbly pray that if you are not a believer you will study the Gospel of John, read and re-read it, until you are saved.

"And many other signs truly did Jesus in the presence of His disciples, which are not written in this book: But these are written, *that ye might believe* that Jesus is the Christ, the Son of God; and that believing *ye might have life through His name*" (ch. 20, vv. 30,31).